THE POLITICS OF
WORKERS' PARTICIPATION
The Peruvian Approach in Comparative Perspective

STUDIES IN SOCIAL DISCONTINUITY

Under the Consulting Editorship of:

CHARLES TILLY
University of Michigan

EDWARD SHORTER
University of Toronto

In preparation

Paul Oquist. Violence, Conflict, and Politics in Columbia

Fred Weinstein. The Dynamics of Nazism: A Study in Psychoanalytic Sociology

Richard C. Trexler. Renaissance Florence: The Public Life of a Complex Society

Samuel Kline Cohn, Jr. The Laboring Classes in Renaissance Florence

Published

John R. Hanson II. Trade in Transition: Exports from the Third World, 1840–1900

Evelyne Huber Stephens. The Politics of Workers' Participation: The Peruvian Approach in Comparative Perspective

Albert Bergesen (Ed.). Studies of the Modern World-System

Lucile H. Brockway. Science and Colonial Expansion: The Role of the British Royal Botanic Gardens

James Lang. Portuguese Brazil: The King's Plantation

Elizabeth Hafkin Pleck. Black Migration and Poverty: Boston 1865-1900

Harvey J. Graff. The Literacy Myth: Literacy and Social Structure in the Nineteenth-Century City

Michael Haines. Fertility and Occupation: Population Patterns in Industrialization

Keith Wrightson and David Levine. Poverty and Piety in an English Village: Terling, 1525-1700

Henry A. Gemery and Jan S. Hogendorn (Eds.). The Uncommon Market: Essays in the Economic History of the Atlantic Slave Trade

Tamara K. Hareven (Ed.). Transitions: The Family and the Life Course in Historical Perspective

Randolph Trumbach. The Rise of the Egalitarian Family: Aristocratic Kinship and Domestic Relations in Eighteenth-Century England

Arthur L. Stinchcombe. Theoretical Methods in Social History

Juan G. Espinosa and Andrew S. Zimbalist. Economic Democracy: Workers' Participation in Chilean Industry 1970-1973

Richard Maxwell Brown and Don E. Fehrenbacher (Eds.). Tradition, Conflict, and Modernization: Perspectives on the American Revolution

Harry W. Pearson. The Livelihood of Man by Karl Polanyi

The list of titles in this series continues on the last page of this volume

THE POLITICS OF WORKERS' PARTICIPATION
The Peruvian Approach in Comparative Perspective

Evelyne Huber Stephens

Department of Political Science
College of the Holy Cross
Worcester, Massachusetts

ACADEMIC PRESS

A Subsidiary of Harcourt Brace Jovanovich, Publishers

New York   London   Toronto   Sydney   San Francisco

ACADEMIC PRESS, INC.
111 Fifth Avenue, New York, New York 10003

United Kingdom Edition published by
ACADEMIC PRESS, INC. (LONDON) LTD.
24/28 Oval Road, London NW1 7DX

Library of Congress Cataloging in Publication Data

Stephens, Evelyne Huber.
    The politics of workers' participation.

    (Studies in social discontinuity)
    Includes index.
    1. Employees' representation in management––Peru.
2. Employees' representation in management.
I. Title. II. Series.
HD5660.P4S73   658.3'152'0985   79–6789
ISBN 0–12–666250–9

PRINTED IN THE UNITED STATES OF AMERICA

80 81 82 83   9 8 7 6 5 4 3 2 1

To the memory of my grandfather
   EMIL WEBER
and to
   JOHN
who stands for the same goals

Contents

3

Origins, Purpose, and Design of Workers' Participation within the Framework of the Peruvian Revolution   79

4

Participation at the Enterprise Level: Its Development and Effects on the Relations among Enterprises, the CI, and Unions   101

5

Dynamics in the Constellation of Sociopolitical Forces I: Opposition against and Mobilization in Defense of the CI   145

Preface

Workers' participation in making decisions in the process of production has been a goal for parts of the Left since the last quarter of the nineteenth century. Because its proponents lacked political strength, however, it never really became salient as a large issue of public debate in Western countries except during a short period of revolutionary upsurge immediately following World War I and during a period of Leftist strength right after World War II. In the mid-1960s, demands for workers' participation were brought to the surface by the wave of radicalism that swept through Western Europe and the United States. As the issue achieved a certain prominence, it came to mean many different things to many different people. The spectrum of meanings and purposes ascribed to it ranges from stimulation of revolutionary impulses through mobilization to integration through human engineering.

Social scientists have responded to the greater importance of the workers' participation issue with a growing number of studies on the subject. Yet, they have generally not addressed the divergence of views on workers' participation that characterizes the political debate. In particular, the empirical literature is dominated by behavioral studies of participation at the enterprise level. Most of these studies treat workers' participation as a problem of organizational behavior detached from the larger social, political, and economic environment. This book explicitly attempts to address the divergence of views in the political debate and to introduce it into the study of workers' participation in the context of social science.

The central argument made here is that workers' participation must be seen as an integral element of a larger social order, that is, of the structure of the economic and political system of a society. Workers' participation affects the distribution of power among social classes, and consequently it is an issue for political conflict. Thus, in order to understand the political debate as well as the possibilities for workers' participation in practice, it is indispensable to elucidate first of all how the introduction of workers' participation and its full development toward workers' control modifies the structure of the politico-economic system as a whole and next to identify which forces in a society promote or obstruct such a development.

Accordingly, this book first describes a conceptual framework for a comparative analysis of the development of workers' participation in a variety of politico-economic systems. This conceptualization is then applied to the analysis of different empirical cases: France, the Federal Republic of Germany, and Sweden, as examples of developed capitalist democracies with varying forms and varying amounts of workers' participation; Yugoslavia, as the most fully developed example of workers' control in the context of a developing socialist authoritarian system; and Peru, as an example of a developing capitalist authoritarian system with a very particular form of workers' participation.

The discussion of the Peruvian experience constitutes a large part of the book. It focuses in considerable detail on processes at the level of national politics as well as at the enterprise level. Empirical evidence is presented which substantiates my contention that workers' participation is an issue of fundamental political conflict and that its development is shaped by the economic and political power of social forces that promote it as part of a transition to a new social order in contrast to those forces that oppose such a transition. Frequent references to the Chilean experience with workers' participation under the Allende regime further highlight the importance of the larger politico-economic context for the development of workers' participation. After a short comparative summary of the evidence from the empirical cases, the book concludes with some speculation about future possibilities for the development of workers' participation.

In two of the countries discussed in this book, Sweden and Peru, I was able to do original field research, and I am deeply indebted to the organizations that gave me this opportunity. My research in Sweden was supported by a grant from the Swedish Institute in Stockholm. For my research in Peru and the subsequent writing of the section on that country, I received a grant from the Social Science Research Council and the American Council of Learned Societies.

In both Sweden and Peru, crucial contributions to this book were made by a large number of persons from all three sides involved in the struggle concerning the development of workers' participation—labor, entrepreneurs, and the state—who were generous with their time and were willing to talk to me about their experiences, hopes, and frustrations. Also, employees in several ministries and private institutions were very helpful in locating and collecting information. Rather than trying to single out a few among these many persons, I will express my thanks to them collectively.

Alberto Bustamante, Peter Cleaves, Zwi Harrell, Luis Pásara, and Martin Scurrah helped me with contacts and advice during the research period and/or read and commented on earlier drafts of the manuscript. Kay Mansfield could always be relied on to help with any practical problem. John Low-Beer and Charles Tilly contributed particularly detailed and constructive comments.

This book owes its existence to a very large extent to Alfred Stepan. He has provided invaluable support from the beginning of the project in the form of insights into Peruvian politics, advice on how to do research in a semi-open environment, intellectual stimulation and criticism, and, last but not least, encouragement to persist in completing it as a book. John David Stephens has offered immense personal and intellectual support, has inspired confidence in the harder moments of research and writing, and has made concrete comments on my work. But his contribution goes much further: Our constant interchange of ideas about politics and social science has been the major foundation for the development of my thinking.

I am deeply grateful for all the support received. I have to assume full responsibility for any errors and weaknesses that remain, as well as for the opinions expressed in this book.

List of Acronyms

France

CFDT   French Democratic Workers' Confederation, *Confédération Française et Démocratique du Travail* (Socialist; formerly Christian)

CGT   General Confederation of Labor, *Confédération Générale du Travail* (Communist)

FO   *Force Ouvrière* (Socialist)

Germany

CDU   Christian Democratic Union, *Christlich-Demokratische Union*

CSU   Christian Social Union, *Christlich-Soziale Union*

DAG   German Salaried Employees' Union, *Deutsche Angestelltengewerkschaft*

DGB   German Trade Union Federation, *Deutscher Gewerkschaftsbund*

FDP   Free Democratic Party, *Freie Demokratische Partei*

SPD   Social Democratic Party, *Sozialdemokratische Partei Deutschlands*

Sweden

LO   Swedish Confederation of Trade Unions, *Landsorganisationen*

SACO   Swedish Confederation of Professional Associations, *Sveriges akademikers centralorganisation*

SR   National Federation of Government Officers, *Statstjänstemännens riksförbund*

TCO   Swedish Central Organization of Salaried Employees, *Tjänstemännens centralorganisation*

Peru

ADEX   Association of Exporters, *Asociación de Exportadores*

APRA   American Popular Revolutionary Alliance, *Alianza Popular Revolucionaria Americana*

CAEM   Center of Higher Military Studies, *Centro de Altos Estudios Militares*

CCUSC   Coordinating Committee for a Unification of Class-Oriented Unions, *Comité de Coordinación y Unificación Sindical Clasista*

CGTP   General Workers' Confederation of Peru, *Confederación General de Trabajadores del Perú* (Communist)

CI   Industrial Community, *Comunidad Industrial*

CNA   National Agrarian Confederation, *Confederación Nacional Agraria*

CNT   National Central Workers' Organization, *Central Nacional de Trabajadores* (Christian-Democratic)

COAP   Advisory Council to the President, *Comité de Asesoramiento de la Presidencia*

CONACI   National Confederation of Industrial Communities, *Confederación Nacional de Comunidades Industriales*

CONACI-CR   National Confederation of Industrial Communities, Reorganizing Committee; *Confederación Nacional de Comunidades Industriales, Comité Reorganizador*

CTP   Confederation of Peruvian Workers, *Confederación de Trabajadores Peruanos* (APRA)

CTRP   Central Organization of Workers of the Peruvian Revolution, *Central de Trabajadores de la Revolución Peruana* (Government-sponsored)

CUOS   Unifying Council of Union Organizations, *Consejo Unitario de Organizaciones Sindicales*

FDRP   Front for the Defense of the Peruvian Revolution, *Frente de Defensa de la Revolución Peruana*

FETIMP   Federation of Workers of the Metal Industry of Peru, *Federación de Trabajadores de la Industria Metalúrgica del Perú*

MIT   Ministry of Industry and Tourism, *Ministerio de Industria y Turismo*

MLR   Revolutionary Labor Movement, *Movimiento Laboral Revolucionario*

OCLA   Office of Labor Communities, *Oficina de Comunidades Laborales*

SINAMOS   National System of Support for Social Mobilization, *Sistema Nacional de Apoyo a la Movilización Social*

SNI/SI   [National] Society of Industries, *Sociedad [Nacional] de Industrias*

1

Theoretical Framework for the Comparative Study of Workers' Participation

The Political Nature of the Problem

In the late 1960s, the issue of workers' participation, or workers' control, moved to the center of the political debate in the East and West, North and South. In Eastern Europe, workers' participation was a central element in the search for new alternatives to the discredited Stalinist version of socialism. In the Western world, participation became a salient issue in the wave of protest movements emerging among workers and students. Demands for participation of workers, students, and citizens in decisions affecting their lives indicated a growing concern with qualitative aspects of life in the context of quantitative growth in developed industrial societies. In developing countries, both the failure of the capitalist way of development to solve the pressing problems of poverty, unemployment, and inequality, and the rejection of the central-command socialist way of development motivated the search for "third ways"—for humanist socialist models of social organization that would facilitate efforts at development and minimize its human costs. The importance assigned to popular involvement in developmental efforts made the potential role of workers' participation a central issue in the political debate.

The political debate about workers' participation, however, has been carried on mainly at the theoretical level, with little grounding in systematic empirical analysis. In part, this is due to the scarcity of empirical cases, where significant schemes of workers' participation have been introduced, and in part to the fact that the empirical studies that have been done have focused mostly on dynamics at the enterprise level. Mainly carried out by scholars approaching the subject from the point of view of organizational behavior or scientific management, these studies have investigated technical aspects of the structural design

1

of participatory decision making—its psychological effects on the participants and its economic effects on the enterprise.[1] Political scientists who have dealt with workers' participation have typically approached the topic as political theorists, either within the tradition of democratic theory or from a critical Marxist point of view.[2]

In this study, I will attempt to improve upon the shortcomings of the two approaches by introducing empirical analysis into the political debate and by showing that empirical observation restricted to processes at the enterprise level, without taking larger political processes into account, does not provide sufficient information to understand the development and effects of workers' participation.

The following statements represent four common, if somewhat stereotyped, positions in the debate on workers' control:

1. Workers' participation in the capitalist enterprise is a means of co-opta-tion and sellout of the working class.
2. Workers' participation in the socialist enterprise is a means for effective downward communication and implementation of directives coming from above.
3. The introduction of workers' participation into the capitalist enterprise is the first step toward socialism.
4. The introduction of workers' participation into the socialist enterprise is the first step toward anarchism.

On a more general level, two basic views of workers' participation can be

---

[1]For an extensive bibliography covering such studies, see Jenkins (1973). The most useful theoretical approach among the ones described in these studies is the "sociotechnical systems analysis" developed by researchers of the Tavistock Institute of Human Relations in London. Their concept of enterprise as an open system leads them to focus on the reciprocity between enterprise organization and conditions in society in general. An example of this approach is Emery and Trist (1965). Espinosa and Zimbalist's (1978) study of structures, processes, and effects of participation at the enterprise level is innovative in that it includes an investigation of political variables.

[2]An excellent normative case for workers' participation in the tradition of classical democratic theory as represented by Rousseau and John Stuart Mill is made by Pateman (1970). She argues that for these theorists the psychological effect of participation in democratic decision making was important, and that in modern societies this effect is greatest in direct participation in decision making at the workplace or the community. Furthermore, spheres such as industry should be seen as political systems in their own right, offering areas for participation in addition to the national level. The most relevant body of literature from a Marxist point of view are the writings of political sociologists and political economists looking at the role of workers' participation in the framework of a socialist transformation. A useful collection of such articles, including some empirical studies, can be found in Hunnius, Garson, and Case, eds. (1973). A notable exception combining the political focus with empirical analysis of self-management in the agrarian sector in Peru is McClintock (1977).

distinguished, ascribing either an integrative or a transformative function to the introduction of workers' participation schemes. The presumed integrative function of workers' participation consists of giving workers a stake in their job in a particular enterprise, fostering an identification of workers with their own enterprise, and thus bringing about acquiescence to their position in the existing social order. The presumed transformative function of workers' participation consists of giving workers some incipient influence over decisions in the enterprise, mobilizing workers to demand an expansion of this influence toward full control, and thus generating pressures for a transformation of the existing social order. The first two positions represent the integrative view; the latter two the transformative view. What is common to most proponents of these views is their assumption that the integrative or transformative effect of a workers' participation scheme can be derived from its structural design.

Here, I will show that no such generalizations about the effects of workers' participation schemes can be made. In some cases they are integrative; in others they are transformative. Furthermore, the integrative or transformative effect cannot be derived from the structural aspects of the design itself. Rather, the development and effects of workers' participation schemes depend primarily on the interaction of sociopolitical forces, which attempt to use workers' participation as an element in a larger strategy of consolidation or transformation of a given social order. The introduction of workers' participation is a profoundly political problem because it modifies the distribution of power between social classes, at least marginally. Workers' participation can be defined as the exercise of certain decision-making rights in the process of production on the basis of the contribution of labor power, as opposed to the contribution of capital. It necessarily transfers power from owners to nonowners of capital and thus affects class relations in a society. Consequently, the introduction and development of workers' participation has to be understood in the framework of the changing distribution of power among sociopolitical forces.[3]

In order to analyze and compare systematically the determinants and effects of workers' participation in different economic and political systems, I will start with a conceptualization of four developmental stages and corresponding dynamics between the development of workers' participation and the strength and action of sociopolitical forces. Subsequently, this general conceptualization will be specified for concrete types of economic and political systems, and will be used in an analysis of five empirical cases to examine its usefulness and explanatory power.

[3] The term *sociopolitical forces* refers to groups of actors (e.g., workers, small shopkeepers, industrial entrepreneurs, the military, the state bureaucracy, etc.) with some common interest based on their position in the social structure and common power resources, which they attempt to use to exert political pressure in the pursuit of their interest.

1. *Origins of workers' participation:* Given that the introduction of workers' participation implies a modification in the distribution of power between social classes, it is unlikely to occur unless preceded by a challenge to the existing distribution of power. Thus the introduction of workers' participation must be seen as a response to a challenge against the established social order.[4] This position clearly contradicts the view that the development of workers' participation is the result of a process of managerial enlightenment. If this latter view were correct, that is, if workers' participation were a phenomenon growing out of scientific management tradition, then one would have to find a substantial proliferation of workers' participation schemes in the United States, the intellectual home of Taylorism and the human relations school. However, the introduction of workers' participation in the United States lags significantly behind many Western European countries. This holds true not only for schemes that emphasize a transfer of decision-making power to the workers but also for those emphasizing job enrichment or job rotation through breaking up assembly lines, etc. Even the latter type of scheme involves some cost and adaptation on the part of management, and consequently it is unlikely to be introduced without a preceding challenge to management's capacity to maintain control and high labor productivity. The introduction of a workers' participation scheme in an individual company, then, has to be seen as a response to a localized challenge, such as from a particularly strong union whose members are in a favorable market position. Similarly, the introduction of workers' participation on a national scale through legislation has to be seen as a response to a more general challenge against the larger social order. Such a challenge can be posed by actual or potential pressures from newly emerging sociopolitical forces, by external threats, by an internal disintegration of the ruling forces, or by a combination of all these.

2. *Purpose and design of workers' participation:* Different schemes of workers' participation promoted as a response to such a challenge are aimed either at integrating workers into their enterprise and the larger social order or at mobilizing workers to press for a transformation of this order. Thus, contrary to views advanced by adherents of scientific management, the designs introduced cannot be understood purely in relation to criteria of technological adequacy, economic efficiency, and social–psychological dynamics. Rather, specific structural designs must be seen in relation to the basic purpose of integration or mobilization that they are intended to serve. Forces oriented to the status quo will promote schemes that they assume will increase job satisfaction and loyalty to the enterprise among the workers. Examples of structural designs,

---

[4]The term *social order* is used as a synonym for "economic and political order," following the usage of "social" as an inclusive term (i.e., seeing the political and economic system as subsystems of a social system).

clearly set forth with an integrative intention and rooted in human relations techniques, are job enlargement, job rotation, improvements in communication, experiments with joint consultation between management and workers, and profit participation as well as individual share-holding schemes.[5] The distinguishing characteristic of these structural designs is their lack of, or minimal amount of, transfer of control to the workers, and their emphasis on joint consultation and mutual accommodation. Change-oriented forces will promote schemes with an emphasis on increasing control over work environment and production decisions, assuming that such schemes will generate interest in and demands for control over a constantly increasing range of decisions at the enterprise level as well as the societal level. Integrative workers' participation schemes, then, are designed to contain pressures through a slight modification of the existing social order, while maintaining the basic principles of social organization and distribution; mobilizing schemes are designed to reinforce pressures for a fundamental transformation of this order, abolishing its basic principles. Consequently, these schemes have to be analyzed in relation to different models of political and economic order that serve as points of orientation to different actors in their attempts to shape policies for the introduction of workers' participation. What type of structural design is actually introduced as an outcome of the political struggle between the proponents of the various designs, pursuing purposes of consolidation or transformation of the existing social order, respectively, is determined by the strength of status-quo-oriented relative to change-oriented sociopolitical forces.

3. *Development and effects of workers' participation:* Once a specific structural design intended to serve integrative or mobilizing purposes is introduced, however, the struggle between sociopolitical forces continues, centering around the implementation of the workers' participation scheme. The actual development and effects of participation processes at the enterprise level are shaped to a much larger extent by the active involvement (or lack thereof) of various actors with links to larger organized forces at the societal level than by the structural design itself. The design structures opportunities for participation, but whether these opportunities simply meet with apathy, lead to integration, or provoke demands for an expansion depends on the degree of mobilizing activity and the ideological orientation of organized forces at the enterprise level.

This is my central departure from the view of other authors, usually Marxists or neo-Marxists, who do analyze workers' participation in the context of class relations and political power. A number of these authors have condemned all

[5]An overview of such attempts is given in Hansson (1974). The following quote from Hansson is typical of the orientation underlying these reforms: "They should achieve increased productivity in such a way that work is consistent with people's needs and interests and that greater job satisfaction is obtained. These objectives, greater productivity and greater job satisfaction, are closely bound up with each other [p. 13]."

participation designs short of full transfer of control rights to the workers as useless or even counterproductive, because of their presumed integrative effects. Gorz is a notable exception among them, drawing a distinction between "reformist reforms" and "not necessarily reformist reforms." He defines a reformist reform as "one which subordinates its objectives to the criteria of rationality and practicability of a given system and policy," as opposed to a reform "which is conceived not in terms of what is possible within the framework of a given system, but in view of what should be made possible in terms of human needs and demands [Gorz 1967:7]." Later on, he qualifies structural reforms (i.e., reforms that modify the relationship of forces or the redistribution of functions and powers) as nonreformist because "the fight for structural reform creates possibilities which point beyond capitalism [Gorz 1967:58–60]." But in the attempt to apply Gorz's qualification to workers' participation schemes, one is left with an ambiguity: According to Gorz's conception of structural (nonreformist) reforms, one has to qualify all structural designs of workers' participation that involve participation in control—even if they transfer only a minimal amount of real power to workers—as nonreformist because they are structural reforms in the sense of modifying the distribution of functions and power within the enterprise. However, a great variety of structural designs for workers' participation are not only compatible with the criteria of rationality and practicability of the capitalist free-enterprise system but also are even introduced with the outright intention of strengthening this system; consequently one would have to qualify them as reformist reforms in Gorz's sense. I intend to show that practically any scheme of participation has the potential to generate challenges to the status quo if a strong and ideologically committed union mobilizes workers to realize fully structurally given participation possibilities.[6] The capacity of unions for long-term, sustained mobilizing activity in turn depends on their strength at the societal level, that is, on their extent of organizational penetration and of organizational and ideological unity. Dynamics at the enterprise level may also have a feedback effect on the societal level, by way of strengthening or weakening the sociopolitical forces involved in the promotion of consolidation or transformation of the existing order. Workers' participation schemes, then, develop in close interaction with changes in the distribution of power in civil society and between civil society and the state.

Here, one can draw an interesting parallel between the development of workers' participation and of strike patterns. In the more recent literature on

---

[6]In a footnote, where he discusses the example of the "counter-plan" advocated by a minority of socialists in France, Gorz admits that in this case it is "impossible to judge a priori if it is reformist [1967:7]." I would argue that this is the case for any reform which constitutes even minimal progress in the direction of workers' control.

strikes, several authors have argued that strike patterns are shaped primarily by societal-level political and economic conditions.[7] Thus, just as strike patterns cannot be explained by the structure of labor relations at the enterprise level,[8] so the development and effects of workers' participation cannot be explained by the structural design of participation introduced at the enterprise level. Both phenomena have to be understood in relation to the distribution of power at the societal level. Strikes are means used by labor to expand its power and share in societal resources for consumption. Strikes can be directed at employers to effect a direct transfer of power and resources or at the government to effect state intervention in the redistribution of power and resources. The use of strikes is rather costly for labor, and consequently alternative means such as political action in the form of mobilization of votes and political bargaining are preferable. Where labor can influence a strong pro-labor government, it can expand its power via workers' participation schemes at the enterprise level and via representation in policy-making bodies at the societal level, and its share in societal resources for consumption via welfare state expansion, taxation, and employment policies. Under such circumstances, then, less frequent use of the strike weapon can be expected. Thus, strike patterns and the development of workers' participation schemes are both shaped by the strength of labor and its political allies relative to other sociopolitical forces.

4. *Supportive policies for workers' participation:* The promotion of specific structural designs of participation has to be seen as an element of a broader political strategy on the part of various sociopolitical forces challenging the established order or responding to such a challenge. Both status-quo-oriented and change-oriented forces pursue a set of policies aimed at consolidating or transforming this order, among which the integration or mobilization of workers occupies a prominent position. Whereas successful integration of workers into their enterprise through a participation scheme may be a sufficient condition to neutralize challenges and consolidate the existing order, successful mobilization of workers through a participation scheme is not a sufficient condition for a process of social transformation; rather it has to be coordinated with

---

[7]Shorter and Tilly (1974); Hibbs (1976); Korpi and Shalev (1979). Though their assumptions and theoretical explanations of the causal linkages differ, all of these authors agree on the basic point that strike patterns are shaped by the political power of labor relative to other sociopolitical forces.

[8]This is not to say that extraordinarily authoritarian relations between management and labor (e.g., lack of communication, etc.) in a given enterprise may not facilitate the outbreak of strikes, particularly wildcat strikes, as proposed by Gouldner (1954). However, the frequency with which such cases occur in a society is dependent on the overall structure of labor relations and thus on wider political forces. Or, to quote Shorter and Tilly: "A society gets, after all, the labor relations system it deserves [1974:27]."

supportive policies that ensure protection of the change process at the societal level. A disjunction between change processes at the enterprise level and the societal level is likely to create economic and political problems, and thus to endanger the progress of a chosen course of the transformation process.

The pursuit of societal level supportive and protective policies for an expansion of workers' participation at the enterprise level is a frequently neglected dimension of the reform process. In particular, members of the New Left who advocate spontaneous action of the masses, such as in factory occupations, and reject organizational centralization of the union movement because of its presumed bureaucratizing and stifling effects on mass mobilization, also tend to de-emphasize coordinated political action for a gradual build-up of protective instruments. Yet, political action to acquire the capacity to exercise control over crucial mechanisms in the national economy, most prominently those affecting investment and employment levels, is indispensable to protect the progressive transfer of control from capital to labor.

Thus, political choice and skill play an important role for the development of workers' participation within given structural conditions set by the strength of status-quo-oriented relative to change-oriented sociopolitical forces. The assignment of priorities among different policies related to workers' participation as an element in a transformation process and the choice of appropriate strategies for the pursuit of a model of a desired alternative social order constitute important determinants of the development and effects of participation schemes. The importance of an adequate choice of strategies, based on knowledge about dynamics that are likely to be set off by policies of social change in societies with different economic and political systems, suggests the need to include the political vision of policymakers as an important variable into an analysis of the development of workers' participation.

In order to understand the role of workers' participation schemes as instruments for integration or transformation, it is necessary to distinguish four different types of politico-economic systems, which serve as points of reference for actors promoting the schemes with one intention or the other. These types are proposed here as general concepts of ideal or pure types, differentiated according to a set of structural variables. Empirical systems approximate these ideal types to varying degrees.

Workers' Participation in Different Types of Political and Economic Systems

The conceptualization of four types of politico-economic systems (see Table 1.1) is based on a combination of distinctions between capitalist and socialist

Table 1.1
Typology of Politico-Economic Systems

System	Liberal-pluralist	Authoritarian-corporatist	Bureaucratic-centralist	Democratic-socialist
Polity	Polyarchy	Nonpolyarchy	Nonpolyarchy	Polyarchy
Legitimacy of organized opposition	High	Low	Low	High
Opportunities for political participation	High	Medium	Medium	High
Economy	Capitalist	Capitalist	Socialist	Socialist
Predominant form of ownership of means of production	Private	Private	Public	Public
Association of exercise Of control rights with legal title of ownership	Close	Medium	Close	Medium
Of income rights with legal title of ownership	Close	Close	Close	Close
Agents exercising dominant share of control and income rights	Private Owners	Private Owners/State	State	State/Workers

economies, and polyarchic and nonpolyarchic polities.[9] The four types are
(1) liberal-pluralist systems, with a capitalist economy and a polyarchic polity;
(2) authoritarian-corporatist systems, with a capitalist economy and a nonpolyarchic polity; (3) bureaucratic-centralist systems, with a socialist economy and
a nonpolyarchic polity; and (4) democratic-socialist systems, with a socialist
economy and a polyarchic polity.

Of the countries that will be discussed in this book, France, Germany, and
Sweden approximate the liberal-pluralist type; Sweden showing some tendencies toward partial assumption of characteristics of the democratic-socialist
type. Yugoslavia exemplifies a case of transition from a system approximating
the bureaucratic-centralist type to a mixed type between the bureaucratic-centralist and the democratic-socialist one. Peru exemplifies the installation of a
system approximating the authoritarian-corporatist type. And Chile, the discussion of which will be restricted to comparisons with certain aspects of the

[9] The term *polyarchy* is used here in Dahl's sense to denote "regimes that have been substantially popularized and liberalized, that is, highly inclusive and extensively open to public con-
testation [1971:8]." The following discussion is very close to his conceptualization. He lists eight
minimal guarantees that such regimes must provide in order to satisfy the requirements of polyarchy: (1) freedom to form and join organizations; (2) freedom of expression; (3) right to vote; (4)
eligibility for public office; (5) right of political leaders to compete for support/votes; (6) alternative
sources of information; (7) free and fair elections; and (8) institutions for making government policies depend on votes and other expressions of preference [1971:3].

Peruvian experience, exemplifies a case of abortive transition from a system approximating the liberal-pluralist type to a democratic-socialist type.

The two types with polyarchic polities are characterized by a high degree of political pluralism, that is, a high degree of legitimacy of organized opposition and broad opportunities for political participation. Legitimacy of organized opposition is particularly crucial as a guarantee for disadvantaged, lower social groups to be allowed to form and join organized movements in order to attempt to gain political power to change the established social order. The access to political power in turn is kept open by broad formal opportunities for political participation in elections and for election to office. In the two types with nonpolyarchic polities, in contrast, opportunities for organized opposition formation and for popular political participation are restricted. Due to the low legitimacy of organized opposition, opportunities for disadvantaged social groups to form movements and attempt to exert political pressure are very small. Opportunities for participating in elections and particularly for being elected to office are narrower than in the two types with polyarchic polities, set within limits defined by the state.

In the two types with a capitalist economy the predominant form of ownership of the means of production is private; in the two types with a socialist economy it is public—that is, the legal titles of ownership of the major means of production are held by private individuals in the former, and by society ("the people") in the latter. Ownership can be conceptualized as a bundle of rights, the two basic types being the right to control the use of property, and the right to appropriate profits generated by its use. Following Pryor's (1973 and 1977) terminology, I am going to refer to them as control and income rights.[10] These two types of rights can be separated from one another and dissociated from the legal title of ownership not only conceptually but also in practice. Either or both of these types of rights can be transferred in varying degrees from the holder of the legal title of ownership to other actors. The degree of closeness of association of the exercise of these rights with the legal title of ownership varies in the different systems. In liberal-pluralist systems, the association is quite close; the major share of income and control rights are exercised by private owners of the means of production, though the state participates to a certain extent in income rights through taxation, and in control rights through general regulations of economic activity. In authoritarian-corporatist systems the regulatory activity of the state in economic as well as political processes is much stronger. Accordingly, the state's participation in control rights is more extensive in authoritarian-corporatist systems than in liberal-pluralist systems, though not its participation in income rights, which remain in the hands of

---

[10] The term *income rights* as used here refers to income from property in the form of interest, rent, or dividends, and has to be distinguished clearly from labor income in the form of wages or salaries.

the private holders of the legal title of ownership. Thus the association between the legal title of ownership and the exercise of control rights in authoritarian-corporatist systems is less close than in liberal-pluralist systems. In bureau-cratic-centralist systems, the association is again very close (i.e., control and income rights are virtually exclusively exercised by the state through the bu-reaucracy, and the state is the representative of "the people," who hold the legal title of ownership.)[11] Applying the same conception of the state as repre-sentative of society, the legal owner of the means of production, to the case of democratic-socialist systems, the association between ownership and the exer-cise of control rights is again less close, insofar as the state delegates a share in the exercise of control rights to the workers in individual enterprises. Associa-tion between ownership and the exercise of income rights remains close, how-ever, insofar as the state appropriates the income produced by the socially owned means of production.

My conceptualization here differs from other conceptualizations of liberal-pluralist, corporatist, and bureaucratic-centralist systems in that it is restricted to structural variables differentiating the four politico-economic systems—omitting the inclusion of normative variables—and it explicitly includes the economic system into the typology.[12] In practice, advocates for the empirical emulation of the various ideal types legitimize their position through ideologies which contain values concerning the desirable character of the social order and of the role assigned to the state in the shaping of this order. For instance, ad-vocates of the liberal-pluralist type value maximum freedom from restrictions for individuals in the pursuit of their interests and assign a passive role to the state, restricted to the protection of a social order arrived at through the inter-action of individuals and social groups in a free market. In contrast, advocates of the democratic-socialist type emphasize social equality and freedom from need as central values and assign an active role to the state, intervening in an equalizing way in the distribution of societal resources.

The differentiation of these four types of politico-economic systems makes it

---

[11]Remember that this is a conceptualization of an ideal type. Of course, one can reject the no-tion that the state in systems approximating the bureaucratic-centralist type is in reality (i.e., not by definition) the representative of "the people." In this case, one would have to argue that the degree of association between the legal title of ownership and the exercise of control and income rights is at a maximum disjunction.

[12]For various conceptualizations of corporatism, which include structural as well as normative dimensions, see Pike and Stritch (1974). Schmitter's contribution to their volume, which is exclu-sively concerned with structural variables, concentrates on the structure of interest articulation (i.e., the political system only). Stepan (1978:3–72) draws attention to the normative and structural dimension of liberal-pluralist and Marxist conceptions of state and society. He also develops the concept of organic statism both as a normative model of relations between state and society, and as an abstract model of governance which resembles the authoritarian-corporatist type proposed here.

possible now to understand the role assigned to workers' participation schemes as instruments for integration or mobilization by sociopolitical forces promoting consolidation or transformation, respectively, of a given empirical system. Change-oriented forces promoting the introduction of workers' participation schemes as an element of a transformation strategy into empirical systems approximating the first three types intend these schemes to create and maintain a momentum for transformation in the direction of the democratic-socialist type.[13] They see the introduction of workers' participation as a step in the process of full socialization of control and income rights, that is, of transfer of these rights from the holders of the legal title of ownership or their representatives to workers and a democratic state. This applies to the liberal-pluralist and the authoritarian-corporatist systems where the primary holders of the legal title of ownership and their representatives are private individuals, as well as to the bureaucratic-centralist system where the nondemocratic state is the representative of society as the formal owner of the means of production. The transformation process thus has several dimensions, according to the type of system: (1) substitution of contribution of labor power for contribution of capital as basis for the exercise of certain decision-making rights in all three types; (2) substitution of the public for private owners in the exercise of income rights in the two types with capitalist economies; and (3) guaranteeing legitimacy of organized opposition while increasing opportunities for popular participation in the political process in the two types with nonpolyarchic polities.[14]

Sociopolitical forces that promote structural changes in a politico-economic system in order to approximate the democratic-socialist type typically also pro-

[13]This is an empirically rather than theoretically founded statement. Of course, change-oriented forces in each of the systems may promote a transformation in a direction other than toward the democratic-socialist type, but in this case they would be unlikely to use workers' participation as an instrument in their transformation strategy. A possible exception to this statement is a transformation attempt from a liberal-pluralist to an authoritarian-corporatist system, in which a workers' participation scheme could be used as part of a "carrot and stick" strategy to prevent lower-class resistance against a curtailment of the legitimacy of organized opposition and political participation, by way of offering some incentives to the previously most mobilized sectors of the working class. However, the workers' participation scheme itself, then, would have an integrative rather than mobilizing character in the sense of containing pressures from workers for a progressive expansion of their control and income rights.

[14]The differentiation of these four types of politico-economic systems also facilitates a clarification of issues frequently raised in the debate about workers' participation. Problems connected to the introduction of workers' participation, such as accumulation versus distribution, moral versus material incentives, and centralization versus decentralization of control rights, pose greater or lesser difficulties depending on the type of system within which workers' participation is developing. Discussions of these issues often obscure more than clarify potential solutions due to a lack of specification of the type of politico-economic system in question. I will deal with some of these issues in later sections.

mote policies to increase social equality. Socialist ideology, which serves as their guide for action and legitimation, contains the achievement of a classless society, free from exploitation and domination as central value. Strategies to achieve this goal are socialization of control and income rights and strengthening of the state's performance of an equalizing function. Thus, in the two systems with capitalist economies, democratic-socialist transformation strategies require that a partial transfer of control rights to workers be linked to a transfer of income rights and a share of control rights to the state. In a bureaucratic-centralist system, they require that the state retain the exercise of income rights and a share of control rights, and that a partial transfer of control rights to workers be linked to a transfer of political decision-making rights from a narrow elite to larger organized forces.[15]

In contrast to workers' participation schemes promoted as elements of democratic-socialist transformation strategies and emphasizing transfers of control rights, workers' participation schemes introduced with integrative intentions into systems with capitalist economies tend to de-emphasize the actual exercise of control rights by workers. In order to be able to assess and compare the extent of control rights exercised by the workers in various structural participation designs, it is necessary to specify different dimensions of control: degree, range, and direction.

Structural Designs for Workers' Participation at the Enterprise Level

The extent of the workers' share in the exercise of control rights depends on the degree of decision-making power transferred to them, on the range of decisions in which they participate, and on the direction in which they can in-

---

[15]This conception of the transformation process and of the democratic-socialist type of system toward which it is directed has to be distinguished clearly from a transformation process involving a joint transfer of the legal title and full exercise of control and income rights from private owners or from the state to the workers in individual enterprises, with minimal or no state participation in control and income rights. Such a transformation process, resulting in the formation of producers' cooperatives, constitutes an obstacle in the realization of the value of social equality, because the members of the different cooperatives enjoy control rights over unequal amounts of capital and thus derive unequal benefits from the exercise of their income rights. It even opens up new possibilities for traditional capitalist types of exploitation, such as the hiring of nonmember workers at low pay. This has happened in the Peruvian sugar cooperatives, which were turned over to the workers after the expropriation of their owners in 1969. Initially, they were praised as the most significant achievement of the Peruvian "Humanist–Socialist Revolution," but then they became frequently attacked examples of "group egoism." McClintock (1977) provides evidence of strong tendencies of group egoism, social inequalities, and resistance against collaboration with government agencies, in particular against compliance with governmental equalization policies in agrarian cooperatives.

fluence the decisions.[16] One can distinguish three basic types of participation according to the degree of decision-making power transferred to the workers: (1) joint consultation, referring to any communications between management and workers about decisions over which workers have less than 50% of the power; (2) codetermination, referring to any decision-making situation where workers and management have equal power and have to find a compromise solution; and (3) workers' control, referring to any decision-making situation where the workers have more than 50% of the power.[17]

The second dimension determining the extent of control exercised by the workers is the range of decisions in which the different types of participation take place. Elaborating Karlsson's (1973) model (see below), we can establish a hierarchical order of decisions within an enterprise. The higher up in this order a decision is, the more importance it has in terms of committing the enterprise's resources and determining the future situation of members of the

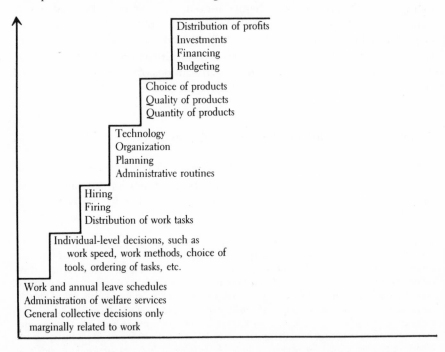

Distribution of profits
Investments
Financing
Budgeting

Choice of products
Quality of products
Quantity of products

Technology
Organization
Planning
Administrative routines

Hiring
Firing
Distribution of work tasks

Individual-level decisions, such as
   work speed, work methods, choice of
   tools, ordering of tasks, etc.

Work and annual leave schedules
Administration of welfare services
General collective decisions only
   marginally related to work

[16] Walker (1975) distinguishes among scope, degree, and extent of participation. Scope refers to the range of managerial functions in which workers take part, degree designates how far workers influence managerial functions, and extent describes how far participation is spread through the workforce of an enterprise.

[17] The participation literature in the field of organizational behavior distinguishes a wide variety of forms of participation, ranging from the right to information to the exercise of full control over decisions. For such scales of participation see Likert (1961:242) and Miller and Form (1964).

enterprise. Thus, the higher up in this model the range of decisions in which the workers participate reaches, the greater the extent of control exercised by the workers over the enterprise.

The third dimension that determines the extent of control exercised by the workers is the direction in which decisions can be influenced through the various types of participation: whether decision-making power granted to the workers is only negative (i.e., making it possible for workers to dispute or veto management's decisions) or also positive (i.e., making it possible for workers to raise issues and initiate decision-making processes). In formal participation arrangements, introduced through legislation or collective agreements between workers and employers, participation tends to include both directions. However, in situations where there are no formal participation arrangements, but plant-level unions or individual work groups are strong enough to force employers to grant them a certain degree of control within the enterprise, such control tends to be exercised primarily in a negative direction, as protection against undesirable management decisions.[18]

These three dimensions determine the extent of formal control rights transferred to the workers, but whether they are actually exercised depends to some degree on the integration of the structural design, and to a much higher degree on the presence of a mobilizing agency, that is, an active union, in the enterprise. Integration of the structural design refers to a link between participation at the different hierarchical levels of decision making and between direct and indirect forms of participation. Direct participation in decision making at lower levels is a favorable motivational condition sustaining interest in indirect participation through representation at higher levels, and effective participation at higher levels is necessary to protect decisions taken at lower levels. In practice, virtually all workers' participation schemes to date fall short of providing such integrated participation possibilities, particularly as far as the extent of real control rights of workers at higher levels of capitalist enterprises is concerned. This holds true for participation designs clearly aimed at integration into the capitalist order, as well as for those arrived at through compromise between sociopolitical forces promoting a capitalist and socialist order respectively. The extent to which deficient schemes result in apathy and leave the status quo unchallenged, or are used as change-oriented instruments realizing potential influence through participation to its fullest and generating pressures for more influence, depends largely on the presence of an actively mobilizing union.

The structural design of a participation scheme never fully determines its impact on the preservation or transformation of a given social order—it only structures possibilities, the full realization and transcendence of which depend on the strength of labor organization at the enterprise level as well as at the

---

[18]Such examples of participation without formal participation arrangements can be found particularly in British and Italian patterns of plant-level labor relations.

societal level, in conjunction with other change-oriented forces. Since the constellation of and dynamics between sociopolitical forces vary according to the economic and political system of a society, I am now going to specify and examine my general conceptualization of dynamics in the four developmental stages for three different types of systems, which approximate three of the concepts of ideal types of politico-economic systems distinguished earlier.

Workers' Participation in Developed Capitalist Democratic Systems

Developed capitalist democratic systems as empirical types approximate the concept of the liberal-pluralist ideal type to varying degrees. In order to be able to identify the important variables for a specification of the dynamics operating in the four developmental stages, it is first necessary to attempt a conceptualization of the constellation of sociopolitical forces in developed capitalist democratic systems, that is, of the distribution of power within civil society and between civil society and the state.

For this purpose, one can distinguish two basic categories of power which can be exercised by social groups: economic and political power. Economic power is based on control over means of production (i.e., control over capital, labor, land, natural resources, and technology). Control refers to the ability of a social group to mobilize the resources at its disposal for purposeful action. This ability is determined by the degree of dispersion versus concentration of the legal title of ownership of resources, the ratio between supply and demand of the resources at the disposal of social groups, the organizational penetration of social groups, and a sustained perception of common interests as a basis for coordinated action.

Political power is based on control over the bureaucratic and coercive apparatus of the state. In polyarchic systems, this control is obtained through winning electoral competitions. Electoral success, in turn, depends on the opinion-making capacity of social groups. Determinants of this capacity are size and organizational penetration of social groups, number of ideologically committed activists, access to communication media, and influence within institutional orders of society. Organizational penetration provides a network for direct personal contacts, a highly efficient means for opinion formation. Thus, organizational strength increases the opinion-making capacity and consequently the political power of social groups directly. It also has an indirect effect insofar as it increases the economic power of social groups by raising their capacity to activate the resources at their disposal for purposeful action. Economic power, in turn, provides access to communication media and influence within institutional orders of society as instruments for opinion formation. Consequently, the distribution of economic and political power is interdependent. The policy output of the state is largely a reflection of the distribution of economic power and opinion-making capacity among social groups. The balance of power between state and civil society is strongly slanted toward civil society.

Challenges to the established order can be a result of changes in the distribution of either one of these two power categories. The type of challenge that is of interest from the point of view of the introduction of workers' participation is the one originating from an increase in power of lower social groups, enabling them to pressure for a transfer of a certain amount of income and control rights from upper social groups. Such an increase can result from the numerical growth of these groups, from a change in the supply–demand ratio of the resources at the disposal of these groups, and, most importantly, from an increase in their organizational penetration as a prerequisite for the activation of their power resources. Taking the example of an increase in the power of propertyless workers as a social group—whose only resource is their labor power—one can identify the following causes: Industrialization leads to a numerical growth of the group of dependent wage earners; high levels of economic growth and full employment cause a favorable shift in the supply–demand ratio of labor; increasing unionization raises the workers' capability for coordinated action and thus for an activation of the power resources resulting from the first two types of changes. On the basis of such an increase in economic power, organized labor can expand its share in income and control rights vis-à-vis owners of capital by way of collective negotiations for wages and working conditions. Or, even if collective negotiation fails to lead to an agreement but organized labor is strong, it can expand its share in control rights de facto by way of noncompliance with managerial directives.

Similarly, changes in the distribution of political power may result from increased organizational penetration of lower social groups, if active mobilization for the pursuit of a common interest is extended to the political sphere. Through electoral support for political parties committed to using state power for redistributive measures, organized lower social groups can extend their share in the distribution of resources. In addition to its direct effect through opinion formation in support of political parties, organization provides indirect access to political power for lower social groups through an increase in their economic power. Economic power is an important prerequisite for sustained political power in two major ways: (1) Economic power provides access to communication media as important instruments for opinion formation; and (2) through their exercise of economic power, social groups can provide or withhold resources from society; in particular, they can create economic difficulties, which are typically blamed on an incumbent government and thus in a polyarchy are highly likely to influence electoral outcomes (i.e., the distribution of political power).

Thus, in developed capitalist democratic systems with strong social and economic institutions, winning legal control over the state apparatus is an insufficient power base to introduce fundamental transformations in the social order, if it is not supported by broad and sustained opinion-making capacity, and thus by a significant share in economic power. In other words, the political path to a redistribution of control and income rights is only viable if it is based on social penetration and sufficient control over means of production to ensure economic stability. [19]

Consequently, the capability of lower social groups to change the existing distribution of control over means of production and of resources for consumption is greatest if their organized activation of economic and political power is coordinated. A highly organized and ideologically united labor movement, with unions as the economic power base and a labor party as the political power base, then, is most likely to successfully expand labor's share in control and income rights, and consequently to effect an equalization in the distribution of resources for consumption.

The two key variables sustaining the successful advance of such a gradual process are long-term incumbency of a leftist party and high centralization of the organizational and collective bargaining structure of the union movement. [20] Political measures for an expansion of labor's share in power and in resources for consumption are not restricted to governmental intervention in direct disputes between labor and capital but rather include a whole range of social and economic policies that cannot produce significant effects in the short run. Centralization of the union movement and of collective bargaining facilitates the consolidation of working class solidarity and the pursuit of a coordinated wage policy. It also renders labor a reliable partner for a leftist government in the attempt to implement a coherent labor market policy and counter cyclical economic policies. If organized labor is assured of government policy gradually but decidedly improving the situation of the working class, and if this assurance can be effectively communicated from the center to the rank and

[19]Using slightly different terminology, this argument states that civil society in developed capitalist democratic systems sets limits to what the state can do. An excellent argument about the relation between the state and civil society in industrial democracies, and its consequences for socialist strategy, is made by Anderson (1965:221–290), drawing heavily on Gramsci. J.D. Stephens (1979) extends this argument and provides empirical evidence in support of it.

[20]Actually, the effect of high concentration of the union movement on an expansion of labor's de facto exercise of control rights at the enterprise level is not unambiguous. Centralization is a prerequisite for a significant transfer of control rights through national legislation, but it may entail a low degree of mobilization at the base and consequently only a partial exercise of legally transferred control rights. In contrast, union movements with low centralization but high mobilization at the base may exercise considerable shop-floor control rights extracted from employers in the best organized enterprises. For a more detailed discussion of this point see Stephens and Stephens (in press).

file, then the likelihood of militant but costly strike action is greatly reduced. Thus, as a result of extended incumbency of a leftist party in alliance with a labor movement characterized by extensive organizational penetration and high centralization, one can expect greater progress towards social equality, with a greater encroachment on control and income rights of capital, lower unemployment, and lower strike frequency.

There is empirical evidence to support these hypotheses: J. D. Stephens (1979) tested the impact of labor organization on the degree of equality in the distribution of resources for consumption for 10 Western industrial democracies and found it to be significant.[21] The percentage of total labor force organized explains between 49% and 81% of the variation in inequality, depending on the measure used, from among the following three different Gini indices of income distribution: pre-tax, post-tax, and post-tax adjusted for the redistributive impact of nonmilitary public-sector spending. The same study also shows the importance of unionization for the electoral strength of left parties: The percentage of total labor force organized explains 76% of the variation in leftist rule, measured by an index of participation of leftist parties in government, according to incumbency as majority or participation in coalition governments. Since these two variables are so highly correlated, it would be very difficult to measure their independent effects on inequality. If only leftist rule is used as predictor of inequality, the number of years of participation of leftist parties in government between 1945 and 1970 explains between 24% and 66% in the variation of the abovementioned inequality indices.

Cameron (1978) introduces expansion of the public economy as an additional variable and shows the same basic relationship in a study based on data for 18 nations: Leftist political strength measured by the percentage of the government's electoral base composed of Social Democratic or Labor parties, 1960–1975, is strongly associated with the increase in all government revenues as a percent of GDP from 1960 to 1975 ($r = .60$). And the increase in the public economy is strongly associated with economic equality, measured by the difference in the proportion of all national income after taxes received by the top and bottom 20% of households ($r = .83$).

These findings support the argument that leftist governments attempt to expand public control over the allocation of resources and to use this control to equalize the distribution of resources for consumption.[22] Size of the public economy, however, does not capture the overall extent of control exercised by the state. Legal measures, such as wage and price regulations, environmental

---

[21]This study also presents evidence for the importance of centralization of the labor movement for its political capacity to effect redistributive policies.

[22]This argument is not the thrust of Cameron's article, but it is supported by his findings. He shows that the openness of the economy (exports and imports as percent of GDP) is the strongest predictor of the growth of the public economy, followed by leftist political strength.

and safety standards, labor legislation, and employment policies, clearly constitute significant forms of public control over the economy and consequently they constitute important instruments for changing the distribution of control and income rights, transferring them to some extent from owners of capital to the state.[23] The significance of these forms of control—like that of different schemes of workers' participation—is hardly quantifiable and subject to statistical analysis. However, a qualitative comparison of such forms of public control, in conjunction with different schemes of workers' participation, will support the argument about the importance of labor organization and leftist rule for a redistribution of control and income rights, and thus for an extension of workers' participation schemes.

Evidence for the relation between leftist incumbency and unemployment is provided by Hibbs (1977). He argues that the low unemployment–high inflation position on the Phillips curve serves the economic interests of lower-income and occupational groups, whereas the high unemployment–low inflation position serves those of upper-income and occupational groups. Subjective preferences of different social groups are more or less in accordance with their objective interests, and the trade-off is clearly perceived by the leadership of various political parties. Hibbs shows that empirical outcomes in 12 Western European and North American nations are consistent with class-related preferences. Nations with predominantly Social Democratic–Labor political rule in the 1945–1969 period (measured by percentage of years with Socialist-Labor parties in the executive) had high inflation rates in the period 1960–1969 $(r = +.74)$ but low rates of unemployment $(r = -.68)$.

Finally, evidence for the impact of effective political representation of the working class on strike behavior is provided by comparative historical and more short-term cross-sectional studies. Shorter and Tilly (1974:328) argue that the distinctive North European strike patterns in the post-1945 period (diminution of strike frequency to virtual insignificance) emerged as a consequence of the access to political power of the working class through participation or domination of leftist parties in government. Hibbs (1976:1054–1055) shows that in the post-1945 period leftist governments in nations with oscillations in leftist rule have not had a moderating impact on short-term upward movements in strike activity. This underlines the importance of medium- to long-term leftist incumbency for the achievement of advances in labor's share of power and means of consumption significant enough to consolidate labor's reliance on political action and render strikes largely superfluous.

---

[23]The existence and extent of such forms of public control does not necessarily imply that they are used to equalize the distribution of resources. This is only the case where there is a leftist government with a strong social base in organized labor. Where labor and the left are weak, public controls can be used for policy formation with highly inegalitarian outcomes, responding primarily to interests of private corporations. The various U.S. regulatory boards are a case in point.

Applying these arguments about the key variables determining the distribution of power in society and policy outcomes to the development of workers' participation, my conceptualization of four developmental stages can be specified for developed capitalist democratic systems as follows:

1. *Origins of workers' participation:* The introduction of workers' participation schemes is a consequence of a challenge to the existing economic and political order resulting from an increase in economic and political power of organized labor, or from interference of external forces in the internal constellation of sociopolitical forces. An example of the latter origins is the introduction of workers' participation through legislation about works councils in most Western and Central European countries right after World War II.[24] Possible future examples might be supranational economic integration agreements that contain provisions about workers' participation. This is only a likely origin for the introduction of workers' participation in relatively small and economically less important countries, though, if such provisions are included in economic integration agreements as a result of pressures from economically dominant countries. Imposition of such provisions on dominant member countries in economic integration agreements by economically less important countries seems much less likely. This points to the importance of internal constellations of sociopolitical forces in economically dominant countries, which account for origins and development of workers' participation there.

Examples of the first type of origins are demands for workers' participation from unions with growing strength directed at employers in collective negotiations or directed at political parties for corresponding legislation. However, increased strength and pressures from labor can be indirect causes for the introduction of workers' participation schemes, even if not demanded explicitly by unions. For instance, high militancy of unions in wage negotiations, or high labor turnover under conditions of full employment, may force employers to make jobs intrinsically more attractive by way of providing some opportunities for workers to participate in the exercise of control rights. Or, it may induce employers to attempt to integrate the workforce into the enterprise through a certain participation in income rights.

2. *Purpose and design of workers' participation:* Workers' participation schemes promoted by status-quo forces as a response to increasing power and pressures from labor are aimed at containing these pressures through integrating workers and their leaders into the capitalist free-enterprise system. Schemes promoted by change-oriented forces are aimed at reinforcing these pressures through increasing labor's share in income and control rights as a step toward

[24]For a short summary of such legislation and its origins, consult ILO (1969a).

gradual but fundamental transformation of the capitalist order. Where different schemes of workers' participation are promoted for purposes of integration by representatives of capital and for purposes of transformation by representatives of labor, the type of structural design introduced and its development will depend on the strength of organized labor relative to representatives of interests of capital as a sociopolitical force (i.e., on its potential for coordinated activation of economic and political power). The greater the organizational penetration of civil society by the labor movement, both through unions and a labor party, and the stronger the ideological unity and commitment of the labor movement to a socialist transformation, the greater the chances for labor to effect legislation that transfers control and income rights from capital owners to workers and/or the state. The smaller the sociopolitical strength of labor vis-à-vis that of capital owners, on the other hand, the greater will be the chances that the need for a political compromise will result in a type of participation scheme with a minimal encroachment on control rights of capital owners.

3. *Development and effects of workers' participation:* Once a specific participation scheme is introduced, its further development in the sense of effective implementation and full realization of structurally given participation possibilities will depend on the relation between the economic and political strength of capital owners to resist, and of organized labor to mobilize for its implementation and active participation. Resistance against or compliance with the introduction of workers' participation on the part of owners and managers depends to a large extent on their perception of its potential effects on the overall share of private investors as a group in the societal-level distribution of control and income rights, as well as on their perception of chances for successful resistance. Attempts to exert actual influence on enterprise decisions, or accommodation, or apathy on the part of the workforce depend only marginally on the specific structural design of participation, and to a much larger extent on the presence of a mobilizing union, on the latter's ideological orientation and larger organizational history and cohesion.

Ideological orientation and active involvement of union leaders and activists at the enterprise level as well as at higher levels of union organization are crucial for the concrete functioning of different structural designs of participation at the enterprise level, and their effects on the workers. Under the same societal-level constellation of sociopolitical forces, the same structural design of participation can result in integration or apathy, or in frustration and militancy, according to the role assumed by the respective union leaders and activists in different enterprises. If union leaders can be co-opted through personal benefits accruing to them from participation in decision-making bodies, chances for integration increase; conversely, if union leaders assume a critical distance or are indifferent toward participation, workers are highly likely to show distrust and apathy toward it. However, if union leaders advocate active participation and point out its impact on decisions affecting the workers' concrete situation, a high degree of involvement is likely, causing the workers to experience the limitations of a given structural design and creating demands for an increasing share in control rights.

There are several types of limitations on participation designs which are typical of the compromise solutions introduced into capitalist enterprises and which can be partly compensated for by strong union activity. For instance, where direct involvement in work organization decisions at the base is weak or nonexistent, the impact of decisions taken by representatives at higher levels is not so immediately obvious as to maintain interest at the base. This, in turn, weakens the position of these representatives vis-à-vis management—and increases the chance of co-optation—by depriving them of pressure they could apply and solidaristic support from below. In these cases, the potential of mobilization and pressure from an active and ideologically strong union can compensate for this weakness. Under exceptional conditions, particularly in crisis situations that endanger job stability, interest in participation through representation at highest levels is generally strong, regardless of opportunities for direct participation at lower levels. However, formal participation in effective control rights at the highest levels is mostly insufficient to allow for significant worker input in the solution of such crisis situations. Again, support from a strong union may at least increase worker input. Another type of limited participation design, where a strong union may provide the missing link, concerns involvement of the base in direct decision making but restricts it to the lowest levels, without any effective power over decisions at higher levels. Examples are arrangements for self-steering groups that may be represented in joint-consultation bodies at higher levels. In such a system, pressure from a strong union in support of demands originating in participation at the base and presented by representatives with joint consultation rights can clearly make it harder for management to reject these demands.

The strength, ideological orientation, and mobilizing activity of a union are crucial not only for the full development of participation possibilities in deficient schemes but even more so for resistance against the devisive and integrative potential built into participation schemes designed to strengthen the capitalist order. Division and integration can take the form of a development of a rivalry between union and participatory bodies, particularly if one of the two is clearly favored as partner by the employer and is capable of providing more concrete benefits for workers. Another possibility is the strengthening of oligarchic tendencies within unions through participative arrangements in which workers' representatives at higher levels are appointed by the union.

Where top union leaders are too remote or are co-opted, the mobilizing role can be performed by lowest-level union leaders or shop-floor activists. The

modal type of reaction, though, and consequently the overall effect on integration of labor versus generation of demands for a transformation of the socioeconomic order, depends on the societal-level strength of organized labor: on
organizational penetration, ideological unity, and available number of activists.
The satisfaction of demands for transformation through corresponding policies
will further depend on the growth of organized labor's sustained capacity for
mobilizing sufficient political support.

4. *Strategies for workers' participation:* Sociopolitical forces that promote
workers' participation in capitalist enterprises as an element of transformation
strategy view its introduction as a step toward the socialization of control and
income rights. Successful progress in this direction depends on a coordinated
strategic approach to encroachment on control and income rights held by capital owners at the societal and enterprise levels. Societal-level protective policies are a prerequisite for the significant transfer of control rights from owners,
or rather from management (as owners' representatives) to workers at the enterprise level. The two most important of these policies in a democratic capitalist
system are protection against capital flight, in order to ensure continued economic stability and growth, and creation of full employment.

Sociopolitical forces promoting workers' participation with the goal of a
democratic-socialist transformation also promote policies to increase social
equality. Policies regulating socialization of control over means of production
and equalizing the distribution of resources for consumption are related not
only for ideological reasons but for practical reasons as well. Equalizing the
distribution of resources for consumption requires redistribution between those
employed and not employed, and between different regions and sectors of the
economy, as well as between different enterprises and skill categories. In the
process of a gradual socialist transformation, such equalization can be pursued
through investment planning, coordinated labor-market and wage policies, and
of course through a progressive tax system and an expansion of the welfare
state. Implementation of these measures requires partial socialization of control
and income rights, that is, partial transfer of these rights from private owners
to the state. Which among the goals of socialization of control rights at the
societal level, expansion of workers' participation at the enterprise level, and
social equality receive priority in policy making in the course of a socialist
transformation is a matter of choice. However, enterprise-level transfer of control rights from owners to workers and equalization of the distribution of resources for consumption cannot be successfully advanced without concomitant
progress of protective policies in transferring control and income rights to the
state.

In Chapter 2, I present empirical evidence to substantiate this specification
of dynamics in the four developmental stages through a comparison of workers'

participation schemes in three different developed capitalist democracies with labor movements of varying sociopolitical strengths: France, the Federal Republic of Germany, and Sweden. In the same chapter, I discuss Yugoslavia, which cannot be ignored in any discussion of workers' participation because it is the most fully developed empirical example of a workers' participation scheme. The Yugoslav scheme of workers' participation developed within a developing socialist system, initially close to the bureaucratic-centralist type. In order to compare the Yugoslav experience to the development of workers' participation schemes in other types of systems, I will now attempt a specification of my conceptualization of dynamics in the four developmental stages for developing socialist authoritarian systems.

Workers' Participation in Developing Socialist Authoritarian Systems

Developing socialist authoritarian systems as empirical types approximate the concept of the bureaucratic-centralist ideal type to varying degrees. They differ from developed capitalist democratic systems in such key dimensions as public versus private ownership of major means of production, low versus high degree of legitimacy of organized opposition, and medium versus high range of opportunities for popular participation. They also differ in a further fundamental respect: conditions of high versus low scarcity of resources. Accordingly, the constellation of sociopolitical forces is fundamentally different: In societies that have gone through a socialist revolution and established a bureaucratic-centralist system, both economic and political power are concentrated in the state. Restrictions on the formation of organized opposition and on opportunities for political participation protect the high degree of autonomy from sociopolitical forces enjoyed by the elite who control the state apparatus. Even more crucial, the power of the state over civil society rests on its exercise of control and income rights over major means of production, that is, on its monopoly of economic power.

Control over organizational penetration of society and over access to communication media confers a significant opinion-making capacity upon the state, and, in particular, impedes independent social groups from gaining an autonomous organizational base and a similar opinion-making capacity, on the basis of which they could compete for political power. The elites who hold state power in such systems typically legitimize their rule with the claim that the establishment of public ownership of means of production eliminates class exploitation and that consequently the state represents and acts in the interests of the working class. Whereas the state enjoys a very high degree of internal autonomy vis-à-vis civil society, its freedom of action may be limited by external forces due to dependence on external resources under conditions of scarcity.

Changes in the existing distribution of economic and political power can originate from within the elite who hold state power or from external pressures. A redistribution of economic and political power in this context can take the form of a democratization of political decision making in the state itself and/or a decentralization of the exercise of control rights over means of production in part to lower-level state agencies and in part to the workers within individual enterprises. The crucial determinants of the direction and extent of such a redistribution process are the strength and ideological unity and orientation of the elite, the priority assigned to the control redistribution process in relation to other policy objectives, and the toleration of the redistribution process by external forces, or the relative capacity of the elite to resist pressures from external forces to the contrary.

If elite cohesion and ideological commitment to a redistribution process oriented toward a democratic socialist transformation are strong, one can expect the following results: sustained progress toward social equality, maintenance of full employment, credibility of the government's claim to represent the working class, and consequently a very low probability of strike action even in the absence of sanctions against it. If elite consensus breaks down and thus opens up greater possibilities for influence from society, this influence is most likely to come from upper occupational groups and to be directed against advances in the redistribution process. In the absence of legitimate autonomous organizations, the working class lacks capacity for coordinated action to exert influence, whereas upper occupational groups are better able to mobilize their resources, such as skills, expertise, connections, to influence various members of the elite. Therefore, deviations from progress toward equality and from full employment can be expected as a result of a breakdown in elite consensus. The concomitant decline of credibility in the representation of working class interests by the government renders labor discontent and its expression through spontaneous localized strikes more likely.

Using the variables identified as important for the constellation of sociopolitical forces in developing socialist authoritarian systems, my conceptualization can be specified as follows:

1. *Origins of workers' participation:* The introduction of workers' participation is a response made by the elite who hold state power to internally or externally induced problems that threaten the existing economic and political order. Such problems can result from internal disintegration of the elite, economic difficulties, social unrest, an overload of the central policy-making machinery, or from external threats. Social unrest refers to spontaneous manifestations of discontent, possibly even violent manifestations, as opposed to challenges resulting from growing economic and political power of social groups and concomitant organized pursuit of demands, as in developed capitalist democratic systems.

2. *Purpose and design of workers' participation:* Workers' participation introduced by the political elite in response to such problems is aimed at either consolidating a bureaucratic-centralist type of system or transforming it into a democratic-socialist type. In the former case, workers' participation as an integrative element will tend to take the form of joint consultation with state-appointed managers through works committees. In the latter case, workers' participation as a transformative element will tend to take the form of a share in the exercise of control rights and to be accompanied by a democratization of economic policy making at higher levels. The type of workers' participation introduced will depend mainly on the relative strength of the advocates of a bureaucratic-centralist and democratic-socialist system among the elite.

3. *Development and effects of workers' participation:* The full development of a specific workers' participation design at the enterprise level will depend on the availability of an organization penetrating society and ensuring the implementation of centrally determined policies. If workers' participation is introduced as an element of a consolidation strategy, such an organization, be it the official party or union, can influence the composition and activities of works councils to ensure collaboration with state-appointed administrators and fulfillment of centrally determined production plans. If workers' participation is introduced as an element of a transformation strategy, bureaucrats and administrators at all levels will have to be convinced or forced to share some of their power with workers or other popular representatives, and also the workers and the population at large will have to be mobilized into participating. Thus the full realization of structurally given participation possibilities presupposes a willingness on the part of the elite to tolerate and even actively support the build-up of an organization reaching down to and stimulating activity at the base. This, in turn, may cause the emergence of pressures on the elite for a further decentralization of control rights and/or democratization of their central exercise through an expansion of opportunities for popular political participation. The effectiveness of these pressures will depend on the ratio of centrally retained to decentralized control and income rights, and on the elite's ideological unity concerning the desirable distribution of economic and political power, particularly the legitimacy of autonomous organization. Thus, the introduction of workers' participation may cause new dynamics between the state and civil society, which influence the further effects of workers' participation on consolidation versus transformation of the existing system. Yet, it is the elite controlling the state that has the initiative and the capacity to channel these dynamics, unless the elite divests itself of this power voluntarily or by default (through failing to reach an agreement on its use).

4. *Strategies for workers' participation:* Workers' participation introduced as an element of a transformation strategy directed toward a democratic-socialist

system requires a coordination of a step-wise transfer of control rights from state-appointed administrators to the workers with a progressive democratization of central decision making. Democratization is not equivalent to decentralization: Central exercise of income rights and overall control rights is necessary to secure the achievement of social equality, a central value for the advocates of a democratic-socialist system, and to ensure purposefully planned use of scarce resources for economic development. However, democratization of the power to exercise central control involves institutionalizing the participation of popular representatives in central decision making by putting the exercise of central decision-making power in their hands rather than those of a small self-appointed elite.

The tension between centralization and decentralization of control rights is a frequently raised issue in the debate about workers' participation in a democratic-socialist transformation. If the introduction of workers' participation is linked to a democratization of central decision making, then the problem becomes essentially one of a trade-off between the extent of direct participation in exercising control rights at the enterprise level and indirect participation through representation at higher levels. The share of control rights exercised by the state relative to the share exercised by workers in individual enterprises depends on the need for central social and economic development planning. Central planning can vary in degree from setting exact guidelines for types and quantities of products and their distribution, which economists consider adequate for lower levels of economic development,[25] to general allocation of investment resources with reliance on the market mechanism as determinant of types, quantities, and distribution of products, deemed economically more adequate at higher levels of development. Similarly, the central performance by the state of equalizing the distribution of resources for consumption can vary from allocating specific types and quantities of resources to individuals and social groups (e.g., through rationing) to the establishment of an equalizing tax system and provision of comprehensive free social services, with choice of types and quantities of consumption left to individuals and social groups through the disposition over their allocated share of income. Again, the level of economic development strongly influences the choice of the type of equalization mechanisms and the degree of "consumer participation" provided for, by way of requiring adaptations to conditions of scarcity.

A further strategic problem in the pursuit of a democratic-socialist transformation is to find a mechanism for distribution which constitutes a compromise

---

[25]"According to this reasoning, a central planning model is very possibly well-suited for an underdeveloped country whose goals include modernization and rapid rates of growth, and which is faced with a low level of technology, small markets, and inelastic supplies of productive factors [Milenkovitch, 1971:293]."

between the basic commitment to social equality and the requirement to offer differential rewards to elicit maximum work efforts. Under equal distribution of resources for consumption and a guaranteed basic standard of living, work efforts tend to diminish unless specially rewarded. This produces a tension between the promotion of social equality and the need to use material incentives whose very logic of operation is based on differential reward. Allocation of such differential rewards at the enterprise level by the workers themselves and central determination of the total amount of resources to be distributed for consumption in this way constitutes a mechanism for distribution compromising a basic commitment to social equality to the least possible extent. This mechanism also avoids the dilemma of accumulation versus distribution. Through central exercise of income rights and determination of the total amount of resources to be allocated for consumption, a constant rate of accumulation can be maintained.

The Yugoslav example of the development of workers' participation is relevant for developing countries which have gone through a socialist revolution and established state control over major means of production. For a substantial number of present-day developing countries, however, the path via a mass-based socialist revolution becomes an increasingly unlikely one to follow as they reach middle levels of economic development. Socialist revolutions have typically occurred in countries at early stages of capitalist economic penetration and development, with a large peasant population and a predominant dependence of the country on agriculture, and with a small industrial working class. Stagnation of further economic development and modernization provided the conditions for radical elites to organize mass-based revolutionary movements and capture state power through armed struggle.[26] Particularly in colonial societies, the exclusion of the indigenous educated elite from all leadership positions was conducive to the formation of radical elites organizing revolutionary movements. And foreign domination constituted a highly visible catalyst for revolutionary action. With the shift from political colonialism to economic neocolonialism, and with growing association between domestic and foreign capital, absorption of the educated elite into privileged political and economic positions, and moderation of the visibility of foreign presence have led to a decrease in revolutionary potential. Furthermore, as economic development, industrialization, and modernization proceed, social differentiation increases and new groups emerge as power contenders with particular interests. This breaks up social polarization to some extent and makes the formation of mass-based

[26]This argument is made convincingly by Tucker (1969). He makes the additional point that most socialist revolutions occurred in the wake of war. Greene (1974) provides a useful discussion of the literature on characteristics and causes of revolutionary movements.

revolutionary movements more difficult. Most importantly, the coercive apparatus of the state (i.e., military force) becomes stronger and more efficient due to technologically advanced equipment and professional training, and thus it becomes extremely difficult for outgroups to organize a militant mass movement against the will of those who control state power and to capture state power by way of destroying the coercive apparatus.[27] Foreign penetration and dependence as a concomitant of capitalist economic development present further crucial obstacles to a socialist revolution, by way of strengthening the position of defenders of the existing order economically and through military assistance.

If the way to necessary changes in the economic and political order of countries at an intermediate level of capitalist economic development via a socialist revolution is unlikely, the way via gradual democratic adjustments through organized mass participation in politics is even less likely. Once popular mobilization has reached a certain level, demands outstrip by far the small resource base available without recourse to massive redistribution, particularly during periods of economic stagnation. This renders democratic competition for these scarce resources unviable. Popular mobilization leads to an overload of demands on the political system, creates disruptive conflicts, threatens the dominant and even middle groups, and thus leads to an authoritarian solution to the problem of distribution.[28]

Since neither violent nor peaceful introduction of changes by lower social groups for a significant transformation of the economic and political order are a likely occurrence in countries at an intermediate stage of dependent capitalist development, the only actors who can be expected to introduce major changes are those actually having access to state power and control over the coercive apparatus of the state. These actors can be either members of the military themselves or a civilian political elite enjoying support from the military. Peru is a very interesting example, in which a military regime took power with the explicit commitment to introduce fundamental structural changes in the social

---

[27]The success of the Cuban guerilla movement seems to contradict this statement, because Cuba in 1956–1959 was at an intermediate level of modernization, but at least two factors can be mentioned which rendered this case exceptional. First of all, the Cuban regular army was neither very disciplined and efficient nor trained in counterinsurgency techniques, like military establishments that have learned a lesson since then. Second, the revolution itself was not a mass upheaval but rather a military victory achieved by a leadership with very heterogeneous support; class polarization was a result of the policies introduced by the revolutionary government after the seizure of power. The alternative way of armed struggle pursued by revolutionary outgroups in countries at medium to advanced stages of industrialization and urbanization is terrorism and urban guerilla warfare, which, however, rest on clandestine small-group activity, without a mass base, and without prospects of capturing state power.

[28]O'Donnell (1973) gives a convincing presentation of this argument.

order, of which workers' participation was to be an essential element. Clearly, the dynamics and problems involved in the introduction of workers' participation into a developing capitalist authoritarian system are different from the other two types of systems already discussed, and my conceptualization has to be specified for this case too.

Workers' Participation in Developing Capitalist Authoritarian Systems

Developing capitalist authoritarian systems as empirical types approximate the concept of the authoritarian-corporatist ideal type to varying degrees. They resemble developing socialist authoritarian systems on the dimensions of scarcity of resources (high), degree of legitimacy of organized opposition (low), and range of opportunities for popular political participation (medium). They differ in the predominant form of ownership of means of production (private versus public).

The distribution of power within civil society and between civil society and the state in developing capitalist authoritarian systems differs from the one in developed capitalist democratic systems in the relative weakness of civil society vis-à-vis the state. The rigorous pursuit of development and industrialization under conditions of late, dependent capitalist economic development and a concomitant lack of a dynamic national bourgeoisie, requires that the state play an essential role in economy and society. The state takes over the entrepreneurial role of the weak national bourgeoisie in the protection of capital accumulation and/or performs supportive and protective functions for certain private-sector economic activities, and mediates in relations between labor and capital. Thus, the state exercises a substantial share of control rights, even where major means of production are privately owned. The economic power base of propertied domestic social groups is weakened by foreign penetration, which results in a dislocation of major economic power centers out of the political system. The economic power base of lower social groups is weak because of a highly unfavorable supply–demand ratio of their only resource, labor, and because of a generally low capacity to activate this resource for coordinated purposeful action. The reasons for this low activation capacity are a low degree of organizational penetration, and/or lack of ideological unity, and/or lack of autonomy from state intervention in organizational activities.

Thus, in developing capitalist authoritarian systems the state has clearly more autonomy vis-à-vis civil society than in developed capitalist democracies. The state's greater share in control rights as well as lower legitimacy of organized opposition, more restricted opportunities for popular political participation and lower organizational density render state action more independent from the economic and political power of social groups. However, just as clearly, the state has less autonomy than in developing socialist authoritarian systems. The state does not have a monopoly of control over means of production; a significant share of control and income rights is exercised by private owners. Furthermore, foreign economic penetration and integration into the capitalist world market limit the capacity of the state to introduce fundamental changes in the domestic social order. Though foreign dependence may also limit the autonomous action capacity of the state in developing socialist authoritarian systems, these limitations are comparatively less severe, due to a partial isolation from the capitalist world market.

The achievement of official control over the bureaucratic and coercive apparatus of the state may or may not involve electoral competition. If it does, the range of participants is restricted, and the limits of the exercise of state power are set by those with actual control over the coercive apparatus, that is, the military leaders. Relative stability and civilian rule may be preserved as long as the dominant groups are in agreement on the use of state power and as long as their resource base is sufficient to incorporate the most mobilized lower-class sectors. Thus, economic power is a source of political power insofar as it is the basis for access to the political arena and insofar as it provides the resources to buy off mobilized sectors in order to preserve relative stability with a minimum of coercion, preventing the guardians of coercive force from intervening and assuming state power independently. Accordingly, the equivalent in these systems to opinion-making capacity in developed capitalist democratic systems for upper social groups is the capacity to pacify mobilized sectors of lower social groups in order to preserve order and stability and thus prevent a provocation of military intervention. The equivalent to opinion-making capacity for lower social groups is the ability to pressure the incumbent elite for special concessions by way of threatening disruptions of the social order and creation of economic difficulties. This ability is determined by the mobilization potential (i.e., the size, organizational penetration, autonomy, and unity of lower social groups).

Serious challenges to the existing order can result from a deterioration of the resource base of dominant social groups due to economic stagnation, or from a fractionalization of dominant groups due to a diversification of their economic power bases, and/or from an increase in the size and mobilization of lower social groups. In contrast to developed capitalist democratic systems, challenges from lower social groups can come from groups other than organized labor. Peasants and urban marginals are large groups with a potential to be mobilized, and since they have often less to lose than industrial workers, their mobilization may take more violent and disruptive forms. Due to the potential disruptive consequences of such challenges, authoritarian state intervention is likely, either to protect the existing order through repression of lower social groups or to transform it through a restructuring of relations between social groups. As long as the dominant social groups are able to reach a consensus on a political course of action, they will most likely also be able to control the coercive apparatus of the state (i.e., to obtain collaboration from the military in the use of physical force to protect the existing order from challenges). If, however, a diversification of interests among the dominant social groups causes a breakdown of political consensus and concomitant vacuum of political power, immobility, and inability to solve mounting problems, the military elite, exercising actual control over the coercive apparatus of the state, is more likely to assume an independent role and either impose a civilian political leadership charged with effecting changes in the existing order or exercise political power directly to effect such changes.[29]

The probability of military intervention is particularly high if governmental inefficiency and popular mobilization threaten the military's corporate interests. Determinants of the redistributive or repressive character of changes imposed by a military elite are the social base and intensity of challenges to the existing order, and the ideological formation of the military elite. A defensive reformist approach including redistributive policies is characteristic for military elites seizing power at early stages of industrialization and in response to social mobilization of limited extent but relatively high intensity. A repressive approach is more characteristic for situations of broad social mobilization intensifying greatly during periods of stagnation at intermediate levels of industrialization.[30] Successful implementation of such changes depends on the internal unity of the elite and on the degree of autonomy from internal as well as external economic power centers.

In the case of elites with high cohesion and a commitment to a reform process involving redistribution of economic and political power, the key variable constituting a potentially serious obstacle to the implementation of the reform

[29]Breakdowns of political consensus among dominant groups in the face of popular mobilization are essential characteristics of the situations mentioned by Fitch (1975) as constituting significant motivation for a military coup d'etat in Latin American countries: pressures for military action from high-status groups antagonistic to the government, large-scale public disorders resulting from anti-government sentiments among politically relevant lower-status groups, lack of support for the government in the civilian sector with which the military most closely identifies.

[30]Stepan distinguishes between "inclusionary" and "exclusionary corporatist" approaches, the former referring to redistributive, the latter to repressive, policy orientations of authoritarian regimes in developing capitalist countries, and argues that "In the specific context of Latin America inclusionary corporatism thus is more likely in the earlier stages of import substitution industrialization. . . . Exclusionary corporatism, on the other hand, is more likely to be attempted if, after the import-substitution phase, the pattern of industrial development begins to stagnate, the political and economic struggle intensifies, and politics is increasingly perceived in zero-sum terms [1978:80]." A similar argument concerning preconditions for reformist or repressive policies of military regimes, though based on different assumptions, is made by proponents of the "middle-class military coup." For a comprehensive discussion of the literature on military intervention in politics, see Nordlinger (1977).

process is external dependence. Given the elite's control over the coercive apparatus of the state, internal opposition can be overcome by breaking the economic power base of small dominant social groups through expropriation. Expression of the elite's commitment to redistribution through policies providing tangible benefits for lower social groups, such as minimum-wage legislation, provision of social services, and reduction in unemployment, can be expected to generate support or at least acquiescence on the part of these groups. However, failure to minimize dependence not only on direct foreign investment but also on any other types of foreign financing will almost certainly force the elite to retreat from the redistributive process. Empirical evidence supporting this contention is rather abundantly provided in studies of prescriptions for economic policies established by the International Monetary Fund (IMF) and implemented by governments in balance-of-payments crisis situations (see Hayter [1971]; Payer [1974]). The forced choice between compliance with IMF conditions or severe economic disruptions due to a sudden cut in import capacity may erode even a previously strong elite consensus.

Erosion of elite consensus, be it due to internal opposition or such external pressures, increases possibilities for predominant influence from upper occupational and property-owning groups, due to the structural weakness of organized lower social groups. Ensuing policy changes in remunerations, employment, social services, even if couched in rhetoric of necessary sacrifices for a continuation of the reform process, decrease the trust of lower social groups in the government's pursuit of their interests. Thus, depending on their organizational capacity, these groups can be expected to resort again to collective actions, such as demonstrations and strikes, aimed at pressuring the government into a resumption of the redistribution process.

This conceptualization of the constellation of sociopolitical forces suggests the following specifications of dynamics in the four developmental stages of workers' participation for developing capitalist authoritarian systems.

1. *Origins of workers' participation:* The introduction of workers' participation is an elite response to challenges to the existing order resulting from increasing mobilization of lower social groups, in particular from a growth of organized labor. Due to the structural weakness of organized labor, however, these challenges tend to be effective in forcing concessions from the elite on a large scale only if they are accompanied by broader mobilization and unrest of lower social groups (i.e., nonorganized workers, urban marginals, or peasants). Yet, it is possible for unions in highly organized and important sectors of the economy to pressure the elite for special concessions, of which workers' participation can be a part. The other two factors mentioned, disintegration of elite consensus and external forces, are possible contributing causes to the introduction of workers' participation, but they only operate in conjunction with pop-

ular mobilization, which is a necessary condition. Disintegration of elite consensus will make it more likely that a large-scale and transformative type of workers' participation is introduced by a new independent elite. But there can also be consensus among the established elite on the necessity to introduce a limited integrative scheme of workers' participation to pacify the most mobilized sectors of organized labor. A threat from external forces might contribute to an introduction of workers' participation designed to strengthen national identification and internal unity as protection against threats of national security. Imposition of workers' participation schemes through supranational economic integration agreements is a theoretical possibility, contingent in practice on the advance of workers' participation in economically dominant countries.

2. *Purpose and designs of workers' participation:* Workers' participation is introduced by the elite either with the aim of consolidating the capitalist order by modernizing it and eliminating the most serious causes of disruption, or with the aim of transforming the capitalist into a socialist order. Accordingly, the structural designs of participation will tend to assume the form of joint consultation and limited participation in income rights in the first case, and increasing participation in control rights in the second case. The type of structural design introduced and its purpose will be shaped by the composition of the political elite (i.e., recruitment on the basis of dominant economic position or on the basis of control over coercive force). In the case of an elite recruited on the basis of economic power, the introduction of workers' participation in response to popular mobilization will be aimed at integrating the best organized and most important sectors of the urban industrial working class into the existing order. In the case of an elite recruited on the basis of control over coercive force, the main determinant of the type of workers' participation introduced will be the relative strength of the capitalist and socialist ideological tendencies within the elite.

3. *Development and effects of workers' participation:* The development of a given structural design and its integrative or mobilizing effects are determined by (1) the elite's unity and commitment to a consolidation or transformation strategy; (2) its effective control over the bureaucratic apparatus of the state to ensure implementation; (3) the strength of entrepreneurs as a group to activate their economic power for coordinated action; and (4) the mobilizing activity of unions and/or political parties. In the case of workers' participation schemes with an integrative purpose, considerable provision of material benefits will be required, and consequently continued economic growth. The effects of any workers' participation scheme for integration of workers or generation of pressures for a transformation toward a socialist order will be strongly shaped by the degree of organizational penetration, ideological unity, and mobilizing ac-

tivity of unions. The same arguments about the importance of the role of unions for the full realization and transcendence of structurally given participation possibilities at the enterprise level made for developed capitalist democratic systems apply here too. At the societal level the development of workers' participation schemes as elements in a socialist transformation will depend on the organizational activity and unity of labor in support of it on the one hand, on coordinated action of entrepreneurs in resistance against it on the other hand, and on the relative strength of both groups vis-à-vis the elite (i.e., on the degree of organizational autonomy reached or retained by labor and on the amount of resources under control of the private sector). Both these latter determinants are in part a result of the elite's general policy approach.

4. *Strategies for workers' participation:* If workers' participation is introduced as an element of a transformation strategy, the most crucial protective policy for a successful transformation is the achievement of independence from foreign economic power centers. A prerequisite for this is the achievement of control over internal resources through a progressive transfer of control and income rights from private (domestic as well as foreign) capital owners in key economic sectors to the state. If workers' participation is introduced as an element of a consolidation strategy, it has to be accompanied by material benefits and by attempts to control autonomous mobilization of unions. Provision of material benefits poses a problem for accumulation: the more serious, the lower the level of economic development of a society and consequently the greater the problem of scarcity.[31] Autonomous mobilization of unions is likely to aggravate this problem by increasing the demand-making capacity of labor, and thus to impede integration by raising the level of social conflict. Autonomous mobilization of unions also poses a problem if workers' participation is intended to contribute to a gradual socialist transformation. Mobilization under conditions of scarcity may force a choice between accelerated redistribution and repression of demands by mobilized sectors.

The promotion of social equality in a process of socialist transformation, of which workers' participation is an element, poses particularly difficult problems in the context of dual economies in developing capitalist systems. Redistribution from the modern to the traditional sector requires a coordinated economic development policy, with emphasis on promotion of agriculture and labor-intensive low-technology industrial production. Such a reorientation of tradi-

---

[31] The problem of a trade-off between accumulation and distribution is often raised by opponents of workers' participation in the context of developing economies. Yet, this is by no means a universal problem; it only arises if participation in income rights remains associated with participation in control rights, typical for capitalist economies. In systems with socialist economies, workers' participation in the exercise of control rights can easily be separated from the exercise of income rights, which is assigned to the state in order to guarantee social accumulation at an adequate rate.

tional capitalist development policy also contributes to the achievement of economic independence, but it is only possible if the major share of control and income rights have been transferred from private capital owners to the state.

Outline of This Study

To examine empirically the conceptualization developed in this chapter, I will first compare the development of workers' participation schemes in three developed capitalist democratic systems with greatly varying strength of their respective labor movements. Next I will discuss the Yugoslav experience as an example of a formally fully developed workers' control scheme developed within the framework of a developing socialist authoritarian system. Then I will analyze the development of workers' participation in the Peruvian Revolution in detail, because it constitutes a highly interesting example for the introduction of a unique scheme of workers' participation in a developing capitalist authoritarian system. Particular attention will be given to the dynamics in the constellation of sociopolitical forces set off by the introduction of workers' participation, their effect on the internal constellation of forces in the elite, and to the factors contributing to the ultimate curtailment of the workers' participation scheme.

Obviously, these discussions can not be regarded as conclusive empirical tests of my conceptualization of dynamics between the development of workers' participation and the strength and action of various sociopolitical forces. I am basing my discussion neither on the universe of empirical systems where workers' participation has been introduced nor on a statistically representative sample of these systems. The purpose of these discussions is to examine the usefulness of my conceptualization as an explanatory tool and as a guide for future research, and possibly political action in the area of workers' participation.

2

Workers' Participation in France, Germany, Sweden, and Yugoslavia

The first part of the discussion in this chapter will deal with three distinctive national patterns in the·development of workers' participation, evolving within the shared framework of developed capitalist democratic systems. The second part will deal with a unique pattern in the development of workers' participation, coming closer to a comprehensive workers' control system than any other empirical case and evolving within the framework of a developing socialist authoritarian system.

France, the Federal Republic of Germany, and Sweden were chosen as examples for the development of workers' participation schemes in developed capitalist democratic systems because they differ greatly in the main variable that I hypothesized to determine the development and effects of workers' participation—the sociopolitical strength of organized labor. The French labor movement is comparatively very weak, the German one of intermediate strength, and the Swedish one among the strongest in Western countries. Accordingly, these countries differ in the origins of workers' participation, which in France and Germany originally came in the wake of World War II, and in Sweden around the same time, but as a result of internally generated changes in the distribution of power in civil society. Later legislation on workers' participation was passed in France in response to labor militancy, and in Germany as well as Sweden in response to political initiative and pressure from the labor movement. The types of participation designs introduced, in particular the extent of control rights transferred to the workers, reflect the differing strength of organized labor.

The strength of labor in civil society has effected corresponding degrees of working class power over state action through incumbency of leftist parties for varying periods of time. This has resulted in policy outcomes responding in different degrees to labor's concerns with increasing social equality and full employment. Also, the three countries have proceeded to a varying extent in the pursuit of system-level protective policies for workers' participation. Longer periods of leftist rule have resulted in an expansion of the welfare state as well as expansion of the exercise of control rights over means of production by the state.

The different political strength of labor has also led to different strike patterns. Organized labor has adapted its strategy for the pursuit of working-class interests to the availability of influence channels. Where channels to exert influence on policy makers have proved to be reliable and effective, the use of the strike weapon has by and large been abandoned. Where no such channels have opened up, militant strike action has remained frequent. The figures in Table 2.1 show various indicators supporting these arguments, which will be analyzed in detail in the separate discussion of each country.

France

The French labor movement is among the weakest in Western Europe in organizational penetration as well as ideological unity. However, the militancy of French unions in terms of strike behavior is comparatively very high, as one would expect on the basis of the arguments about political strength (or lack thereof) and availability of political action as an alternative to strike behavior.[1] The strength of French labor as a sociopolitical force is low due to a relatively small union membership and lack of organizational and political unity. Only 15% of the total labor force is organized, partly because of the large agricultural sector, but partly also because of the political divisions and consequent competition within the labor movement. A further factor that keeps labor organization at a low level is the type of structure adopted by French unions, in that they put more emphasis on placing some militant activists in many enterprises than on organizing all workers in an enterprise.

The biggest central union organization is the communist CGT (*Confédération Générale du Travail*, General Confederation of Labor), followed by the formerly christian-democratic CFDT (*Confédération Française et Démocratique du Travail*, French Democratic Workers' Confederation) which changed its name and orientation in 1961. Third, there is the social-democratic FO (*Force Ouvrière*) adhering to free trade unionism. Only since 1966 has competition between the unions given way to some collaboration between the CGT and the CFDT, but on the important issue of workers' participation there is still no

[1]Clearly, this argument only applies to labor movements with the necessary organizational capacity for collective action, and under conditions of freedom of organization. Repression may weaken labor to the point of no militancy at all, regardless of lack of any action alternatives.

Table 2.1
Unionization, Left Rule, Size of Public Sector, Income Inequality, Unemployment, and Strike Activity in France, Germany, and Sweden

	France	Germany	Sweden
Percentage of labor force organized[a]	15	30	75
Political unity of the labor movement	Split	United	United
Incumbency of socialist parties, 1945–1976[b]	4	7	30
Current government expenditure as percentage of GDP, 1976[c]	40.0	41.7	49.8
Percentage change in GDP composed of all governments' revenues, 1956–1973[d]	14.5	18.0	50.0
Percentage of post-tax income received by[e]			
Top decile	30.4	30.3	21.3
Bottom decile	1.4	2.8	2.2
Gini index for inequality in post-tax income distribution[e]	0.414	0.383	0.302
Unemployment as percentage of civilian labor force[f]			
Average, 1964–1977	2.5	1.6	1.9
Average, 1975–1977	4.1	4.1	1.6
Average number of days lost through strikes per 1000 employees per year[g]			
1963–1967	364	34	26
1968–1972	277	74	62
Average number of strikers per 10,000 persons in the nonagricultural labor force per year, 1946–1976[h]	1,367	92	36

[a]*Source:* European Communities, Press and Information Service (Summer 1971), Trade Union News from the European Community.

[b]*Source:* Stephens and Stephens (in press). A score of 1 was given for every year of incumbency of the Social Democrats and their leftist allies. For coalitions with the right, the number of seats held by the socialists was divided by the total number of seats held by the coalition, yielding a fractional score.

[c]*Source:* OECD *Observer*, March 1978. Figure for Germany is for 1975.

[d]*Source:* Cameron (1976).

[e]*Source:* Sawyer (1976:14). The years are 1970 for France, 1973 for Germany, and 1972 for Sweden.

[f]*Source:* OECD *Labor Force Statistics*, 1967–1975, and OECD *Observer*, 1977–1978.

[g]*Source:* Barkin (1975:371).

[h]*Source:* Korpi and Shalev (1979).

unity. The CGT is fundamentally opposed to participation, seeing it as a means of co-optation of workers into the capitalist system.

After a period of relative strength right after World War II, both union membership and strength of leftist parties as participants in government declined rapidly. Due to their role in the Resistance, labor unions and leftist political parties enjoyed great legitimacy, whereas most of the nation's military, bureaucratic, and business elites were discredited by their accommodating behavior. In the first two years after liberation a large part of the social and economic reforms contained in the program of the National Council of the Resistance were implemented. At the same time unions were going through a process of revival and intense organization; union membership in 1947 had reached 7 million, as compared to 3.5 million in 1939; however, already by 1954 union membership had dropped back down to the low level of 2.5 million.[2]

The introduction of workers' participation came in 1945 as part of the general reform program which included nationalization of some key industries and a significant reorganization and expansion of the social security system. Workers' participation extended to both the national and the enterprise level, taking the form of representation in national economic planning and policy agencies on the one hand, and election of works committees on the other hand. Though one might expect that a workers' participation design with a transformative character and actual transfer of control rights to workers would have been introduced, given labor's political strength at that point, the tasks assigned to these works committees resembled those assigned to works councils introduced in most countries in Western and Central Europe during that period. These tasks were essentially of an integrative nature, as the works committees were charged with cooperating with management on the improvement of general working and living conditions of the workforce, and were given minimal participation in control rights. The explanation for the fact that only such a weak scheme of participation was introduced despite labor's temporary strength lies most probably in a lack of preoccupation among unions with workers' participation in capitalist enterprises, as they were putting more emphasis on nationalization, economic reconstruction, and labor's participation in political decision making, which all seemed within reach at that point.

Under the 1945 legislation, all enterprises employing at least 50 workers are required to have a works committee, the members of which are elected by the workers. Participation in decision making by the works committee is extremely limited, extending only to the lowest levels in the hierarchical order of decisions and involving a minimal transfer of actual control to workers. The committee is in charge of the administration of welfare schemes and social organization, but it has no influence whatsoever on production-related decisions. Through several amendments to the original legislation, the spheres for participation were extended to joint consultation on major changes in working hours, annual leave schedules, rules of discipline, and long-range developments of the enterprise, particularly redundancy.

Due to the organizational weakness and passive or even negative attitude of unions vis-à-vis participation, this highly limited structural design of participation resulted predominantly in apathy on the part of the workers. In the ab-

[2]A discussion of this period, in the framework of a general history of the French labor movement, is given by Lorwin (1954).

sence of union leaders or activists mobilizing workers into participating and insisting on their legal rights, information provided by management to the works committees remained very scarce and important decisions frequently were concealed until after the fact. Many enterprises simply ignored the law and in the absence of pressure from the workforce either did not form such a committee or let it slowly disintegrate by depriving it of any function. Consequently, according to Asplund (1972:30), the number of works committees declined from 21,000 in 1954 to about 10,000 in 1964, a decline which was fought by legislation in 1966 strengthening enforcement provisions. Though the legislation provides for inclusion of unions in the design of participation by stipulating that lists of candidates for works committee elections be presented by trade unions, the unions failed to become major actors who fully utilized the limited opportunities for participation and generated pressures for their extension.

Thus, the works committees remained largely without any effect at all. They provoked neither challenges to the existing distribution of power nor did they serve the purpose they had been designed to—integrating workers into the enterprise and improving labor relations. In a study of eight enterprises over 15 years, Montuclard (1963) found that the committees had elicited a certain interest for questions of production planning and organization among the union representatives elected to the committees. Particularly in times of crisis, enterprise committees put forward suggestions and demands for the protection of their enterprise or branch of industry. In the case of mergers, the committees proposed certain conditions that would ensure continued employment for the workforce, etc. These are issues that in other countries have given rise to strong union demands for an effective extension of participation, but the French labor movement failed to take them up. Consequently, works committees that put forward such suggestions had no power base behind them that enabled them to exert any pressure to overcome the limitations of joint consultation, and they remained ineffective in their attempts. This also holds true for workers' participation in nationalized industries, where the administration council has a minority workers' representation, appointed by the state upon recommendation by trade unions, and where there are some specialized joint committees for personnel and safety questions. Given this general lack of effective influence and the passive role of unions, the widespread disillusionment and lack of interest in the works committees is not surprising.

In addition to their ideologically grounded indifference toward participation, the passive role of unions vis-à-vis the works committees is partly due to their generally weak position at the enterprise level. Up to the Grenelle Accord of 1968, which provided for representation of all major union federations in enterprises with 50 or more employees, employers had refused to recognize officially unions at the enterprise level. The basic union unit is at the local level, representing one industry in one municipality. These units are affiliated to national industrial and/or interindustry departmental federations, which in turn form a confederation. The collective bargaining system is weak. National interindustry or industry-wide negotiations seldom lead to binding agreements. but rather take the form of joint declarations of principle. Wage negotiations take place mainly at the regional level, but they only set minimum standards, leaving room for local-level bargaining. However, multiple unionism and reluctance on the part of employers to conclude wage agreements have created a situation where for most workers actual wages are not set through negotiation by their union.[3] This weakens the dependence of workers on their unions and thus the control of unions over their members. Multiple unionism also makes it very difficult for unions to use the strike weapon to force employers into negotiations and wage concessions. Strike calls which are followed by part of the labor force of an enterprise only are not very effective in bringing economic pressure to bear on employers.

As a result of labor's weakness at the enterprise level and as a sociopolitical force at the national level, rank and file militancy has been comparatively high in the post-World War II period in the context of Western European countries.[4] Given the weakness of unions vis-à-vis employers, union action was primarily oriented toward provoking favorable government action. Through determination of family allowances, social insurance levels, and fringe benefits, the government directly influences a large proportion of workers' total remuneration. Also, the legal prerequisites for direct government intervention in labor disputes exist. However, labor's influence on government policy through incumbency of leftist parties has been very ineffective since 1947, when the immediate post-World War II coalition government broke apart and the Communists went into opposition. The Socialists continued to be represented in most cabinets in the Fourth Republic, but their strength was never sufficient to shape government policy decisively.[5] Thus there were no reliable and effective channels available for organized labor to influence policy outcomes through persuasion and mobilization of political support. This caused unions to resort frequently to militant strike action. As Shorter and Tilly (1974:326) show, the French strike pattern in the post-World War II period is characterized by high frequency, large size, and short duration of strikes. They interpret this pattern as typical for a situation where the working class is politically impotent but determined to use the strike as symbolic action in the struggle for power. Mobilization for collective political protest in the form of short strikes with large numbers of participants is the most feasible way open to an economically weak, organizationally fragmented, and politically powerless labor movement to attempt to influence government action.

[3]For a description of the French collective bargaining system, see Reynaud (1975).
[4]Ross and Hartman (1960:116) claim that: "Clearly, French workers have been the most strike-prone of any in the world."
[5]As early as 1946, the Socialists lost a considerable number of seats in the National Assembly; their 1945 share of 150 out of 586 seats dropped to 105 out of 618 in 1946.

This high degree of militancy has caused the government to search for reforms that would secure industrial peace. Accordingly, a scheme for participation in profits (i.e., in income rights rather than control rights) was introduced by law in 1967, applying to all enterprises with more than 100 workers. In 1971, CGT and FO issued a joint statement condemning the profit-sharing arrangement as a sheer statistical procedure that would not change the global share of wage earners (Asplund 1972:50). Clearly, this was possible due to the lack of any type of participation in control rights through workers' representatives at higher managerial levels who would have a right to inspect company books and supervise the calculations for profit sharing. Spontaneous manifestations of demands for workers' control emerged in factory occupations, particularly in May 1968, and were subsequently promoted as demands for economic democracy by the CFDT. However, since the CGT still opposes workers' participation in decision making in capitalist enterprises as co-optative reform, no significant progress toward its extension can be expected unless a Socialist–Communist coalition manages to win national elections and link workers' control to significant extension of state control over means of production.

Given the very limited transfer of control rights from capital owners to workers at the enterprise level, there has been a low need for system-level protective policies. The extent of state participation in the exercise of control rights was greatest right after World War II, when a significant portion of French industry—such as coal, gas, electricity, Renault automobiles, the Bank of France, and the largest insurance companies—was nationalized to bring the economy back on its feet. In 1959, 25% of national gross fixed investment was accounted for by the state-owned industrial sector (Lowell 1963). The early 5-year development plans provided for considerable state intervention, but an increasing proportion of control rights was transferred back from the state to private owners, particularly through a reduction of wage and price controls and of state control over distribution of credit.[6] Thus the decline in political strength of labor and left parties after 1945 impeded advances in transfer of control and income rights from private owners to both the state and the workers.

The lack of sociopolitical strength of the labor movement also resulted in little progress toward social equality and toward full employment. The extractive capacity of the state, measured in current government revenue, is comparatively high, 42.4% of GDP,[7] but this public control has not been used to equalize distribution of means of consumption. The inequality index (i.e., the Gini index of post-tax income distribution) is .414 for France, highest among 12 capitalist industrial countries (Sawyer) 1976:17). The system of financing

---

[6] MacLennan *et al.* give an account of declining state intervention in the economy; see MacLennan *et al.* (1968).

[7] OECD *Observer*, March 1978.

of public sector expenditures severely limits its impact on equalization. The French tax system is highly regressive (Heidenheimer et al., 1975:227 ff.), and tax evasion, which benefits mostly higher income groups, is notoriously high (Wilensky 1975:60). Unemployment between 1964 and 1977 stood at an average of 2.5% of the labor force, reaching a high of 4.2% in 1976, as compared to an average of 1.6% in West Germany and 1.9% in Sweden in the same period (see Table 2.1).

Since the late 1960s, an awareness of the need for political unity of the left has led to increasing collaboration between unions as well as between political parties. Electoral gains of the leftist coalition have brought the issues of transfer of control and income rights from private owners to the state and to the workers to the forefront of political discussion. The Common Program agreed on in 1972 by Communists, Socialists, and Left Radicals was aimed at breaking monopoly control of the economy through nationalization of nine large industrial trusts and of all financial institutions. It also provided for the possibility that the government propose nationalization of other industries, if demanded by the employees. State-owned enterprises were to be managed by tripartite boards, with equal numbers of representatives of government, workers, and consumers. This example, it was assumed, would generate demands from workers in the private sector for the same type of management and thus set off dynamics toward a socialist system with full workers' control.

The defeat of the left in the 1978 parliamentary elections again demonstrated how limited the organizational and ideological penetration of French society by the labor movement is. The combined opinion-making capacity of organized labor and the leftist parties was not sufficient to transform a general sentiment of popular discontent with existing social and economic conditions into electoral support for the leftist coalition. Even if the left had won the elections, chances for success of the Common Program would not have been great, given the weakness of the labor movement and the dominant control of middle and upper social groups over societal institutions. Though the Socialist–Communist coalition relied on its ability to check capital flight through control of foreign credit and exchange, economic problems would have been unavoidable.[8] These most likely would have antagonized the middle class despite explicit provisions in the Program to give the middle class initially a material stake in the regime.

The political consequences are obvious if one considers that less than 60% of the left's electoral support in the 1973 legislative elections came from the working class (see, e.g., Ehrmann 1976:233). Thus, in the absence of strong backing from a united labor movement to compensate for devisive pressures

[8] In fact, capital flight had started already well before the 1978 elections, as a consequence of leftist gains in local elections in 1976, which confirmed prospects for a possible electoral victory of the left in 1978. For instance, total deposits in the French state savings bank dropped 23% between June 1976 and June 1977. Newsweek, June 13, 1977.

and middle-class defections, such a coalition government would hardly have been able to resist the opposition of propertied groups, and it might have been forced to delay the implementation of its program even before losing the election at the end of its term.[9]

Federal Republic of Germany

The German labor movement is generally considered powerful, achieving high benefits for workers at the bargaining table without having to resort to open struggle through industrial action. In terms of absolute size, organizational unity, and financial security, German unions appear strong in comparison with those in other Western industrial democracies, but within German society labor's strength relative to other sociopolitical forces is rather limited. Three factors contribute to this limitation: (1) stagnation in membership; (2) lack of ideological unity on a desirable socioeconomic alternative with concomitant ideological education and mobilization; and (3) internal structural deficiencies.

Membership figures have been stagnating as unionization has not kept up with expanding white-collar sectors. In 1977, 29% of the total German labor force were unionized, the same percentage as in 1950 (*Statistisches Jahrbuch für die Bundesrepublik Deutschland*). The vast majority of employees are represented by only three trade union organizations: the DGB (*Deutscher Gewerkschaftsbund*, German Confederation of Trade Unions), the DAG (*Deutsche Angestellten Gewerkschaft*, German Salaried Employees' Union), and the German Association of Civil Service Officials. The German Commercial Employees' Union and the Confederation of Christian Trade Unions of Germany have only rather small memberships. Consequently, though interests and positions of blue- and white-collar unions may diverge, labor is not weakened through competition among unions with different political affiliations. However, the labor movement lacks a shared strong ideological base on which to mobilize members in support of an alternative to the capitalist free-enterprise system. The 1949 program adopted by the founding Congress of the DGB was a socialist program, calling for nationalization of key industries and codetermination in all decisions about management and design of the economy. However, ideological penetration of the rank and file with this program was not achieved, and the DGB programs of 1955 and 1963 constituted clear adaptations to neocapitalism, assigning priority to economic growth over issues of workers' participation. Only due to ideological rejuvenation through influence from younger leftists in the late 1960s, both within the labor movement and within the SPD (*Sozialdemokratische Partei Deutschlands*, Social Democratic Party) did the is-

[9]An additional problem in the French case, of course, would have resulted from the constitutional structure in that a leftist-controlled legislature would have faced a hostile president.

sue of social control over means of production at the societal as well as enterprise levels assume renewed importance.

The limited organizational and ideological penetration of German society by the labor movement kept electoral support for the Social Democratic Party at an insufficient level to obtain governmental power up to the formation of the Grand Coalition with the CDU/CSU (*Christlich-Demokratische Union/Christlich-Soziale Union*, Christian-Democratic Union/Christian Social Union) in 1966, and finally the coalition with the FDP (*Freie Demokratische Partei*, Free Democrats in 1969.[10] Accordingly, little progress was made in the transfer of income and control rights from owners to the state and to workers from the introduction of workers' participation between 1946 and 1952, to new participation legislation in the 1970s. Germany's model of *Mitbestimmung*, or "codetermination," was for a long time the most significant model of workers' participation developed in any Western industrial democracy. Yet it has serious weaknesses both in its structural design at the enterprise level, consisting in a lack of integration between representation at the top and participation at the bottom, and in its relation to the societal level, insofar as it is restricted to the coal, iron, and steel industries and not supported by public control over more comprehensive economic decisions.

The origins of workers' participation in Germany, as in France, can be seen as a result of a temporary impact of external forces on the internal constellation of sociopolitical forces. Legislation concerning workers' participation goes back to the period of Allied administration of Germany right after World War II. Codetermination was introduced then as a response to pressures from organized labor, in a moment of relative, sectorally limited, strength of unions vis-à-vis entrepreneurs. Business leaders, particularly in the coal, iron, and steel industries, were largely discredited because of their support for Hitler, and strong demands were made by miners in the *Ruhrgebiet* for the nationalization of these industries and their administration by the workers.[11] However, on a national level unions were just reemerging and still organizationally weak—too weak as a sociopolitical force to achieve an implementation of their conception. As a compromise solution that reflected more the conception of business than of labor, a scheme of codetermination was introduced in 1947, in the steel industries only, and in 1951 in coal and iron mining. By that time, representatives of capital interests had regained their legitimacy and political allies, such that their weight in the constellation of sociopolitical forces effected the implementation of a very weak compromise with labor's demands for an exten-

[10]The growing electoral strength of the Social Democratic Party can be seen in part as a result of greater political unity among the working class, as a considerable number of Catholic workers switched their vote from the CDU/CSU to the SPD after Vatican II.

[11]For an account of developments in this period, with extensive references, see Deppe *et al.* (1969).

sion of the codetermination model, in the form of a structural design with highly limited participation possibilities in all enterprises outside of the iron, coal, and steel industries. The DGB attempted to mobilize pressure in support of legislation introducing codetermination through the threat of a general strike. The Adenauer government responded with harsh public attacks, accusing the DGB of staging an illegal attempt to impose its will on the democratically elected parliament. The DGB retreated, and instead of codetermination, the Works Constitution Act of 1952 introduced a joint-consultation type of workers' participation in all enterprises with more than five workers through the creation of works councils.

Both schemes of workers' participation, codetermination as well as joint consultation under the Works Constitution Act, are integrative in their intention. They are explicitly designed to benefit the enterprise as well as the workers by requiring collaboration between the employer and the works council which exists in both schemes, within the framework of existing collective agreements, in conjunction with the trade unions and employers' associations. The works council is elected by secret ballot, by blue- and white-collar workers separately, unless they agree to vote as a group, and lists of candidates are submitted by the trade union. The works council has control over a very limited range of decisions, and codetermination rights over some others, but mostly it is a body for joint consultation. Control is limited to the lowest stage in the hierarchical model of decisions (i.e., mainly regulation of daily working hours and breaks, leave schedules, administration of welfare services). Codetermination rights now—after their extension through the 1972 revision of the Works Constitution Act—include questions of propriety and behavior on the job, determination of rates for piece work, recruitment, redeployment, transfers, and dismissals (i.e., management decisions in these areas cannot be made without prior approval by the works council). If management and the works council are unable to reach an agreement, the dispute is settled by a mediating body set up according to the law—or as a last resort by a Labor Court. Decisions belonging to the third and higher levels of the model, however, are only subject to joint consultation.

The difference between participation under the Works Constitution Act and under the codetermination legislation in coal, iron, and steel lies in the degree of control rights transferred to workers' representatives at highest levels. Under the Works Constitution Act, workers' representatives hold one-third of the seats in the *Aufsichtsrat*, the board of supervisors, which has roughly the same position as the board of directors in an American company. This arrangement is one of joint consultation, then, in contrast to the one under the codetermination law, where labor and capital have an equal number of representatives on the board of supervisors. Together, they appoint a neutral outside member to avoid deadlocks. Also, the personnel director, a member of top management, cannot be appointed against the will of the labor representatives on the board of supervisors. Half of these labor representatives are appointed by the union from outside the enterprise and half are elected by the works council. In order to promote integration and protect enterprises from disruptive conflict as a result of codetermination, the law stipulates personal liability of all board members for damage caused to the enterprise (e.g. by indiscretion), but no accountability of labor representatives to the workers.

Developments at the enterprise level have been shaped by the role assumed by unions, which for a long time provided support for participation but failed to engage in active mobilization at the base. The overall position taken by the unions has been to participate in the works councils and coordinate union functions with activities in these councils. For instance, in 1965, 83% of all works council members were members of DGB-affiliated unions (Bergmann and Müller-Jentsch 1975:250). However, the legal separation of functions between union and works council, which prevents the union from acting as representative of workers' interests within the enterprise, has weakened the position of the shop stewards at the enterprise level. Works councils are in charge of representing workers in all social and personnel affairs, and they also participate in the setting of internal pay scales, piece rates, etc. Basic wage rates and working conditions are negotiated by unions, but not at the enterprise level. The structure of collective bargaining is highly centralized, corresponding to the organizational structure of the union movement. Local unions are affiliated to district organizations, which in turn form the national federations of industrial unions. Bargaining takes place for industry-wide agreements either at the national or the district level. Internal power is highly concentrated at the top of the national federations in the hands of the presidium. The presidium has the right to make all decisions about wage policies, and collective negotiations are handled by the national presidium jointly with the district leadership. This has generated a tendency toward bureaucratization and lack of involvement at the base.

Since wage contracts negotiated at the district or national level are oriented toward average profitability of the firms in a particular industry, it has happened that works councils in highly profitable enterprises conclude local agreements with management for higher wages. Yet these agreements can be unilaterally revoked, and the works council is legally prohibited from resorting to industrial action by a peace obligation. Thus works councils have mainly become an instrument for communication and collaboration with management, where management is willing to accept the works council as a body for consultation. Particularly in bigger enterprises, where works council members exercise their functions as full-time jobs, tendencies toward bureaucratization and professionalization have led to a loss of communication with the rank and file and a concomitant loss of interest among the latter. For the ordinary workers, participation consists in taking part in elections for the works council and for representatives on the board of directors. There is no direct participation of workers at the lowest levels. In terms of the discussion of integration of the structural design in Chapter 1 this means that there is a disjunction between the top and bottom levels of decision making and that participation occurs only through representation. As could be predicted, the result is apathy at the bottom. In general, works councils have become instruments for the accommodation and integration of workers into the enterprise, rather than for an extension of workers' decision-making power. Tendencies toward integration through apathy at the base have occurred in enterprises with codetermination as well, since they have the same disjunction between top and bottom, and workers' representatives—particularly those appointed by the union from outside the enterprise—are far removed from the base.

Studies carried out to assess the effect of codetermination on the attitudes of workers have consistently found lack of information, disinterest, or even cynicism. In general, the attitude toward codetermination has been found to be closely associated with the workers' relation to their union. Involvement in and satisfaction with union activities mostly carried with it the same attitude toward codetermination.[12] These findings again highlight the crucial role of unions for the development of any scheme of workers' participation. For a long time, the German unions failed to perform the role of a mobilizing agent, providing a link between the workers' direct experience and the questions discussed in codetermined boards. On the contrary, it has happened that top union leaders occupy positions as board members in several enterprises, enjoying extremely high monetary benefits accruing from these positions. Clearly, this strengthens oligarchic tendencies within unions and in some cases has had highly integrative effects, causing union representatives to set the interest of the enterprise above those of the workers and to develop a strong interest in maintaining their own positions and consequently the status quo. Again, it has to be emphasized that codetermination as a structural design of participation need not necessarily result in integration, if unions are ideologically strong and organizationally active enough to mobilize workers into active participation, to make the limitations of codetermination clear and to push for an expansion of participation rights.

The failure of German unions to perform such a mobilizing function is an inherent characteristic of their general deradicalization and low militancy since 1950. The German post-World War II strike pattern is very similar to the Scandinavian one, showing extremely few official strikes. However, German

---

[12]A review and criticism of four such studies can be found in Dahrendorf (1963). An early study focusing on the attitudes toward codetermination in relation to workers' general attitudes toward work and their world-view, is Popitz and Bahrdt (1957).

labor has by no means enjoyed the same access to reliable and effective channels for political influence as, for instance, the Swedish labor movement has. The following factors can be mentioned to explain why the German labor movement has been less strike-prone than one would expect on the basis of its limited influence on government policy. First, the years of fascist rule effected a certain break in the socialist tradition within the working class, particularly among younger rank-and-file workers. They also left a heritage of distrust and apathy vis-à-vis mobilization for collective action. Thus it was difficult for the initially radical DGB leadership to penetrate the membership ideologically. When the leadership adapted its ideological position to "socially responsible action" within the existing politico-economic system and moderated wage demands in the interest of national reconstruction, it did not have to face radical challenges from the base. Second, union action is subject to a highly restrictive legal system, defining legitimate strike action very narrowly, which was a result of government policy dominated by pro-business political forces. Rather than challenging this legal system, union leaders have shown a highly legalistic orientation. Their carefulness to maintain union action within legal boundaries has certainly been strongly conditioned by the prevailing public opinion. Through their control over mass media and a variety of societal institutions, particularly religious and educational ones, pro-status-quo forces were able to instill a strong pro-law-and-order orientation in public opinion. Third, the Cold War and Germany's division into East and West weakened the legitimacy of militant labor action. Finally, continued economic growth and low unemployment facilitated the achievement of relatively high real-wage gains through well-consolidated collective bargaining procedures, without the need to resort to strike action.

However, over the long run, internal centralization of the union movement and the pursuit of a moderate, "socially responsible" wage policy led to the emergence of discontent among some parts of the rank and file. In 1967, the unions agreed to "concerted action" proposed by Minister Schiller and the Grand Coalition government between Social Democrats and Christian Democrats. "Concerted action" consisted in voluntary coordination of wage and price policies through negotiation between the government, employers, and unions. By 1969 it had become clear that wage gains were falling behind increases in corporate profits and that no significant rewards in the form of social policies were forthcoming. As a result, a wave of wildcat strikes broke out. This strike wave occurred at the same time as a general wave of political activism and ideological radicalization of parts of the labor movement and the Social Democratic Party. In 1972–1973 new waves of wildcat strikes broke out, and this general increase in militancy also motivated local union representatives for greater mobilizing activity for participation through works councils.

In the 1972 works council elections, shop stewards ideologically committed to an extension of effective control of workers in several cases placed new and militant candidates on the list to challenge well-established works council members who had been in their positions for years and had adopted a managerial point of view facilitated by apathy at the base. Since candidates for works council elections are nominated by the union, it was possible for militant shop stewards to put equally militant workers in favorable positions on the list. In several large enterprises in chemical, automobile, and metal industries, former works council members presented their own list—which was technically a violation of rules—and were defeated by the new more radical candidates (Jacobi *et al.* 1973). These elections demonstrated that accommodation and integration of workers was not an unavoidable effect of the integrative German schemes of participation but that this effect had been mediated by the weak position and passivity of union representatives at the enterprise level and the overall accommodative behavior of unions.

The increase in mobilizing activity at the enterprise level was accompanied by a general process of ideological reorientation within some major national unions. In particular, unions have shown growing militancy in the pursuit of a redistribution of control and income rights from private owners to workers and the state. In 1969 the DGB put forward demands for participation of labor in social and economic decision making at the societal level, and for an extension of the codetermination model to all enterprises.[13] The demands for an extension of codetermination initiated a long and hard process of bargaining within the SPD–FDP coalition government. The FDP managed to gain more and more influence on this legislation. The compromise that was finally accepted in 1975—to be enacted in a 2-year transition period starting in June 1976—clearly preserves the ultimate decision-making right for representatives of capital. Though there are equal numbers of representatives of capital and labor on the board of supervisors, the chairman of the board, who cannot be elected against the will of representatives of capital, has the decisive vote in deadlocks. Furthermore, "leading employees," legally defined as employees entrusted with entrepreneurial functions (i.e., top management) are entitled to one of the seats held by representatives of labor.[14] However, even this limited type of codetermination may develop into a significant participation of workers in control rights and may generate renewed pressures for a further transfer of control rights if the DGB persists in its ideological aggressiveness and maintains an intensive mobilization activity. The precondition for these pressures to effect legislation for a further extension of workers' participation is an increase of labor's sociopolitical strength, in order to mobilize sufficient electoral support for an exclusively Social Democratic government, independent of a coalition

[13]An analysis of labor's conception of various forms of participation at the societal level is given by Otto (1971).
[14]For a discussion of the legislation, see *Der Spiegel*, No. 50, 1975.

partner. Such an increase in labor's organizational and ideological penetration of society would have to include a growth of white-collar unionization.

Under the Social Democratic–Free Democratic government, some progress in the transfer of control and income rights to the state and in the pursuit of social equality has been made, though within fairly narrow limits. Despite the existence of workers' participation schemes, the decisive share of control rights at the enterprise level—except in steel, coal, and iron—is still exercised by private capital owners, as are income rights. This has enabled representatives of capital interests to mobilize their economic and political power to resist successfully an encroachment on these rights by the state as well. Government regulation of the economy, particularly control over investment resources, is still highly restricted. Legislative proposals for investment planning have met with decided opposition from entrepreneurs.[15] Economic intervention mainly takes the form of tax incentives and persuasion for collaboration. For instance, the attempt at "concerted action" promoted by the Grand Coalition under Minister of the Economy Schiller in 1967, in order to fight inflation and a developing recession, remained at the level of voluntary cooperation among the state, the unions, and the employers' association. The state did not impose any legally binding action parameters then, and proposals for economic stabilization measures in 1973 met with stern opposition against any state interference into the free enterprise system. The strongest measures that could be implemented in 1973 were a temporary investment tax and a stabilization levy to be frozen in a special account in the German *Bundesbank* (Schoenbach 1974:78–83). Similarly, measures against capital flight as protective policies for an extension of workers' participation have hardly been developed.

Somewhat more progress has been made in the pursuit of social equality. The public sector expanded by 18% from 1956 to 1973. This is higher than in France but much lower than in Sweden. Though the percentage of total income after taxes received by the top decile is as high as in France, and the total amount of GDP accounted for by government expenditure is only slightly higher, the German system of expenditures on income maintenance renders the resulting distribution of resources for consumption more equal.[16] The bot-

[15]For the internal dispute within the SPD, see *Der Spiegel*, No. 40, 1975. The long-range program, *Orientierungsrahmen 1985*, of the SPD proposed only tax incentives, direct subsidies, and prohibitions to establish enterprises in certain locations as a means to guide investment (*Der Spiegel*, No. 7, 1975), but even these were strongly opposed by business interests.

[16]Schnitzer (1974) shows that the German tax transfer system modifies the inequality in income distribution, as taxes and social security contributions amount to about 16% of average monthly income in the highest income class, whereas transfer payments account for only 7% of total income of this income class; in the lowest income class, taxes and social security contributions amount to 2.5% of average income, while transfer payments account for 80% of total income of this income class.

tom decile's share is 2.8% as compared to 1.4% in France, and the Gini index is .383 as compared to .414 for France (see Table 2.1).

However, in another policy area of central importance to organized labor—full employment—the record of the SPD–FDP government has not been very favorable. Due to the strength of the German economy, unemployment remained at very low levels up to 1974 (an average of 0.85% in 1964–1973) without the need for government intervention through a purposeful labor market policy. In fact, labor shortages led to the immigration of large numbers of foreign workers. When economic growth decreased significantly in 1974, unemployment rose from 1.0% in 1973 to 2.2%; and in 1975 it reached 4.1% (see Table 2.1). Had it not been for the "export" of a certain percentage of unemployment in the form of foreign workers returning to their home countries, these figures would have been even higher.[17] Despite labor's insistent demands for government intervention to alleviate the unemployment problem, government policy has shown more concern with avoiding inflationary stimulation of the economy than with job creation. This demonstrates that the political influence of the German labor movement is still quite limited, despite 10 years of Social Democratic incumbency. The limits to changes in the distribution of control and income rights through legislation are mainly a result of the limited social penetration and consequent opinion-making capacity of the labor movement. This forces the Social Democratic government into collaboration with the liberal and reform-minded, but pro-capitalist, representatives of middle- and upper-middle-class interests. A typical example for this forced political collaboration is the compromise for the new codetermination law, where organized labor's strength as a sociopolitical force was simply not sufficient to have its conception prevail over competing ones.

Sweden

The Swedish labor movement is exceptionally strong in organizational penetration as well as in political unity and ideological commitment. Sweden has the highest unionization rate of any Western industrial society; 75% of the total labor force is organized. Whereas unionization rates stagnated or even declined in the post-World War II period in France and Germany, as they did in many other Western countries, they continued to increase steadily in Sweden, as shown in Table 2.2. This continuous growth in Sweden is primarily due to the extraordinary expansion of white-collar unionization. Over 70% of the white-collar workers are union members in Sweden. In contrast, Table 2.2 indicates

---

[17]Between September of 1969 and 1974 the number of foreigners had increased from 2,381,100 to 4,127,400; by September of 1976 this figure was reduced to 3,948,300. *Statistisches Jahrbuch für die Bundesrepublik Deutschland.*

Table 2.2
Unionization

Year	France	Germany	Sweden
		Percentage of total labor force organized	
1950	22	29	51
1960	11	30	60
1970	15	30	75
		Percentage of wage and salary earners organized	
1950	47	44	69
1960	17	39	73
1970	20	37	87

Source: J. D. Stephens (1979).

that unionization failed to keep up with the expansion of white-collar sectors in France and Germany. There are two major central organizations, the LO (*Landsorganisationen*, Swedish Confederation of Trade Unions) for blue-collar unions, and the TCO (*Tjänstemännens Centralorganisation*, Central Organization of Salaried Employees) for white-collar unions. Two other central union organizations, one for federal government employees and one for employees with higher educational degrees, are very small in comparison to the LO and TCO. The ties between the LO and the Social Democratic Party are very close, both organizationally and ideologically, as the Social Democratic Party and LO consider themselves two branches of the same tree, the labor movement. TCO is officially politically neutral, and many white-collar union members vote for the center parties. This is of political importance insofar as it moves center parties toward the left on issues of concern to dependent wage earners. If the LO and TCO agree on a certain type of legislation, which is promoted by the Social Democrats, the center parties can hardly oppose it. Workers' participation, or "democracy at the workplace" in Swedish terminology, is an example of such legislation.

The organizational and ideological penetration of Swedish society by the labor movement kept a Social Democratic government in power for more than 40 years. During this period, Sweden advanced further toward a redistribution of control and income rights at the societal level and the enterprise level, as well as toward social equality than any other Western industrial democracy. The Swedish schemes of workers' participation originated in response to pressures from organized labor and developed with labor's growing organizational penetration and consequent sociopolitical strength. Significant advances toward transfer of control rights to workers at the enterprise level have been made since the late 1960s, due to a reorientation of labor's pressures from transfer of control and income rights at the societal level to workers' participation at the enterprise level.

The origins of workers' participation in Sweden lie in a collective agreement between unions and the employers' association about the establishment of works councils. This agreement was concluded in 1946 when workers' participation was introduced through legislation in most other European countries, and in contrast to other countries it was less a result of the impact of external factors than a response on the part of employers to a changing internal constellation of sociopolitical forces. Union membership had increased from 36% of the total labor force in 1940 to 44% in 1945 and kept growing, reaching 50% in 1950 (figures from J. D. Stephens, 1979). Yet, these works councils had mainly joint consultation functions similar to the ones in Germany and therefore were of equally limited significance. The unions' primary concern was with improvement of wages and working conditions, security of employment, and wage-equalization policies. They pursued these goals both through central collective bargaining with the employers' association and through political action in collaboration with the Social Democratic Party.

The two key components of the labor movement's strategy were (1) to improve the situation of the working class through social and economic policies, and (2) to ensure continued long-term incumbency of the Social Democratic Party as a precondition for an expansion of public control over the economy. Thus unions and the Social Democrats pursued a coordinated set of policies designed to promote economic growth, full employment, and redistribution through the welfare state. Unions readily accepted rationalization measures and structural changes in industry because of their reliance on labor market policies that would make society as a whole bear the costs of such adaptations, not the working class or the groups of workers affected. In cases of shutdowns, layoffs, etc., which in other countries have been a major issue in demands for an expansion of workers' control, labor representatives are involved in a different type of participation. The National Labor Market Board and local branches, which include governmental and labor representatives, provide assistance in relocation and retraining to affected workers. The state also sponsors projects for the creation of employment and, when considerations of social costs outweigh economic costs, companies in crisis may be subsidized at least temporarily to ease the adaptation process of the labor force. Labor's receptivity to technological changes facilitated the development of internationally competitive industries, crucial for a country with a high export dependence like Sweden. Continued economic growth and prosperity under the Social Democratic government in turn facilitated the expansion of the welfare state, and full employment strengthened the position of labor in society.

In the mid-1960s, a variety of reasons caused an increasing concern of organized labor and the Social Democratic Party with workers' participation at the enterprise level. Though they had always remained ideologically committed to a transformation of society toward an egalitarian ideal, they had not always seen a clear, consistent, and viable strategy to effect a gradual democratic socialist transformation. But at this point, the transfer of control rights at the enterprise level became an element of central attention and gave new substance to the pursuit of a transformation strategy in the form of "economic democracy" as a goal. High labor turnover and occasional wildcat strikes alerted LO's leadership to the importance of quality of worklife as a necessary complement to satisfactory wage settlements. Employers on their part, equally concerned about high labor turnover, absenteeism, and wildcat strikes, took the initiative to introduce various work humanization experiments. On the political scene, the Liberal Party took the initiative for the establishment of a Delegation for Industrial Democracy, which the Social Democratic government took up and implemented in the form of a committee of researchers charged with exploring possibilities for introducing changes in the work organization in state-owned companies. What is significant in view of the argument about the importance of white-collar unionization is the fact that the Liberals, a center party, took the initiative in pursuing the issue of workers' participation, because this issue is of great concern to TCO members, who form an important constituency of the center parties. In order not to lose any support to competing conceptions in their pursuit of a comprehensive scheme of workers' participation by introducing democratization of decision making in the enterprise as part of a strategy to advance toward full economic democracy—that is, a socially controlled economy—both LO and the Social Democratic Party developed intensive mobilization activities. The program adopted by the LO Congress in 1971 reflects the renewed ideological strength and reorientation toward the control issue, as it calls for "Industrial Democracy . . . as an integral part of the labor movement's struggle to reform society as a whole [Swedish Trade Union Confederation LO 1972]."

In the mid-1960s, the structural design of participation at the enterprise level in Sweden was quite similar to the one in Germany, outside the iron, coal, and steel industries, as was the position of the local union representatives. However, subsequent developments were rather different, due to the greater organizational, ideological, and political strength of the Swedish labor movement. In 1966, a new agreement on works councils was concluded between LO and the employers' association, which emphasized that consultation take place prior to managerial decisions. However, the functions of the works council remained restricted to joint consultation, as in Germany under the Works Constitution Act. Though the local union was given increased responsibility for the functioning of the works council through the 1966 agreement, local union representatives were insufficiently prepared to perform a mobilizing function and to press for effective participation. The role of the local union representatives had mainly been one of intermediaries between the rank and file and higher leadership levels.

Bargaining centralization is even greater in Sweden than in Germany. Collective negotiations take place at the national level between the LO and the employers' association, which conclude a frame agreement for the whole Swedish private sector. This frame agreement forms the basis for bargaining of national industrial unions. Due to this highly centralized bargaining procedure, the LO was able to successfully pursue a coordinated wage policy of solidarity aimed at equal pay for equal work and decreasing pay differences for different types of work. However, another consequence of this high centralization was that the role of the local union representative was of relatively small importance. In contrast to Germany, though, the works councils did not develop into an alternative or even rival institution for the representation of workers' interests. For instance, the wage-drift phenomenon, that is, deviations from centrally negotiated wage rates, occurred in Sweden, too, but local agreements were concluded with the local union, not with the works council. Despite their relatively restricted role, local union representatives remained the principal actors handling labor relations at the enterprise level. The reason for this difference between the Swedish and German case is the greater hegemony of unions in Sweden as the sole legitimate representative of workers' interests, which in turn is based on their comprehensive organizational penetration. Through subsequent legislation in the 1970s, the role of local union officials was greatly expanded and their position strengthened.

As a result of the union movement's collaboration with the incumbent Social Democrats in the pursuit of economic growth, full employment, and expansion of the welfare state, Sweden had the lowest strike rate among Western industrial countries in the 1950s and 1960s. The high degree of bargaining centralization ensured compliance of member unions with the coordinated wage policy. By the late 1960s, however, this centralization caused the Swedish union leadership to experience criticism about loss of touch with the base and manifestations of discontent in wildcat strikes, just as their German counterparts. In 1969 and 1970 unauthorized strikes assumed quite significant proportions. According to van Otter, the 216 officially recorded wildcat strikes for 1970 underrepresent the real extent of industrial conflict, because by no means are all such strikes reported.[18] These strikes constituted a considerable challenge to the apparent success of the Swedish labor movement in decisively improving the situation of the working class. In particular, they highlighted the discontent resulting from the continued subordinate position of workers in authoritarian control relations at the enterprise level. Unlike Germany, in Sweden the union leadership could activate power resources and thus was capable

---

[18]van Otter (1975:213). Korpi (1968, cited in van Otter) presents figures from a special study of 46 plants in the metal industry from 1955 to 1967, which show that out of 34 wildcat stoppages and 60 collective demonstrations, only 15 were known to the union and only 9 were recorded in official statistics.

of responding to this challenge by opening up new channels for participation at the workplace, enhancing the importance of local unions, and embarking on a massive education and mobilization campaign.

Following the tradition of minimal direct state intervention in labor–management relations, the unions first attempted to expand workers' participation through negotiations with employers. When demands went beyond experiments with different forms of joint decision making, however, extending to real transfer of control rights over decisions at higher hierarchical levels from management to workers, the way of collective negotiation failed because of the decided resistance of employers. At this point, the strength of labor as a sociopolitical force proved crucial, as workers' participation could be extended by way of legislation. The interesting aspect of the Swedish conception of participation in comparison with other countries is the explicit concern with the preservation of the antagonistic positions of capital and labor. Rather than a type of codetermination with the potential of leading to an integration into the existing structure of distribution of control, stepwise transfer of full control over an increasing range of aspects and collective negotiations about others has been demanded. In 1973, for example, the position of the local safety officers and committees was strengthened. They were granted the right to stop work and summon the Labor Inspectorate in case of dangerous working conditions, as well as the right to participate in the planning of working premises, methods, and the purchase of machinery, which requires that they be provided with all relevant information, including investment programs and production plans.

Another law passed in 1973 entitled workers in companies with more than 100 workers to at least two representatives on the board of directors, to be appointed by the local union.[19] Though unions had previously been opposed to such minority representation on the board of directors, they changed their position and used this right as the basis for further demands. They claimed that this representation could only be meaningful with the assistance of an economic expert who would have the same rights to the inspection of company accounts and other documents as a shareholder's auditor. Under the threat of legislation to satisfy this demand, employers accepted a collective agreement in 1975, which also stipulates that the cost for the work of this economic advisor is to be paid for by the enterprise. To maintain the independence of the union vis-à-vis the enterprise and prevent possible co-optation, the worker representatives were prohibited from participating in decisions about labor–management conflicts and collective agreements.

The latest legislation concerning "democracy at the workplace," which went into effect in January 1977, has greatly extended workers' participation in a

---

[19]This law, extended in 1976, applies to all industrial enterprises with 25 or more employees, as well as to banks and insurance companies.

highly integrated way by opening up possibilities for direct as well as indirect participation at all levels of decision making within the enterprise.[20] The structural design follows the pattern of preserving the antagonistic positions of labor and capital by providing for participation through collective negotiation. According to this law, employers no longer have any unilateral decision-making rights.[21] Rather, all decisions in an enterprise can be taken up as issues for negotiation either by the local union or by individual workers. If no agreement can be reached, workers have the right to resort to industrial action during an ongoing contract period. In case of a dispute about a collective agreement, the interpretation right belongs to the local trade union except if the dispute concerns wages. In that case, the interpretation right will go to the workers after a period of 10 days, unless the employer asks for central negotiations. Trade unions are entitled to all the information they demand on the company's situation; and if the employer is considering any changes that affect employees, he is obliged to initiate collective negotiations before carrying out these changes. Composition and functions of decision-making bodies within each enterprise are also to be regulated by collective agreements, in order for them to be properly adapted to local conditions.

Clearly, this type of legislation, relying completely on collective negotiation, can only be meaningful in a context where labor is strong organizationally and ideologically, and where socioeconomic conditions are supportive in terms of high employment rates and relatively high qualification of the labor force. Since these conditions exist in Sweden, however, this legislation will open large areas to workers' control. Experts agree that it will take years to exploit fully all the potential for control that this legislation has opened up—a task that will require great efforts for training of shop-floor union activists. These efforts had already started at the time of the adoption of the Industrial Democracy program by the 1971 LO Congress. Lower-level union leaders and activists were trained in courses designed to prepare them to assume functions that would be transferred to them upon implementation of the program.[22]

[20]For an excellent discussion of this legislation and its political significance, see Martin (1977).

[21]The way this legislation was passed exemplifies the political importance of white-collar unionization very well. A legislative study commission composed of members of the various political parties and representatives of employer and labor organizations came out with a majority report with suggestions for rather limited workers' participation. The representatives from LO and TCO wrote a dissenting minority report, which was taken as a basis for the legislation introduced by the Social Democratic government. Constrained by their dependence on the white-collar vote, the Liberals and the Center Party finally supported this legislation in Parliament as well.

[22]In 1974–1975, for instance, 83,000 union members attended study circles on trade union subjects organized by the union educational organizations, and 15,000 union members attended residential courses by the LO; 4000 among them attended longer training courses for safety stewards and worker representatives on corporate boards. (Translated into an American order of magnitude in proportion to the total population, this would amount to roughly 2,450,000 people attending

The strong position already achieved by unions and the crucial role assigned to them in this participation scheme have caused critics to predict that in the not-too-far future Swedish industry might be run as undemocratically as it is today, only by union oligarchs handing directives down to the enterprise level instead of by businessmen. Two main characteristics argue against this prediction: First of all, the design of the new participation scheme provides for maximum flexibility for local participation, relying on the mobilizing activity of local unions, and it gives individual workers the right to take up questions directly, not only through the union. Second, top- and middle-level union leaders have a strong ideological commitment to a socialist transformation, involving democratization of control over means of production and equalization of the distribution of resources for consumption.[23] Due to its social and political strength, the Swedish labor movement could have become a status-quo-oriented force long ago if power did necessarily corrupt. On the contrary, Swedish labor, in close alliance with the Social Democratic Party, has upheld the goal of a democratic socialist transformation of society.

The 1975 program of the Social Democrats emphasized that the third phase of societal transformation, the installation of economic democracy, was to be effected, as political democracy and social democracy (i.e., the establishment of the welfare state) had been achieved. More progress toward an expansion of democratic control over the economy has been made in Sweden than in any other developed capitalist democratic system. As discussed earlier, societal-level supportive policies involving transfer of control rights from private capital owners to the state have preceded the transfer of control rights to workers at the enterprise level. Transfer of control rights was not done through nationalization (i.e., transfer of the legal title of ownership to the state) but through dissociation of control rights from the legal title and their transfer to the state; or, in Swedish terminology, socialization of functions.[24]

The main areas of state exercise of control rights are investment resources

---

union courses.) The LO Congress of June 1976 established that all union members must be given basic trade union education and that new employees, especially, should be given a course of education dealing with the problems of their workplace sponsored by their unions during paid working hours. See Viklund (1977).

[23]That this is not pure rhetoric but a genuine practice can be seen, for instance, in the material benefits that top union leaders derive from their positions, which are very modest in comparison to other countries. Despite the fact that the Swedish labor movement is socially and politically stronger than any other Western labor movement, the income of a top union leader is not much higher than the one of a skilled Swedish worker. For instance, the income of the president of one of the largest Swedish unions was 65,000 crowns (about $16,000) in 1973, as compared to an average income of 50,000 crowns for a skilled worker. Figures from J. D. Stephens, 1976.

[24]This notion was developed and corresponding policies advocated by Social Democratic theoreticians and politicians; for more background information, see Adler-Karlsson (1967).

and legal regulation of economic activity. The state sector accounts for only 5% of the value of production in mining and manufacturing, but state control over the credit market amounts to about 50%, through the government-owned PK Bank and the Public Pension Funds. The Public Pension Funds amounted to over 80 billion Swedish crowns in 1974 ($20 billion), almost twice the value of the total stock of shares registered on the Stockholm stock exchange (Sodersten 1975). The management of the Public Pension Funds is professional, under the supervision of a board which consists of government and trade union representatives. So far, their investment policy has been very cautious, the funds being used mainly to finance a massive housing construction program. In 1973 a law was passed which allowed the Pension Funds to allocate a certain limited amount to the acquisition of shares of private companies. Clearly, these pension funds constitute a powerful instrument for public control over means of production and an important protection against capital flight and investment strike on part of the private sector in protest against an expansion of workers' participation. A further instrument of control over investment is a system of company-owned but in part publicly controlled investment funds. This system allows the government to stimulate investments in periods of downturn and restrain them in periods of high business activity.[25]

Social equality has been pursued politically through a strong welfare state, a progressive tax system, and the already mentioned active labor market policies. Combined national and local taxes on corporate profits are around 55% in addition to which employers pay a 29.2% payroll tax for various social insurance schemes. Personal income taxes are highly progressive. Government revenue for 1976 amounted to 57% of GDP (OECD *Observer*, No. 90, March 1978). The public sector expanded by 50% from 1956 to 1973 and performed a significant redistributive function. Schnitzer, in his comparative income distribution study based on data for the early 1970s, states flatly that: "In terms of per capita money income, (Sweden) ranks second only to the U.S. in the world; in terms of a more equitable distribution of real income, it ranks second to no country [Schnitzer 1974:62]." Labor's coordinated pursuit of an equal-

[25]The system of investment funds was first introduced in 1938, with current provisions dating from 1963. Every company is permitted to allocate up to 40% of its profits before taxes in any one year to an investment fund. Of this allocation, 46% is to be deposited with the Bank of Sweden in a blocked account, on which no interest is paid. Since the combined national and local tax on company profits comes to around 55%, it is to a company's advantage to make allocations to the investment fund if its only other distributions of retained earnings are subject to tax and if the company does expect to be required to draw on its accumulated investment funds in the future. Five years after an allocation to the investment funds, a company can use up to 30% of it for purposes specified by the law. The release of the remainder of the funds is subject to government authorization, which facilitates a practical timing of investments to combat recession. The Swedish Institute, December 1973.

izing wage policy through centrally negotiated collective agreements has also contributed to decreasing social inequality by reducing income differentials.[26] However, white-collar resistance against these equalizing policies has been growing, which constitutes a potential danger for ideological unity within the labor movement and consequently for its strength as a sociopolitical force. So far, labor is united in its support for a progressive transfer of control rights from private owners to workers at the enterprise level, and for protective policies at the societal level.

Through strong labor market policies, the Social Democratic government was able to maintain a consistently very low level of unemployment, despite Sweden's high export dependence and consequent vulnerability to fluctuations in the world market. Average unemployment during the period 1964–1977 was 1.9%. Though this is slightly higher than the 1.6% for the corresponding period in Germany, several factors have to be considered in interpreting this difference. First of all, labor force participation rates are higher in Sweden than in Germany (75.2% versus 68.9%),[27] mainly due to higher employment levels among women (61.9% versus 47.5%). Second, Sweden has fewer foreign workers than Germany, and those who are there are granted more rights than their counterparts in Germany, such that Sweden could not "export" part of the unemployment. Third, people who are unemployed receive significant assistance not only for their living expenses but also for retraining and locating new jobs. And finally, Sweden is more dependent on foreign trade than Germany (exports in 1976 accounting for 25% of GDP versus 21% in Germany, and imports for 26% versus 18% [OECD *Observer*, No. 86, 1977]) thus finding it more difficult to protect the domestic economy from external influences. The difference between the two countries in labor's influence on full-employment policies becomes visible in a comparison of the years 1975 and 1976, when unemployment in Germany rose to 3.7% and 3.6% despite strong protests from the unions, whereas unemployment in Sweden during this period was kept at 1.6%.

The potentially most significant reform leading toward a democratic socialist transformation is a proposal for the establishment of so-called wage earner funds, which is currently being debated.[28] Essentially, this proposal provides a concrete policy instrument for a viable democratic socialist transformation strategy, in that it suggests policies for the long-range socialization of ownership

[26]In collective bargaining LO consistently negotiated special funds for raising wages in lower-paying industries and plants. As a result, the differential in average hourly earnings between contract areas declined from 30% in 1959 to 15% in 1972. See van Otter (1975:210).

[27]Participation rates are calculated on the basis of the total population 15–64 years. OECD *Labor Force Statistics*, 1964–1975.

[28]For the history of the proposal, see Meidner (1978).

of capital without direct expropriation of private owners. A study report sponsored by the LO in 1975 suggested a system of funds based on a yearly percentage of company profits, owned by workers as a collectivity, and administered on a branch of industry basis. These funds were to serve several medium-range purposes as well: to increase capital formation and facilitate a continued pursuit of the wage policy of solidarity without undesirable distributional consequences, and to prevent potential capital flight in reaction against the full development of the participation reform from causing serious economic problems. Under the proposed system, public control over industry could be achieved in roughly 30 years. Though there has been no agreement reached even among the proponents of the system about the exact nature of the administration of the funds—whether through union or community representatives—and though the proposal has been relegated to low priority by the bourgeois governments which have been in power since the September 1976 elections, it is an indicator of the dynamics favoring increasing social control over means of production. Whether these dynamics can be sustained will depend to a large degree on the mobilizing activity of the unions and the sustained unity of blue- and white-collar organized labor on the issue of transfer of control and income rights from private capital owners to the state and the workers. Unity on this issue will be a crucial determinant of the labor movement's capacity to mobilize sufficient political support to bring the Social Democratic Party back into power.

Analyses of the 1976 elections have shown that the narrow defeat of the Social Democrats was not due to a backlash against the welfare state nor against the workers' participation program, which after all had received broad support in Parliament (Korpi 1977; Sifo 1976). The issue dominating the campaign, particularly in the final weeks when the crucial swing took place, was nuclear energy. The Center Party was able to build itself up as the champion of environmental protection, whereas the Social Democrats advocated limited use of nuclear energy to guarantee continued economic growth. In addition, a series of minor scandals, mainly around the tax authorities, produced a certain backlash against bureaucracy and thus against the Social Democrats as the dominant party in the bureaucracy. The key problem for the Social Democrats was that they lacked an issue on which to countermobilize support. The "democracy at the workplace" legislation was widely approved by the electorate, but the Center and Liberal parties' support of it rendered it ineffective as a campaign issue. Also, full employment and inclusive welfare state policies had come to be taken for granted.

The debate about wage-earner funds is still going on and will not be resolved until the 1980s. If, however, the LO and TCO will be able to agree on common principles for the wage-earner funds, this issue could provide the basis to mobilize sufficient electoral support to return the Social Democrats to power. Legislation on wage-earner funds, then, would constitute a significant step on the legal road toward a democratic socialist transformation.

Yugoslavia

Compared to the experience in these developed capitalist democratic systems just discussed, where the growing sociopolitical strength of organized labor effects a gradual transfer of control and income rights from private capital owners to the state and the workers, the Yugoslav experience constitutes a stark contrast in that the elite in control of the state initiated a process of gradual transfer of control and income rights from the state to the workers, whose rights as a group have come to resemble those of capital owners. Despite this fundamental difference, the Yugoslav experience has one important aspect in common with the three others: the failure of workers' participation schemes to develop fully in practice without supporting activity from an agency mobilizing workers at the base into exercising their structurally given participation rights.

Yugoslavia in the 1950s embarked upon a transformation from a system approximating the bureaucratic-centralist type in a democratic socialist direction. Though Yugoslavia has probably moved further in this direction than any other country, the Yugoslav system in the 1970s differs from the ideal type of a democratic socialist system in two fundamental respects. First, the polity is nonpolyarchic: Legitimacy of organized opposition is very low. Second, the state has divested itself of the exercise not only of most control but also of income rights, which are exercised by the workers in individual enterprises. This has produced inegalitarian results in the distribution of resources for consumption, because workers' income depends on the capital intensity and market position of their enterprise, and because the labor market maintains stratification within enterprises. It has also produced inegalitarian results in the distribution of power due to monopolistic positions of some enterprises and financial institutions. Furthermore, the ideological commitment of the elite to social equality and the pursuit of corresponding equalization and full employment policies are rather weak, despite proclaimed adherence to the ideal of a classless society.

Workers' participation originated as a response of the elite to a threat from external forces. The course of its subsequent development was strongly shaped by a disintegration of elite consensus and by increasing foreign indebtedness, and thus dependence on continuing Western financial aid. Yugoslavia's expulsion from the Cominform in 1948 left the leadership in a state of deep confusion and in urgent need to find a new legitimacy formula and unifying ideology to substitute for the originally followed bureaucratic-centralist Soviet model. Accordingly, a doctrine of direct socialist democracy was developed, calling for an immediate beginning of the state's withering away and the re-placement of bureaucratic-centralist decision making with direct participation of the population in the decision making, based on a system of self-managing political and economic units. Given the monopoly of sociopolitical power of the Communist Party, the main task of the leadership in facilitating the imple-mentation of this design was to reduce the direct control of the party over the whole social and economic life, restricting its function to indirect political and ideological guidance. With this purpose, the Communist Party was trans-formed into the League of Communists of Yugoslavia (LCY) in 1952.[29] Slowly, the two-track system of control was dismantled by preventing League officials from holding government positions at the same time.

Supreme decision-making authority within the enterprise was transferred in the early 1950's from party-appointed administrators of enterprises to workers' councils. Production planning was decentralized to individual enterprises, whereas enterprise autonomy was still limited through central investment plan-ning and certain price controls. Through successive reforms, both economic and political control were more and more decentralized to the lowest levels. In 1958, a system of social self-management was introduced, with considerable autonomy of communes in economic, cultural, and educational affairs, and social services. The Constitution of 1963 adapted the political system to this social self-management structure, in the form of representative democracy with chambers representing people as citizens and producers at the local and re-gional as well as the national level.[30] The indirect political guidance role of the League, of course, remained very strong. However, decreasing elite consensus led to decentralization of decision making within the League also. The process of economic and political decentralization and the consequent growing in-equalities between regions in turn reinforced centrifugal tendencies in Yugo-slav society, aggravating the nationality problem.

Initially, the design of workers' participation consisted of a full transfer of control rights from administrators to the workers over decisions taken at the enterprise level, with preservation of the major share of income rights and a substantial share of control rights for the state, through limitations on the range

---

[29]An analysis of the circumstances under which the pursuit of a bureaucratic-centralist model was abandoned is given by Hoffman and Neal (1962) and Rusinow (1977).
[30]The assembly system consisted of two chambers at the communal and republican level (i.e., one council elected on a one-man-one-vote base and one council elected by workers in enterprises on the territory of the commune or republic, and by agricultural producers and members of co-operatives). At the federal level, there were five assemblies: (1) the federal council as representative of citizens in republics; (2) the economic council; (3) the council for culture and education; (4) the council of social and health services; and (5) the council for organizational policy. Roggemann 1970:235. With subsequent strengthening of the autonomy of republics, the five-chamber system was introduced at the republican level too.

of decisions taken at the enterprise level. First, this range was extended to include daily production decisions. Subsequently, a disintegration of national political consensus on priorities in economic development, particularly concerning the allocation of resources among regions at different levels of development, led to the abandonment of central investment planning.[31] Instead, the economic reforms of 1965 introduced predominant reliance on market determination of investment, through the substitution of the investment funds formerly in the hands of communes, republics, and the federation by a system of self-financing and credits provided by banks on business principles. These reforms, which included other economic liberalization measures, were advocated by a coalition of political leaders and managers in the developed republics. Other members of the political elite, particularly officials in less developed republics, opposed the reforms, which were only fully implemented after the purge in 1966 of the former chief of the Secret Police, an old guard bureaucratic centralist (see Milenkovitch 1971:175).

The 1965 economic reforms also have to be seen in connection with the increasing association of the Yugoslav economy with Western markets and Yugoslavia's increasing indebtedness to Western creditors. When trade with the East bloc was shut off in 1948, the Yugoslav leadership turned to the West for imports to implement their heavy industrialization program. By 1950, foreign exchange reserves were depleted, and Yugoslavia was in dire need of foreign aid. In 1952, an aid agreement was concluded, involving the United States, Britain, and France, and establishing Western control over the use of aid.[32] Throughout the 1950s, large sums of aid flowed into Yugoslavia. The continued trade imbalance and growing debt burden brought the balance of payments under great strain in the 1960s. In order to preserve her trading position in Western Europe, Yugoslavia applied for full GATT membership in 1960. This required a currency reform as well as liberalization of imports, which aggravated the trade balance even further. In 1965, $290 million were due in repayment for Yugoslavia's debt, and consultations with the IMF and creditor countries about debt rescheduling and new credits involved the package of liberalizing reforms as well (Payer 1974:132). These reforms included devaluation, end of subsidies to inefficient enterprises, and a rise in the percentage of earnings to be retained by the enterprises from 51% to 71%. They also allowed enterprises to lend to others directly and receive flexible interest rates. These

[31]Milenkovitch's (1971) and Farkas's (1975) analyses support the argument that political factors were main determinants in the progressive decentralization of economic decision making in Yugoslavia.

[32]Payer (1974) makes a convincing argument for the important impact of Yugoslavia's reliance on foreign aid on the process of economic liberalization. She shows how successive reforms were developed in consultation with the IMF and in accordance with the latter's policy preferences. The following discussion relies heavily on her study.

measures were designed to render Yugoslav enterprises competitive in Western markets and able to respond quickly to changing export possibilities. The results were shutdowns of inefficient enterprises, increasing unemployment, and increasing income differentials between workers in more and less profitable enterprises and more and less developed regions.

The 1965 reforms, then, implied a substantial transfer of income rights from the state to worker-managed enterprises. However, the state still retained a share in income rights in the form of charges for the use of social property, that is, socially owned land and capital. Only the abolition of interest on social capital and rental fees for capital equipment in 1970 constituted a reassociation of control and income rights and their exercise by the same group of people, the workers in individual enterprises. This put members of enterprises in the position of collective capital owners. They came to enjoy group property rights insofar as all enterprise income, including the part generated by socially owned assets, could be distributed by members of the enterprise.[33] The disappearing role of the state in the economy generated further dynamics similar to the ones in capitalist market economies, such as concentrations of wealth and economic power based on monopolistic positions.

The structural design of workers' self-management provides for an equal distribution of control rights among members of an enterprise, but in practice the exercise of these control rights developed rather unequally. The workers' council, elected on a one-man-one-vote basis by secret ballot is the supreme authority within the enterprise. It elects a managing board for supervision of day-to-day operations, as well as the director of the enterprise, who is subject to recall from the workers' council. However, despite this egalitarian design, differences in power and rewards have remained associated with different positions in the enterprise and have tended to reinforce themselves over time. Though the Yugoslav design of participation provides for relatively extensive participation through various specialized committees and the requirement of rotation in office,[34] there is no direct participation at lowest levels. For regular workers without specialized skills, who became heavily underrepresented on workers' councils from 1960 to 1970,[35] participation is thus mainly restricted

[33]For a discussion of this "privatization" of property rights and an assessment of its significance for the socialist character of Yugoslav society, see Milenkovitch (1971:265–273).

[34]The term of office as a member of the workers' council is restricted to two years, and reelection is only permissible after two years off the council. Estimates are that over one million Yugoslav workers served on workers' councils and other committees between 1950 and the early 1960s, which amounted to about one-third to one-half of all workers in the Socialist sector of the Yugoslav economy. Cited in Blumberg (1968:245).

[35]Jovanov (1972:62–96) shows that the proportion of workers' council members made up of workers from all skill categories declined from 76% in 1960 to 68% in 1970; among all these workers, only the highly skilled improved their rate of representation, from 15% in 1960 to 17% in 1970.

to electoral activities. The degree of job control directly exercised by the lower skilled worker is small, as the line of managerial administrative authority continues to function in a hierarchical manner. Skilled and highly skilled workers are more heavily represented on the workers' councils. According to Denitch, they constituted 50.9% of workers' council members in 1970, and they manage to influence particularly decisions on wage scales and on expenditures for social purposes.[36] Still, on the whole, even their influence on important enterprise decisions as well as their direct participation in work organization are restricted. In order to raise the level of direct participation, enterprises were broken up into smaller units, the "basic organizations of associated labor," a concept which was incorporated into the 1974 Constitution. Also, in order to raise workers' effective influence on all decisions of the workers' council, the 1974 Constitution forbade the election of managerial and technical staff to the councils (Rusinow 1977:329). Yet, these provisions are unlikely to reduce the influence of managerial–technocratic groups, which can be exercised through informal channels. Nor do they affect the predominant decision-making role of the director.

In survey studies investigating the perceived influence of different groups on decisions within the enterprise, the influence of unskilled workers was ranked lowest, and the one of the union second lowest (e.g., Rus 1970:148–160). These same studies also found a discrepancy between actual and desired distribution of influence. However, discontent resulting from this discrepancy on the part of lower categories of workers found no channel for organized expression. There was no agency mobilizing these workers into active participation to remedy their grievances via the workers' council, as unions failed to perform this function.

Thus spontaneous short strikes provided a major outlet for open manifestations of discontent. From 1958 to 1969, a total of 1750 strikes occurred. A nationwide study on strikes from 1966 to August 1969 showed that about one-third of them lasted less than three hours, and less than a quarter of them lasted more than one day.[37] The immediate complaints expressed in practically all of the strikes concerned personal income levels. It seems reasonable to assume that the expression of such complaints grew in frequency and intensity due to the increase in inequality rather than the development of absolute income levels. The number of strikes increased greatly in the early 1960s and remained higher throughout the decade than in the late 1950s, when absolute income levels had been clearly lower. This increase was not due to a legaliza-

---

[36]Denitch (1976:156–161). He argues that despite some shortcomings in practice the norm of workers' self-management has been widely accepted and has helped to legitimize the Yugoslav regime.

[37]Jovanov (1972). The figures concerning strikes in Yugoslavia presented in the following discussion are drawn from this source.

tion of strikes either, as they remained illegal up to 1971. Rather, it appears that the demonstration effect of much faster growing income levels of those employed in more privileged sectors of the economy clashed with the expectations raised by the egalitarian rhetoric of self-management. Though the internal spread of basic wages in most enterprises has remained comparatively narrow,[38] the differences between enterprises and between sectors of the economy have become considerable. Thus, unfulfilled aspirations for social equality and for effective influence on decision making in the enterprise caused discontent among disadvantaged groups. One can also assume that growing inequalities between sectors of the economy weakened the government's credibility as representative of the interests of the working class as a whole. This is not to argue that these strikes were political strikes in the sense of organized expression of political protest, but rather that trust in the government's acting to promote the welfare of all sectors of the working class had lost some effectiveness as a restraining factor.

Most strikes broke out among production workers in industrial enterprises; none broke out among employees in banks, enterprises dealing with foreign trade, and public administration, where income levels are comparatively high. For most of the enterprises that experienced strikes, difficult market situations were reported. Since market forces are no appropriate target for complaints and strikes, management became the target. Though the director and his assistants are formally subject to the authority of the workers' council, they exercise in reality predominant influence on decision making about business operations, and they are primarily responsible for it in the eyes of the workers. The perceived, and in most cases real, weakness of lower blue-collar workers vis-à-vis highly skilled groups, technicians, experts, and management in the self-management organs of the enterprise has given rise to action outside these channels. Only in about a quarter of the strikes, resolution of the conflict through the formal channels was attempted. Even more indicative for the experience of powerlessness in these channels due to underrepresentation of lower categories of workers is the fact that in about 85% of the cases striking workers were joined by their representatives on the various self-management organs. However, only 11% of the strikes were supported by unions.

In the post-World War II period of installation of the Yugoslav regime, unions had been built up as simple one-way transmission belts, in charge of supervising the implementation of party policies at the workplace. Though this supervising function lost its importance with increasing autonomy of the enterprise, trade unions have not managed to recover importance as sociopolitical actors in the defense of workers' interests. Tendencies toward a more autono-

[38]Vuskovic (1976) cites figures based on information from the Yugoslav Federal Bureau of Statistics, which show that in 1970 almost three-quarters of all enterprises had a spread of basic wages of 1:4 only.

mous and critical position of unions have emerged, but they found their expression mainly in resolutions at meetings rather than in concrete actions. In particular, unions have failed to reorient their activity toward mobilizing lower-level workers into participation.

The role of trade unions in a worker-managed enterprise is a theoretically much disputed issue. Clegg (1951) argues that under workers' self-management, unions would struggle with the workers' council about genuine representation of workers and unavoidably try to capture control over the self-management organs. This would lead to a loss of function of unions, which—according to Clegg—consists in opposing management analogous to independent opposition in a political democracy. Blumberg (1968:162), on the other hand, points out that there can be a separation of functions between the workers' council, as representative of workers' interests as producers, and the union, as representative of workers' interests as wage earners. I would basically agree with this second position, but add a further dimension to the role of unions under workers' self-management: the mobilization of lower categories of workers into active participation and the defense of their interests vis-à-vis the managerial-technocratic stratum.

Survey research carried out in Yugoslavia shows that socioeconomic status, measured by education and income, and organizational affiliation are the crucial determinants of participation in communal and enterprise self-management organs (Verba and Shabad 1978). Research in many other countries has consistently found these two variables to be strong predictors of the level of political participation.[39] Socioeconomic status in most cases has a double effect, insofar as it raises participation directly as well as indirectly by increasing the likelihood of organizational affiliation. Thus lower social groups are doubly barred from participating. However, if there are strong organizations penetrating lower social groups, such as the union movement in Sweden, they can eliminate this effect and raise participation levels of these groups up to those of higher social groups.[40] In Yugoslavia, membership in the League of Communists raises participation in self-management organs significantly among all socioeconomic groups. Yet, membership is highly skewed toward upper educational and income groups (Verba and Shabad 1978). Only an organization specifically attempting to recruit and mobilize lower categories of workers could compensate for this double advantage of higher status groups. This again underlines what a crucial deficiency the lack of a strong union movement is for the full realization of workers' self-management.

[39]See, e.g., Nie et al. (1969), and various voting studies.

[40]Participation levels in Sweden show virtually no class differences (e.g., analysis of data from the 1964 election survey carried out by the Institute of Political Science at the University of Goteborg showed 84.4% voting participation for manual workers, and 85.5% for nonmanual workers).

The tendencies toward underrepresentation of lower categories of workers and lack of effective influence of workers' councils were aggravated by the growing approximation of the Yugoslav to Western capitalist market economies. The economic reforms of 1965 greatly strengthened the position of the managerial–technocratic elite, both within the enterprise and in the political system. The more competitive economic environment and closer relations to foreign business tended to reward faster, more complex and innovative decision making, and consequently entrepreneurial expertise. Thus, most empirical studies have found that directors, technicians, and other high level employees have a high degree of autonomy and exert a dominant influence on the decisions of the workers' council, despite their formal subjection to the authority of the council.[41]

Commensurate with the growing importance of their role, the managerial elite increasingly came to enjoy special privileges. Despite a continued relatively narrow spread of basic remunerations within the enterprise, if compared with Western capitalist enterprises, rewards for employees in leading positions have grown considerably. They take the form of use of cars, travel abroad, liberal expense accounts, etc.

Yugoslavia's increasing closeness to Western market economies manifested itself in still other respects. Both central democratic guidance and equalization policies were more and more abandoned, as elite ideological consensus on the pursuit of a democratic socialist order had disintegrated.[42] Policy making came to respond primarily to needs and interests of dominant economic sectors, filtered from the republican up to the national level, as the political role of the managerial elite grew in importance. The influence of the managerial elite works through the economic chambers, the formal channels for representation of economic interests, and through a variety of industrial associations and special advisory committees. Particularly at the republican level representatives of big enterprises exercise strong influence.[43] Thus economic policies have been shaped more by the articulation of particularistic interests than by a coherent developmental design for a socialist society. In fact, compared to the pursuit of protective policies for a socialist transformation in capitalist democracies, Yugoslavia to some extent went through a reverse process. The divestment on part

---

[41] For example, Obradovic (1972:137–164). Farkas (1975:26) confirms that "the lion's share of the decision-making power and responsibility for decisions made have come to rest in the hands of the director [president/top manager of a firm]."

[42] Farkas observes "a decrease in the number of purely political criteria for solutions to basic problems" and "a pragmatism that pervades the system"; he finds that in general "the direction away from rigid ideological prescriptions is in evidence throughout the system [1975:123]." One certainly can interpret these observations as indicators of the abandonment of the pursuit of a clearly defined social order.

[43] Farkas (1975) strongly emphasizes the importance of the political role of the managerial elite.

of the national political elite of economic power through the decentralization of virtually all control and income rights caused the emergence of new "group–private" economic power centers based on monopolistic positions.[44] It also opened the possibility for "group–capitalist exploitation" through appropriation of surplus generated by workers in other enterprises in the form of high interest rates on loans, or monopolistic price setting for inputs needed by other enterprises. Particularly banks and companies involved in foreign trade developed into crucial mediating agencies and were able to concentrate control over an increasing amount of resources in their hands. By 1971, banks controlled 51% of gross investment, and due to the great need for investment loans, they were in a position to set their interest rates in some cases as high as 20 or 30% (Supek 1975:23). By 1972, there were only 15 banks in existence, and the 6 largest banks had a market share of 70%. This meant that these 6 banks were exercising great influence over the Yugoslav economy, operating on the basis of capitalist business principles rather than considerations of development needs of society.[45] Thus, due to the lack of a central regulating and overall guiding mechanism, production became less oriented toward criteria of socio-economic rationality and more toward narrow criteria of profitability.

A corollary of these developments was an increase in regional differences in economic and social development, and in income differentials between branches of industry and individual enterprises.[46] The principle of "to each according to his work" became inoperative, as monopoly advantage and differential access to socially owned resources assumed increasing importance in the determination of enterprise revenues and consequently personal income (Milenkovitch 1971:264–265). Regional differences were particularly aggravated through foreign exchange revenues from tourism, which can be retained and used for imports in part by the enterprises and in part by the republics receiving them. Furthermore, in 1967 Yugoslavia first decided to allow foreign investment of up to 49% in joint ventures, and in 1971 this decision was revised to allow for foreign majority ownership.[47] Clearly, foreign investment is

[44]In 1971, only 1.4% of all productive, transport and trading firms accounted for much more than one-third of the total gross revenue of the Yugoslav economy, 3.3% of industrial enterprises accounted for close to half the total gross revenue of Yugoslav industry, only 1.7% of trading firms accounted for over a third of total trade in Yugoslavia. *Yugoslav Survey*, Vol. XII, No. 4, November 1971, p. 93.

[45]In order to curtail the power of banks, the 1974 Constitution provided for their control by the enterprises that subscribed to their capital. See Rusinow (1977:329ff).

[46]In 1969, Croatia had an income per capita of $370, Slovenia of $515, and Kosovo of $100.

[47]Information about foreign investment in Yugoslavia and about curtailments of the sphere of decision making for workers' councils in joint ventures can be found in Farkas (1975:31; and 104–110).

again most likely to flow to the more developed regions which can offer adequate infrastructure.

In accordance with the weakening of the state's central guiding role in the pursuit of equalization policies, the pursuit of an active employment policy was assigned very low priority. Instead of developing labor-intensive industrial production and domestic agricultural production, the government let economic development and demand for labor be shaped by market forces. As a result, large numbers of workers migrated to Western European industrial countries. By the end of 1975, about 1.2 million Yugoslavs were working abroad. Nevertheless, domestic unemployment stood at 10% of the labor force in the public sector at that point (ILO *Yearbook of Labour Statistics*). Besides alleviating domestic unemployment, the migration of Yugoslav workers to Western Europe is an important source of badly needed foreign exchange revenue for the Yugoslav economy in the form of savings remitted from abroad.

Continued balance of trade deficits and the pressing debt burden forced a renewed devaluation in 1971. In 1972, Yugoslavia's foreign debt amounted to $2.5 billion, and new loans had to be raised to meet debt service payments. A succession of stabilization programs, closely modelled after the typical IMF fiscal austerity recommendations, was introduced. Clearly, under these conditions of dependence on continued foreign loans, and thus subject to conditions from foreign creditors, a reversal towards more socialist, equality-oriented policies would be extremely difficult, even if greater political consensus on such a course could be achieved.

In view of the disintegration of political consensus and the concomitant fractionalization of the political elite, the question emerges as to which sociopolitical forces might shape policies through pressures on the weakened political decision-making center after Tito's death. Organized labor is weak at the enterprise level, and even more so as a sociopolitical force due to its lack of an autonomous organizational base, linking lower-level workers horizontally and providing mobilization capacity for political pressure. A potentially more effective sociopolitical force is the managerial–technocratic elite, particularly in coalition with regional political elites. Such a coalition emerged in the Croatian crisis of 1971, actively supporting expressions of popular discontent. Due to Tito's intervention, central authority prevailed over the centrifugal tendencies manifesting themselves in this crisis. In 1973, Tito effected a recentralization of decision making within the LCY. Also, toleration of dissent was restricted, and the party's control over the state was strengthened.[48] However, economic decentralization was left unaffected, and consequently inequalities and result-

---

[48]See Rusinow's discussion (1977:308–342) of Tito's reaction to the Croatian crisis and of the changes in the following two years, endorsed by the 10th Congress of the LCY in May 1974.

ing tensions have persisted. In the post-Tito era, the military seems to be the force most capable of guaranteeing central guidance and unification of Yugoslav society. If a reversal in the decentralization of economic and political decision making in Yugoslav society in the direction of a bureaucratic-centralist system were to be favored by the military, little effective popular opposition in defense of the system of workers' self-management could be expected.[49] Rank-and-file workers with an interest in the preservation and improvement of the system lack an organizational power base. And whereas the managerial–technocratic elite will certainly favor preservation of enterprise autonomy, they are less likely to resist a retransfer of control rights from workers to an authority in charge of managing an enterprise. This elite might well have a potentially influential ally in the IMF. IMF influence in consultations with the Yugoslav government has consistently worked in the direction of greater enterprise autonomy and relaxation of all restrictions on the free operation of market forces. As long as Yugoslavia remains committed to living up to debt obligations, and thus dependent on renegotiations, this influence can be expected to prevent a deviation from a free enterprise–free market system. However, there is no reason to expect that it will prevent a deviation from the self-management model toward a more traditional managerial authority structure. Certainly, a military-dominated government is as unlikely to strengthen trade unions as a government dominated by an alliance between party and managerial–technocratic elites. Thus even if the system is left formally unchanged, it will remain far from being a fully developed workers' control model.

The discussion of these four empirical cases has provided evidence for the usefulness of my conceptualization of dynamics in the four developmental stages of workers' participation. It has shown how workers' participation developed in interaction with the strength and action of sociopolitical forces. This interaction operated at two levels: at the level of national politics and at the enterprise level. The constellation of sociopolitical forces varied in accordance with the type of politico-economic system, and thus different actors played the crucial role at the national level. In France, Germany, and Sweden, the developed capitalist democratic systems, the balance of forces in civil society determined state action. Legislation on workers' participation and corresponding policies reflecting working-class interests and preparing the way for a gradual socialist transformation advanced only under pressures from an organizationally strong and ideologically united labor movement. In Yugoslavia, the developing socialist authoritarian system, the state initially dominated civil society, and the initiative for the introduction of workers' participation came from the elite controlling the state apparatus. As the elite divested itself of much of its

---

[49]A crucial factor determining developments in Yugoslavia will clearly be the extent to which independence from the U.S.S.R. can be retained.

central economic and political control, forces in civil society gained strength and started to shape the development of workers' participation along with other economic policies. Under the influence of new groups of managerial–technocratic elites without a countervailing influence from organized lower social groups, policy formation deviated from socialist principles. The Yugoslav case also showed how dependence on foreign trade, financing, and technology renders developing countries susceptible to outside influence, on a wide range of important domestic policies, from foreign national and international agencies.

The discussion also showed that the requirement for full implementation of workers' participation at the enterprise level was the same in all four cases. Structurally provided possibilities for participation were only fully taken advantage of and their limitations challenged where a strong union was present to mobilize workers to exercise all their given participation rights. The probability of the presence of such a strong mobilizing union in turn was dependent on the strength and autonomy of labor organization at the societal level. France, Germany, and Sweden differed in the degree of strength of labor at the societal level, in the extent of mobilizing activity by local unions for participation at the enterprise level, and accordingly in the extent to which participation designs met with apathy or were fully implemented and ultimately transcended. In Yugoslavia, the lack of strong and autonomous labor organization at the societal level and of mobilizing union activity at the enterprise level led to a highly deficient exercise of control rights by a large proportion of the workers despite the fact that the Yugoslav design transferred a maximum degree of control rights to the workers.

Now I am going to turn to a new case, to the development of a unique scheme of workers' participation in a developing capitalist authoritarian system, Peru. I will apply my conceptualization to an analysis of the Peruvian experience, in the course of which I will draw on the previously discussed cases for occasional comparison. Also, I will make extensive reference to some aspects of the Chilean experience. On the basis of my conceptualization of the constellation of sociopolitical forces and the concomitant relations between state and civil society in developing capitalist authoritarian systems, the following dynamics can be expected in the Peruvian case. Civil society is weaker in relation to the state than in developed capitalist democracies but stronger than in developing socialist authoritarian systems. Accordingly, the decisive impetus for the introduction of workers' participation can be expected to come from the elite controlling the state apparatus, but policy formation and developments at the national level will be affected by pressures from both private capital owners and organized popular forces. And constraints from foreign economic power centers can be expected to limit the action capabilities of the state. Thus the elite's general relations to these various forces and the handling of concrete pressures will be of particular importance for the advance of workers' participation and related policies of socioeconomic change. At the enterprise level, the degree of effective participation and its integrating or demand-generating effects can also be expected to depend on the presence of a mobilizing union and its political orientation. And the density and strength of mobilizing unions at the enterprise level will in turn reflect variations in the strength of organized popular forces and other change-oriented sociopolitical forces at the societal level.

Chapter 3 will deal with the emergence of the Revolutionary Government of the Armed Forces under President Velasco in 1968, with its initial power relative to civil society, with the nature of its ideological commitment to socioeconomic change, and with its purpose in introducing and developing workers' participation. Chapter 4 will focus on the development of participation at the enterprise level, in particular on the involvement of unions and on the effect of the participation arrangement on integration or mobilization of the workforce. In Chapter 5, I will investigate the effects of the workers' participation scheme on the behavior of sociopolitical forces, on their efforts to resist or protect its further development, and on the government's reaction to these efforts. This investigation will continue in Chapter 6 with special focus on the government's attempts to bring unforeseen and unwanted mobilization and militancy of organized labor under control. The economic crisis, the polarization between sociopolitical forces, and the forced choice between acceleration and reversal of the reform process, and of the development of workers' participation as part of this process, will be discussed in relation to the neglect of the pursuit of protective policies in Chapter 7. In the concluding chapter, the experiences in the different systems will be compared in the light of my conceptualization of dynamics in the four developmental stages, in order to point out implications for possible future developments of workers' participation.

3

Origins, Purpose, and Design
of Workers' Participation
within the Framework
of the Peruvian Revolution

Origins: Background for the Revolution

The introduction of workers' participation in Peru has to be understood as an integral element of the reform process carried out by the self-proclaimed Revolutionary Government of the Armed Forces.[1] Consequently, the question of its origin is really a question of the reasons accounting for the seizure of state power by a military government with the commitment to carry out a process of fundamental socioeconomic change. These reasons are to be found in a challenge to the established socioeconomic order resulting from changes in the constellation of sociopolitical forces, on the one hand, and in institutional developments predisposing the military to respond to this challenge through direct intervention on the other hand.

Peru in 1968 was at a low to intermediate stage of modernization, industrialization, and political mobilization within the Latin American context.[2] Oligarchic domination had been eroding, as economic power had shifted from the land-holding oligarchy toward mining, fishing, and manufacturing sectors. The coastal export-oriented sugar plantation owners were the economically most powerful group among the old oligarchy, who as a whole managed to

---

[1] Officially, the "Peruvian Revolution" is divided into two phases: the First Phase from 1968 to 1975 under President Velasco; and the Second Phase, beginning with the coup against Velasco and his succession by Morales Bermudez in 1975. Actually, it would be more accurate to call the Second Phase the "Peruvian Counterrevolution." All the important reforms were introduced in the First Phase, and several of them were reversed or modified in the Second Phase. Thus, when I refer to the "Revolution," the statements apply to the First Phase and its legacy.

[2] Palmer (1973) constructed a composite index of indicators of social mobilization, on which Peru ranked 16th among 20 Latin American countries in the mid-1960s.

retain an amount of political power incommensurate with their economic importance, due to the over-representation of rural departments in the Peruvian
Congress, the political importance of Congress, and the oligarchy's continued
high influence over mass media. A large amount of resources in the new important economic sectors were under foreign control and thus not concentrated
in the hands of a new dominant social group capable of establishing a hegemonic position in civil society and firm control over the state apparatus.[3] In
the 1950s, new moderately reformist political parties, largely based on middle-
class support (e.g., Popular Action and the Christian Democrats) started challenging the political domination of the formerly dominant conservative forces.
This led to a virtual stalemate among the participants in the political arena, to
governmental inefficiency and inability to respond to pressures from increasing
mobilization of lower social groups.[4] This mobilization occurred both in the
urban and in the rural sector: Between 1957 and 1968 there was a considerable
proliferation of peasant unions, and land invasions took place on a rather large
scale in some areas.[5] Unions were strong in the sugar plantations, where 85%
of the land was cultivated by unionized workers.[6] Though urban labor was
weak as a sociopolitical force at the societal level, it had reached considerable
organizational penetration in crucial sectors of industry. The major sources of
weakness were high unemployment, which made it easy for employers to fire
militant workers, union legislation that prescribes an establishment-based instead of enterprise-based structure of unions, and political divergences that severely limited the capacity for coordinated action due to coexistence of unions
with different affiliation in the same branch of economic activity or even
within the same enterprise.

In the 1960s, the control of the APRA[7] trade union confederation CTP

---

[3]Ownership patterns in Peru are investigated by Malpica (1974). A documentation of penetration
of foreign investment into the export and domestic manufacturing sectors is given by Anaya Franco
(1975). Uriarte and Torres (1972:68, 91) present data for the participation of foreign firms among
big manufacturing enterprises, which show that 41 foreign-owned companies accounted for
roughly 30% of fixed investment and 33% of gross value of production in the manufacturing sector
in 1968.

[4]A discussion of conditions in pre-1968 Peru can be found in Bourricaud (1970), Astiz (1969),
and Jacquette (1971); the background conditions for the coup are analyzed by Cotler (1970, 1972)
and by Lowenthal (1976).

[5]According to Bourque and Palmer (1973), the figure reported by Lima newspapers of 103 invasions of haciendas between 1959 and 1966 underrepresents the real figure, and Handelman
(1971) reports 150 invasions in Pasco, Junin, and Cuzco alone between July and December 1963.
Cotler and Portocarrero (1969) also deal with this increasing peasant mobilization.

[6]Figure from Matos Mar et al. (1970:138).

[7]APRA (Alianza Popular Revolucionaria Americana, American Popular Revolutionary Alliance)
has been Peru's only mass-based party. In its early years, the 1920s and 1930s, it took a radical
reformist stand. During that period, frequent confrontations between APRA and the military laid

(Confederación de Trabajadores Peruanos, Confederation of Peruvian Workers) which had been dominating the labor movement since the 1940s, was eroding and new more leftist tendencies were gaining influence. Already in the years of the economic crisis, 1958–1959, a Committee of Union Reorganization was formed under the leadership of bank employees, metal workers, and construction workers. This Committee failed to gain control over the central CTP leadership, and was destroyed through repression of its leaders after the banking and metalworkers' strike in 1964. However, in 1966 a new Committee was formed, which founded the new central union organization CGTP *(Confederación General de Trabajadores del Perú,* General Workers' Confederation of Peru) under leadership of the Communist Party. During the economic crisis of 1967, when the CTP tried to hold down union demands for wage raises, the number of unions affiliated to the CGTP grew rapidly.[8] When the CGTP was officially recognized by the military government in January 1971, it counted 267 affiliated base unions in manufacturing industry out of a total of 870 officially recognized unions in that sector.[9] For the most part, these unions were located in the key branches, which account for the largest proportion of value of production, such as metalworking, food production, beverages, and chemical products. Table 3.1 shows the absolute figures for value of production in the various branches of manufacturing industry, and Table 3.2 shows the Federations which were affiliated to the CGTP at the moment of its recognition. In the textile branch, which also accounts for a high percentage of the total value of production in manufacturing industry, most unions were still affiliated to the CTP in 1971, though by 1976 the CTP leadership had lost all control over them, such that the strike called in February 1976 was a total failure *(La Prensa,* February 2, 1976).

Thus, internal strength and unity of the labor movement were low, and its size was about average in comparison to other Latin American countries. In 1968, according to official figures, 19% of the economically active population

---

the ground for lasting animosity between them. In particular, the massacre of military officers in an APRA-instigated uprising in Trujillo in 1932 left deep-seated feelings of hostility against APRA among the military. These feelings have remained strong throughout the 1970s, though APRA has adopted a clearly conservative orientation since 1956. Many observers argued that APRA nevertheless had remained the largest and best-organized political force in Peru. In particular, it had retained strength among middle-class and student activists. Their presence became very visible with their leading role in the street disturbances of February 1974. Reports in *La Prensa* and *La Crónica* identified APRA members as instigators of mass demonstrations and looting. The contention about the breadth of APRA support was borne out by the 1978 elections to the Constituent Assembly, in which APRA won a plurality of votes and 37 out of 100 seats. See *Latin America, Political Report,* June 1978. For a discussion of Peruvian parties, see Neira (1972) and Astiz (1969); on APRA see in particular North (1973).

[8]For a history of the Peruvian labor movement, see Sulmont (1974, 1975).
[9]Register of Recognized Union Organizations, Ministry of Labor, Lima.

Table 3.1

Gross Value of Production by Sector of Manufacturing Industry, 1970 (in 1000 soles)

International Standard Industrial Classification	Rank	Gross value of production
20 Food and kindred products	1	23,870,489
21 Beverages	6	6,256,507
22 Tobacco	19	1,504,600
23 Textiles	2	11,916,876
24 Shoes and clothing	10	3,644,341
25 Lumber and wood products	18	1,520,853
26 Furniture	17	1,669,729
27 Paper and allied products	12	2,889,896
28 Printing	13	2,779,505
29 Leather	20	940,415
30 Rubber products	16	1,922,569
31 Chemicals and applied products	3	11,705,154
32 Petroleum refining and related industries	4	8,257,868
33 Non-metallic minerals	9	3,590,596
34 Basic metals	5	7,967,956
35 Simple metal products	8	3,877,086
36 Non-electrical machinery	15	2,460,574
37 Electrical equipment and supplies	14	2,715,772
38 Transport equipment	7	4,674,082
39 Miscellaneous industries	11	3,369,894
Total		121,519,097

Source: Ministerio de Industria y Turismo, Evolución Industrial Manufacturera Peruana, 1971–1972, Lima, 1974.

were organized.[10] But sectoral demand-making capacity was considerably higher than this figure might lead one to expect. The phenomenon of economic and organizational concentration caused high unionization rates in key sectors of the economy. In 1963, there were 1461 enterprises with more than 20 workers (the legal limit for the establishment of a union) in manufacturing industry, and 503 recognized unions, which means that 34% of these enterprises were unionized. Together, they employed 69% of the labor force in manufacturing industry, but the 323 existing enterprises with more than 100 workers alone employed 45% of the labor force and contributed 72% of the gross value of production in the sector. Given that the bigger the enterprise,

[10]Venezuela, Cuba, and Argentina had much higher unionization rates, and Colombia, Chile, Mexico, Bolivia, and Uruguay were roughly comparable to Peru, with the remainder of Latin American countries having clearly lower unionization rates (*Statistical Abstracts of Latin America*, 1968). One certainly has to have certain reservations concerning the accuracy of these figures. They are best regarded as careful estimates, useful mainly for general cross-national comparison.

Table 3.2

Union Federations Affiliated to the CGTP at the Moment of Its Official Recognition in 1971[a]

1. Federation of Workers of Puno
2. Federation of Workers of the Brewing Industry of Peru
3. Federation of Workers of the Metal Industry of Peru
4. Federation of Workers of Civil Construction of Peru
5. Federation of Bakery Workers Progress and Justice of Peru
6. Federation of Workers in Mineral Water Beverages and Similars
7. Federation of Workers of the Fishing Industry of Peru
8. Federation of Workers of Cuzco
9. Federation of Bank Employees
10. Regional Federation of Mining and Metalworkers of the South of Peru

Source: Register of Recognized Union Organizations, Ministry of Labor, Lima.
[a]As explained in the text, it is legally possible for federations with different affiliations to coexist in the same branches. In fact, in 1971 the CTP still had formally federations in some of the above branches, but the CGTP clearly had the only significant mobilization potential. For evidence concerning the mobilization potential of the different Confederations, see Chapter 6.

the more likely its workers are to be unionized, it is safe to assume that by 1963 between one-half and three-quarters of the value of production in manufacturing industry came from unionized enterprises.[11] From 1963 to 1968, a total of 1221 new unions were recognized, among which 447 belonged to the industrial sector, an indicator of continued mobilization.

A further factor contributing to social mobilization of lower social groups, and consequently to a potential for political mobilization, was rural–urban migration, which let the percentage of Lima's squatter population grow from 20.2% in 1961 to 27.2% in 1972 (Collier 1975).

In this situation of disintegration of the traditional order due to pressures from increasing mobilization at the bottom and stalemate at the top, the military's role as guardians of the constitutional order became more and more controversial within the military leadership.[12] Particularly the repression of the guerilla movement in 1965–1966, when the military crushed the guerillas in the Sierra in a short but very cruel campaign, made a lasting impression on the military. This campaign pointed to the threat of a potential mass-based socialist revolution, among whose prime victims, of course, was going to be the traditional military apparatus. The recognition on the part of military leaders that the causes for this revolutionary potential lay in the existing socioeconomic order was based mainly on ideas presented and insights gained in courses in the Center of Higher Military Studies (CAEM). The curriculum in

[11]Calculations by the author on the basis of data from the Ministry of Labor.
[12]Einaudi (1973), Stepan (1978), and Villanueva (1970, 1971) discuss institutional developments and experiences which shaped the political views of the Peruvian military. For an article reviewing the literature on the Peruvian Military, see Malloy (August 1973).

CAEM comprises social science courses in addition to technical and traditional military training courses. The "new professionalism"[13] links the concern with external security to internal security, both comprised in the notion of integral security.[14] Thus the structural causes of popular unrest were perceived as a major threat to national security, and since the civilian political elite was unwilling and unable to effect the necessary changes, the military elite seized power with the intention of introducing fundamental structural changes in Peruvian society. As part of this revolutionary process, relations between labor and capital were to be transformed through the introduction of a worker's participation scheme. In order to understand the basic purpose of this scheme, one has to analyze it in relation to the elite's ideology, or, rather, the ideological struggles underlying the whole revolutionary process.

Ideology of the Peruvian Revolution

The most salient characteristic of the Peruvian Revolution was the lack of clarity of its ideological definition. According to the government's self-characterization, they were following a "noncommunist, noncapitalist, humanist–socialist" third way to economic development and social justice. Different observers have varied widely in their interpretations of the government's ideology and policies. The government was criticized by the left for simply modernizing a dependent capitalist economic system (Quijano 1971) and creating a control-oriented corporate political system (Cotler 1972), as well as by the right for creating a climate of uncertainty about the future of private ownership of means of production and therefore stifling private entrepreneurial initiative.

Stepan (1978) characterized the regime's ideology as organic-statist, differentiating organic statism as a third major ideological approach to the state from the liberal pluralist and classical Marxist approach. He differentiates the organic-statist from the other two approaches on several dimensions. First, organic statism has a strong normative component, assigning to the state the role of interpreting and promoting the common good, and of creating a harmonious integrated community in which subsidiary parts play a vital role (Stepan 1978:37). Second, from a structural point of view, organic statism is characterized by limited pluralism, and by a "decisive role [for the state] in constructing the parameters, rules, and infrastructure of a market economy" and ". . . a key role for intermediate self-managing 'labor-capital' functional groups [Stepan

[13]This concept was developed by Stepan (1971) in his study of the Brazilian military, and applied to the Peruvian one as well (1978).

[14]For an elaboration of this concept, see Mercado Jarrín (1974:145–161).

1978:41]." In the structural aspects of limited pluralism and of strong state intervention, organic statism resembles the authoritarian-corporatist type of politico-economic system characterized in Chapter 1. As a normative conception, organic statism rejects class struggle, but not the existence of social classes itself. In practice, then, the state's interpretation of the "common good" determines the share of power and of resources for consumption that the various social classes are legitimately entitled to. And it was on this point that the Peruvian military government had considerable internal disagreements. In terms of concrete policies, the class issue created debates about the desirable dominant form of ownership of major means of production; about the share of private capital owners, the state, and the workers in the exercise of control and income rights. Thus, the divergence of opinion about the "Peculiar Revolution," as it was called by Hobsbawm (1971), was in large part a result of the coexistence of different tendencies within the government, some favoring a development toward a socialist transformation, others favoring a consolidation of the capitalist order through the institutionalization of a system approximating the authoritarian-corporatist type.

Clearly, this lack of ideological consensus was a major weakness in the Peruvian Revolution, as it deprived the leadership of a clear guide for political action and a moral basis for legitimizing this action.[15] The essential elements of an ideology are a shared value image of a future socioeconomic order, an analysis of the deficiencies of the present order, and a set of strategies to transform the present into the desired order.[16] The Peruvian military government by no means had arrived at such a coherent view of the revolutionary process, and policymaking developed rather as an action–reaction sequence than as pursuit of a clearcut strategy. Frequently, the introduction of a specific reform created new unforeseen problems which called for additional legislation.[17] Thus the Peruvian process cannot be analyzed as an attempt to implement a grand vision of a new socioeconomic order and a corresponding politico-economic system, but rather as a process of structural change shaped by diverging tendencies within a state elite whose primary uniting goal was the creation of a stable sociopolitical order, that is, the achievement of integral security. The indispensable requirements for the achievement and preservation of integral security were seen as national integration and independent, permanent, self-sustained

---

[15]In Apter's (1964) terms, ideology as a link between action and fundamental belief performs the social function of creating solidarity and the individual function of providing identity, both of which combine to legitimize authority.

[16]Himmelstrand (1970) and J. D. Stephens (1976: 165–166) have used this definition of ideology and discussed its role as guide for action of political elites.

[17]The introduction of workers' participation and the ensuing Law of Security of Employment are one example of such an action–reaction sequence, which produced further unforeseen and undesired dynamics; those will be discussed later.

development (Mercado Jarrín 1974:145–163). National integration was to be brought about by a strong state breaking the economic and political power of small groups and overcoming the marginalization of the masses, so as to avoid class struggle and link all social groups to the state.

As a means of achieving these objectives, redistributive measures aimed at weakening the power base of the old oligarchy and raising the standard of living of the poorest groups were to be applied, and base organizations under control of the state bureaucracy were to be created to avoid any economic and political power concentration outside the state. Consequently, redistribution of wealth and power was a means to achieve other objectives, rather than an end in itself.

The second cornerstone of national security, the capacity for independent, permanent, and self-sustained economic development, required increased investment, economic planning, and efforts to increase production. The means to achieve these objectives were increased state control over resources formerly under foreign or domestic private control, reform of the state apparatus, stimulation of initiative and qualification of workers, and the elimination of conflicts between capital and labor.

Clearly, within this rudimentary framework of objectives, contradictions were likely to arise between different means or between means and other superordinate objectives, such as increased investment and raised consumption of the lowest social groups, in which case the higher ranking objectives would prevail. Also, opinions were likely to diverge on the choice of concrete policies as a means to achieve the objectives, based on different assessments of their relative costs and benefits. In fact, opinions did diverge greatly within the military government. Stepan's (1978) analysis of the ideological, educational, and institutional evolution of the Peruvian military shows that before 1968 an institutional consensus had been reached about two fundamental objectives only: the land reform and the nationalization of key resources under foreign control, particularly the International Petroleum Company. What eventually became accepted as the program of the Revolution, the Plan Inca, was elaborated on the request of Velasco by a small group of colonels with ties to the Intelligence Service (i.e., with career patterns slightly different from the military mainstream).[18]

Examining the Plan Inca as the ideological blueprint for a revolution, one finds high-level abstract values and low-level concrete objectives and strategies for action in 28 areas, but no middle-level coherent vision of a social, eco-

---

[18] The version that the Plan Inca was elaborated by these colonels before the seizure of power is given by Zimmerman (1974). Other commentators argue that it was not written until much later. Whatever the time period when it was written, the point is that it was written by a small group of colonels and thus did not have the approval of a solid majority of the higher military leadership. Also, it lacks the essential elements of a coherent ideological framework.

nomic, and political order. The Revolution is defined as "nationalist, independent, and humanist, insofar as it is not linked to existing ideologies, political parties, or power groups . . . and is aimed at the full realization of man
within a solidary community, whose essential and inseparable values are justice
and liberty [Plan Inca, p. 11]." Going from these general values to concrete
reform strategies, elements of an organic-statist design can be found in the 28
areas outlined, the most important of which are a strong planning and super-
visory role for the state in all sectors of the economy, creation of necessary organs for active and full participation of the population in the activities that national development requires (Plan Inca, p. 39), and achievement of just labor
relations that make dignity, security, and welfare of the worker compatible with
efficiency of the workplace and socioeconomic development of the country
(Plan Inca, p. 36). Nowhere, however, is the desirable result of structural
change for relations between the state, the private-sector capitalist entrepreneurs, and labor addressed in terms of the fundamental question of their relative share in the distribution of control and income rights. Statements in the
early years of the regime referring to the socioeconomic order contain the term
"pluralist economy, where cooperatives, self-managed, and state enterprises
would flourish side by side with private enterprises [Velasco, April 6, 1970, in
1972:213]." As the reform process advanced, the problem became inescapable,
because the private sector started withholding investment, complaining about
total uncertainty of its future, and strongly demanding a clarification of the
rules of the game. Finally, in his Message to the Nation on July 28, 1971,
Velasco announced that a social property sector, to consist of socially owned
worker self-managed enterprises, would have priority in the future mixed economy. This announcement, however, did not in any way clarify the issue, as
the term "priority" (*prioritario*) was interpreted by different members of the
government according to their personal views and preferences. Three distinct
positions concerning the desirable form of economy and society crystallized
within the government.

The conservative conception envisioned some modifications, but basically a
preservation of the traditional relations between labor and capital. On the one
hand, the worst forms of exploitation were to be eliminated through more protective labor legislation, and on the other hand labor discipline and labor peace
were to be ensured through a system of corporate controls over unions, particularly an elimination of "politicized" unionism. The state was to assume an
overall guiding and protective role, stimulating investment and providing infrastructure, but not to enter into competition with the private sector as
entrepreneur.

The mainstream, or "moderate," conception envisioned an harmonious integration of capital and labor, with capital retaining the predominant role in
control over means of production but giving labor a fairer share in the profits

generated, in order to stimulate productivity. The state was to perform not only an important regulatory and supportive but also active, entrepreneurial function. In particular, the state was to substitute foreign entrepreneurial groups in the control over the nation's key resources. Social property enterprises could receive priority in attention and stimulation of popular initiative for the creation of employment, but not in capital investment. Essentially, private exercise of control and income rights based on ownership of means of production was to remain important, but within general parameters set by the state through its exercise of a larger share of control rights to ensure "permanent and self-sustained development."

The "radical" conception envisioned a slow development toward equality of capital and labor in the exercise of control rights, and inequality in favor of labor in the distribution of profits generated in the private sector, that is, in the exercise of income rights. Simultaneously, the social property sector was to be developed in close collaboration with the state sector, which was assigned an important regulatory as well as entrepreneurial function. Investment was to go primarily into the social property sector, and conversions of existing enterprises into social property enterprises were regarded as a definite probability and necessity in order to make the sector grow significantly. Due to these simultaneous developments, means of production were to pass rapidly to a large extent under social control; the exercise of control and income rights was to be shared by the state and the workers; and only an insignificant proportion of control and income rights was to be retained by private owners of capital.

Though this radical conception was held by a relatively small group among top military leaders—the group connected to the authors of the Plan Inca—it seemed to gain preponderance due to Velasco's support of it. After the coup replacing him with Morales Bermúdez, however, the moderate conception rapidly came to prevail and developments in 1976 decisively strengthened the conservative tendency within the new government.

These divergent conceptions not only considerably weakened the government by making formulation and implementation of policies difficult but also caused tensions within the armed forces in general through the formation of internal opposition groups. Though such conflicts were openly admitted for the first time in the purge of conservative Navy ministers in June 1974, (Peruvian Times, June 7, 1974), several mini-crises and rumors about plots had emerged before. In March 1970, Velasco warned that a division in the armed forces over the issue of leftist influence could lead to civil war. This warning gave substance to the rumors that General Montagne Sánchez, the moderate commander-in-chief of the army, was under house arrest on suspicion of plotting with the conservative opposition to the military government (Peruvian Times, March 27, 1970)—rumors that were never confirmed. The crisis during Velasco's illness in March 1973 foreshadowed the disintegration that was finally going to lead to an end of the Revolution after the coup against him.

Purpose of Workers' Participation

The purpose of the workers' participation scheme, then, has to be understood in relation to the government's minimal consensus on the achievement of integral security. As explained previously, integral security was seen as based on national integration and permanent, self-sustained, independent economic development. Both of these goals were to be realized under guidance of the state. In order to perform such a role, the state needs autonomy from and power over civil society. If a government rejects coercion and repression as a principal means to achieve and maintain such power, which the Peruvian government did in the First Phase of the Revolution under President Velasco, the alternatives are incentive strategies to elicit voluntary compliance of social groups and strategies designed to reduce the power base of social groups through slow encroachment on the control over resources of upper social groups and through weakening the organizations of lower social groups. Three major strategies through which organizations, the only power base of lower social groups, can be gradually weakened, are (1) to "divide and rule"; (2) to co-opt leaders; and (3) to provide incentives through alternative channels so as to make the old channels superfluous. Co-optation, the provision of incentives through alternative channels, and general provision of incentives to elicit compliance, however, require distribution of at least some resources for consumption. This may present a problem where the goal of rapid industrialization calls for high investment.

The introduction of workers' participation was a typical case of multipurpose incentive strategy. It was intended to stimulate labor productivity, induce private entrepreneurs to increase investment, reduce conflict between capital and labor, and deprive traditional class-based labor organizations of their function through providing new channels for interest articulation by the workers. It was hoped that this would cause a loss of power of existing unions without a need for repression. The government's officially expressed expectation was that "relations of ownership and production will change in such a clear manner that the workers will end up considering a redefinition and reorientation of unions necessary [Velasco, July 28, 1971, in 1972:117]." In a conversation with journalists, Velasco used more concrete terms: "Politically, there will be problems. There are well-organized unions, but from now on they will see that if they stage strikes, they will go against themselves [*La Prensa*, November 13, 1970]."

It is important to emphasize that none of the three groups holding distinctive ideological positions within the government promoted workers' participation with the deliberate intention of increasing working class mobilization. Obviously, the conservatives favored outright demobilization of labor, if necessary through legal restrictions, as an essential prerequisite for consolidation of the existing order and promotion of private enterprise. The moderates also opposed autonomous organization and mobilization of labor, but they favored the incentive strategy for the integration of labor. Labor was to be given a fairer share in the private enterprise, as part of a larger strategy for partial structural modification in the existing order.

Even the radicals were ambivalent about the desirability of autonomous labor organization and mobilization. Though they promoted workers' participation as an element in a strategy of transformation in a socialist direction, this transformation was to be guided and controlled from above. They recognized the need for popular involvement in the transformation process and supported the establishment of SINAMOS[19] (Sistema Nacional de Apoyo a la Movilización Social, National System of Support for Social Mobilization) as agency in charge of organizing the population for such involvement. However, they also perceived increased autonomous popular organization, particularly labor organization, as a potential threat to the state's autonomy and capacity to determine the pace and direction of the transformation process. Thus they failed to fight a decided internal battle, in defense of SINAMOS and popular mobilization, against those sectors of the government and the state bureaucracy that started sabotaging SINAMOS activities and intervening directly to split, manipulate, and weaken popular organization.

At least part of the initial staff of SINAMOS, many of them radical civilians, was committed to genuine mobilization policies and attempted to raise labor organization and consciousness in the course of the implementation of the reform process. At first, conservative sectors in the government set up rival agencies to restrict the area of operation of SINAMOS, and, finally, leading SINAMOS officials were removed from their positions.[20] Their radical supporters in highest government circles did not regard the issue as crucial enough to activate all their potential influence, which at least up to 1973 was quite considerable, to protect popular mobilization. They apparently failed to recognize that strong working-class organizations might constitute a counterweight to the power of the private sector and thus might partly neutralize the pressures put on the government by the latter. These pressures eventually effected a shift in the internal power distribution in the government away from the radical members. Contrary to the dominant official deemphasis of labor

[19] For a discussion of the general purpose, structure, and activities of SINAMOS, see pp. 152–153.

[20] An insider's account is given by Béjar (1976).

mobilization, however, the reaction of entrepreneurs and unions to the participation reform caused mobilization to remain a central point of tension and concern for the government.

The incentives provided through the workers' participation scheme included participation in profits and ownership (i.e., in income rights as well as control rights).[21] This participation in income rights meant that incentives for labor were not taken from direct redistribution of existing wealth but rather from future wealth that was to be generated, and that consequently the success of this incentive strategy was going to depend on economic growth.[22]

As will become clear in the further course of this discussion, the incentive strategy failed vis-à-vis private investors as well as vis-à-vis labor. Private capital owners withheld new investment in purposeful resistance against the government's reform policies and also created obstacles for the implementation of the workers' participation scheme. Both this entrepreneurial resistance against workers' participation and deteriorating economic conditions, which neutralized the effect of the material incentives, contributed to a continued reliance of workers on their traditional organizations, the unions. In fact, the conflicts created and the organizational opportunities provided through the workers' participation scheme led to an increase in the number of unions, as the need to form or join one for the collective defense of their interests became obvious to a great number of workers.

A further reason why the participation scheme failed to provide alternatives to unions as a means of interest articulation by the workers was that its structural design kept workers from articulating the concerns most salient to them in their condition as dependent wage earners. Such concerns were explicitly excluded from the competence of participatory bodies, as belonging to the sphere of labor relations and consequently under the competence of unions, which in turn were legally excluded from the participation arrangements. The role assigned to workers' representatives through the structural design of participation was to represent workers' interests as co-owners, or entrepreneurs. However, the participation design simply failed to change the structural conditions

---

[21]Exact characteristics of the structural design of the participation scheme will be discussed in the next section.

[22]The most significant redistributive measure, and the only direct one, introduced in the course of the Peruvian Revolution, was the agrarian reform. Like the workers' participation reform, it was also intended to serve a double purpose (i.e., to deprive the members of the old oligarchy of their major economic power base, and to appease peasant unrest). By July 1974, roughly 200,000 families had benefitted from the allocation of 5 million hectares, and these figures were to increase to 340,000 families and 11 million hectares by 1976. See Harding (1976:220). By September 1976, this goal had not been reached, as 8.5 million hectares had been distributed, benefitting 285,000 families, which corresponds to about 35% of agricultural land and 24% of all rural farm families. McClintock (1976). Nevertheless, the land reform was declared basically completed.

of workers within the enterprise enough to override their identification as dependent wage earners and provide them with an identification as co-owners.

The Structural Design of Participation: Compromise among Competing Conceptions

The structural design of participation was arrived at through a compromise in a long and difficult policy-making process. Basically, the integrative conception prevailed and shaped the major aspects of structure in the participation design, but some aspects of participation conceived of as an element in a strategy for socialist transformation remained. These latter aspects consisted of the growth up to 50% of workers' participation in ownership and control rights, and the indefinition of further developments at that point.

Initially, the extent of power transferred to workers through the structural design was minimal, restricted to joint consultation through one or two representatives at the highest level, but it was supposed to grow with increasing ownership of the workers. The increase in ownership was based on a share of workers in the profits of the enterprise, an additional part of which was to be distributed in cash to the workers.

According to the law, every industrial enterprise with six or more workers and/or more than one million *soles* gross annual income had to form an Industrial Community[23] (CI: *Comunidad Industrial*), to which all the full-time employed personnel belonged. The enterprise was obliged to give 15% of before tax net profits to its CI as a collectivity and to distribute 10% in cash to individual workers. The 15% could either be part of a reinvestment program of the enterprise, or be used to buy shares from existing shareholders if no reinvestment program had been presented to and approved by the Ministry of Industry. This participation was intended to grow up to 50%, after which point the 15% of profits would be used by the CI for investment in other firms. Initially, the CI was entitled to one representative on the board of directors, and this representation was to grow according to the percentage of ownership until it would reach 50% and end in a situation of codetermination. At this point, the chairman of the board of directors was to be elected by a majority among the members of the board, and in case of a deadlock by lot (Article 48).

The CI was self-managing in its internal affairs. The General Assembly,

---

[23]Workers' participation was first introduced in the industrial manufacturing sector only; in 1971 it was extended to mining, fishing, and telecommunications, and the generic name became Labor Community (*Comunidad Laboral*). However, the commerce and service sectors remained exempt from the requirement to establish a Labor Community, which opened the way for various evasion attempts on the part of industrial enterprises.

consisting of all members of the CI (i.e., all full-time employed persons of an enterprise), was the supreme authority in charge of electing the president and the council of the CI as executive organ. The members of the council, on their part, elected the representative(s) of the CI on the board of directors. The main tasks of the General Assembly, which was required to meet twice a year, were to approve the report of activities of the council and the accounts of the CI and to decide about the use of the part of the General Fund that was legally left to the CI's free disposition. The General Fund was to consist of income of the CI—from its shares in the enterprise. Its use was partly specified by the law; most importantly, it was to be used for compensation of CI members who were leaving the enterprise, and for administrative costs of the CI. The remainder could be used for cultural, educational, or social activities of the CI, or distributed in cash to individual members of the CI.

The main tasks of the council were to carry on the day-to-day administration of the CI, particularly of its General Fund, and to advise and supervise the representative(s) of the CI on the board of directors. The representative(s) had to act as delegates of the council, charged with bringing questions and demands which the council and/or the General Assembly had decided on, to the attention of the board of directors. The president of the CI and one further member of the council were to act as official representatives of the CI vis-à-vis public administration. For this activity, they were entitled to half a day per week of time off from their job, without loss of remuneration. All other activities of the CI were to be carried on outside of working hours. Whereas this type of internal self-management provided some training and experience for workers in administrative affairs, it was not complemented by any opportunities for direct participation in decisions related to the concrete work situation in the enterprise. Participation of rank and file workers in enterprise decisions was restricted to indirect election, via the CI council, of representatives with joint consultation rights at the highest level.

As already indicated, the structural design of the CI was a compromise, between competing conceptions. The major disagreements between proponents of workers' participation as a means for integrating workers into the private enterprise, and thus consolidating the existing order, and those promoting it as an element in a strategy of fundamental societal transformation, concerned the extent of ownership and control rights to be transferred from private capitalists to workers. The formula of a gradually increasing share of participation in ownership and in management was a last-minute compromise solution reached in a difficult policy-making process.

In his inaugural speech to the Latin American Congress of Industrialists in April 1970, Velasco outlined that in the future other types of enterprises would coexist with the private one, namely cooperatives, self-managed, and state enterprises (Velasco, April 6, 1970, in 1972:212). There was no mention of a reformed private enterprise or codetermination. The draft for a General Industries Law (Anteproyecto de Ley General de Industrias) published in May 1970 did not even mention the CI. During that period, a much wider project for the reform of the whole private sector—not only in industry—was elaborated in the Ministry of Industry (MIT; Ministerio de Industria y Turismo).[24] This project considered a broader range of participating actors, in combination with a categorization of enterprises according to their social importance. In enterprises of local importance, the directing body would have included representatives of the municipality, and, in those of wider importance, zonal, regional, and national political organs, in a relation of 60% to 40% to the workers of the respective enterprise.[25]

COAP (Comité de Asesoramiento de la Presidencia, Advisory Council to the President) insisted that some type of enterprise reform should be included in the General Industries Law, or else that this whole project be returned to the MIT. The enterprise reform suggested by the MIT for inclusion in the General Industries Law went much further than the final CI Law and was clearly conceived of as an element of socialist transformation. The CI would have started with a strong initial capital base and would not have been limited to 50%. The initial capital base was to be the indemnization fund which every enterprise is required to have by law, and since this fund constitutes generally a large part of the capital of an enterprise, particularly in older enterprises, its capitalization in favor of the CI would have resulted in a significant participation in ownership to begin with.[26] This project was presented by the MIT to COAP, and by COAP to the other ministries for comment, where it met with very strong resistance. The polar counterposition was to introduce the whole enterprise reform not as a law but as a tentative experiment to be revised after some experience. According to this position, there ought to be participation in profits—cash and some individual shares—but not in management.

The disagreements, then, fundamentally concerned the alternatives of integration or transformation; of adjusting the enterprise to the capitalist system with full preservation of private control rights over the means of production and a minimal transfer of income rights to the workers, or radically changing

[24]In the period of the establishment of the CI, this ministry was still the Ministry of Industry and Commerce, until the Ministry of Commerce became independent and the old MIC was transformed into the Ministry of Industry and Tourism. For reasons of consistency, the abbreviation MIT is used here for the whole time period.

[25]Interview with Dr. Virgilio Roel, ex-advisor to the ex-Minister of Industry, Dellepiane.

[26]Enterprises are legally required to set one monthly pay per worker aside every year to accumulate an indemnization fund, from which a worker who leaves the enterprise receives a certain amount as compensation.

the structure of this system, transferring control and income rights to the workers and the state. These internal differences of opinion about the CI reform were so fundamental that the project was virtually deadlocked, and only Velasco's personal commitment to and intervention in favor of an enterprise reform pushed through the eventual compromise solution, elaborated by COAP. Even after the articles about the CI had been included in the General Industries Law, however, disagreements about their interpretation persisted. In an exposition on television on July 30, 1970 (printed in *El Peruano*, July 31, 1970), Minister of Industry Dellepiane explained what would happen at the 50% point: The CI would then be substituted by a cooperative, which would be a partner in the enterprise owning 50% of the capital. The process of reinvestment of the 15% would start again until the CI would reach 50%, and then a second cooperative would be formed, which would own 25% of the total capital, such that the workers would own a total of 75% of the capital (50% through Cooperative #1 and 25% through Cooperative #2), and the private shareholders 25%. The process would go on until the percentage of capital owned by private shareholders would become negligible. This exposition alarmed the private sector, and Velasco had to reiterate publicly on August 16, 1970, that the CI would not go further than 50%.[27]

Though the issues—particularly the 50% limit—were further clarified in the CI Law (*Decreto Ley, D. L.* 18384, September 1, 1970), differences of opinion among members of the government about the final purpose and role of the CI continued to manifest themselves publicly. In March 1971, a minor scandal was prompted by the accusation that presentations in a seminar for promoters of CI organization given by the MIT had propagated class struggle through the CI.[28] This was obviously a frontal contradiction to the prevailing integrative conception, which found its expression in the main objective ascribed to the CI by the Law: "To strengthen the industrial enterprise through the unitary

[27]A further indication of lack of a clear vision as to where and how fast the CI should lead was the absence of an officially agreed upon estimate for the average time period within which the 50% limit could be reached, and of the factors upon which this would depend. On their own initiative, some economists at the Universidad del Pacífico did a study and found, through simulation models, that the profitability of an enterprise would be the most important factor in determining the CI's speed of progress in ownership. However, as will be seen in our subsequent discussion, profitability is to a certain extent subject to manipulation by accounting techniques (i.e., the declaration of profits could be kept to a minimum in order to slow down the growth of the CI). A second factor determining the relative advance of the CI was of course the proportion of profits reinvested by the enterprise, which had been designed as an incentive for private investment. This study was done by de las Casas *et al.* (1970) and a similar one by Llarena *et al.* (1972).

[28]The two officials, one of whom was Virgilio Roel, Minister Dellepiane's advisor and main author of the initial radical proposal for an enterprise reform, were subsequently removed from their functions.

action of the workers in management, in the production process, in ownership of the enterprise, and in reinvestment, as well as through the stimulation of constructive forms of interrelationship between capital and labor [Article 3a]."

Both the prevalence of the integrative over the transformative, or radical, conception, and the weak impact that the officially proclaimed noncapitalist component of the Peruvian Revolution had on the structure of the participation reform, manifested themselves in the fact that ownership of capital remained the basis from which the right to control the enterprise as well as the right to the appropriation of 75% of before tax net profits was derived.

After the scandal around the MIT seminar, and the forced resignation of the Minister of Industry, Dellepiane, about a month later, all official statements as well as enforcement policies for the participation scheme came to reflect the integrative conception. Workers were explicitly supposed to adopt capitalist attitudes:

> Therefore, the CI tries to transfer to the worker the responsibility that the capitalist also has by virtue of possessing interests in the enterprise.

> The CI gives a patrimony to the worker; it seeks to motivate the Peruvian citizen who works in an enterprise by way of giving him a reason to struggle in life, because he who has nothing doesn't fear to lose anything.

> When our workers will know that they are owners of a patrimonial good, they will have to defend this good, they will have to make efforts for this good, because it is the guarantee of subsistence of their children, of their households, tomorrow when they will disappear [General Graham Hurtado, April 14, 1971; published in La Prensa, April 15, 1971].

Yet, as my conceptualization stipulates and the previously discussed cases show, the effects of participation on integration of workers or on the generation of pressures for a transformation of the given order are not determined by the structural design of participation arrangements, but rather by the reactions and strength of sociopolitical forces relative to each other and relative to the state. For a developing capitalist authoritarian system, the relevant actors besides the elite in control of the state are entrepreneurs, with their ability to use their control over resources to create difficulties for the implementation of participation policies; organized labor, with its ability to mobilize workers into participating and to defend participation rights through coordinated action; and the state bureaucracy in charge of enforcing the legally correct implementation of participation policies. Now, I am first going to discuss general attitudes and initial reactions of entrepreneurs and organized labor to the introduction of the CI. In the next chapter, I will focus in more detail on concrete processes in the development of participation at the enterprise level, and in the later chapters I will deal with the effect of the participation scheme on dynamics between entrepreneurs and unions as sociopolitical forces at the societal level and on their interaction with the government.

Reactions of Entrepreneurs and Unions

As a result of the difficulty and secrecy of the policy-making process, both unions and entrepreneurs were taken by surprise by the CI legislation. Given the explicit expectation on part of the government that the CI would reduce the importance of unions, it is not surprising that the initial reactions to the CI legislation on part of the unions were cautious. The APRA-controlled CTP supported the cash participation in profits but rejected the participation in management with the argument that it would fail due to the lack of qualification of the workers. The Communist CGTP supported the CI, but immediately pointed out that the reform needed to be extended and that the CI was in essence a transitory stage to social ownership of the means of production. In practice, union leaders of all confederations soon discovered that the CI could be used in the defense of the interests of the workers, both directly to obtain the material benefits that the law granted to the workers, and indirectly as a source of information for the union or a shelter for organizing a union where none had existed before. The law separated the roles of union and CI leaders by preventing any union official from being a member of the CI council. Therefore, many experienced union leaders gave up their union positions and took on positions in the CI. Where union leaders did not do that initially but rather were indifferent or hostile towards the CI, with the result that higher-level employees were elected for leadership positions in the CI, internal conflicts within the CI were highly likely to emerge later, and union leaders to run in the second election of the CI council, as will be shown in the next chapter.

Entrepreneurs on their part immediately started attacking the CI[29] and creating obstacles to its implementation. Besides large-scale firings intended to create a climate of social and political unrest, and the withholding of investment, they applied all kinds of techniques to avoid the establishment and growth of a CI. First, there was a possibility to break up enterprises such as to fall below the limit of six workers and avoid the establishment of a CI altogether. This was done, but it never became a major issue for struggle and public attention, because it obviously was possible only in enterprises of rather small size to begin with. A second, much more widely used avoidance measure, was to break up big enterprises into manufacturing (with CI) and commercializing or service enterprises (without CI). With appropriate accounting techniques, the profits could be channeled to the commercial or service enterprise, and the CI received nothing or a totally negligible amount as their participation in profits. Other measures used to minimize the declaration of profits—particularly in family-owned and managed enterprises—were expense

---

[29]A summary of reactions from private sector representatives to the CI is given by Bustamante (1974:67–94). Garcia (1975) describes the development of relations between government and entrepreneurs from 1968 to 1973.

accounts for higher management, relatives as phantom-employees on the pay-roll, and astronomical salaries for management. The only limit set by the orig-inal law to such techniques was Article 47, stipulating that no type of voluntary extra payment, which would not constitute payment for services rendered (ob-viously a flexible concept), could be considered costs of the enterprise. How-ever, the CI originally did not have the opportunity to check the enterprise accounts, unless their representative on the board of directors had the necessary expertise, until a law (D.L. 19262) in January 1972 granted the right to the CI to inspect all books assisted by outside advisors, within the offices of the com-pany. Even then, of course, lack of experience and money to hire auditors pre-vented the CI in most smaller enterprises from detecting irregularities. Further conflicts developed around the sale of shares by the enterprise to the CI, or the capitalization of the 15% reinvested by the CI. Only in August 1972 was a definite procedure for determining the value of shares fixed by law (D.L. 19419), whereas the time period within which the capitalization was to be completed was not fixed by law.

It has to be pointed out that in most cases these conflicts did not arise from clear violations of the law, but rather from the use of legal loopholes to impede full functioning and deny full rights to the CI. One might expect that such managerial resistance and lack of power on the part of the workers to overcome this resistance would have caused apathy and withdrawal from participation, except for enterprises where an ideologically committed union would mobilize workers into participation. The reason why this did not occur to any great ex-tent (unlike in the case of the equally powerless French works committees, for instance) but rather interest in participation was strong even in the absence of a union, provided the workers were informed about the legislation, obviously lies in the monetary nexus between participation and ownership as well as cash distribution of profits provided by the CI. The importance of representation on the board of directors was based on the necessity of supervising compliance with the law on part of the enterprise. The need for supervision of the correct calculation and distribution of profits in order to ensure progress of ownership toward the 50% point explains the considerable interest of the workers in the activity of their representatives. Assemblies of the CI elicited most interest and participation where there were funds to be allocated for some collective purposes.

Clearly, hostility and evasion attempts on the part of the entrepreneurs re-quired workers to turn to leaders with organizational experience to exercise ef-fective supervision and to defend their interests. Where there was a strong union, it was the obvious institution to seek support from, and where there was none, the need to organize one became more apparent. Since the CI did not change structural conditions in the enterprise so as to override workers' expe-rience as dependent wage earners with an identification as co-owners, the concerns expressed in assemblies of the CI, which it was the responsibility of the CI representative to bring to the attention of the board of directors, were to a large extent with wages, working conditions, and other personnel questions. This means that it was very common for CI representatives on the board of directors to bring up questions and demands that the enterprise would object to as belonging to the realm of labor relations. The fact that the CI was prohibited by law from performing the function of defending the interests and needs of the workers as wage earners contributed to the continued reliance of workers on old and new unions, and thus enhanced rather than reduced the importance of the latter.

Reliance on unions and industrial action in the pursuit of workers' interests was further increased by the lack of effective enforcement of participation rights legally granted to the CI. The only way for the CI to defend itself against violations was to complain to the Office of Labor Communities (OCLA, *Oficina de Comunidades Laborales*)[30] in the Ministry of Industry, the agency in charge of supervising the establishment, registration, and functioning of the CI. However, there was no agency with the legal power to apply sanctions in order to enforce the law. All OCLA could do to resolve conflicts between enterprises and their CI was to write letters, urging either or both of the two sides to comply with certain regulations and interpretations of the law. Consequently, certain conflicts were carried on over several years due to the intransigence on part of the enterprise to accept the directives from OCLA. Furthermore, OCLA not only lacked the legal means to enforce the rights of the CI in conflicts but frequently also the commitment to doing so, as the officials adhered to the integrative conception.

The following detailed analysis of the development of participation at the enterprise level will clarify and expand upon these remarks concerning the reaction of entrepreneurs and unions to the introduction of the CI. And it will provide a basis for the subsequent analysis of effects of the development of the CI on relations between labor, capital, and the state.

---

[30]Despite its generic name, OCLA in the MIT only dealt with Industrial Communities.

4

Participation at the Enterprise Level: Its Development and Effects on the Relations among Enterprises, the CI, and Unions

The structural design of participation itself plays only a minor role in my conceptualization, which links the origins, development, and effects of workers' participation schemes at every stage to the strength and action of various sociopolitical forces. What happens at the enterprise level upon the introduction of a given participation design depends on the interaction between various groups with linkages to sociopolitical forces at the societal level. In the last chapter, I indicated that the structural design of the CI caused considerable interest in participation among workers due to its link to monetary incentives. However, in this chapter I am going to show that the actual development of the participation process and its integrative or mobilizing effects were determined by the roles assumed by the various actors, most importantly the unions. Thus, despite its general interest-generating quality, one and the same structural design of participation had different outcomes depending on the presence and involvement of various actors.

The process of introduction of the CI and its further functioning were most strongly shaped by the capacity of the workforce to overcome entrepreneurial resistance, as well as by the nature of this resistance. This capacity on part of the workforce depended mainly on their degree of organizational experience (i.e., on the presence of a union). A second factor raising this capacity was the sheer size of the workforce, not only indirectly by increasing the likelihood of the existence of a union, but also directly by decreasing the opportunities for paternalistic domination of blue-collar workers by the employer and/or white-collar employees and by raising the blue-collar workers' subjective sense of strength. The crucial importance of union involvement is further highlighted by the fact that relations between enterprise and CI differed according to the type of union present in the enterprise, whether the union had existed before the introduction of the CI or was formed afterwards, and whether there was only a blue-collar or mixed union or a white-collar union as well. Also, there is indirect evidence for the influence of the political affiliation of the union on its role in the enterprise, which supports the argument about the importance of linkages between actors at the enterprise and the societal level.

The influence of particular types of entrepreneurial behavior on the relations between CI and enterprise is harder to differentiate analytically, because it varied less in practice than the behavior of workers. It varied in degree, but not in kind, as the basic entrepreneurial reaction was hostility and resistance against the CI. Resistance varied from passive forms, such as lack of collaboration, to outright violations of the law, such as fraudulent accounts and exclusion of the CI representative from meetings of the board of directors. But the various degrees of resistance assumed relevance only in relation to the capacity of the workforce to react against them, and consequently the latter was the crucial variable determining the extent of open conflict in the relations between enterprise and CI.

One general characteristic of the enterprise which shaped relations to the CI was nationality of majority ownership. In foreign-owned and mixed companies, relations to the CI were in general more subject to conflict than in national companies. This was the case despite the fact that foreign-owned companies were generally more modern, under professional management, and consequently showed a more flexible attitude toward the introduction of workers' participation than national companies, which were generally older and run by more traditional management, in particular those which were family-owned and run. Thus the reason has to be sought in factors outside the enterprise that would heighten the probability of conflicts between the CI and foreign-owned companies. The chief of these outside factors was the general revolutionary atmosphere created through rhetoric with strong emphasis on anti-imperialism, national dignity, and economic independence.

The final actor with strong influence on the development and effects of participation within the given structural design was the state bureaucracy. The Office of Labor Communities in the Ministry of Industry and Tourism was charged with officially recognizing and registering each CI, and with exercising general supervision to ensure their legally correct functioning. Due to entrepreneurial hostility on the one hand, and workers' attempts to enforce their rights and/or extend them on the other hand, the OCLA was forced into the role of mediator and arbitrator between the two sides. Initially, the OCLA personnel was predominantly committed to the conception of the CI as an element in a socialist transformation, and consequently supported workers' efforts to fully develop participation through the CI. Personnel changes following the resignation of Minister Dellepiane in April 1971, however, caused a change in policies on the part of the OCLA, insofar as adherence to and enforcement of the integrative conception of the CI became predominant. Concretely, this meant that CI representatives found it more difficult to get access to and obtain support from the OCLA in complaints against their enterprise. Though this moderating role had little effect in the case of an organizationally experienced and militant workforce, it could keep CIs in smaller, nonorganized enterprises from articulating latent conflicts and fighting for their solution.

Data Base

Clearly, the nature of the questions asked (i.e., the influence that the various actors had on the development of participation at the enterprise level) required information about attitudes and behavior of all three sides involved: entrepreneurs, workers, and the state bureaucracy. On the workers' side, further differentiations needed to be made between elected organs of the CI (i.e., council, president, and board representative[s]) and blue- and white-collar unions. Also, information about financial background data of the enterprise was essential in order to assess the significance of the monetary benefits distributed to the CI.

Several alternative approaches seemed possible in the attempt to collect this information. The first, most straightforward and scientifically respectable approach that would come to the mind of a social science researcher is a survey study, based on interviews with entrepreneurs or management, workers and CI and union leaders, in a representative sample of enterprises. However, this approach was completely ruled out due to the highly politicized and conflict-ridden atmosphere. It would have been virtually impossible to get access to all sides involved, and even if access could have been obtained, the quality of answers would have been highly questionable. The only existing survey study, carrying out interviews with all the actors in a representative sample of enterprises, suffers from this latter weakness. Access was obtained on the basis of official sponsorship by the Ministry of Industry and Tourism, but the answers to attitude questions obviously reflect the official doctrine of the CI rather than its reality.[1] The most useful parts of this study are factual questions, concerning knowledge about the law of the CI on the part of the workforce, and benefits distributed through the CI by the enterprise. Occasionally, I will draw on these parts of the study for comparison with my own data.

A second possibility to collect information about the development of the CI

---

[1]The study was carried out by the research center of the Universidad del Pacífico. Unfortunately, it was not made publicly available, but it was semipublic enough for me to be granted permission to look at it and take notes of the findings in the offices of the research center.

would have been through case studies in selected enterprises. Participant observation combined with interviews with the persons available and willing to grant them could have provided valuable insights into the dynamics of participation. However, the weakness of this approach would have been its limited reliability as a basis for generalizations, as it would have been hard to differentiate typical from atypical characteristics of the respective enterprise and actors. I did use this type of interview–conversation with several actors within some enterprises in addition to my main approach in order to gain in-depth insights into the dynamics of interaction around the CI.

A further possible approach would have been through a systematic analysis of newspaper articles on aspects of relations among enterprise, CI, and the unions. Again, however, the problem of generalization would have imposed itself. Such reports and consequently the analysis would have tended to be based on particularly interesting cases, neglecting developments in the "silent majority" of enterprises.

There seemed to be only one possible approach to obtaining both representative and reliable information, and that was through access to the source where comprehensive information was collected for administrative purposes of the state bureaucracy. This source was the MIT, with predominantly the OCLA as the official agency in charge of CI affairs, and the Office of Industrial Statistics as the agency in charge of collecting basic statistical information about the whole industrial manufacturing sector.[2] The OCLA not only held the register of all CIs in the country but also the whole correspondence between enterprises, CIs, and various agencies in the MIT that had been carried on since the introduction of the CI in late 1970. Since a letter of complaint to the MIT was the only possible action for the CIs to defend their rights against entrepreneurial intransigence, this correspondence constituted a valid indicator for the degree and nature of open conflict between CIs and enterprises.

However, this correspondence lacked comprehensiveness in one aspect: It only provided selective information about the role of unions, as the latter were only mentioned if they took an openly and officially active part in a conflict. This did not occur very frequently, because unions were legally excluded from taking part in CI affairs. Thus an additional source of information was needed, from which exhaustive and reliable data about unions and their behavior could be obtained. Again, the only place where such information was held was the state bureaucracy, the Register of Unions and the Statistical Office in the Min-

---

[2]The industrial manufacturing sector (*sector fabril*) is defined as comprising all enterprises in Categories 20–39 of the International Standard Industrial Classification that employ five or more workers. Enterprises with one to four workers are classified as belonging to the artisan sector. In 1971, the industrial manufacturing sector employed 34.8% of the total manufacturing labor force in the country, and the artisan sector 65.2%. Sulmont (1972:11–12).

istry of Labor. The former could provide information about the presence or absence of one or more blue- or white-collar unions in an enterprise, as well as their year of formation, and the latter about all strike action occurring in an enterprise.

Needless to emphasize that this information was collected mainly for internal use of the state bureaucracy, and that its potential politically controversial character made accessibility particularly problematic. The most easily accessible part of the information was the data from the industrial statistics, which by itself could only serve as a basis for research on economic aspects of enterprises and CIs. The register of CIs and the files with all the correspondence concerning their interaction with their enterprise and the state bureaucracy were rather closely guarded, because the OCLA was at the center of the struggle around the CI and its performance was under attack from both left and right. And the most crucial source of information for a completion of the picture of dynamics set off by the CI—the detailed data on strikes in every enterprise—was regarded as classified. The apparent reason for this secrecy was that the government attempted to maintain an official image of harmony in labor relations, or at least to prevent the dissemination of an image of class struggle. Yet this attempt did not quite seem worthy of the effort, as aggregate strike figures were made public by the Society of Industries. The reasons for secrecy were much more obvious in the case of a final source of information about conflicts generated by the introduction of the CI. This information concerned the interference of OCLA officials in the national organization formed by CIs as solidaristic base for a defense of their interests. The interference of OCLA officials in this organization, which will be discussed in the next chapter, was of an openly manipulative character and ran partly contrary to the official government policy towards this organization. Consequently, the OCLA had a strong interest in keeping access to this information highly restricted. Yet, through a combination of tenacity, luck, and invaluable help from friends I was able to obtain access to the Ministry of Industry and the Ministry of Labor. Throughout periods of ups-and-downs of bureaucratic goodwill I finally managed to collect the relevant data from all the sources of information just described.

On the basis of the 1973 industrial statistics I chose a sample of 438 industrial enterprises, which is representative for the whole industrial manufacturing sector under the administrative competence of the MIT.[3] For these enterprises, I collected economic background data, including profit distribution to the CI and ownership of the CI, pertaining to the state of enterprise and CI in 1973. I read and coded the whole correspondence that went on between the enter-

---

[3]A description of the sample procedure and a comparison of my data base with official statistics is given in Appendix I.

prises in my sample, their CIs, and the MIT in the 5 years of existence of the CI, from late 1970 to January 1976.[4] From the official register of unions, I could find out whether a blue- and/or white-collar union existed in the respective enterprise, and when this union had been established. And finally, I could complete the data set with information about all strikes and the number of man-hours lost in the enterprises in my sample in the years 1973–1975.

In order to complement this information and gain a deeper understanding of motivations of actors at the societal level, I carried out a number of elite interviews with representatives from all three sides: labor, business, and the state. They included the top leaders of the major union confederations and of the national organization of industrial communities; executives in the Exporters' Association, the Peruvian Institute for Enterprise Management, and several companies; advisors to policy makers, and the former (that is, 1970–1974) Minister of Labor. Also, I attended an evening seminar extending over several weeks for CI presidents and representatives on boards of directors, which provided insights into the legal, administrative, financial, personal, and political problems confronted by lower-level leaders.

Besides the already mentioned MIT–Universidad del Pacífico study, only one other study of developments at the enterprise level was available as a basis for comparison with my own findings. Santistevan did a study of conflicts between CI and enterprise in the first one and a half years of their existence, based on the same correspondence from the Office of Industrial Communities, but with a different sample of enterprises and without information on union involvement (Santistevan 1974:153–192). Pásara studied dynamics at the societal level, focusing on the emergence of a new actor, the national organization of industrial communities (Pásara 1974:195–262). Both of these studies were published by the DESCO research institute and thus are easily available, in contrast to the Pacífico study.

An interesting basis for cross-national comparison is provided by Espinosa and Zimbalist's (1978) study of worker's participation in Chile during the Allende years. Though the political context in Chile was quite different from the Peruvian one, and though the study uses a somewhat different approach from mine, the essential findings are strikingly similar. Variables measuring working-class mobilization, political unity, and ideology are found to be the strongest predictors of the level of participation developed in an enterprise. Since their study is restricted to enterprises in the social property sector, however, it does not address the question of integrative or mobilizing effects of different designs introduced to consolidate or transform a given order. The Chilean design was clearly introduced as part of a strategy of societal transformation to-

[4] The coding scheme is given in Appendix II.

ward a democratic-socialist order. Nevertheless, comparisons with this study will add interesting perspectives at various points in the following analysis.

General State of Labor Relations

In order to understand the dynamics resulting from the CI, it is essential to consider the conditions into which it was introduced, particularly the traditional patterns of labor relations and degree of unionization. Labor relations in Peru have traditionally been characterized either by paternalistic domination, or, if a union was present, by strong antagonism and conflicts, solved more frequently by intervention of the Ministry of Labor than by direct negotiation. Official intervention and legislation have provided the only protection for workers against the virtually unlimited power of management. Consequently, no tradition of rational interaction and mutual accommodation between management and workers had developed and the design of the CI stood in fundamental contradiction to established patterns of behavior. In particular, accepting the CI representative on the board of directors as something like an equal partner meant for management an untolerable reduction of social distance and loss of prerogatives. Workers on their part, except where relations to the employer were of a paternalistic nature, saw employers predominantly as their antagonists in a zero-sum game and the CI as a means to enlarge their share of rewards at the expense of the employers, rather than as an institution designed to facilitate cooperation of the two sides. Entrepreneurial hostility and attempts to evade the law confirmed this view, and thus the CI by no means served to smooth labor relations and to deprive unions of their function, but on the contrary increased workers' reliance on unions.

Union activity in Peru, like in other Latin American countries, is intrinsically linked to the state bureaucracy.[5] For instance, upon initiating collective negotiations, the union has to present a list of its demands to the employer and at the same time to the Ministry of Labor, which approves new contracts, if they are reached in direct bargaining, or else mediates in the second stage of negotiation, or finally resolves conflicts through binding arbitration. The same holds true for all types of grievances, which have to be presented in the form of a complaint (*denuncia*) to the Ministry of Labor in order to be settled through mediation or an administrative resolution. This means that union leaders have a certain experience in dealing with official bureaucracy and perceive complaints to the Ministry as the appropriate way for the solution of con-

---

[5] A variety of articles discussing this trilateral relation among workers, employers, and the state, can be found in Davis and Goodman (1972).

flicts. Therefore, when conflicts arose between CI and enterprise in unionized enterprises, the workers knew which steps to take and followed the same pattern as in union affairs, writing letters of complaint to the Ministry of Industry. In order to assess the overall defensive capacity of workers, then, and the potential for open conflict upon introduction of the CI, one has to look at the degree of unionization reached in 1970.

Table 4.1 shows that unionization in 1970 was very low in enterprises with less than 100 workers, but that over half of enterprises in the size category of 100–500 workers had a union, and almost all enterprises with more than 500 workers did. Consequently, the workforce in the majority of bigger enterprises had the organizational capacity to push for the implementation of the CI, and to insist on their rights as CI members. By January of 1976, this capacity had expanded considerably, to three-fourths and above, of enterprises with 50 or more workers. In many formerly nonunionized enterprises a union was formed between 1970 and 1976, and in many already unionized enterprises a second or third union was formed. These additional unions could be either white-collar in addition to blue-collar unions, or unions in other production centers belonging to the same enterprise, because under Peruvian law unionization is structured on an establishment-wide rather than a company-wide basis.

Several reasons account for this steep rate of increase in unionization, and the CI is one of them. A major reason was the Law of Security of Employment (D.L. 18471), decreed in November of 1970 in order to stop the massive waves of firings started by entrepreneurs in protest against the creation of the CI. The law postulates that after an initial trial period of three months, a worker can only be fired for serious misbehavior. This made it impossible for employers to resort to their traditional strategy of using intimidation and actual firings to prevent the formation of a union in their enterprise. Another factor raising the

Table 4.1
Unionization before and after 1970 by Size of Enterprise

Number of workers in enterprise	Percentage of enterprises where a union was established			Percentage of enterprises in size category	N	Percentage of workers employed by enterprises in size category
	Before 1970	After 1970	By 1976			
Under 20	0	0	0	28.9	(577)	4
20–49	4	22	25	32.5	(648)	11
50–99	23	51	74	17.0	(339)	13
100–499	51	57	78	19.3	(385)	42
500+	93	41	98	2.2	(44)	30
All	17	28	38	100.0		100.0
N	(338)	(551)	(758)	(1993)		(190,762)

degree of unionization was the government's extensive use of revolutionary rhetoric and ambiguous mobilization policies, which will be discussed in more detail in Chapter 5. The introduction of the CI itself contributed to this union-ization process in two ways. First, it provided an organizational shelter for union organizers to reach sufficient numbers of workers in a situation where social pressure could overcome traditional fear and reluctance of individual workers to sign the membership list needed for official recognition of the union. Second, the hostility of entrepreneurs toward the CI in most cases sharpened the perception of a conflict of interests and consequently of a need for collective defense of their interests on part of the workers. Yet, for the dis-cussion of the initial development of the CI, it has to be kept in mind that the majority of enterprises in Peru are small (i.e., 79% of the enterprises in my sample had less than 100 workers) and that their unionization rate in 1970 was very low. Looking at the percentage of the labor force, an estimate based on the figures in Table 4.1 indicates that a little more than half of the workers in the industrial manufacturing sector were employed in unionized enterprises in 1970.

Ignorance, Uncertainty, and Opposition vis-à-vis the CI, and the Role of the OCLA

The determining impact of the capacity of the workforce to overcome entre-preneurial resistance on the one hand, indicated by size of the workforce and presence of a union, and of the intervention of the OCLA on the other hand, on the development of the CI was already clearly visible in the phase of its establishment and recognition. Given that unions as well as all other actors concerned were surprised by the CI legislation, and entrepreneurs immediately started opposing it, it was to be expected that the establishment and official recognition of the CIs would get off to a slow start. According to the law, the employee with the highest administrative position was supposed to call and pre-side over the meeting to establish the CI. The law also prescribed that this meeting was to be held within 60 days from the day of promulgation of the law, September 1, 1970, and was to elect an organizing committee. This com-mittee was to elaborate the statutes and call a new meeting for the election of the CI council within the following 30 days. The CI council was to immedi-ately demand the official registration of the CI in the OCLA. However, by December 1, 90 days after the promulgation of the law, only 2.4% of the CIs in the sample had been recognized, and by January 1, 1971, only 32%. As predicted, speed of establishment and recognition was dependent on the size of the workforce; by February 1, 1971, only 59% of enterprises with less than 20 workers had a recognized CI, as compared to 84% of enterprises with more than 500 workers. One explanation is that the smaller the enterprise the more likely the employee in the highest administrative position would be to identify with the employer, who in practically all cases would be opposed to the establishment of the CI. And the smaller the enterprise the less likely the workers were to have the organizational strength and experience to demand the establishment of the CI. Table 4.2 shows that size made a consistent and considerable difference for speeding up recognition in nonunionized enterprises, whereas this difference was practically eliminated by the presence of a union. An overall comparison of speed of recognition of CIs in unionized and nonunionized enterprises in the size group 20–499 workers shows a consistent difference in the predicted direction:[6] Presence of a union increases the likelihood of earlier recognition of the CI. However, in the early and middle stages this difference is neither fully consistent within the various size groups nor very big. A consideration of administrative procedures involved in official recognition suggests the following explanation. Unions—or rather, experienced leaders— pressed for the establishment of a CI from the beginning and took an active part in preparing the documents required for getting the necessary bureaucratic formalities accomplished. However, one of these formalities was official approval of the statutes of the CI by the OCLA, and this caused a delay in the recognition of many of these CIs that were established early under the pressure of union leaders. Pásara (1974:133–152) showed that one of the main reasons for the OCLA to ask for revisions of statutes were articles referring to the relationship between CI and union. Accordingly, by February 1, 1971, there was almost no difference in the percentage of CIs recognized in unionized versus nonunionized enterprises in the size categories between 50 and 499 workers. A month later, however, probably after adequate revisions of statutes in many cases, there was a consistent and visible difference in all size categories, and on the whole 91% of unionized enterprises had a recognized CI, as compared to only 58% of nonunionized enterprises.

The role played by unions was also found to be of major importance for the introduction of the participation scheme in the enterprises belonging to Chile's social area.[7] The situation there was fundamentally different from the Peruvian

[6]The reason for excluding enterprises with less than 20 and more than 500 workers from Table 4.2 is that there is no variation in unionization in these two size categories. According to the law, a union can be formed only in enterprises with 20 or more workers, because a union has to have at least 20 members. Furthermore, a union has to present signatures from at least half the workers in an enterprise to apply for official recognition from the Ministry of Labor, which is indispensable for a union to perform any function. At the other end of the scale, 93% of enterprises with more than 500 workers had a union in 1970.

[7]The social property sector of the Chilean economy, the so-called social area, comprised fully and partly state-owned, intervened, and requisitioned enterprises. At the time of Allende's overthrow, there were 420 enterprises in the area. For a discussion of the development of the social area, of the structural design of workers' participation, and of its introduction, see Espinosa and Zimbalist (1978:46–56).

Table 4.2

Speed of Recognition of CI by Size and Union Presence

| Number of workers in enterprise | Percentage of enterprises with and without an old union which had a CI recognized by the following dates | | | | | |
| | January 1, 1971 | | February 1, 1971 | | March 1, 1971 | |
	With	Without	With	Without	With	Without
20–49	46	12	54	44	96	44
50–99	18	33	58	57	84	74
100–499	43	44	82	78	93	85
20–499	37	23	73	53	91	58
N	(109)	(225)	(217)	(524)	(270)	(576)

one with respect to the role officially assigned to unions. The Chilean government elaborated the participation design in collaboration with the leadership of the CUT (*Confederación Unica de Trabajadores*, Central Workers' Confederation) the central national union organization. Unions were in charge of organizing initial elections and educating workers about the participation scheme. They were also given a role in the new participatory bodies, as they were to preside over the General Assembly and coordinating councils. However, a complete fusion between unions and new participatory bodies was prevented by barring union officials from being elected to management councils and production committees. In some cases, this created suspicion and hostility among local union leaders against the participation scheme, and where this occurred, implementation tended to be slow and deficient.

The reason why such local variations in the behavior of unions were possible was the weakness of the Chilean labor movement in organizational penetration and centralization, and in political unity. Collective bargaining was legally restricted to the local level, and federations were illegal. Furthermore, different parties were competing for the political loyalty of unions. Thus the influence of the central CUT leadership over member unions was very tenuous, not to mention effective control over their behavior. Where local unions were organizationally strong, politically united, and well informed about the participation scheme through good communication with the CUT and/or political parties, the introduction of participation went swiftly, as no resistance from private entrepreneurs had to be dealt with. In some cases, state-appointed administrators did offer resistance, but the workers had the power to overcome such resistance—if necessary by firing the administrator—provided the workers had sufficient organizational strength and experience (Espinosa and Zimbalist 1978:56).

In Peru, many nonunionized enterprises managed to delay the establishment of a CI for a considerable time, and a few of them managed to escape it alto-gether. For approximately one-fourth of enterprises in my sample with less than 20 workers, no recognition of a CI could be found in the OCLA register by early 1976; the same was true for 14% of nonunionized enterprises with 20–49 workers; but all enterprises with a union also had a recognized CI. In January and February 1971 the OCLA started a campaign sending out pro-moters to organize the CI where it had not been established yet. This was par-ticularly important in the provinces, where the bulk of recognitions came later than in the Lima–Callao area. By February 1, 1971, only 23% of enterprises located in the provinces had a recognized CI, as compared to 61% of enter-prises in the Lima–Callao area.

After the campaign for establishment and recognition of the CI, an actual promotion campaign would have been needed, explaining the law and their rights through the CI to the workers. It was in the initial stages of this promo-tion campaign that the scandal around the MIT seminar, where class struggle supposedly was promoted, broke out. This brought the campaign to a halt in March 1971. After the change of minister one month later, only a few edu-cational activities were undertaken, and those few were directed mainly toward entrepreneurs. In July 1971 SINAMOS was created, and became the agency in charge of supporting the activities of the CI, but when the mobilization cre-ated by SINAMOS among the CIs seemed to get out of control, all education and training activities relating to the CI were reserved for the MIT by decree in June 1972. Yet, the activities undertaken by the MIT were of rather limited significance; if not in scope, so at least in depth. Data for the period 1973 and 1974 were not available, but if we assume that an equal number of workers was reached through some sort of training activity in each of these 2 years as in 1975, we come to a total of 30,600 workers, which corresponds to roughly 15% of all CI members in the country. About half of these workers, however, were exposed to no more than a lecture in their enterprise.[8] How low the knowledge about the provisions of the law still was among workers, after almost 5 years of existence of the CI, is shown in the Pacífico Study: 56% of the blue-collar workers simply did not know anything about the rights granted to them as members of the CI, and among the 44% who knew something, there were many with very rudimentary or even incorrect ideas about their rights.

A generally low level of education and knowledge among workers, and the

[8]The training activities in 1975 comprised technical–economic accounting courses with 2940 participants, basic courses about the CI with 1272 participants, integral courses in collaboration with Federations of CIs with 530 participants, a course about the newly created court with juris-diction in conflicts between CI and enterprise, the *Fuero Privativo de Comunidades Laborales* with 258 participants; lectures were given in various enterprises, which a total of 5185 CI members at-tended. Consequently, a total of 10,212 CI members were reached through some form of educa-tional activity by the MIT in 1975. Program of the Office of Education of the MIT, March 1976.

lack of clarifying propaganda efforts on the part of the OCLA aggravated the state of general confusion among those concerned with the implementation of the CI. This confusion mainly resulted from the complexity of certain provisions in the law and the vagueness of certain definitions, and it created a heavy burden on the OCLA as interpreter of the law, in addition to its function as mediator and arbitrator in conflicts. Particularly in the first year of existence of the CI, a large number of letters with requests for clarification were written to the OCLA.[9] Most of these questions concerned the exact way of distributing the 10% cash participation in profits. According to the law, half of this amount was to be distributed evenly among the workers, the other half proportional to their basic remuneration. This provision was objected to by numerous CIs, who asked for equal distribution, which the MIT refused to allow, demanding proof of proper distribution. Other questions about this distribution concerned the definition of "basic remuneration" for people working on bonus systems or piece rates, etc. Consultations about these questions as well as about calculations of the total sum of profits to be distributed, and procedures for reinvestment of the 15% of profits came from both CIs and employers. Employers were in charge of distributing the 10% and capitalizing the 15% in favor of the CI, and CIs had an interest in watching over correct application of the law. A further area of uncertainty and conflict was the internal functioning of the CI (i.e., rules concerning elections, procedures in assemblies, application of fines for the members, number of representatives on the board of directors, etc.).

Table 4.3 shows how frequently such questions were brought to the OCLA, particularly by CIs or enterprises with a large work force. Since these questions were equally likely to occur in small as in big enterprises, the difference in the number of questions brought to the OCLA leads one to assume that in smaller enterprises management just decided to solve these questions according to their interpretation of the law, as the CI would not be capable of challenging this interpretation anyhow. The comparatively lower number of questions concerning the calculation of profits and the procedures for the 15% ownership participation is not an indicator for greater clarity of the law on these points, but rather for the high probability of the emergence of conflicts about them. Most communications to the OCLA about these points involved explicit discrepancies between the interpretations made by the enterprise and by the CI, which caused them to be coded as "complaints," rather than "questions."

For many of these questions and complaints there was no clear answer to be derived from the law, but legal advisors of the OCLA established certain precedents which then became the basis for standard interpretations. In certain

---

[9]The criterion for coding some communication as question rather than complaint was the absence of expressed controversy between CI and enterprise about the correct interpretation of a certain provision.

Table 4.3

Questions from CIs or Enterprises to the OCLA by Size and Subject Matter[a]

Number of workers in enterprise	Percentage of enterprises or CIs with one or more questions about the following			
	Distribution of 10%	Internal functioning of CI	Calculation of profits	Investment capitalization of 15%
Under 50	7	12	0	0
50–99	25	46	6	17
100–499	56	68	18	18
Over 500	73	85	30	45
All	22	32	6	11

[a] N = 1756.

cases, however, opinions of various offices within the MIT differed considerably, and internal consultations went back and forth. Occasionally, there were even disputes about which Ministry was to pronounce an opinion on certain matters—the MIT, the Ministry of Economy and Finance, or the Ministry of Labor. Such cases were rather frequent, as 12% of enterprises posed problems about which one additional agency was consulted by the OCLA, and 21% of enterprises posed problems that required consultation of two or more additional agencies. Yet, all these different agencies could do was to pronounce an opinion—which occasionally was disregarded by enterprises as "just the opinion of some officials [Pásara 1974]." In many cases, the OCLA sent supervisors to the enterprise in charge of ensuring compliance with the official directives for the solution of a conflict. Of all enterprises with a recognized CI, 59% received one or more visits from a supervisor; and 90% of enterprises with more than 100 workers were visited. In contrast, less than 30% of enterprises with less than 20 workers and a recognized CI were visited, which indicates the low degree of enforcement of the law in enterprises of this size. Yet these supervisors had no legal authority to sanction continued violations of the law and of official guidelines.

A further step taken by the OCLA was to summon representatives of the respective enterprise and CI to meet with an official in the MIT and work out a compromise. In certain cases, this was done repeatedly, sometimes still without success. Again, there was a strong difference in the frequency of such summons to the MIT according to the size of the workforce. Only 5% of CIs with less than 20 workers were asked to send a representative to the MIT for a conciliation meeting, as compared to half of the CIs with more than 100 workers. Of CIs with more than 500 workers, 37% even had their representatives called to the MIT twice or more. Yet, despite these conciliation efforts, some conflicts were carried on over several years, until a special court for Labor Communities (Fuero Privativo de Comunidades Laborales) was established in July 1975.

Reasons for Complaints

Though lack of knowledge about and a certain vagueness of the law hindered the development of the CI, purposeful avoidance on the part of enterprises of granting benefits to the CI was by far the greatest obstacle. How successful this avoidance was can be seen from the extent of actual benefits received by the CI. The Pacífico Study found that in almost 5 years of existence, only 42% of the CIs had been receiving all three types of benefits prescribed by law (10% in cash, 15% in ownership, and representation on the board of directors), whereas 26% had been receiving no more than one of these benefits, in most cases the cash participation in profits. Forty-nine percent of the CI presidents in their sample knew the percentage of capital the CI owned in their enterprise, 25% said that they had been receiving the 15% of profits for the acquisition of shares but did not know how much that was, and 26% had not received any participation in ownership. My data show that by the end of 1973, the recognized CIs owned an average of 6.4% of capital in their enterprises. Though this is lower than the officially given average of 9%, this is probably still an overestimate, because information about their participation in ownership was missing for 34% of the CIs in my sample. It seems reasonable to assume that these were mostly CIs with a low participation in ownership, because the data are based on the declaration of industrial statistics filed by the enterprise, which had an interest in pointing out the progress of the CI in ownership as an indicator for compliance with the law.

My figures on cash participation in 1973 profits also tend to overestimate the benefits that individual blue-collar workers got from the CI. The real amount they received was smaller than the figures reached by dividing the total amount of cash to be distributed by total number of workers in the respective enterprise (the only calculation possible with my data), because half of the 10% were distributed according to basic remunerations.[10] The overall cash benefits received by CI members were the following; one-fifth of enterprises distributed nothing or a nominal amount as cash participation in profits to the CI members; 14% of enterprises distributed between 2000 and 4000 *soles* per member, which corresponded to roughly 1 month's minimal legal wage for a blue-collar worker; one-third of enterprises distributed between 4000 and 8000 *soles* per CI member—roughly the average monthly wage of a blue-collar worker;[11] and 31% of enterprises distributed more than 9000 *soles* per CI member (this clearly can be regarded as a very significant benefit granted to the workers through the CI re-

[10]This provision was changed to equal distribution through *D. L.* 21310 in November 1975.

[11]If these figures are corrected for the unequal method of distribution, they amount to roughly 1500 to 3000, and 3000 to 6000 *soles* per blue-collar worker respectively; the minimal legal wage in industry in Lima in 1973 was 2400 *soles* per month according to the Resolution of May 22, 1972; and the average remuneration of blue-collar workers in my sample was 4200 *soles* in 1973 for the whole sample and 4500 *soles* for those in enterprises with more than 20 workers.

form). However, these enterprises constituted a minority, and the general picture was one of struggle to obtain the legally granted benefits from the enterprise on part of the CI.

Initially, all the CI could do in the struggle against entrepreneurial attempts to avoid granting benefits was to complain to the OCLA about the amount of profits distributed by the enterprise, but after a law (*D.L.* 19262) in January 1972 granted the right to the CI to inspect all company books, with the help of an outside advisor, audits were carried out in 22% of enterprises. Since outside auditors had to be paid, the capability of a CI to have the books audited depended on its financial strength (i.e., on the amount of money accumulated in the General Fund of the CI[12] or on voluntary contributions from its members)—and thereby indirectly on the size of the enterprise. Whereas less than 10% of CIs with less than 20 members had the books of their enterprise audited, over 50% of CIs with more than 500 workers did. As expected, a comparison of unionized with nonunionized enterprises with 20–499 workers shows that presence of a union increased the likelihood of an audit to be carried out: 36% of CIs in unionized enterprises had audits carried out, as compared to only 20% of CIs in nonunionized enterprises. How reluctant enterprises were to grant access to information demanded by the CI can be seen in Table 4.4, which shows that 24% of CIs complained to the OCLA once or more about this problem—a higher percentage of complaints than about any other single subject matter.[13]

Analyzing the frequency of complaints according to the broader areas of conflict to which they pertained, one can see that each of the three major areas of conflict caused complaints from roughly 30% of CIs: (1) 29% of CIs complained about general maneuvers of the enterprise to avoid progress of the CI in ownership of enterprise capital; (2) 28% of CIs complained about attempts

---

[12]The General Fund of the CI consisted of dividends received from the shares owned by the CI, so if the CI did not get any ownership participation to begin with, it did not have funds to pay for an audit, either. Among other purposes, this fund was to be used for compensation of members who were leaving the enterprise. In case that the General Fund was too small to compensate these members, the enterprise had to make a repayable loan to the CI out of its indemnization fund for compensation purposes. (Articles 19 and 20 of the Law of CI).

[13]The variety of techniques used to keep information from the CI, mentioned in the letters of complaint to the OCLA, were amazing. For instance, in one case the enterprise transferred the whole accounting department to a different location and hired an accounting firm to handle all financial matters, and this firm simply ignored requests from the CI for information. In another case, a CI was kept from carrying out its planned audit with the argument that the enterprise accountant was using the books for a special report and that no copies of the documents could be made. Or, since the CI was legally required to carry out an audit within the offices of the enterprise, some enterprises just did not make any physical space to work in available to the auditors. In other cases, personal intimidation, layoffs, or firings for "insubordination" were used to keep CI representatives from pursuing requests for certain information.

Table 4.4
Frequency of Complaints from CIs and Enterprises to the OCLA[a]

Code	Subject matter	Percentage of recognized CIs or enterprises with the following number of complaints	
		1	2–51
Complaints from CIs			
(1) Not received 10%		14	3
(2) Not received 15% or shares		15	3
(3) Maneuvers to impede growth of the CI		13	4
(4) Decapitalization of the enterprise		6	3
(5) Refusal of access to information/documents		17	7
(6) Irregularities on board of directors		10	4
(7) Irregularities in accounts/books		8	12
(8) Maneuvers to disturb functioning of CI		12	6
(9) Noncompliance with agreements		3	0
(10) Firings		6	1
(11) Other labor relations problems		6	2
Complaints from enterprises			
(12) Irregularities in internal affairs of CI		2	1
(13) Undue intervention of CI in enterprise		2	2
(14) Labor indiscipline, low productivity		4	0
(15) Political agitation		1	0
(16) Use of CI for union affairs		1	1

[a]$N = 1758$.

of the enterprise to keep the CI from obtaining information about and participating in enterprise affairs; (3) 30% of CIs complained about general maneuvers of the enterprise to minimize the participation of the CI in profits.[14] Table 4.4 also shows that in a comparatively small number of enterprises management complained about the respective CIs to the OCLA. However, these complaints hardly ever initiated a dispute, but rather were made in the course of a conflict, as a counterattack on the CI. Accordingly, the distribution of complaints from the enterprise corresponds to the distribution of complaints from the CI (i.e., the zero-order correlation between them is $r = .50$), and both of them are related to the size of the enterprise. Size of the workforce of an enterprise shows totally consistent relations with all indicators of conflict between

[14]Particularly in family-owned enterprises, practices to minimize the declaration of profits were abundant. For instance, some letters of complaint mentioned that domestic servants of the owners' family were put on the payroll of the enterprise, or that family trips abroad were declared as enterprise representation costs, or that suddenly a large number of "consultants" were hired by the enterprise, mainly relatives of the owner.

enterprise and CI in my analysis as well as in Santistevan's (1974:153–192) study. This can be explained partly by the simple probability that the higher the number of actors, the greater the amount of interaction, and therefore the higher the potential for conflict. However, the crucial factor mediating the impact of size on the level of conflict was the capability of the CI to defend its interest. On the one hand, this capability increases with pure numbers of workers, insofar as numbers give a feeling of strength and consequently willingness to fight out conflicts. In fact, size does have a certain influence regardless of any other factor on the total number of complaints, as will be shown in a regression analysis. On the other hand, the defensive capability of the CI increases with organizational unity of the workforce and experience of the leadership resulting from unionization. Table 4.5 shows that both size and presence of a union had a consistent impact on the total number of complaints directed to the OCLA by CIs.

When one looks at the benefits received from the CI and the general economic situation of the workforce, one can see that CIs in smaller enterprises in fact would have had more reasons for complaints, but that they lacked the capacity for self-defense. Bigger CIs owned a higher percentage of capital in their enterprise, received higher amounts as the 10% participation in profits, and were generally higher paid (Table 4.6). Two basic types of reasons can be adduced as explanation for the fact that bigger enterprises provided generally higher monetary benefits for their workers: The economic situation of these enterprises and the demand-making capacity of their workforce. A straight economic explanation would be that bigger enterprises tended to be more capital intensive, in a stronger market position, and consequently more profitable than smaller ones. This explanation received some support from my data, though the relationships were not very strong: The zero-order correlation between size and capital assets per worker in my sample was .19, and between size and profits declared per worker in 1973, .11. The low correlation between size and profits declared, of course, is likely to be the result of intentional distortion of

Table 4.5
Impact of Size and Unionization on Complaints from CIs

Number of workers in enterprise	Percentage of recognized CIs in size category with one or more complaints	
	With union	Without union
Under 20	—	31
20–49	66	29
50–99	57	49
100–499	73	50
Over 500	97	—

Table 4.6

Impact of Size and Unionization on Average Remunerations and Benefits Received through the CI in Enterprises with a Recognized CI

Number of workers in enterprise	Average remuneration of blue-collar workers			Average percentage of enterprise capital owned by the CI			Average cash distribution of profits per CI member[b]		
	All	Without old union	With old union	All	Without old union	With old union	All	Without old union	With old union
20–49	42.8	42.9	42.5	6.0	5.9	7.5	5.6	5.3	10.6
50–99	50.2	47.5	60.9	6.7	7.0	5.7	9.1	8.9	9.9
100–499	67.9	66.8	68.9	6.5	7.2	5.9	18.4	21.3	15.8
Over 500	102.7	83.3	108.8	9.5	13.2	82.	18.9	10.1	22.2
All over 20	54.3	49.2	69.8	6.5	6.6	6.2	10.7	9.3	14.7

[a] In 1000 soles per year.
[b] In 1000 soles.

the profit figure by the enterprises. My data from the industrial statistics reflect the official figures provided by enterprises, on the basis of which the 10% and 15% share of the CI was calculated.

Another possible explanation, based on the demand-making capacity of the workforce, is that bigger enterprises were more likely to be unionized, and particularly to have a longer tradition of unionization. This higher degree and longer tradition of unionization in bigger enterprises was already demonstrated (Table 4.1). In fact, unionization did raise remuneration levels,[15] as the average blue-collar yearly remuneration was consistently higher in enterprises where a union had existed since before 1970, with the exception of the size category 20–49 workers, where, however, only 4% of enterprises had a union established before 1970 (see Table 4.6).[16] Yet, the figures for the percentage of enterprise capital owned by the CI and the amount of cash distributed by the enterprise to CI members show that unionization had no consistent impact on these benefits. Its impact varied in different size categories. Nevertheless, if all enterprises with more than 20 workers, with an old union, are compared to those without an old union, the impact of unionization shows up clearly in cash distribution of profits, though not for CI capital ownership. This can be explained by the fact that progress of the CI in capital ownership depended on two separate aspects of enterprise behavior: undistorted calculation of profits and due transfer of shares to the CI every year on the one hand, and amount of reinvestment by the enterprise on the other hand. Whereas union pressure could certainly influence the former, it cannot be assumed to have had a consistent effect on the latter.

The impact of size on benefits received from the CI becomes somewhat less consistent when unionization is controlled for, but its general direction remains clearly visible. Two complementary interpretations are possible: the economic one, just mentioned, and one based on the previous argument that demand-making capacity of the CI vis-à-vis the enterprise due to sheer number of CI members was of importance, and thus had a certain impact on the amount of benefits obtained independent of the presence or absence of a union. The assumption underlying this explanation is that complaints from the CI to the OCLA, which were made much more frequently by bigger CIs,

---

[15]Payne's (1965:22–23) analysis also shows the impact of unionization on wages. He gives comparative figures for real wages in related industries with and without extensive unionization. They show that workers in the unorganized garment and foodstuffs industries received higher real wages in 1939 than workers in the highly organized textile and beverage industries, whereas by 1959 workers in the highly organized industries received 45 to 85% more.

[16]The reason why the impact of the presence of an old union (i.e., one established before 1970) is chosen for investigation is that the data on remuneration level, cash distribution, and accumulated capital ownership are for 1973. A union established 1970 or later could hardly be expected to have had a major impact on the state of the CI in 1973.

made it harder for their enterprises to avoid granting the legally prescribed benefits to the CI members, because the complaints forced the OCLA to at least insist through formal letters that the enterprise comply with the law.

A regression analysis on the amount of cash distributed by the enterprise to the CI members showed that all these factors mentioned (i.e., economic situation of the enterprise and defensive capacity of the workforce, due to both unionization and numerical strength) had an independent impact. Capital assets per worker were entered as first variable, with a Beta weight of .23, presence of an old union as second variable (Beta = .11), and number of CI members as third variable (Beta = .08).

The assumptions about economic situation of the enterprise and differential efforts to enforce the law could also explain the fact that CIs in foreign and mixed enterprises received higher amounts of all three types of benefits: participation in ownership, cash distribution of profits, and average wages (Table 4.7).[17] A combination of two factors probably contributed to stricter enforcement of the law in foreign and mixed than in national enterprises. First, foreign and mixed enterprises tended to be concentrated in the bigger size categories. Whereas less than 10% of industrial manufacturing enterprises with fewer than 100 workers were foreign-owned or mixed, 26% of enterprises with 100–499 workers were, and 35% of enterprises with more than 500 workers were.[18] This means that foreign and mixed enterprises tended to have a bigger workforce with a stronger demand-making capacity, more frequent complaints to the OCLA, and consequently greater pressure for enforcement of the law. Second, foreign enterprises were subject to generally greater bureaucratic supervision due to the fade-out requirements they had to comply with on the basis of the articles from Decision 24 of the Andean Pact, which had been incorporated into Peruvian law in 1971 (*D.L.* 18900 and 18999).[19] In particular, the requirement that an agreement be concluded between the state and each foreign enterprise about a schedule for partial ownership transfer to nationals necessitated a stricter adherence to the law than for national enterprises. A law (*D.L.* 18900) dated June 30, 1971, stipulated that all foreign-owned enterprises had to reach a 15% participation of national investors in ownership by

[17]The ownership categories are defined as follows: (1) national enterprises: less than 20% foreign capital; (2) mixed enterprises: between 20% and 49% foreign capital; or more than 49%, if in combination with at least 30% state ownership and control; and (3) foreign enterprises: more than 49% of foreign capital (definitions from *D. L.* 18350).

[18]Foreign and mixed enterprises together constitute only 10% of all enterprises in the sample, but they account for 28% of capital assets and employ 23% of the workers, as they are typically large, capital-intensive, modern enterprises.

[19]For an analysis of the issues in the Andean Pact agreements on treatment of foreign investments, see Ffrench-Davis (1978) and Vaitsos (1974). Stepan (1978:273–277) draws attention to the combined impact of the Andean Pact and CI legislation on foreign-owned enterprises in Peru.

Table 4.7
Average Remunerations, Benefits Received through the CI, and Complaints from CIs by Ownership Category

Ownership category	N	Average remuneration of blue-collar workers[a]	Average percentage of enterprise capital owned by the CI	Average cash distribution of profits[b]	Average number of complaints from CI
Foreign	121	70.2	7.6	33.3	3.3
Mixed	81	68.1	7.7	27.1	2.9
National	1550	48.3 ⎤	6.1 ⎤	6.6 ⎤	2.1 ⎤
		⎬ 49.2	⎬ 6.1	⎬ 6.8	⎬ 2.2
National (large)	25	106.4 ⎦	7.4 ⎦	16.8 ⎦	10.6 ⎦
State	5	61.2	1.0	1.9	2.4
State/mixed	2	85.8	8.2	48.5	0.0
	1784				

[a]In 1000 soles per year.
[b]In 1000 soles.

June 30, 1974; 45% by 1981, and 49% by 1986. Another law (D.L. 18999) followed on October 19, 1971, with the provision that in case of noncompliance with the transfer of shares and/or the conclusion of a contract with the state within the established time periods, foreign shareholders would be required to gradually transfer their shares to the CI until the necessary proportions would be reached. The CI would be required to buy these shares, and in case of lack of funds, the enterprise would have to grant the necessary amount as a loan to the CI. This combination of requirements clearly contributed to closer supervision of the progress of the CI in ownership of enterprise capital in foreign-owned than in national enterprises.

This explanation poses an apparent paradox: If foreign enterprises were less able to avoid compliance with the law of CI, why did their CIs complain more frequently to the OCLA than the CIs in national enterprises? Part of the reason may have been the larger average size of foreign and mixed enterprises, but part of it certainly was the anti-imperialist revolutionary sentiment mentioned in the introductory remarks to this chapter.[20]

[20]In the letters of complaint to the OCLA, this sentiment was frequently expressed in formulations such as "the bad, mal-intentioned foreign entrepreneurs are doing damage to the enterprise, the workforce, and our nation's economy." One might be inclined to interpret this as purposeful use of the government's own rhetoric to force the state bureaucracy into active intervention to protect the rights of a CI, but the style and spelling of most of these letters would invalidate the assumption of such sophistication and rather underline the genuine nature of these sentiments on the part of the authors.

Determinants of the Overall Number of Complaints

Having established that the introduction and development of the CI was a highly conflict-ridden process, and that a variety of factors contributed to the emergence of conflicts, it becomes necessary to assess the relative importance of the various factors for the overall level of conflict. In particular, I am going to show that the role of unions was as crucial for the development of CI–enterprise relations as my conceptualization implies. This point is confirmed by a regression analysis on total number of complaints from the CI to the OCLA over the whole time period 1970–1976, for all enterprises with more than 20 workers, as the presence of a union established before 1970 turned out to be the strongest predictor (Table 4.8). As second variable size was entered, which gives support to the argument that number of actors increases the potential for conflicts to be brought into the open and fought out through complaints to the OCLA.

Some interesting comparisons with the Chilean experience can be drawn here. The total number of complaints from the CI to the OCLA can be regarded as an indicator of high interest and involvement of the workers in participation. Though one might rather want to interpret it as an indicator of the intensity of entrepreneurial opposition, I would contend, as argued earlier in this chapter, that with few exceptions entrepreneurial opposition was rather generalized and only assumed relevance for open conflict in relation to workers' efforts to overcome it. The extent of these efforts in turn depended on the involvement of workers with the participation scheme and on their capacity to act collectively. Whereas there was little opportunity for active participation in Peru other than complaining to the OCLA about violations of the law, high involvement could be channeled into high activity in various decision-making bodies in the enterprise in the Chilean case. Accordingly, the measure for intensity of participation used by Espinosa and Zimbalist (1978:112) is a cumulative index of participation in decision making, execution of policies, and

Table 4.8
Regression on Total Number of Complaints from CIs with More Than 20 Workers[a]

Independent variables	Beta	Simple r
Presence of an old union	0.36	0.43
Number of CI members	0.17	0.33
10% cash distribution of profits through CI	−0.14	−0.03
Presence of a new union	0.12	0.14
Average blue-collar remuneration per year	0.12	0.25
Proportion of enterprise capital owned by the CI	−0.06	−0.09
Increase in average remuneration, 1971–1973	0.01	0.10

[a] $R^2 = 0.27$; N = 1075.

control and evaluation of these policies. They find that the level of labor mobilization prior to the introduction of participation, the attitude assumed by
unions vis-à-vis participation, and the political loyalties of workers are the
strongest predictors of the level of participation. Together, the three variables
explain 64.9% of the variance in their participation index. Thus their results
confirm that the presence of an actively mobilizing union at the enterprise
level with ties to supportive outside forces is crucial for the full exercise of
structurally given possibilities for participation. When technological variables
are added to the political ones in their regression equation, they show no independent impact on the level of participation. The effect of the technological
variables, which appears in a separate regression on participation, is neutralized
by the overwhelming importance of the political variables.

Espinosa and Zimbalist include size of the enterprise in their investigation
of the effect of organizational structure on participation. They find that size
and three additional variables indicating organizational structure explain 9.8%
of the variance in participation, and they argue that "if the relationship between technology and organizational structure is weak, the relationship between organizational structure and worker participation is even weaker
[1978:95]." The apparent discrepancy between this finding and interpretation
and my findings, which show a consistent and strong impact of size on
the development of participation, can be explained easily. I have argued that
size of the enterprise was important because it increased the capacity of the
workforce for collective action in defense of their rights as CI members. Frequent and exclusive interaction among large numbers of blue-collar workers
generated a subjective feeling of strength and capacity to confront capital owners and their managerial representatives. In Chile, the situation was essentially
different in that the conflict between labor and capital in the social area enterprises had been eliminated through the transfer of the enterprise to this area.
Thus the development of participation was not a matter of confronting a hostile
entrepreneur in a struggle to obtain legally granted benefits, but rather of mobilizing workers into active involvement in a variety of participatory bodies.
Only in the case of strong resistance from state-appointed administrators would
one expect size of the workforce to play a similarly important role as in Peru.
But cases where such resistance was strong and led to protracted conflicts did
not occur very frequently. Rather, administrators seemed to adapt to pressures
from the workers, as those in enterprises with a more mobilized workforce
tended to be more favorably disposed toward participation (Espinosa and Zimbalist 1978:114–117). The difference between stern entrepreneurial resistance
in Peru and adaptation on the part of administrators in Chile was very significant for the effects of high involvement of the workers in participation, in particular for its effects on strike behavior. I will turn to a comparison of these

effects in more detail after concluding the discussion of determinants of complaints from the CI.

The third strongest predictor of the total number of complaints was the amount of cash distributed by the enterprise to the CI members, showing a moderating impact. This could mean simply that the CIs in enterprises that did pay the due participation in profits to the workers, without trying to get around it, had less reason for complaints. However, it could also mean that the CIs in less profitable enterprises complained in general more, despite compliance with the law on part of the enterprise, just because the benefits received by the CI were small. This second interpretation is based on the assumption of relative deprivation, the reason for which could be either a comparison with benefits received by CI members in other enterprises or simply a raise of expectations caused by official propaganda about the CI. On the basis of the available data no clear decision between the two explanations can be made, because there is no objective indicator for compliance or noncompliance on part of the enterprise. However, additional evidence, to be presented here later, gives support to the second explanation, based on the assumption of relative deprivation.

The fourth variable entered in the regression was presence of a union established since 1970. The considerable progress of union organization in the years since 1970 has been mentioned already. The reason why presence of a union established before 1970 had a greater impact on the total number of complaints directed to the OCLA by the CI is first of all that these unions could provide advice on the basis of experience with bureaucratic procedures, as well as organizational cohesion of the workforce from the beginning, as basis for action in the defense of CI interests. In enterprises where a new union was established, this process most probably absorbed time and energies of the most experienced and active members of the workforce at least for a while; and only after the new union had been firmly established would their efforts be concentrated on CI affairs.

The fifth variable entered in the regression was the average remuneration level of blue-collar workers, showing a positive relation to the overall number of complaints from the CI. Two explanations for this relationship are possible: a psychological one, based on the assumption of relative deprivation, and one based on assumptions about consistency in the behavior of the blue-collar workforce. The explanation based on relative deprivation states that the higher the average remuneration of blue-collar workers in an enterprise, the higher their expectation of benefits from the CI, and the higher the number of complaints from the CI due to unfulfilled expectations. The other explanation states that blue-collar workers who assumed a tough stand in wage questions would do the same in CI affairs. Since the effect of union presence was controlled for in the regression, this explanation pertains to differences between unions in their combativeness and mobilizing activity, or (though a much less likely occurrence in practice) to differences in the assertiveness of nonunionized workers.

As sixth variable, percentage of enterprise capital owned by the CI was entered in the regression, showing a weak moderating impact on complaints. Again, compliance with the law might be thought of as the explanatory factor, but CI capital ownership is a weak indicator of this because of its additional dependence on the amount of capital reinvested by the enterprise. Rather, relative deprivation can be assumed to be the motivating factor here, too. The rank order of importance of CI capital ownership compared to cash distribution of profits is understandable if one keeps in mind that, from a psychological point of view, the amount of cash received through the CI was more important to the workers and consequently likely to determine the behavior of CI members to a greater extent than the amount of capital collectively owned, the concrete benefits of which were much less visible. Consequently, a subjective comparison of cash received resulting in relative deprivation or gratification would have a greater impact on the number of complaints than a comparison of progress in capital ownership.

The following argument and evidence provide additional support for the contention that the phenomenon of relative deprivation or gratification influenced the propensity of CIs to bring complaints to the OCLA. Relative deprivation or gratification of members of a given CI can be assumed to result from a comparison of the benefits they received through their CI with the benefits distributed through the CIs in similar types of enterprises; the criterion for similarity being size of the enterprise. Obviously, other criteria for similarity might be relevant for the workers' choice of other CIs for comparison with their own situation, such as type of goods produced, or proximity in location, etc. However, I would argue that similarity in size is a necessary criterion for the choice of other CIs for comparison, though it may not be a sufficient one. The data available lend themselves to an examination of the phenomenon of relative deprivation among CIs of comparable size. Accordingly, one would expect greater satisfaction and less complaints among those CIs that received comparatively greater amounts of benefits from their enterprise than among those CIs that received comparatively lower amounts of benefits within a given size category. Comparing the average number of complaints received from the CIs with highest to those with lowest amounts of cash received and percentages of capital ownership achieved within the various size categories, this expected relationship in fact appears for all size groups over 20 workers (Table 4.9).

The pattern in the size group with 10–19 workers is reversed in both cases for cash distribution and capital ownership. This can be explained by a change in the direction of causality: Among the smallest CIs, those who did not com-

Table 4.9
Impact of Cash Distribution of Profits and Capital Ownership on Average Number of Complaints within Size Groups

Number of workers in enterprise	Mean number of complaints from CIs within size group that received			
	Under 2000[a]	Over 9000[a]	Under 5%[b]	Over 10%[b]
10–19	0.1	1.3	2.4	3.1
20–49	1.1	0.5	0.9	0.2
50–99	1.5	1.3	1.8	0.8
100–499	10.8	3.1	6.2	4.1
Over 500	13.8	6.6	8.6	4.1

[a] *Soles* per CI member.
[b] Percentage of capital ownership in the enterprise.

plain did not receive any benefits. The generally low number of complaints from CIs in enterprises with less than 20 workers, among which 70% never complained to the OCLA, is an indicator of the highly marginal situation of these CIs.[21] In my sample, only 37% of CIs in enterprises of this size had a file in the OCLA and a further 35% were officially recognized and registered, but for 28% of enterprises the recognition and registration of their CI was lacking. The CIs that did exist received extremely low benefits (e.g., 79% of these CIs owned less than 5% of the capital of their enterprise, and 48% of these enterprises distributed less than 4000 *soles* in cash per CI member). Also, workers received generally low wages: an average of 3700 *soles* per month, as compared to an average of 4500 *soles* for workers in enterprises with more than 20 workers. The obvious reason for this unfavorable situation was the lack of union organization and experience, which resulted in a state of acquiescence and inability to demand compliance with the law through complaints to the OCLA. An experienced advisor of CIs states that it was in these small enterprises that the most flagrant violations occurred and that ignorance about the fundamental rights of the CI was most frequent (Santistevan 1974:158). Consequently, the law about small enterprise passed in March 1976, which raised the limits for exemption from the requirement to establish a CI, can be seen primarily as an adaptation of the law to reality. Though the already existing CIs in the enterprises that fell below the new limits were to remain in existence, they could be

[21] Enterprises with less than 20 workers constitute 29% of my sample, and employ 4% of the workers. However, this size category is somewhat underrepresented in my sample because its response rate in industrial statistics, which is the basis for my sample, is lower than that of bigger size categories. Therefore, a greater number of industrial workers than the 4% appearing here were actually in this situation of marginality in relation to the CI.

expected to make even less progress than before, due to less outside official support, which would be absolutely essential for their development.

Effect of the CI on Strike Behavior

For an assessment of the general effect of the CI on the level of conflict between capital and labor, one has to go beyond the analysis of complaints from the CI. The conflicts manifesting themselves in these complaints were created by the law introducing the CI, and one might assume that the high degree of conflict was an indicator of the great interest taken in the CI by the workers. Hopeful promoters of the CI might even argue that a transformation of labor relations was taking place, insofar as workers tried to advance their interests through the CI by way of orienting union activity towards the CI and participation in the enterprise.

The answer to this argument, and to the question about the extent to which workers identified as co-owners and co-managers of their enterprise, has to be sought in an analysis of strike behavior. Did strikes decline due to the introduction of the CI? Did the distribution of high cash and ownership benefits through the CI have a moderating effect on strikes?

Ideally, one would like time series data on strikes to answer these questions. However, strike statistics with strikes per enterprise as unit of analysis have only been systematically collected since 1973. Therefore, one has to take global figures for the industrial sector as an indicator of a potential moderating effect of the introduction of the CI. Table 4.10 shows an interesting pattern of variation: Between 1969 and 1971 the number of strikes declined in all sectors compared to the last years of the Belaúnde government, but the relative decline in the industrial manufacturing sector was steeper than the relative decline in the economy as a whole. During these years, highly advantageous wage settlements were reached by unions, allowing wages in the modern urban sector to grow by 5% annually (Webb 1975:112–113). One might even argue that the CI contributed to this decline in 1970 and 1971 through an initial "wait-and-see" moderating effect. But in 1972, already the number of strikes started increasing, and in 1973 a tremendous increase in the number of strikes as well as in the total number of workers involved and man-hours lost in the industrial sector paralleled the increase in the economy as a whole. This was after the CI had been in existence for 2 years and could have had a moderating impact. Clearly, it is impossible to single out the effect of the CI as causal factor for the development of strikes since 1970, as the CI was but one element in a reform process which introduced various types of changes. The main reasons for the great overall increase in the number of strikes were the general process of mobilization and union organization which took place under the military gov-

Table 4.10
Total Number of Strikes, Man-Hours Lost, and Workers Involved, 1965–1975; All Sectors, and Manufacturing Only[a]

Year	All sectors						Manufacturing only			
	Strikes		Man-hours lost		Workers involved		Strikes			
	Number	Index	Number[b]	Index	Number	Index	Number	Index	Man-hours lost[b]	Workers involved
1965	397	100.0	6,421	100.0	135,586	100.0	191	100.0		
1966	394	99.2	11,689	182.0	121,232	89.4	191	100.0		
1967	414	104.3	8,373	130.4	142,282	104.9	207	108.4		
1968	364	91.7	3,378	52.6	107,809	79.5	198	103.7		
1969	372	93.7	3,889	60.6	91,531	67.5	143	74.9		
1970	345	86.9	5,782	90.0	110,990	81.9	136	71.2		
1971	377	95.0	10,882	169.5	161,415	119.1	184	96.3	3,140	42,577
1972	409	103.0	6,331	98.6	130,643	96.4	259	135.6	4,430	62,119
1973	788	198.5	15,688	244.3	416,251	307.0	423	221.5	5,335	112,196
1974	570	143.6	13,413	208.1	362,737	267.5	316	163.9	4,597	86,507
1975	779	196.2	20,269	315.7	617,120	455.2	427	224.1	5,431	133,942

Sources: Ministerio de trabajo, *Las huelgas en el Perú, 1957–1972.* Lima, 1973; and calculations by the author on the basis of unpublished statistics from the Ministry of Labor and from the ILO *Yearbook of Labor Statistics,* 1976.
[a]Index for base year 1965 = 100.0.
[b]In thousands.

ernment, intensifying rather than eliminating class struggle, within enterprises as well as at the level of national politics.[22] The deteriorating economic situation also contributed to the higher strike rate. Though the economic crisis did not make its full impact felt until 1975, its first tangible signs for workers came in 1974, when the steady increase in real wages since 1968 was suddenly reversed. Two arguments about the impact of the CI on the development of the strike rate may be made. First, it failed to counteract the impact of deteriorating economic conditions and wages on strike behavior, insofar as it failed to transform the identification of workers as dependent wage earners into an identification as co-owners of the enterprise. Second, the CI contributed to the process of mobilization and organization, and thus had an indirect impact on the increasing strike rate by raising the workers' potential for collective action. Of course, one might also argue that the contribution of the CI to this mobilization and organization process was small, and that overall the number of strikes would have increased even more without the supposedly integrative effect of the CI. This argument can only be supported or contradicted by a cross-sectional analysis comparing the effect of differential amounts of benefits distributed by the CI on strike behavior in comparable enterprises.

Two measures for strike activity could be computed on the basis of my data: total number of strikes within an enterprise from 1973 to 1975 and total number of man-hours lost per worker by an enterprise in this time period. Since both measures showed generally the same relationships with the independent variables in the analyses, and since the second one combines several dimensions into one statistic, giving an indication of the depth of conflicts, this measure is used for the presentation of the results.

A highly obvious relationship exists between size of the workforce and strike-proneness: Enterprises with less than 20 workers lost no man-hours at all; and 96% among those with 20–100 workers lost less than 2 days per worker; but 54% of those with 100–499 workers lost 2 or more days per worker, and fully 88% of those with over 500 workers lost that much. One might suspect the relation between size and strikes to be a spurious one, caused by presence of a union. In fact, Table 4.11 shows that where there was no union, there was practically no strike activity, with the exception of one size category.[23] However, this table also shows that the relationship with size holds up when the

---

[22]A more detailed discussion of strikes and their causes will follow in Chapter 6.

[23]The most probable explanation for this exception is that there is a union without official recognition in these enterprises, which would be coded as absence of a union in my data, because the data base is the register of unions in the Ministry of Labor. The existence of a nonrecognized union is a very rare case, because the union cannot bring any affairs to the Ministry of Labor, where most labor relations questions are settled. However, in certain cases recognition has been withheld for a considerable time, or withdrawn from a union for political reasons.

Table 4.11
Strike Activity in Manufacturing Industry by Size and Type of Union Presence

	Mean number of man-hours lost per worker, 1973–1975, in enterprises within size category:			
Type of union present in the enterprise	20–49	50–99	100–499	Over 500 workers
Unionized	39.7	12.4	69.2	137.1
Not unionized	0.5	0.1	18.4	0.0
Only old union	0.0	6.1	57.2	138.1
New union (only, or in addition to old union)	46.3	15.2	73.6	143.7
Only blue-collar or mixed		12.2	52.7	134.2
Blue-collar or mixed *and* white-collar union		39.7	97.7	153.5

presence of a union is controlled for. Bigger enterprises with a union still had considerably more strikes than smaller ones with a union.

This finding was confirmed in a regression analysis on the total number of man-hours lost per worker, where size of the workforce turned out to be the strongest predictor, entered as first variable (Table 4.12). This is not surprising from a comparative point of view: There are frequent references in the literature on industrial relations to studies in different settings which have shown that size of enterprise is an important determinant of strike activity.[24] One explanation relates strike activity to industrial morale and makes the assumption that morale is generally lower in bigger enterprises. Another explanation states that paternalism, which serves as a restraining factor on strike activity, is less likely to occur in bigger enterprises. I would argue for the importance of an additional factor: The subjective sense of strength and capacity for successful strike action. This confidence can be assumed to grow with the pure number of co-workers and with frequency of interaction and communication among blue-collar workers exclusively, without interference from management, which is facilitated by greater size of the enterprise. This is essentially the same argument which can be used to explain the greater militancy of the CI in bigger enterprises, the common dimension being a sense of capacity for collective action.

The second variable entered in the regression was presence of a new union (i.e., a union formed after 1970). This is different compared to the role of old and new unions in the CI, where presence of an old union increased militancy measured in total number of complaints decidedly more than presence of a

---

[24]Cleland (1955) makes this point in a study of industrial enterprises in the Trenton area, and Revans (1960) bases the same conclusion on a comparison of British coal mines.

Table 4.12
Regression on Total Number of Man-Hours Lost per Worker in 1973–1975, in all Enterprises with a Recognized CI and more than Twenty Workers[a]

Independent variables	Beta	Simple r
Number of CI members	0.27	0.37
Presence of a new union	0.21	0.25
Average blue-collar remuneration per year	0.12	0.26
10% cash distribution of profits through CI	−0.11	0.02
Presence of an old union	0.08	0.19
Proportion of enterprise capital owned by the CI	0.06	0.04
Increase in average remuneration 1971 to 1973	0.06	0.15

[a] $R^2 = 0.20$; $N = 1075$.

new union. Militancy in strike behavior, however, was higher among new than among firmly established unions—a phenomenon that can generally be observed in all countries.[25] For the Peruvian case, the following explanation was given by the Minister of Labor who had been in charge during this period.[26] For most newly recognized unions, their first action was to go on strike in order to gain respect both among the workers and management. Then, the dispute would be brought to the Ministry of Labor, where long delays occurred due to an insufficient capacity to handle all these new cases, and a new strike was called to protest against these delays. The difference in strike proneness between old and new unions also appears in Table 4.11, which shows a consistently higher average of man-hours lost for enterprises with new than with old unions only, within each size category.

As further explanation for higher strike rates in bigger enterprises the degree of unionization of white-collar workers could be mentioned. White-collar unions existed almost exclusively in enterprises with more than 100 workers. Only 1% of enterprises with 50–99 workers had both a blue-collar or mixed and white-collar union, whereas 30% with 100–499 workers and 56% with more than 500 workers did.[27] Enterprises with both types of unions in fact did show a consistently higher average of man-hours lost per worker than did those with only blue-collar or mixed unions (Table 4.11).

The third variable entered in the regression was the average blue-collar remuneration level. Several explanations can be offered for the fact that better-off workers were more strike prone. Higher paid workers are generally in a bet-

[25] See Ross and Hartman (1960) on this point.

[26] Interview with General Sala Orosco, Minister of Labor from 1970 to 1974, Lima, April 1976.

[27] The reason why blue-collar and mixed unions are grouped into one category for this analysis is that mixed unions were almost exclusively dominated by blue-collar workers. A mixed union provided the possibility for white-collar workers to join, which was not done frequently in practice, though.

ter position to endure loss of income through strikes, thanks to a stronger material base. Also, enterprises with higher average remuneration levels can be assumed to have a more skilled workforce; and skilled workers have greater organizational capacities to carry out strikes. And finally, reverse causality may be operating: Enterprises with a more militant workforce in 1973–1975 probably had had a comparatively more militant workforce before, which therefore had obtained higher remuneration levels by 1973.

Finally, as a fourth variable, the amount of cash received by the workers from the enterprise through the CI was entered, showing a moderating effect on strike behavior. This indicates that the CI had at least a certain potential to develop into an integrative institution. The main factors that kept this potential from developing on a large scale were purposeful evasion of profit distribution on the part of entrepreneurs, and the general increase of mobilization and organization resulting from the reform process.

The rank order of importance of the different variables emerging from this regression, though, indicates that this organization process would probably have offset the integrative effect of the CI even given greater compliance with the law on the part of entrepreneurs. The rapid proliferation of unions involved a high degree of mobilization, and it entailed the institutionalization of a greater capacity for collective action of the working class. The development of solidaristic ties between unions constituted a potential for activation of this capacity for purposeful coordinated action, particularly if connected to the fostering of a shared commitment to a socialist transformation among the new unions. This was clearly recognized by the government, and efforts were made to prevent such an organizationally and ideologically independent development of union organization (see Chapter 6).

A comparison with the Chilean experience highlights the importance of entrepreneurial resistance against the CI for high strike militancy in Peru. In both countries, labor organization and mobilization increased during the period of development of workers' participation. Enterprises in the Chilean social area, however, provided possibilities for workers to exercise real influence through the participation scheme. Thus increased mobilization stimulated fuller development of effective participation. High rates of worker participation in the various decision-making bodies led to social and economic changes in the enterprise, which in turn increased productivity and worker discipline and lowered strike rates in these enterprises.[28] This stands in stark contrast to developments in Peru. The Peruvian participation design did not provide any possibilities for workers to exercise real influence on decision making within the enterprise. Where mobilization led to greater demands for real participation, or just for

---

[28]Espinosa and Zimbalist (1978:127–175) show that high rates of participation had a variety of effects, such as changes in work organization, in product lines, in wage determination, in absenteeism, thefts, strikes, etc.

full implementation of the CI law, entrepreneurial resistance stiffened even further. Blocked demands and unfulfilled expectations resulted in frustration, and thus the increase in labor mobilization caused an escalation of conflicts and of militant strike action.

Obviously, this difference was conditioned by the larger political process, in particular the form of ownership of the enterprises in which workers' participation took place. If greater possibilities for real participation had been granted to the workers through legislation in Peru, entrepreneurial resistance would most likely still have thwarted workers' capacity to effect changes significant enough to moderate even temporarily the conflict between labor and capital. Furthermore, autonomous mobilization by unions with links to political forces committed to a socialist transformation would have sustained pressures on the government for transfer of an ever larger share of control rights to the workers. Therefore, the unavoidable full confrontation with the private sector over an extension of workers' participation rights was regarded as a politically undesirable trade-off by a majority of members of the military government.

In Chile, on the other hand, the full development of workers' participation in the social area enterprises was regarded as politically desirable by a majority of the members of Allende's government, the notable exception being members of the Communist Party. Resistance from state-appointed administrators found little outside support, and it happened that under strong worker pressure such administrators were fired and a worker from the factory appointed in their place. Political support for participation, then, had a moderating effect on resistance from administrators and thus on conflicts and strike activity in the social area in Chile,[29] whereas the lack of it had a reinforcing effect on entrepreneurial resistance and thus on conflicts and strike activity in the reformed private sector in Peru.

The variable entered as fifth in importance in the regression was presence of an old union, which means that old unions were not acquiescent, but that they were clearly less strike prone than new ones. The sixth variable entered was percentage of capital ownership of the CI, showing a positive relation to strike activity. The rank order of importance of this variable confirms the argument made in relation to its impact on the total number of complaints from the CI: Percentage of capital ownership of the CI had less importance for the behavior of workers than the amount of cash received by them through the CI. One way to explain the positive relationship between capital ownership and strike prone-

[29]Strike activity in the Chilean private sector, however, increased greatly during the Allende years, as will be discussed in Chapter 6. No participation design was introduced into privately owned enterprises. The very steep increase in unionization and strike activity was a reflection of the political struggle between the forces defending the status quo and those promoting a socialist transformation.

ness is to assume that strike proneness rather than capital ownership was the causal variable. Consistent behavior of a militant workforce would manifest itself in strikes as well as in pressures on the enterprise to comply with the law and transfer the due amount of shares to the CI. The problem with this explanation is that the percentage of enterprise capital owned by the CI was influenced not only by compliance with the law, which could be affected by pressures from the workforce, but also by the amount of reinvestment on part of the enterprise.

Another way in which one might want to explain this relationship is in terms of Korpi's power difference model of conflict. He proposes a curvilinear relationship between the differences in power resources between two parties and the probability of manifest conflict between them (Korpi 1978:40). If one regards the percentage of enterprise capital owned by the CI as a power resource available to the workforce, then strikes should have been more likely to occur in enterprises where the CI owned a greater percentage of capital. This explanation is problematic as well, because the capital owned by the CI did not really constitute a power resource. It entitled the CI to receive dividends, which went into the General Fund. Only part of this fund could be freely disposed of by the CI, however, and it could absolutely not be used for union purposes, least of all as a strike fund. There were some instances where CIs gave or lent money to a union, nonunionized CI members complained, and the MIT reacted sharply, insisting on immediate return of the money. The fact that all employees of an enterprise, including nonowner members of management, were CI members, virtually guaranteed that such irregularities in the use of CI funds would be detected, reported, and censured. Thus the first explanation offered here appears more appropriate, despite the weakness of capital ownership as indicator of compliance of the enterprise with the law.

The last variable entered in the regression—the difference between average remuneration levels in 1971 and 1973—was intended to measure the impact of workers' satisfaction with their present situation on strike behavior. The assumption underlying this measure was that aspirations and consequently relative deprivation or gratification would be determined by past experience. If relative gratification or deprivation did have an influence on strike behavior, one would expect a negative relationship between the average increase in remuneration levels from 1971 to 1973 and strike proneness. However, the relationship emerging in the regression was positive. This might be interpreted by again resorting to the explanation used for the positive relation between absolute level of average blue-collar remuneration and strike proneness (i.e., a reversal in the direction of causality). Greater militancy in 1973–1975 was related to militancy in 1971–1973, which in turn caused greater average wage increases between 1971 and 1973.

In separate regressions, I examined the impact of two further variables as indicators of relative deprivation or gratification on strike behavior.[30] One indicator I used was the difference between average blue-collar and white-collar remuneration levels in the same enterprise. The second indicator was "CI importance," based on the assumption that the importance of the cash distribution from the CI would depend on its amount compared to a worker's general income level. The measure for "CI importance" was calculated by dividing cash distribution per worker in 1973 by remuneration per worker in 1973. Both of these indicators of psychological state turned out to be the weakest variables in the regressions; size and presence of a new union remained consistently the most important determinants.

Given that both strike behavior and militancy of the CI through complaints were to the largest part determined by the presence of unions, the actual relationship between CI and union(s) as two legally separate institutions has to be examined more closely. Entrepreneurs complained that the CI in practice was nothing but an extended arm of the union and a weapon for class struggle, quite contrary to the intention of the legislators to clearly separate the two institutions and to have the CI serve an integrative function.

Relations between the CI and Unions

A comparison of patterns of militancy of the two institutions within the same enterprise does show a clear consistency; enterprises with militant unions tended to have militant CIs. The zero-order correlation between total number of complaints from the CI and total number of man-hours lost per worker is .41. Examining this relationship within the different size categories, one can see that CIs in enterprises where 2 or more days per worker were lost through strikes brought a higher average number of complaints to the OCLA than CIs in enterprises with less strike activity—a consistent relationship within each size category (Table 4.13).

The same difference appears between average number of man-hours lost per worker in enterprises with zero or one complaint, and in those with two or more complaints. This relationship can be explained in two complementary ways: First as a straight result of the degree of organization, cohesion, and experience reached by the workforce; and second, as a result of the interaction of the strength of the workforce and the type of attitude assumed by the employer. If one assumes uniform resistance from entrepreneurs against the CI, one can

[30]The reason why I had to perform separate regression analyses with these variables was the problem of multicollinearity. Since these variables were derived from the same basic measures, they were highly correlated with each other and thus could not be entered in one and the same regression. For reasons of space and repetitiveness I am not going to present these separate tables.

Table 4.13

Militancy of Workforce in Complaints of CI and Strikes by Size[a]

Total number of man-hours lost per worker	Average number of complaints from CIs within size group:			
	20–49	50–99	100–499	Over 500 workers
Less than 2 days	0.85	1.8	2.1	4.7
2 and more days	2.4	4.7	8.6	9.3
Total number of complaints from CI	Average number of man-hours lost per worker in enterprises with:			
	20–49	50–99	100–499	Over 500 workers
0–1	8.6	12.0	29.3	118.6
2 and more	22.1	4.0	79.6	139.6

[a]N = 1758.

argue that the degree of strength of the workforce, indicated by its capacity for strike action, also determined its capacity for action in defense of the CI. If the workers had learned to exert pressure on the employer through strikes, they could be expected to defend their rights as CI members through complaints to the OCLA. If one assumes certain variations in the behavior of employers toward the CI, related to their behavior towards labor in general, one can make the following argument. If the employer was a hard negotiator vis-à-vis the union, he could be expected to adopt an equally inflexible and hostile attitude vis-à-vis the CI, and thus a strong workforce could be expected to react with high militancy in strikes and in complaints. If, on the contrary, employer and union had worked out a less conflictual relationship, the same type of relationship could be expected to prevail between CI and employer, thus reducing militancy in both strikes and complaints.[31] This finding and interpretation, however, only imply that the general character of labor relations found its

[31]This second interpretation of my findings would support the hypotheses about four probable types of relations between CI and employer, based on the type of capital–labor relations within the enterprise, formulated by Santistevan and Pásara. They distinguish four basic possible constellations, depending on the nature of the workforce and the attitude of the employer. They dichotomize into organized and unorganized workforce, and traditional and flexible attitude of the employer. They hypothesize that in the case of an organized workforce and a traditional employer conflicts are most likely to emerge, as workers try to use the CI as a weapon in the struggle for better working conditions, and employers try to obstruct the development of the CI. In the case of an organized workforce and a flexible employer, they predict a more routinized collaboration, with the possibility for serious conflicts only in crisis situations that might threaten layoffs. An unorganized workforce vis-à-vis a traditional employer is assumed to either remain under authoritarian domination in the CI, or feel the need for the formation of a union to defend their rights as CI members. In the case of an unorganized workforce and a flexible employer, they predict a reduction of disputes to a minimum and a passive role of the CI. Santistevan and Pásara (1973:127–142).

expression in strikes as well as complaints from the CI; it does not imply that the directing bodies of the CI were totally manipulated by the union as most employers complained. Accordingly, the question of relations between CI and union requires some further discussion.

The Pacífico Study claims that the CI in fact had a high degree of autonomy, based on answers of CI leaders and members to the question of who would control or take the initiative in the CI: 88% of CI leaders claimed that it was they as leaders, or the workers themselves who would do so; 7% said it was the government, SINAMOS, or CONACI[32]; 5% said it was the management of the enterprise, but none said it was union leaders. CI members responded slightly differently: 74% mentioned leaders or members of the CI; 10% the government, SINAMOS, or CONACI; 9% management; and 7% union leaders. However, one has to keep in mind that these were the officially correct answers, which could be expected to be given in an interview for a MIT-sponsored project. Therefore, a more penetrating investigation of the relation between CI and union is needed.

One factor, which was definitely an obstacle to total domination of the CI by the union was the CI membership of all persons employed in the enterprise, including highest level management, unless they were shareholders in their company. The relation between CI and union(s) then depended on the activity and orientation of white-collar employees and the presence of white-collar unions, as well as on the interest taken in the CI by blue-collar unions.

Unfortunately, my data on relations between union and CI are not exhaustive, because only active collaboration or conflict that appeared in correspondence to the OCLA could be included. Yet, in about one-third of all unionized enterprises, active collaboration or conflict between union and CI was mentioned in this correspondence. In addition to conflict between union and the CI, a high incidence of internal conflict in the CI was reported, which included cases where a group of members complained to the OCLA about the CI Council or other members trying to impose their will on the CI. Since it could not always be determined whether the union was or was not involved at least informally in such disputes, conflicts between union and CI were also coded and included as internal conflict. This raises the percentage of enterprises with a union, for which some type of collaboration or conflict was reported to about half (Table 4.14).

On the whole, there was a slightly higher percentage of collaboration than conflict between CI and union. The fact that both collaboration and conflict appear to have been higher in bigger enterprises is probably a result of the greater number of complaints from these CIs to the OCLA, which of course

---

[32]CONACI stands for *Confederación Nacional de Comunidades Industriales*, National Confederation of Industrial Communities. For a discussion of its emergence and role, see Chapter 5.

Table 4.14
Relations between CI and Union(s) by Type of Union Presence and by Size[a]

| | Percentage of CIs within size group reporting: | | | | | | | | | | | | | | |
| Type of union present in the enterprise | Collaboration between CI and union(s) | | | | | Conflict between CI and union(s) | | | | | Internal conflict in CI | | | | |
	All	20–49	50–99	100–499	500+	All	20–49	50–99	100–499	500+	All	20–49	50–99	100–499	500+
Only blue-collar or mixed union	19	7	16	30	50	9	13	0	16	25	24	14	25	28	81
Blue-collar or mixed and white-collar union	22	—	—	14	63	30	—	—	33	21	49	—	—	47	63
All unionized	19	7	16	24	55	13	13	0	22	21	29	14	25	35	69

[a] N = 756.

raised the probability of collaboration or conflict being mentioned in the correspondence. However, the incidence of internal conflict was in reality probably also higher in bigger enterprises, due to (1) the number of actors in interaction raising the probability of conflict, and (2) the higher probability of active participation of higher white-collar employees as a group, and/or of lower- and middle-level white-collar employees through a separate union. In smaller enterprises, the social distance between higher-level employees and blue-collar workers caused a certain reluctance among the former to participate in assemblies of the CI, particularly where the blue-collar workers were organized and a paternalistic domination of the CI by these higher-level employees was impossible. Also, in smaller enterprises there were no separate white-collar unions. In bigger enterprises, however, higher-level employees could act as a group and make at least their voice heard as a sizeable minority, even if the governing bodies of the CI were dominated by an organized blue-collar workforce. Such participation clearly raised the probability of internal conflict in the CI, given the diverging views and interests of the two groups. Furthermore, in bigger enterprises the existence of separate white-collar unions was more likely.

The role of white-collar unions seemed overall somewhat ambiguous. In earlier sections of this chapter, I showed that presence of a white-collar union increased the average number of man-hours lost per worker through strikes (Table 4.11). However, it did not increase the average number of complaints from the CI. CIs in enterprises with 100–499 workers, where both a blue-collar or mixed and a white-collar union existed brought an average of 6.2 complaints to the OCLA, as compared to 6.6 complaints from CIs in enterprises with a blue-collar or mixed union only. CIs in enterprises with more than 500 workers even had a lower average of complaints when a white-collar union was present: 7.2 complaints from CIs in enterprises with, and 12.0 complaints from CIs in enterprises without a white-collar in addition to a blue-collar or mixed union. This casts doubt on the assumption of greater capacity for collective action based on greater solidarity among the workforce due to unionization of both blue- and white-collar workers. This doubt is reinforced by the overall somewhat higher incidence of conflict between CI and union, as well as of general internal conflict reported for enterprises with both blue-collar or mixed and white-collar union than for those with blue-collar or mixed union only (Table 4.14). The alternative assumption to the one of solidarity and mutual support in struggles with the enterprise would be that blue- and white-collar unions tried to promote their particular interests through the CI, just as they promoted their separate interests through independent strikes. As an example for a legally structured divergence of interests, the original mode of distribution of the 10% of profits in cash can be mentioned: Blue-collar unions had been demanding equal distribution, whereas white-collar unions had been mostly in favor of keeping the original mode of distribution, based partly on basic remuneration.

Apart from these divergencies of interests reinforced by the distinction between blue- and white-collar labor legislation, the lack of solidarity between blue- and white-collar unions has to be seen as a result of the political legacy weakening the Peruvian labor movement. In the period under study, many white-collar unions were still affiliated to the APRA-controlled white-collar union federation CSEPP *(Central Sindical de Empleados Particulares del Perú,* Central Union Organization of White-Collar Employees of Peru), whereas most industrial blue-collar unions were affiliated with the Communist-controlled CGTP. The hatred and therefore impossibility of collaboration between these labor organizations was probably greater than that between APRA-controlled unions and the employers.

However, not all white-collar unions were APRA-controlled, and not in all cases did presence of a white-collar union increase the reported incidence of conflict between CI and union, and of internal conflict in the CI. For instance, among enterprises with more than 500 workers, greater collaboration and fewer conflicts were reported if both blue-collar or mixed and white-collar unions were present (Table 4.14). This variation from the overall pattern can be interpreted as indicating the importance of the attitude assumed by individual unions—both in relation to the CI and in relation to the idea of worker solidarity—for the development of relations between blue- and white-collar unions and thus between CI and unions. Since these attitudes are predominantly shaped by the central organization to which individual unions are affiliated, this interpretation in turn supports the point about the impact of societal-level linkages on enterprise-level processes.

This point is also supported by Espinosa and Zimbalist's findings in the Chilean context. They measured political party support among the workforce by calculating the percentage of votes for candidates with different party affiliations in the 1972 elections to the national union leadership. Their expectation that large numbers of votes for the Communist and the Christian Democratic candidates would have a restrictive effect on the development of participation was borne out. A combined measure for the size of the two types of votes explains 40.6% of the variance in their participation index. In contrast, a large vote for the Socialist Party and other left parties had a reinforcing effect on participation. The authors argue that the influence of the political parties worked via ideological influence as well as via concrete actions taken by elected officials affiliated to a party at the enterprise level (Espinosa and Zimbalist 1978:105–108). Thus the societal-level strength of the various parties, that is, their total number of members and sympathizers, shaped the overall development of participation significantly. And power struggles between the parties at the societal level were reflected in struggles at the enterprise level: Where political loyalties of the workforce were split among various parties, conflicts tended to emerge and have a negative effect on the development of participation.

In the Peruvian case, a further factor, in addition to the role of white-collar unions and the divergence of interests among different members of the CI, according to their position in the enterprise, can be mentioned as explanation for the generally high incidence of conflict between CI and unions and of internal conflict within the CI: initial indifference or hostility toward the CI on the part of a certain number of unions. Where unions failed to recognize the potential usefulness of the CI and to support candidates in the first council elections, higher-level employees were able to dominate the CI Council in the beginning. Many of these employees would either identify with the company or employer due to their position in the internal hierarchy, or they could be co-opted into collaboration (e.g., into accepting fraudulent accounts that showed low profits to be distributed to the CI). In most of these cases, unions started to attack such councils and managed to have their candidates win the second council elections, which according to the law had to be held after 2 years. This explanation then suggests that there would have been less collaboration and more conflict between CI and union in the early years of the CI, before the union would gain influence over the CI council by way of having its candidates elected. My data allowed for a partial examination of this expected relationship only, as time periods could not be separated for the majority of enterprises in the sample.[33] However, for 486 enterprises they could be separated, and 333 among them had a union established before 1970 and consequently lent themselves to an examination of this question. The expected relationship in fact did occur: In the earlier period, a higher percentage of conflict between CI and union was reported than in the later period—17% compared to 5%, and more collaboration was reported in the later than in the earlier period—17% compared to 6%. In a similar way, reported internal conflict also declined from the earlier to the later period—from 27% to 17%.

Summary and Implications

The analysis of the development of the CI reform at the enterprise level first of all confirmed that the introduction of the CI as participation design had the opposite effect from the integrative that a majority of the government intended it to have. Instead of reconciling interests of capital and labor and harmonizing

[33]The reason is that in general I analyzed and coded the information for the whole time period without keeping track of the dates. For these enterprises, however, the information for the earlier period was physically separated and had to be collected from a Central Archive, which resulted in separate notes that made this comparison possible in the analysis stage.

labor relations, the CI created a great number of conflicts about its implementation, and it failed to impede a tremendous increase in strike activity. Insofar as the conflicts between CI and enterprise sharpened the workers' perception of a basic conflict of interests and consequently the need for collective action through the formation of unions, the CI even contributed to the increases in strike activity.

Again, a short reference to the Chilean experience is instructive. In both cases, the introduction of workers' participation and the whole reform process raised mobilization, and this mobilization gained a certain momentum that escaped the control of the government and had effects that were contrary to the government's intentions. Though the Chilean reform had never been intended to have an integrative, class-conciliatory effect, it had an at least partly unintended and undesired demonstration effect on workers in the private sector. It contributed to the occurrence of factory occupations and takeovers at a faster pace than was acceptable to a majority of the political leadership, given their commitment to respecting legality in the process of socialist transformation. In Peru, the growing intensity of demands for an acceleration of the reform process toward a socialist transformation made by strengthened working-class organizations constituted a threat to the government's capacity to control the pace and direction of the process. And the use of the strike weapon to reinforce pressures for satisfaction of labor's demands rose way beyond what the government considered tolerable.

The findings in the analysis of developments at the enterprise level consistently pointed to the domineering impact of two factors: the role of unions and the size of the workforce. The role and impact of unions varied according to their length of existence and the degree of consolidation they had reached, as well as according to the presence of white-collar unions. The varying impact of white-collar unions on relations between CI and unions, and on the degree of internal conflict in the CI, suggested that the ideological position assumed by unions, and consequently their affiliation to a central organization with a given political position, was important in the development of participation processes at the enterprise level. Further evidence for the impact of the linkage of unions to central national organizations will be presented in the analysis of their strike behavior in Chapter 6. The point to be emphasized here is that the analysis of relations between CI and enterprise provided evidence in support of my contention that the effects of any given structural design of participation depend on the dynamics between sociopolitical forces in societal-level processes by showing (1) that the amount of benefits received by the workers through the CI had a small impact on the development of relations between CI and enterprise in particular, and labor relations in general; (2) that the development of participation at the enterprise level was predominantly shaped by the involvement of unions, whose behavior varied according to their links to actors at the societal level; and (3) that general governmental policies vis-à-vis foreign investment had an impact on the relations between CI and enterprises under foreign ownership.

Thus participation through the CI at the enterprise level was strongly shaped by dynamics at the societal level, but the CI also had a feedback effect on the constellation of sociopolitical forces. By contributing to the overall process of mobilization and organization, the CI raised the level of open conflict in relations between labor and capital. This increase in conflicts could not be regarded as temporary, even if a revision of the CI legislation had eliminated the major violations causing conflict. The increase in unionization and the emergence of a new organization of CIs at the national level[34] led to the institutionalization of a higher level of social conflict, and to a permanent change in the relations between sociopolitical forces. Greater unionization brought with it a higher potential for collective action of urban labor, and consequently a greater potential strength of labor as a sociopolitical force. However, this potential failed to be fully activated and consolidated so as to provide an actual and permanent power base through which labor could effectively demand a progressive redistribution of control and income rights. Purposeful policies on the part of the government successfully impeded a decisive strengthening of labor as a sociopolitical force capable of pressuring for a socialist transformation. Instead, interests of domestic and foreign capital owners gained increasing influence on governmental policies, until they finally brought the reform process to a halt, and caused partial reversal. This struggle between sociopolitical forces at the societal level, mobilizing their resources in resistance against basic changes in the capitalist order, or in defense of the reform process and in support of an acceleration of fundamental changes toward a socialist transformation, as well as the government's interference in this struggle, will be the focus of discussion in the following two chapters.

---

[34]The emergence of this organization will be discussed in Chapter 5.

5

Dynamics in the Constellation of Sociopolitical Forces I: Opposition against and Mobilization in Defense of the CI

In order to understand why the reform process took a more and more integrative course, away from fundamental transformations and toward a clear consolidation of the capitalist order that ultimately resulted in a curtailment of the participation scheme, it is necessary to investigate the interaction between the government and the major sociopolitical forces (i.e., private sector capitalists on the one hand and labor on the other hand). This investigation will focus on the resources at the disposal of these groups, on their intentions for purposeful use of these resources, on their capacity to act accordingly, and on the effectiveness of governmental intervention designed to reduce this capacity.

The introduction of the CI not only contributed to the mobilization and militancy of workers through the creation of conflicts at the enterprise level but also contributed to an overall increase in labor organization by generating a need for an organized defense of workers' participation rights and providing an organizational shelter for unionization activities. These dynamics contained a potential for growing strength of labor as a sociopolitical force pressuring the government to direct the reform process toward a socialist transformation.[1] The realization of this potential would have required the development of coherence, autonomy, and ideological unity among old and new labor organizations. Clearly, such a growing strength of labor presented a threat to the gov-

---

[1]An interesting parallel can be drawn to the abortive attempt at creating harmonious entities and demobilizing peasants through the establishment of agrarian cooperatives. Despite the fact that peasants were the owners of the cooperatives, union activity increased rather than decreased there, too. Social inequalities persisted, and conflict continued to manifest itself in hostilities against technicians and directors. Also, an increase in political activity occurred as peasants learned to articu-

ernment's goals of structuring relations between social groups from above and maintaining an autonomous arbiter position between them. And it was obviously completely unacceptable to the adherents of the integrative conception of participation. The internal divergencies of opinion within the elite about consolidation of the capitalist order or transformation toward a socialist order manifested themselves in bureaucratic competition concerning policies toward popular organizations, varying from support for mobilization to control and containment. As the integrative tendency gained the upper hand in this internal dispute, policies of containment of autonomous organizational growth came to dominate the government's relations to the urban working class.

The introduction of the CI constituted a major catalyst for entrepreneurial opposition and resistance against changes in the existing capitalist order. Before the CI, entrepreneurs had expressed moderate opposition against what they perceived as unnecessarily strong state interference in the economy. Upon introduction of the CI, however, the private sector started launching frontal attacks against the government's reform course, both because of the encroachment on their control and income rights through the CI itself, and because of the lack of credibility and clarification of the "rules of the game." Aside from frequent and harsh public attacks through the press, the private sector engaged in a virtual economic war with the government, purposefully withholding investment in order to prevent the implementation of governmental plans for economic development. The government's response consisted in attempts to elicit compliance and collaboration through persuasion and incentive strategies. Two major reasons prevented the government from resorting to more effective measures, such as greater transfer of control and income rights from the private sector to the state. The moderate and conservative members of the government insisted strongly on maintaining a relationship of dialogue and collaboration with the more flexible group among entrepreneurs. And the government as a whole had to be concerned about reactions from foreign capital and probable consequences in the form of economic sanctions. The government's failure to establish greater effective control over resources in the private sector, however, rendered entrepreneurial opposition against changes in the existing capitalist order increasingly effective.

---

late demands and channel them to regional authorities. This newly gained political capacity was frequently used against the government, that is, to resist implementation of government policies. The characteristic contrast between the political mobilization effects of the CI and the agrarian cooperatives lies in the pressures for socialist transformation generated by the former, compared to the conservative resistance against further changes generated by the latter. Whereas the CI sharpened class conflict and thus strengthened working-class solidarity, with the exception of a few cases, the cooperatives created a spirit of group solidarity among the owner-members and generalized hostility against outsiders. See McClintock (1977).

Entrepreneurial Opposition

Entrepreneurial opposition against the government's reform policies in general and the CI in particular manifested itself in three major ways: (1) through public attacks in the press questioning the legitimacy of the government's approach; (2) through the maneuvers to obstruct the functioning of the CI discussed in the last chapter; and (3) through a virtual investment strike. The arguments used to delegitimize the CI were couched in terms of its negative consequences for national development and of its collectivist nature alien to principles of the Peruvian Christian tradition. "In the proposed scheme, the property granted the workers is collective and not individual, thus excluding them from the right to private property; a right granted to man, as individual, by this Creator [from a communiqué of the SNI *(Sociedad Nacional de Industrias,* National Society of Industries), *El Comercio,* August 4, 1970]."

Predictions of stagnation of economic development and aggravation of the problem of unemployment due to the uncertainty about the future of private investors' control and income rights contained barely hidden threats of economic noncooperation on the part of the private sector. The government was accused of making an outright attempt to destroy private enterprises in Peru, the proof being that the rights of the CI in state enterprises and in others declared as strategic for national development were more restricted than in all other private enterprises.[2]

The government responded to this criticism and opposition with appeals to "progressive, dynamic, open-minded sectors" among entrepreneurs for open dialogue and collaboration in the interest of the nation's development, but initially it showed no susceptibility to pressures through policy changes at all. In his speech to the Annual Conference of Executives in October 1970, President Velasco proposed the formation of a National Front Against Underdevelopment, which was to bring the government, entrepreneurs, and labor representatives together for discussions of economic policy. However, despite support for the proposal from the private sector (see, e.g., *La Prensa,* November 20, 1970) and several subsequent trilateral meetings, the Front remained without any impact on the basic entrepreneurial opposition against the government's policies. The government, in turn, showed no willingness to formalize the Front in the sense of official interinstitutional negotiations, which would have run counter to its policy of weakening the organizational and institutional power of social groups. Consequently, the meetings simply stopped and the

---

[2]In state-owned and strategic enterprises, the CI received bonds issued by the National Development Corporation (COFIDE) instead of partcipation in ownership of enterprise capital, and participation in decision making was restricted to two representatives on the board of directors.

Front vanished. Whereas some entrepreneurial sectors, principally in export-oriented enterprises,[3] maintained an open dialogue with the government, the great majority rejected all further appeals for private sector contributions to national economic development.

Entrepreneurs started to make purposeful use of their resources, capital, in order to obstruct the implementation of the government's plans for economic development. By withholding investment, they intended to create economic difficulties and thus force the government to abandon its chosen course of reform. The proportion of private investment declined over all (Table 5.1), and particularly strongly in the industrial manufacturing sector (Table 5.2). The private capital that was invested in industrial manufacturing was mainly reinvestment in already existing enterprises in order to retain control vis-à-vis the advance of the CI in ownership. In 1973, 76.9% of private industrial investment went into already existing enterprises, and in 1974, 66.2% (*Ministerio de Industria y Turismo*, May 1976). Yet, according to Fitzgerald (1976:73–74), private investment was barely enough to cover replacement.

Instead of putting their resources to productive use, private sector capitalists channeled them into real estate speculation, construction for private purposes, into luxury items and conspicuous consumption. As Table 5.2 shows, private investment in housing showed no decline, but most of this construction was for upper-class and upper-middle-class consumers.

The fact that most investment was reinvestment in already existing enterprises had a number of negative consequences from the point of view of national economic development. The General Law of Industries (*D. L.* 18350, July 27, 1970) had categorized industrial activity according to its importance for permanent, self-sustained industrial development, assigning priorities to the various industrial sectors. First priority was assigned to production of basic industrial inputs and of capital goods, and to research and development of industrial technology. Second priority was assigned to production of goods to satisfy essential needs of the population and to serve as inputs for productive activities in other sectors. Third priority was assigned to production of nonessential consumer goods, and "no priority" to production of superfluous luxury consumption items. Basic industry (i.e., the production of basic industrial in-

---

[3]Two main reasons can be mentioned for this special relation between exporters and the government: first, favorable policies for stimulation of nontraditional exports in order to improve the trade balance; and second, personal rivalries within the National Society of Industries. These rivalries led to the formation of the Association of Exporters (ADEX) as a separate institution from the SNI in July of 1973, a period when relations between the government and the SNI had deteriorated to an absolute crisis point. Thus the government was favorably disposed toward the formation of this organization as a new channel of communication with the private sector. Also, export-oriented enterprises were mainly modern ones, frequently with professional management trained abroad, who were less threatened by the idea of worker's participation than were traditional entrepreneurs.

Table 5.1
Decline of Private Investment

Investment	Gross fixed capital formation as percentage of GDP			
	1960–1964	1965–1968	1969–1972	1973–1974
Private	14.6	10.7	7.7	7.5
Public	3.6	4.6	4.9	7.3
Total	18.2	15.3	12.6	14.8

Source: Fitzgerald (1976:22–23), Tables 14 and 15.

puts) was reserved for state-owned enterprises, or for private enterprises under a contract with the state. The measures used to promote first and second priority industrial activities were tax incentives concerning taxes on imports and reinvestment, differential credit policy on the part of the state development bank, and preferential treatment through public infrastructural, commercial, and technological assistance.

These incentives clearly failed to attract private investment in high priority sectors, since entrepreneurs were decided on jeopardizing the government's development plan, even if it was to their own short-term economic disadvantage. Through reinvestment in already existing enterprises they managed to obstruct rather than promote permanent, self-sustained development. First of all, this reinvestment led to a perpetuation of existing production patterns geared to middle- and upper-class consumption, and consequently to further industrial growth in low priority sectors. Second, it led to a growth of idle capacities in certain sectors, where the market had reached a point of saturation. Third, it hardly contributed to the creation of new jobs, as reinvestment was predominantly used to modernize equipment. Fourth, by perpetuating existing production patterns, which were heavily based on foreign technology and frequently even imports of industrial inputs, it aggravated the balance of payments prob-

Table 5.2
Fluctuations in Sectoral Allocation of Private Investment

Sector	Private investment as percentage of GDP	
	1965–1968	1969–1972
Manufacturing	2.2	1.2
Transport equipment	1.7	1.5
Housing	2.8	2.8
Other	4.0	2.2
Total	10.7	7.7

Source: Fitzgerald (1976:23), Table 16. These figures are estimates; Fitzgerald notes that no data about capital formation are published in aggregate sectoral form in Peru.

lem. And finally, it left the financial burden for the development of high priority industrial sectors to the state.

The two principal solutions to the problem of financing such investments sought by the state were public borrowing abroad and the creation of special mixed enterprises with state and foreign private capital. The creation of special mixed enterprises seemed to be the only possibility of attracting new foreign investment in industry. The combination of the fade-out provisions from Decision 24 of the Andean Pact with the law of CI constituted highly restrictive conditions for foreign investment in comparison to other Latin American countries. Not only were the activities of foreign enterprises subject to close supervision and the amount of their profit repatriation limited but their loss of control was more certain than in other member countries of the Andean Pact, due to participation of the CI. Consequently, foreign capital could only be attracted through provision of special protection, such as partnership with the state. Special mixed enterprises were supposed to become an important solution for reconciling the problems of need for foreign investment on the one hand and protection of national interests on the other hand. However, negotiations between the state and foreign capital turned out to be rather difficult and lengthy, such that by 1975 only three special mixed enterprises had been established, whereas negotiations for other projects had either not been concluded or not even been initiated yet.[4]

An alternative type of special protection (instead of majority state participation in ownership) that could be provided in order to attract foreign investment was the declaration of an enterprise as "strategic for national development." This meant that the enterprise was exempt from the requirement of granting participation in ownership and increasing participation in management to the CI. However, this form of solution was only applied in one case, for Bayer. In this company, the state participated initially with only 18.5% of capital; in 1972 this participation was raised to 30%, and at the same time Bayer's production of acrylic fibers as input for the textile industry was declared strategic for national development. Bayer provided the largest foreign private industrial investment under Velasco's leadership of the military government. However, Bayer remained a singular case, and consequently direct foreign investment under special agreements with the state supplied only a small proportion of Peruvian investment resources, the largest proportion being supplied by foreign loans to the government.

---

[4]The three special mixed enterprises were *Tractores Andinos*, with 49% Canadian capital; *Motores Diesel*, with 48% capital from Volvo and Perkins; and *Máquinas Herramientas* with 49% Rumanian capital. A list of 22 projects was presented to the World Bank in May 1974 (*Peruvian Times*, May 24, 1974). A general analysis of the treatment of foreign investment by the Peruvian government is made by Hunt (1976:302–349); and Durand (1975) discusses in particular the emergence of special mixed enterprises.

The implications of this reliance on foreign borrowing for the further course of the reform process will be discussed in Chapter 7. The point of the discussion here was to show how purposeful resistance on the part of private entrepreneurs succeeded in creating serious difficulties for the implementation not only of the workers' participation scheme, but of the government's economic development and reform program as a whole. Whereas the government seemed unable to weaken entrepreneurial capacity for resistance, or rather, unwilling to face possible consequences of such action, it showed greater ability in preventing the growth of labor's capacity to pressure for an acceleration and deepening of the reform process in the direction of a socialist transformation.

Labor's Countermobilization

The only possibility for workers to gain strength for the defense of the CI and other rights vis-à-vis entrepreneurial opposition and bureaucratic indifference was through the development of an organizational power base. The increase in unionization·strengthened labor's capacity for the pursuit and protection of rights in the area of wages and working conditions in particular, and also for assuming a generally assertive position vis-à-vis entrepreneurs. But since unions were legally excluded from handling any CI affairs, the need for the formation of a separate organization for the defense of rights in the area of participation was strongly felt. An organization legitimately linking individual CIs to each other was needed to provide assistance and solidaristic support in conflicts, as well as to represent CIs as a collectivity vis-à-vis the state bureaucracy and to act in the collective pursuit of CI interests as a pressure group. Clearly, leaders with experience in organizational and bureaucratic affairs gained through union activity were most prone to building up this new organization, and consequently the indirect influence of union presence was visible from the beginning throughout the whole development of the new organization.

Early contacts for common efforts in the defense of workers' rights as CI members were initiated by leaders of several large CIs, when the first presentation of enterprise accounts with the share of profits for the CI made the many violations of legal rights of the CI obvious, and a clear lack of effective protection of these rights on part of the state bureaucracy was experienced. Some of these large CIs formed a loose association, called CONACI (*Confederación Nacional de Comunidades Industriales*, National Confederation of Industrial Communities), which acted as representatives of member CIs in complaints to the OCLA and announced plans for the formation of a national organization as early as February 1971 (*Expreso*, February 4, 1971). As already indicated, these first contacts were initiated by CI leaders with previous union experience, and in October of 1971 a meeting was held in the local of the Federation of

Bank Employees (at that time affiliated to the Communist-controlled central union organization, CGTP).[5] In this meeting the decision was taken to organize a national congress out of which a national organization was to emerge, and an organizing committee was elected. The aim was primarily to bring public pressure to bear on the authorities for a clearer protection of rights already granted to the CI, and for an extension of these rights. In order to obtain support for these organizational efforts, the committee initiated contacts with SINAMOS, the governmental agency in charge of support for popular mobilization. However, the MIT was also needed as a participant in the organization process, because the OCLA as agency legally in charge of CI affairs had important functions such as requesting time off for delegates to organizational meetings from their respective employers. In December of 1971, the head of SINAMOS, Leonidas Rodríguez, and the Minister of Industry, Jiménez de Lucio, announced in a press conference their support for the organization of the congress, with the wish that "the discussions center around the exact spirit of the law, the principal aim of which is the integration of the enterprise in order to achieve its economic and social progress [*La Prensa*, December 18, 1971]."

Governmental Reactions

Despite this official expression of unanimous support for the integrative conception of the CI, bureaucratic conflict and competition emerged between the MIT and SINAMOS, the former promoting integration of workers into the capitalist order, and the latter mobilization for a socialist transformation. SINAMOS was set up in July 1971 as "System for Support of Popular Mobilization" in charge of organizing the population to "achieve the conscious and active participation of the national population in the tasks that economic and social development demand." Its purposes were (1) training, orientation and organization of the national population; (2) development of entities of social interest; and (3) communication and, particularly, dialogue between the government and the national population (*D.L.* 18896, July 2, 1971). Though the heads of eight out of ten regional SINAMOS offices were military officers (Palmer 1973:94), SINAMOS as a newly created agency drew most of its higher- and middle-level personnel from young radical civilians. Most of them

[5]Pásara (1974:196–198), who gives a very detailed account of the course of the congress, its preparation, and the later developments of CONACI, argues that there was no dominant political tendency, neither Aprista nor Communist, among the initiators of these efforts. The original CONACI, together with the CI from the newspapers *La Prensa* and *El Comercio*, formed the core group of organizers.

were young university graduates without party ties, and some of them were politically noncommitted technocrats, but others had held leftist political beliefs and commitments, though they declared their support for the Revolution above their other loyalties.

The Labor Area of SINAMOS was initially set up to support the implementation of workers' participation through the CI, both through organizational activities at the enterprise level, and through training courses for workers and their elected representatives. Several members of the Labor Area had worked as CI organizers in the OCLA under Minister Dellepiane and had left it after his resignation. They were adherents of the mobilizing conception of participation, and in their direct contact with workers, they propagated a class analysis of society and predominant social ownership of means of production. A national organization for the defense of the CI reform fit well into their conception of the main purpose of SINAMOS, which they saw as promoting the organization of lower social groups, particularly labor, in order to build a sociopolitical power base strengthening the radical forces in the government and constituting a counterweight to the power of capitalist groups. Theirs was a "bureaucratic guerilla strategy" aimed at changing the balance of forces in civil society by building up popular organizational power to pressure the government into radicalizing the reform process. This approach, and the emergence of a national organization of CI's, clearly conflicted with the moderate and conservative positions to which MIT officials were strongly committed.

MIT officials as adherents of the integrative conception of participation advocated class conciliation and collaboration between labor, the private sector, and the state in the interest of economic development and industrialization. Consequently, their attitude toward the emergence of a national organization of CIs was highly negative, because of its potential class character and demand-making capacity constituting a challenge to governmental autonomy. Instead, the MIT tried to promote the constitution of a vertical, class-integrated organization, in the form of a national association of enterprises with representatives from both employers and CIs. Through a decree, the requirements for the establishment and official recognition of regional and national associations of industrial enterprises were modified. (*El Peruano*, June 6, 1972). Enterprises were to be represented by delegates elected by the board of directors of the enterprises, but these delegates had to be members of the CI, which excluded owners and members of management who were private shareholders of enterprises. Furthermore, all governing bodies of these associations were to include delegates elected by Industrial Communities, proportional in number to the average participation reached by the CIs in the capital of the enterprises affiliated to the association. Resistance from the National Society of Industries, the existing entrepreneurial association, was so strong that these new associations failed to be constituted. The only measure the government took was to with-draw official recognition from the SNI and prohibit it from using the term "National" in its name, such that it changed its name to Society of Industries in 1973.

Despite its basic hostility toward the emerging organization of CIs, the MIT was forced to become involved and to try to keep the organization within the parameters of the integrative conception. The struggle between forces promoting integration and transformation, respectively, manifested itself in the whole development of CONACI. Though the bureaucratic competition between SINAMOS and the MIT was decided in favor of the MIT after the transfer of General Leonidas Rodríguez from his position as head of SINAMOS in January 1974, and clear attempts at containing mobilization efforts and breaking organizational and ideological autonomy started dominating policies towards CONACI, the original radical tendencies survived among CIs that were capable of resisting these manipulative policies.

The evolution of policies towards CONACI followed a pattern which in a similar form was also followed in the government's policies toward unions. Initial attempts at co-optation gave way to direct organizational intervention, and finally to the use of legal controls to restrict the influence of autonomous forces within CONACI. As one would expect, these policies proved most successful in sectors with predominantly small, marginal, inexperienced CIs and met most resistance among sectors with organizational experience and a class-oriented ideology. The relative success of these restrictive integrative policies over radical tendencies favoring a socialist transformation manifested itself in the resolutions adopted by different federations of CIs, particularly concerning the relation of the CI to private owners. Successfully encapsulated federations supported harmonious collaboration between CI and entrepreneurs in the interest of the development of the enterprise, which, in the context of strong entrepreneurial hostility toward the CI, amounted to nothing less than acquiescence of the workforce. Federations that had managed to retain their autonomy, on the other hand, supported the CI as first step toward the elimination of exploitation and emphasized the need for an effective protection of CI rights and progress. They accepted and defended the CI as a transitory form of organization to give way to social ownership of the means of production in the future. This conception was dominant in the resolutions of the First National Congress of Industrial Communities in March 1973. Though its main proponents successfully resisted later intervention attempts, they were deprived of access to major communication channels, and the conception had lost much of its power as public expression of an underlying sociopolitical force by August 1975, when the coup replacing President Velasco with Morales Bermúdez initiated the second phase of the Revolution.

Failure of the Government's Attempts to Prevent the Emergence of Tendencies Promoting a Socialist Transformation

Though the government's attempts to contain the autonomous expression of tendencies pressuring for a socialist transformation in the Congress of Industrial Communities failed, the dependence of CONACI on state agencies, which later was to facilitate organizational intervention and manipulation, had its roots in the long preparation phase for this congress. The main reason for this dependence was financial, since the long organization process as well as the congress itself, which finally took place from February 23 to March 2, 1973, involved substantial costs.

Originally, the organizing committee had insisted on self-financing through contributions from CIs, but on a voluntary basis this was clearly impossible. The only way would have been through a legal provision for a mandatory deduction of a contribution from all CI members, which would have given CONACI clearly more independence than state agencies were willing to grant. Accordingly, the demand for such a legal provision remained a major issue in the preparation for a Second National Congress in 1976,[6] eliciting frequent but finally unkept promises for satisfaction.

Dependence of the congress on state agencies, however, was much more comprehensive than just financial, extending to the preparation of the agenda for the congress. As basis for this agenda, a questionnaire was prepared and sent out by SINAMOS to all CI's, to be discussed in the congresses at the branch and regional levels, which were held in 1972, and in which delegates to a new organizing committee were elected. Pásara points out that during this phase a lot of time and energy were wasted in fruitless discussions resulting from power struggles among different members of the original organizing committee, a characteristic which further facilitated later manipulation by state agencies (Pásara 1974:198–212).

The strong dependence of the congress on state agencies caused critics like Quijano (1973) to call the event "a controlled and manipulated meeting between workers, executives, enterprise officials and state officials [p. 48]." Yet, this criticism misses the important point about the whole event: the prevalence of autonomous tendencies over the parameters set by state agencies in the discussions and resolutions adopted by the congress. These resolutions were a clear embarrassment to the MIT, as far as demands for a revision of the CI legislation as well as an explicit censure of MIT intervention were concerned.

[6]In 1976, this congress was first postponed and then cancelled altogether in order to avoid public manifestations of opposition against the revision of the CI legislation, and the general conservative shift in government policies.

They were strongly oriented toward the transformation of the existing capitalist into a socialist order, and as such toward transcendence of the CI as desirable model of enterprise organization. The reasons why the resolutions did not reflect the "exact spirit of the law" aimed at integration and harmonious collaboration between workers and entrepreneurs lie first of all in the nature of concrete experiences with the CI, and second in the difference in attitude between the MIT and SINAMOS, which impeded the exercise of coordinated control and containment of autonomous expressions of demands resulting from such experiences.

The resolutions adopted by the congress in no way implied opposition to the government; on the contrary, the congress was characterized by expressions of strong support for the military government and its reforms. One has to keep in mind that in those years the radical transformative tendency within the government was still strong, and that therefore the demand for an economy based on social ownership of means of production did not necessarily imply a deviation from the official conception of the revolutionary process. Already in 1971, President Velasco had announced that the sector of social property enterprises was to be the base for the future society:

> Because we attempt to create a social democracy of full participation. The economy of this future society will consequently neither be the private enterprise, nor bureaucratic and total domination of the state over the productive apparatus. This economy will be based on the contrary, on social property enterprises, directed by those who within them create the wealth of all Peruvians. [October 3, 1971, in 1972:240–241].

In his concluding speech to the congress, Prime Minister Mercado Jarrín underlined the radical conception by pointing out that "the capitalist enterprise reformed by the CI is not, and does not pretend to be, the model of the industrial enterprise that the Revolution attempts to organize in the country [*La Prensa*, March 2, 1973]."

Resolutions of the Congress of CIs

Strong tendencies toward a socialist transformation found clear expression in a variety of resolutions: The law of the CI was considered to be in principle beneficial to the working class, but in practice deficient as means for fundamental change, as it

> does not suppress exploitation of man by another man; social classes and their struggle persist; [the CI] does not represent destruction of the capitalist system but a reform of the capitalist enterprise; consequently, by itself, it cannot be the way to a

New Society. Given that today the ownership and participation of workers is minimal, and in certain cases nonexistent yet, crude exploitation of the working class by the capitalist class persists [*Confederación Nacional de Comunidades Industriales* 1973:6–7].

It was clearly perceived that for an advancement of fundamental change toward a new society without exploitation, coordinated action of working class organizations (i.e., collaboration of CIs with unions) was indispensable. In the introductory *Declaration of Principles* in the congressional resolutions, the "irreplaceable role of unions" was stressed, as well as "the necessity to strengthen blue- and white-collar unions as a guarantee for the correct functioning of the CI." Specifically, the resolutions stated that union and CI were to collaborate in solidarity for the correct application of legal provisions in favor of workers; that, where there was no union, the CI was to assume the defense of workers' rights in case of a labor conflict and to actively promote the formation of a union; and that the CI was to support the union in its just claims, making sure that the documentation and information needed for the success of the union's struggle for improvements would be made available to the union. These resolutions, of course, stood in frontal contradiction to the official doctrine of strict separation of functions between CI and unions, and as such indicated the prevalence of experience over official ideological indoctrination.

Resolutions concerning the need for collaboration with unions in support of societal-level changes explicitly mentioned the importance of ideological and organizational independence of workers, and the permanent and decided struggle for the socialization of means of production under control of the workers. As part of the active role of workers' organizations in support of an acceleration of the process of transformation toward a socialist society, participation in state decision-making bodies, such as in regional and national bodies of the National Institute of Planning, was demanded.

The emergence of these demands for participation in decision making at higher societal levels supports the contention made in my conceptualization that the promotion of workers' participation at the enterprise level by mobilized sectors of the working class and their political representatives has to be seen as part of a larger strategy for societal transformation. The transfer of control rights to the workers at the enterprise level is one aspect of a global process of socialization of control and income rights, and of democratization of decision making in society. The same phenomenon could be observed in Chile, where the social area enterprises with the most mobilized workforce and the most developed system of participation put forward demands for participation in sectoral and national planning with greatest insistence (Espinosa and Zimbalist 1978:186).

The first step toward assigning a role as participant in societal level decision-making bodies to CONACI would have consisted in its official recognition by the MIT. The fact that it took 2 years for the MIT to recognize federations of CIs—upon fulfillment of its own requirements—is indicative of the extremely low degree of positive impact all of these resolutions had on government policies. This was true not only for resolutions concerning societal-level policies for a socialist transformation but also for resolutions concerning a protection and extension of workers' participation rights at the enterprise level.

The major characteristic of resolutions concerning an improvement of the CI was the demand for a higher degree of integration of the structural design with emphasis on transfer of greater effective control rights to workers. The considerations in Point 3.3 of the resolutions indicate the fundamental weakness of the CI as a scheme of participation restricted to sharing in profits and ownership and being represented at the highest level. They state that "in several organs of management and control of the industrial enterprise the participation of the CI is (rudimentary) minimal, and in others practically non-existent." Accordingly, an extension of participation was demanded in several dimensions: (1) in the degree of participation at the highest level, substituting codetermination in important matters for practically nonfunctioning joint consultation; and (2) in the scope of participation at intermediate levels, including general work organization and personnel questions. Concretely, the demands included an immediate increase of CI representatives on the board of directors to 50%, with decisive vote of the CI representatives in decisions crucial for the future development of the enterprise, like expansion of the capital base, modification of statutes, dissolution or merger with another enterprise, acquisition of foreign technology, agreements about royalties and credits, and the establishment of a committee in charge of management functions in which the CI would participate. The financial aspect of participation through the CI was to be protected through additional legal provisions making the application of profit evasion techniques on part of employers impossible. Examples are demands for the establishment of an upper limit for travel, representation, and other expenditures of executives to be charged as enterprise operation costs, as well as a maximum relation of 1:10 between the lowest and highest remuneration on the enterprise payroll. For the same reason it was demanded that subdivisions of enterprises and the establishment of service enterprises to obtain exemption from the CI be declared illegal, retroactively to the date of CI legislation.

Practical experience had shown that the MIT's performance as enforcement agency was completely deficient due both to its weak commitment to an effective protection of CI rights vis-à-vis entrepreneurs and also to its lack of legal sanctioning power. To fill this vacuum, the creation of a special court was demanded, with equal numbers of representatives from state agencies and

CONACI. This demand was the only major one[7] among the many contained in the congress resolutions that was satisfied through the creation of the Court for Labor Communities (*Fuero Privativo de Comunidades Laborales*) in May 1975. How badly needed this innovation was is indicated by the number of cases brought to it in the first months of its existence. By December 1975, there were already 304 cases before the court in Lima alone (*La Prensa*, May 8, 1976), and the first decisions that were taken ended disputes that had gone on over several years. These decisions were widely acclaimed by representatives of Labor Communities and unions as precedents for the protection of rights of the CI, but they remained isolated incidents in a context of continued general disregard for the resolutions of the First Congress on the part of the state bureaucracy. Despite frequent official repetitions of promises for an imminent revision of the CI legislation, with serious consideration of the congressional resolutions, internal differences of opinion in the government about the nature of this revision impeded its implementation until the forces promoting the transformative conception were definitely defeated in 1976.

Obviously, the resolutions of the congress carried the imprint of the most politicized and organizationally experienced participants, and it would be a wrong conclusion to assume a corresponding political consciousness among the base, but for an assessment of the constellation of sociopolitical forces, the tendencies dominating in this congress were highly relevant. An important reason for the predominance of this class-conscious, union-oriented and militant attitude was the heavy representation of the big CIs among congress participants, whose leaders for the most part had long experience in the union movement. The originators of the organizing effort in 1971 had been from bigger CIs, and subsequently other big CIs could most easily be motivated to participate, for instance through personal contacts based on union connections. Also, as shown in the last chapter, bigger CIs were more militant and had more resources enabling them to send delegates to meetings, etc. Furthermore, the original CONACI leaders and SINAMOS as major congress organizers attempted to have as large a number of CI members, not of CIs, as possible represented in the congress.

It was exactly this disproportionate representation of bigger CIs that later provided MIT officials with the justification for intervention into the national organization founded in this congress. Through a change of statutes[8] and the or-

---

[7]Another minor demand that was satisfied was the one for equal distribution of the 10% cash participation in profits.

[8]The original statutes of CONACI, adopted by the congress, postulated the formation of 25 branch federations of CIs, comprising all the CIs within their respective branch of industry if located in the Lima–Callao area, and nine regional federations comprising all the CIs within their respective regions. The statutes based representation on the number of CI members at the federation as well as national level. The quorum in the National Congress consisted of the sum of del-

ganization of new federation-level congresses, the representation of smaller CIs was increased in order to neutralize the political influence of the original leaders of the organization. A second argument used by state officials to justify the reorganization attempt was the "oligarchic, sectarian, nonparticipatory" character of the original leadership. This allegation did have some foundation in the leadership's failure to maintain close interaction with the base, and in the political and personal divergencies among the five members of the collegiate presidency of CONACI (Pásara 1974:239–243). Though the former problem was inherent in the situation, given the leadership's action possibilities, it was mainly the combination of the two problems that rendered CONACI vulnerable to intervention.

Division through Direct Organizational Intervention

In the first year after the congress, the CONACI leadership concentrated their efforts mainly on the achievement of official recognition by the government as the organization representative of all CIs. The MIT, however, persisted in basic opposition to this national organization, and the resulting policy was a de facto recognition, but a denial of official recognition. This de facto recognition consisted in consultations of ministerial committees with CONACI representatives, concerning the elaboration of a revision of CI legislation, and mediation in concrete cases of serious conflicts between enterprises and their CI. Quite rightly, the CONACI leadership considered legislative changes as the only way to achieve progress of the CIs, and consequently considered the task of promoting such legislation as much more important than the provision of practical assistance and advice to CIs. This concentration of efforts in interactions with the state bureaucracy, however, led to a scarce contact of the national leadership with the base. At the branch level—at least in some federations—some more practical advisory services were provided to member CIs, mainly under the guidance of SINAMOS personnel. These activities as well as the costs for the national headquarters and secretarial services were practically completely funded by SINAMOS. The organizational life of most regional federations depended exclusively on a small leadership group, for whose activities contacts with SINAMOS were more important than those with the national CONACI leadership. Obviously, this almost total dependence put SINAMOS in a strategic position for direct intervention into the internal life of CONACI, which was taken advantage of under a new top SINAMOS leadership in 1974.

---

egates that would represent half plus one of all the CI members in the country. The criterion for representation—and in July 1975 for official recognition of federations—used by the MIT was number of CIs.

The change in the top SINAMOS leadership was a major success in the struggle of moderate and conservative factions in the government against all mobilization policies supporting the growth of popular organizations with strong grass-roots involvement. This struggle, which had originated with the creation of SINAMOS and its staff recruitment, was fought out inside the government over questions of delimitations of competence between SINAMOS and other state agencies. For instance, according to Béjar (1976:86), the decree which reserved the exclusive right to training and education of CI leaders and members for the MIT was passed by the Council of Ministers after the congress of CIs in a session where Leonidas Rodríguez, then still head of SINAMOS, was absent. In society, the struggle was fought out between SINAMOS organizers, officials of various ministries, leaders of popular organizations with various political affiliations, and semi-clandestine agents in the service of conservative government factions, particularly the Ministry of the Interior.[9] The Intelligence Service was heavily agitating against presumed Communist infiltration in a variety of popular organizations, and even in certain parts of the state bureaucracy. Thus agents in charge of organizing new rival popular organizations and/or infiltrating existing ones were provided with massive financial support, and, depending on the nature of the task, with official backing. In the case of unions, the major support agencies were the Ministry of Labor and the Ministry of the Interior. In the case of CONACI, it was the Ministry of Industry and SINAMOS after "Communist infiltrators and sympathizers" had been purged.

The immediate motive for intervention into CONACI was a certain radicalization and planned mobilization of the base by the CONACI leadership, disillusioned by almost a year of fruitless efforts spent in bureaucratic contacts and negotiations. The CONACI delegates to a joint committee with MIT officials resigned, arguing in a letter to the Minister of Industry that "given the repeated promises formulated by high state officials, particularly you, to find solutions shortly, of which we can see nothing so far, we have to come to the conclusion that we cannot remain in this committee a minute longer."[10] In March 1974, the national leadership decided to call for assemblies in each CI, and for extraordinary congresses of federations, for the election of a new leadership and deliberation of future policies.

At that stage, the intervention began with a withdrawal of all material support from CONACI. Taking advantage of the internal disunity of the leadership, SINAMOS and the MIT sponsored a Reorganizing Committee, (CR, *Comité Reorganizador*), among whose apparent leaders one of the members of

---

[9] McClintock discusses contradictory tendencies within SINAMOS itself, between SINAMOS and the Ministry of Agriculture, and between SINAMOS and peasant leaders in the implementation of the agrarian reform (1977:16–17).

[10] Copy of the letter, dated February 20, 1974, from CONACI archive.

the original collegiate presidency of CONACI figured prominently. On June 1, 1974, a communiqué signed by 17 federations out of a total of 34 existing ones was published, which announced an imminent reorganization of CONACI in order to overcome "the institutional crisis" which had been caused by "the sectarianism of a tiny leadership group."[11] The strategy pursued by the MIT and SINAMOS through this reorganizing committee was aimed at gaining control over the leadership of federations in extraordinary congresses, and from there over the elections of a new national leadership. The method generally used by SINAMOS and MIT agents in the preparation of a federation congress was to visit as many enterprises of a given branch or region as possible. Particular efforts were made to induce the smaller CIs that had not participated in former congresses and consequently were uncommitted to either the CR or CONACI, or even ignorant about the struggle between them, to affiliate themselves to their federation and send delegates to its extraordinary congress. Obviously, such delegates were highly susceptible to influences favoring a vote for support of the CR. The MIT solicited permission from the enterprises for workers to participate in these congresses, and SINAMOS contributed financial resources for transportation, congress costs, etc. Particularly in the provinces, only this direct intervention and mobilization made it possible at all to link individual CIs to a higher-level organization, which in turn could hardly develop any autonomy from these tutelary agencies.

In all the extraordinary congresses held in 1974, MIT agents were present and wrote exact reports about proceedings, dynamics among delegates and leaders, political tendencies, and union contacts of leaders. In several cases, they managed to isolate delegates with "undesirable political views" through prior contacts and "political education" of other delegates.[12] By the end of 1974, extraordinary congresses had been held in 19 federations: 12 of them had voted in favor of the CR, and 7 were either neutral or split; the remaining 15 federations had not held extraordinary congresses in protest against the CR. Both factions claimed to be the authentic majority representatives, as the total of federations supporting the CR supposedly affiliated a greater number of CIs than the total of federations adhering to CONACI, but the latter affiliated bigger CIs and therefore, a greater number of CI members than the former. This was a result of both the greater capacity for resistance to direct intervention on

---

[11]This communiqué was published in *Expreso* and *La Crónica*, with the additional information that the Ministers of Industry, Labor and the Interior, as well as the head of SINAMOS, had participated in the meeting where the reorganizing committee had been constituted. This indicates clearly that the reorganization attempt was well-coordinated at highest governmental levels, though apparently without the explicit consent of President Velasco. In a press conference on June 26, 1974, he declared that "Government officials who talk to one group should also talk to the other group. I will gladly look into the problem. We are all Peruvians. There should be neither time nor bile spent in this mess. [*El Peruano*, June 27, 1974]."

[12]This information is taken from the documentation on CONACI held in the MIT, of which these reports are part.

the part of bigger CIs, with a more organizationally experienced and ideologically educated labor force, and of their higher rate of participation in the first congress and consequent commitment to the original principles and leadership of CONACI.

The data on adherence of the CIs in my sample to one of the two factions, which were taken from the documentation in the MIT, clearly show that presence of a union increased the probability of the CI to participate actively in federations either in congresses or in assemblies that decided not to hold a second congress (Tables 5.3 and 5.4). The 54% of CIs for which no information was recorded were not mentioned as participants in these reports. The CIs in the categories "split" and "neutral" participated in congresses or assemblies where the federation was either split or decided to remain neutral vis-à-vis the two factions.

It seems reasonable to assume that part of the CIs not mentioned in these reports, which are predominantly small ones, were in fact represented in federation congresses supporting the CR, because otherwise the CR could hardly have managed to get a majority vote in 12 federations. MIT agents were obviously more likely to specifically mention the participation of "instransigent" CIs which supported CONACI in their reports. However, for a majority of bigger CIs, information was recorded, and most of them adhered to CONACI. Thus CONACI clearly represented the largest proportion of CI members: 46% as compared to 18% for the CR. The branch federations that successfully resisted intervention were those with a high number of CIs from big and well-unionized enterprises: chocolate production, shoes and leather, textiles, metal-mechanics, glass, automobile manufacturing, breweries, printing, and machine industries. The three regional federations that managed to resist intervention were from geographical locations where strong regional union federations existed, Ancash, Cuzco-Puno, and Piura.

From August 1974 on, public controversy between the original CONACI and the CR was carried on extensively in the newly expropriated newspapers.[13] When it became clear that the CR tendency would not manage to gain preponderance among the federations, official government policy changed from full support of the CR to a call for unification.[14] The head of COAP, the pres-

---

[13]In July 1974, the major Lima daily newspapers were expropriated in order to be transferred to organized popular sectors, such as peasants, labor communities, the educational community, etc., after a 1-year transition phase under state-appointed administrators–directors. Despite strong support for the government, some of these newspapers took a critical stand on certain issues. By the end of the First Phase, several directors, editors, and journalists were fired on the basis of accusations of having succumbed to Communist infiltration. In the Second Phase, even the more moderate directors were too critical for the government, and in March 1976 all of them were substituted by persons with known conservative orientations. See *Expreso* and *La Prensa*, March 16, 1976.

[14]Public demonstrations of this full support were, for instance, a dinner of the CR leadership and delegates from the base with the Minister of Industry and the head of SINAMOS on September 2, 1974. *La Prensa*, September 3, 1974.

Table 5.3

Participation of CIs in Federation Adhering to CONACI versus CR by Unionization

	Percentage of recognized CIs				
Participation in federation adhering to:	All	Nonunionized	With old union	With old and/or new union	Percentage of CI members represented
No information	54	72	26	32	26
CONACI	28	18	45	41	46
CR	9	6	12	12	18
Split	4	2	8	6	5
Neutral	5	2	8	9	5
	100.0				
N	(1758)	(1002)	(337)	(756)	(185,176)

idential advisory committee and political body closest to President Velasco, declared that the government did not support the division of CONACI (*La Prensa*, December 19, 1974), and the Minister of Industry followed suit by manifesting the support of the MIT and SINAMOS for reunification of CONACI, and not for either one of the two groups (*La Prensa*, December 24, 1974). However, this manifestation remained only verbal, and heavy material support for and consequent influence over the CR continued into 1976. After a long and difficult unification process through the constitution of a provisional committee, a new National Directive Committee was to be installed in July 1975.[15] In this meeting, resolutions proposed by the CONACI faction were gaining consistent majorities in votes, which led to intervention of MIT and SINAMOS agents and consequent withdrawal of some CR federations. This incident ended the reunification contacts and activities until the neutral federation of Basic Chemicals reinitiated them on its own initiative in November of the same year. This attempt at reunification proved finally successful. The deteriorating economic situation of industrial workers and the apparent strengthening of antilabor forces in the government made the need for an autonomous and unified organization for the defense of rights of CIs even more obvious than before, and among organizationally inexperienced and nonideo-

[15] The two sides agreed on a provisional National Executive Committee (CEN) composed of presidents of 29 federations on May 3, 1975. (The nonparticipating federations were non-alcoholic beverages, automotors, shoes and leather, and Cuzco-Puno; all of them of the original CONACI.) In the case of three divided federations, representatives of both sides were integrated into the committee. The formation of the committee was officially acclaimed, and on May 30, the Minister of Industry handed a draft law for a revision of the CI legislation over to the committee, for public discussion and suggestions to the MIT.(*La Prensa*, May 31, 1975.) This draft law was the result of a long process of compromise finding in which the integrative conception had finally prevailed. However, a further shift in the internal balance of power in the government to the conservative side occurred before this law was put into effect.

Table 5.4

Participation of CIs in Federation Adhering to CONACI versus CR by Size

Participation in federation adhering to:	Percentage of recognized CIs						
	Under 9	10–19	20–49	50–99	100–499	Over 500	All
No information	83	76	73	36	22	21	54
CONACI	0	12	11	36	61	51	28
CR	17	6	7	10	11	9	9
Split	0	6	2	6	4	9	4
Neutral	0	0	7	12	2	9	5
	100.0						
N	(60)	(356)	(578)	(339)	(382)	(43)	(1758)

logical CI leaders as well. On March 15, 1976, an Interim Directive Committee was constituted, as well as an organizing committee for the Second National Congress to be held within the following half year. Due to the declaration of a state of emergency in July, however, this congress was postponed indefinitely. The revision of the CI legislation announced in November, finally, made it altogether undesirable for the government to grant permission to hold this congress, as it would certainly have brought up strong criticism of the new legislation.

Emargination through Legal Restrictions

The formal transfer of the expropriated newspapers to the "organized sectors of the population" that was to take place on July 28, 1975, made the official recognition of federations of CIs on part of the MIT unavoidable. In order to elaborate a scheme of representation of base organizations in the governing bodies of *La Prensa*, the newspaper assigned to the Labor Communities, relative weights for representation of labor communities from the industrial, mining, fishing, and telecommunications sectors had to be established. Within the industrial sector, representatives had to be elected by delegates from officially recognized federations. Quite predictably, the requirements for recognition were designed to reduce the weight of big and politicized CIs: A federation had to present proof of affiliation of 51% of all CIs in the respective branch or region, irrespective of the number of individual CI members that these CIs represented. Just how unrepresentative the result of this criterion for recognition could be becomes clear if one considers that 50% of all CIs had less than 20 workers, but accounted for only 14% of all CI members. In Chapter 4, I argued that these small CIs functioned highly ineffectively because the workforce lacked knowledge about the law as well as organizational capacity for the defense of their rights. Consequently, their participation at higher levels of organization was likely to be equally ineffective, or even more so.

By July 1975, 29 federations had been officially recognized and could participate in the election of delegates to the governing body of La Prensa. The 5 unrecognized federations (textiles, metal-mechanics, plastics, automotors, and machine industry), which together accounted for roughly 30% of all CI members, were all from among those who had resisted the intervention attempt. The final representation of CIs and CI members in the governing body of La Prensa was further biased by the rule that each federation had equal weight in the vote for representatives, whereas the number of CI members represented by a federation reached from about 1000 (jewelry) to 10,000 (clothing). The 14 elected delegates came predominantly from smaller federations, which together represented 64,200 CI members, roughly 32% of all CI members in the country. Nine of the federations belonged to the CR, two to CONACI, and three were either split or neutral.[16] Clearly then, the legal requirements for recognition proved successful in emarginating the more radical tendencies among the CIs from access to a potentially important communication channel. However, the potential of this channel was never realized, because editorial policy remained the responsibility of the state-appointed directors. The change of directors in March 1976, which put personalities with known conservative leanings in charge, and the indefinite suspension of the transfer of newspapers following in July, rendered the legal emargination of the radical forces in CONACI a rather superfluous success.

Potential and Weaknesses of CONACI

With the successful containment of the influence of radical forces in CONACI, the moderate and conservative forces within the government not only managed to prevent the emergence of a strong autonomous sociopolitical force capable of pressuring the government for an acceleration and radicalization of the reform process but also obstructed the full development of structurally existing participation possibilities through the CI. With support from SINAMOS, CONACI would have had the potential to develop into an organization providing advice to individual CIs, spreading knowledge about legislation, and mobilizing workers into taking advantage of the limited opportunities available for participation. Through this activity, it could have reduced the space for violation and evasion of the CI legislation at the enterprise level and established communication channels for CIs to enlist support from the

---

[16]Information about the elected delegates is taken from La Prensa, July 31, 1975.

state bureaucracy in the enforcement of their participation rights. However, this would have required a unified commitment to the CI as reform design on the part of government bureaucracies, particularly the MIT, which in turn would have involved a change in the latter's relation to its private sector clientele.

The successful pursuit of the policies of containment was facilitated by certain internal weaknesses of CONACI on the one hand, and the superiority of material and symbolic resources available to state agencies on the other hand. The lack of participation from the base was the crucial weakness of CONACI from the beginning, because it restricted organizational life by and large to leadership activities and made it heavily dependent on interactions between different personalities. Consequently, MIT and SINAMOS agents could capitalize on rivalries within the top leadership in their intervention attempt. This lack of participation from the base was mainly a result of the widespread ignorance about the CI legislation, which could only have been overcome by mobilizing activities of the leadership, stimulating active participation and involvement among the base, a task whose fulfillment was impossible due to the limited availability of resources. Ignorance about the CI legislation as well as about the reorganization attempt could be found even among federation leaderships, as was mentioned repeatedly in the reports of MIT agents. Most of these leaders were blue-collar workers, carrying out organizational tasks outside of working hours, except for special occasions for which the MIT solicited permission from their employer. As a result, attendance at leadership meetings in many federations was very low, and several federations were not functioning at all in the first year after the National Congress. Consequently, in these federations, MIT and SINAMOS agents were not faced with the task of eliminating certain tendencies and personalities from the leadership organs, but simply with organizing them. Also, there were hardly any competing mobilizing agents except in the best-organized federations, where the original leadership tried to reach nonaffiliated smaller CIs. And even in some of these cases, the superiority in material resources, time, and personnel made it possible for MIT agents to reach more small CIs and organize a CR-supporting constituency among them, thus splitting the federation into two factions. Given the material and symbolic resources available to the agents promoting the CR, only the experience and ideological formation of the most politicized CI leaders provided an effective protection of relative organizational autonomy.

Compared to similar policies aimed at weakening unions, the ones directed towards CONACI were clearly more successful. The organization succumbed to the intervention attempt and was actually split. This effectively impeded publicly visible coordinated action even within the two factions. Time and energy were largely spent in competition between the two leadership groups, which left no opportunity for building up a strong organizational infrastructure and active internal life. Thus the lack of internal organizational life with involvement of the base, which had made CONACI so susceptible to intervention to begin with, was perpetuated. There was no organizational infrastructure that could be relied on to mobilize the base in unified opposition to outside intervention. Nor was there a shared experience of mutual assistance and success in conflicts, which was definitely present among unions, as will be shown in the next chapter. However, these are problems characteristic for newly emerging organizations in general, which suggests the conclusion that it is easier to keep new organizations from developing a strong power base than to reduce the power base of already existing ones. This conclusion emphasizes again the importance of the involvement of established working-class organizations (i.e., unions) for the development of workers' participation schemes, as they are a potentially more effective force than new organizations emerging with the purpose of supporting the development of participation schemes.

In conclusion, it should be reiterated that the power of entrepreneurs to obstruct the implementation of changes in the existing order introduced through the reform process was left largely unimpaired, whereas the sociopolitical strength of labor was kept low through policies aimed at impeding the growth of an organizational power base. These policies were quite successful in the case of CONACI, and somewhat less successful in the case of the unions, but overall they prevented labor from developing into a strong sociopolitical force capable of mobilizing for coordinated, unified, political action. Consequently, the balance of forces in civil society remained skewed toward capital-owning social groups, whose pressures on the government contributed to an internal shift toward prevalence of the moderate and conservative forces. Under economic crisis conditions accompanied by strong external as well as internal pressures, these moderate and conservative forces effected a stagnation and even partial reversal of the reform process. This shift in the reform process in turn required an even further debilitation of labor's mobilization capacity, and where more subtle policies of containment had failed, the government resorted to outright repression. The next chapter will deal with the application of these various policies toward unions, and with the unions' response.

6

Dynamics in the Constellation of Sociopolitical Forces II: Increase in Unionization and Strike Activity, and the Government's Response

The analysis of the interaction between the government and organized labor will start with a focus on the various strategies used by the government in the attempt to contain the growth of labor's strength as a sociopolitical force. First, a repetition of a conceptual clarification is in order. Labor's capacity to use its organizational power base for the mobilization of workers into coordinated purposeful action has to be differentiated from pure militancy at the enterprise level. In the initial theoretical chapter, I contended that in a developing authoritarian capitalist system pressures for an improvement of labor's situation are principally aimed at impressing the political elite by threatening serious disruptions of production and public disturbances. The crucial determining factors of labor's strength, then, are the extent of its organizational penetration of the industrial working class and its ideological unity, as basis for its ability to mobilize workers into acting collectively in a purposeful manner. An increase in organizational penetration and militancy per se does not constitute an increase in this ability, if organizational and political unity are lacking. Growing organizational penetration and capacity for militant action at the enterprise level are necessary but not sufficient conditions for a growth of labor's strength as a sociopolitical force.

One of the crucial factors obstructing the growth of labor's strength in the Peruvian Revolution was in fact political fractionalization, resulting from historical developments as well as from attempts on the part of the government to deepen political divergencies through purposeful "divide and rule" policies. The other crucial factors were additional governmental policies designed to restrict organizational autonomy and action capacity of unions. As in the formation of policies toward CONACI, elite consensus concerning the policy

169

goals and the choice of strategies toward organizational growth of unions was low. Accordingly, a variety of strategies was applied both alternatively, through centrally determined government policy, and simultaneously, by different government agencies under the personal influence of certain ministers. These strategies, in part similar to the ones applied towards CONACI, ranged from persuasion and provision of incentives to selective repression. In particular, one can distinguish the following approaches:

1. *Divide, co-opt, and rule* through balancing autonomous union organizations against each other and coopting union organizations and leaders by provision of official recognition and frequent interaction.
2. *Setting up a new government-sponsored union organization* with strong material support.
3. *Exerting control through legal provisions* that limit the scope of organization and range of action of union organizations.
4. *Exerting selective repression* and tolerating limited violence.

The frequency of use of these strategies shifted from the first to the last between 1968 and 1976, as the ratio of the government's resources to the effective demand-making capacity of the unions deteriorated.

The Situation in 1968

The Plan Inca analyzes the situation in the area of union organization as "politicized unionism with corrupt leaderships," requiring the "reorganization of the union system for the benefit of the workers themselves [pp. 35–36]." In fact, the links of unions to political parties have been close, and though these links are clearly divisive, weakening organized labor as a sociopolitical force, they have been perceived as a potential threat by the military government.

These links are the result of historical developments, since the Peruvian labor movement, like most labor movements in Latin American countries, has been dominated by political forces since its origin.[1] Benefits for labor have been obtained predominantly through labor legislation, rather than bargaining between unions and employers. And where bargaining takes place, the labor authorities usually play a very important mediating role. The first unions in Peru were organized by anarchists, but with the founding of APRA by Haya de la Torre, and the Socialist Party by José Carlos Mariátegui in the 1920s, the

---

[1]This argument is made, for example, by Alexander (1965) and Alba (1968) for labor movements in Latin America, and by Millen (1963) for labor movements in developing nations in general. For a history of the Peruvian labor movement and its relation to political parties and different governments, see Sulmont (1975) and Payne (1965).

labor movement came under their influence and increased its level of national organizational centralization. In 1929, the Confederation of Workers of Peru was founded, but in November of 1930 it was already repressed, together with the Socialist Party, which had been transformed into the Communist Party earlier in the same year (Sulmont 1975:143). From then on, the labor movement developed principally under APRA leadership through alternating periods of free organization and of repression.

In 1944 the Confederation of Workers of Peru (CTP) was founded, which is still APRA-controlled today. The erosion of APRA-control over the labor movement started with the *"convivencia"* (i.e., the collaboration between APRA and the pro-oligarchic and pro-imperialist Prado government from 1956 to 1961). In these years, relatively more democratic freedoms allowed an increase in unionization; from 1956 to 1962 a total of 625 new unions were recognized. However, APRA's attempt to play a mediating role between popular organizations and the oligarchy caused a loss of its mobilization potential among the urban industrial working class. This loss continued during the *"super-convivencia"* (i.e., the coalition between APRA and Odría against the Belaúnde government), which clearly subordinated the defense of workers' interests to the pursuit of political power for the APRA party leadership. Unionization kept increasing, with 1221 new unions recognized from 1963 to 1968, and under the influence of leftist political forces, more class struggle oriented unions united against the APRA leadership. Out of attempts at union reorganization by these forces emerged the General Confederation of Workers of Peru (CGTP) under Communist leadership.[2] The two sectors where the CTP resisted the challenge from the leftist unions most successfully were the sugar plantations in the north and the textile industry, where the APRA-controlled unions had achieved comparatively high benefits. Their major achievement was a decree in 1945 that established an automatic adjustment of textile workers' wages to the official cost-of-living index. This legal provision proved very advantageous, as can be seen in Table 6.1, which shows that average wages in the textile industry were higher than the general average in manufacturing, at least up to 1961. However, with the crisis of the textile industry in the 1960s, textile workers lost their comparative advantage and large numbers of textile workers were laid off due to bankruptcies of enterprises. When the APRA-controlled Federation of Textile Workers concluded an agreement with representatives of the textile industry, which gave employers large possibilities for rationalization, opposition among affiliated unions against the federation leadership grew strong. Several large unions disaffiliated themselves from the federation. By February 1976, the federation leadership had apparently lost all

[2]For the developments between 1958 and 1968, see pp. 80–83.

Table 6.1
Average Wages in the Textile Industry Compared to Other Industries in Peru

| | Blue-collar average daily earnings[a] | | |
Year	Textile workers	Workers in other branches in manufacturing industry	Difference
1938	2.98	3.11	−0.13
1950	25.02	19.97	5.05
1960	52.18	37.57	14.61
1961	56.00	42.00	14.00

Source: Gomez Cornejo (1976:61).
[a] In current *soles*.

control over the textile unions, as a call for a strike remained practically unnoticed, and the leadership was censured by assemblies of affiliated unions (*El Comercio*, February 3, 1976; *Expreso*, February 4, 1976).

According to Peruvian union legislation, five or more unions in the same type of economic activity can form a federation, and ten or more federations can form a confederation. Consequently, it is possible for different federations to coexist in the same branch of industry. Since there is neither a legal requirement for exclusive representation of all workers in the same branch by one federation nor a practical one, such as industry-wide collective bargaining, a large number of unions are not affiliated to any federation or confederation. The functions of the federations and confederations are primarily to provide legal advice and assistance in collective negotiations or with individual grievances to affiliated unions. In addition, the better-organized federations (e.g., the Federation of Metal Workers, FETIMP), use solidarity strikes to exert pressure on employers and the Ministry of Labor for favorable solutions to collective negotiations and particularly serious conflicts between enterprises and affiliated unions, such as in cases of layoffs or firings. Furthermore, both federations and confederations take political stands and include certain legislation or change of labor authorities in their list of demands. Again, this is an obvious result of the dominant role that the state plays in industrial relations, both through labor legislation and direct mediating intervention. However, the degree of politization in union demands has contributed to the military government's perception of growing unionization as a challenge to its autonomy, requiring that the organizational power of unions be kept in check.

Divide, Co-opt, and Rule

In the attempt to weaken the labor movement through division and co-optation, the government was able to take advantage of these differences in political orientation. As a measure to weaken the influence of APRA, the military's historical adversary[3] through the CTP, the government formally recognized the CGTP in January 1971. Besides prestige, this official recognition granted the right to CGTP officials to advise and represent affiliated unions in the processing of labor relations affairs in the Ministry of Labor. A few months after the CGTP, the very small Christian Democratic-oriented CNT *(Central Nacional de Trabajadores,* National Central Workers' Organization) was also recognized. This meant that three different political tendencies were balanced against each other in the labor movement. In addition to granting formal recognition to these confederations, a policy of open doors was pursued by Minister of Labor Sala Orosco, who took office in September 1970, in an attempt to establish close personal relations with union leaders. This attempt was clearly integrative, intended to turn important union leaders into loyal brokers between the government and their constituency, a strategy which has shown successful results in Mexico, for instance.[4] Initially, this attempt was supported by considerable benefits granted to the leaders on behalf of their constituency. The years 1971 and 1972 brought comparatively highly favorable wage settlements for unions. This attempt succeeded in generating strong support for the government's general reform policies among CGTP- and CNT-affiliated unions, whereas the CTP was more critical, demanding an active role in the shaping of policies, though it was cautious not to enter into open opposition to the government.[5] However, the attempt failed in co-opting union leaders into the role of brokers delivering unconditional compliance of their constituency with decisions of the Ministry of Labor in exchange for selective benefits.

A comparison with Mexico suggests that favorable wage settlements and establishment of close personal relations with union leaders were relatively inefficient means of co-optation. Some of the more effective means applied in the Mexican case were appointment of union leaders to governmental positions from which they derive prestige, a certain amount of power, and extra income. Also, unions frequently are dependent on financial assistance from the government for organizational maintenance and activities. Furthermore, corruption

[3]See Chapter 3, n. 7, for reasons underlying this enmity. For a history of relations between the military and the APRA Party, see North (1973) and Villanueva (1957).

[4]Two scholars who support the view that most of Mexico's labor leaders are loyal collaborators with the government and with management, often corrupt and oligarchical, are Handelman (1976) and Stevens (1974).

[5]The support from CGTP and CNT, as well as the hidden opposition from the CTP, are expressed in their own publications and were confirmed in my personal interviews with the secretary generals of the CGTP and the CTP. The CTP has supported some of the government's reforms, but has consistently pointed out that only a democratic system can provide real social justice—clearly understandable as a strategic position in support of APRA's demands for governmental elections. A compilation of official positions of the four confederations on various issues is given in Aparicio *et al.* (1975).

pervading the whole organization gives leaders at all levels a stake in their position, thus keeping them from forming internal opposition groups to pacification policies of co-opted leaders.[6] In the Peruvian case, both the means applied by the government to co-opt top union leaders and the means available to these top union leaders to control middle- and lower-level leaders were much weaker. Accordingly, unions' compliance with governmental wishes for acceptance of wages and grievance settlements issued by the Ministry of Labor remained far from unconditional.

Though the number of strikes remained comparatively low up to 1973, they by no means disappeared. The CGTP leadership, fully aware of the need to support the government as a whole for lack of any further leftist alternative, and hoping for a strengthening of the radical faction within the government, tried to find solutions to labor conflicts that would neither provoke the government through costly strikes nor compromise vital interests of the base. However, due to the low degree of centralization of collective bargaining and of control in the confederation, the CGTP leadership was unable to impose its line on member unions. In several cases, the CGTP was very hesitant to support strikes of affiliated unions that were regarded as unnecessarily militant.[7] As a result, extreme left tendencies gained influence, and a number of unions defected from the CGTP, attacking it as revisionist and a sellout to the government.[8] These autonomous tendencies, as well as a continuous increase of labor's demand-making capacities due to the formation of new unions, caused the government to seek additional means to extend its influence over the labor movement.

Setting Up a Government-Sponsored Organization

As a counterweight to existing unions guarding their autonomy in the pursuit of working-class interests, a government-sponsored union organization was set up and was expected to adopt a class-conciliation attitude and renounce all militancy in favor of "constructive dialogue." This expectation was borne out, but the organization failed to acquire legitimacy and influence among the most important sectors of the urban industrial working class. Partly, this was due to the fact that the organizational space was already filled to a high degree and

[6]Everett (1967) describes these co-optation mechanisms in detail. In several ways, co-optation is closely linked to legal controls, particularly through the mechanisms of official recognition.

[7]Examples are the miners' and teachers' strikes in 1971, and the strike in SIDERPERÚ, the state-owned steel company, in May 1973.

[8]These unions formed a new loose association, the CCUSC (*Comité de Coordinación y Unificación Sindical Clasista*) in October 1973, which also attracted several textile unions that were in opposition to the CTP federation leadership. For more information, see *Cronología Política*.

that existing unions competed with government sponsorship in organizing and affiliating new unions.

Again, a comparison with Mexico strengthens the argument about the importance of preexisting unions for the chances of success of the establishment of a government-sponsored central union organization. In the early 1930s, when large-scale union organization was started in Mexico, there were relatively few unions in existence, organizing a total of 294,000 workers, which amounted to 5.6% of the active workforce. Thus the Mexican government under President Cárdenas was able to incorporate largely unorganized sectors of the urban industrial working class into the newly created union structures. The number of union members tripled from 1930 to 1940, amounting to 878,000 in 1940, or 15.4% of the active workforce (Handelmann 1976:269). In contrast, the Peruvian government in 1970 was faced with a relatively greater number of existing unions, which had organized an estimated 20% of the active workforce, and had reached a high degree of penetration among workers in the most crucial industrial sectors. The existence of these unions and their activities also had a certain demonstration effect on unorganized workers, providing an example with which to compare the new government-sponsored union organization. Such a comparison contributed to the failure of the new organization to acquire legitimacy and influence by making evident the obvious lack of responsiveness of the central leadership to demands from the base for support in the defense of their interests. Particularly under the impact of the economic crisis in 1975, the leadership came under increasing criticism, and base unions started to act autonomously in the defense of their demands. Significantly, the "100 bases of Lima" (i.e., unions most directly exposed to a demonstration effect from the behavior of other unions) demanded a National Congress for the renovation of the top leadership, which they publicly censured as corrupt and manipulatory (*Marka*, October 16, 1975).

The impetus for the creation of a government-sponsored central union organization came from President Velasco himself, apparently as a reaction to the protracted strikes among miners in 1971 (Béjar 1976:70). In the beginning of 1972, the Council of Ministers appointed a committee in charge of organizing such a new national structure of unions. Members of the committee were the Ministers of the Interior, Industry, and Labor, and the head of SINAMOS. SINAMOS was to be the organizational tool to set up this new union structure, but disagreement about procedures soon caused the other ministers to get their own officials involved in the organizing process. SINAMOS insisted on actual mobilization and organization from the base, and on a concomitant elimination of the notorious corruption among officials in the Ministry of Labor, with whom the new unions would have to deal. The radical members of SINAMOS rightly perceived that this was the only way for the new union structure to acquire legitimacy among large sectors of the working class. In

October 1972, the leftist political group *Frente de Izquierda Revolucionaria* (Front of the Revolutionary Left) published an article (*Revolución Peruana*, No. 50, October 1972) citing a SINAMOS organizer who revealed the plan of setting up "revolutionary" (i.e., identified with the ideology of the Peruvian Revolution) union nuclei in work centers, out of which official "revolutionary" unions were to be formed, which then would be linked into a national organizational structure, the Central Organization of Workers of the Peruvian Revolution (CTRP, *Central de Trabajadores de la Revolución Peruana*). This way of totally new organizing was obviously going to be a long and slow process.

The procedures pursued by SINAMOS, not to mention the insistence on elimination of corruption in the Ministry of Labor, were opposed by the other members of the ministerial committee. They favored a faster procedure, based on the co-optation of already existing organizations for the formation of the new government-sponsored national organization. When the head of the labor area of SINAMOS refused to have his officials participate in such operations, officials from other ministries, particularly agents from the Ministry of the Interior, were put in charge of putting together the CTRP. However, their identity was semisecret, and frequently they identified themselves as SINAMOS organizers, such that SINAMOS was held publicly responsible for the organization of the CTRP.[9] After the already mentioned changes in the top SINAMOS leadership in 1974, SINAMOS did in fact get closely involved and started providing strong support for the CTRP.

The new central organization was built on the basis of the fishermen's federation, which had disaffiliated itself from the CGTP in 1969 due to its failure to obtain support for the call of a general strike. In December of 1972, the Constituent Congress of the CTRP took place, with 14 federations that had been recognized in a very short time by the Ministry of Labor. Massive material and organizational support from ministerial agencies, as well as favorable treatment of requests for official recognition by the Ministry of Labor, facilitated fast growth of the CTRP. Organizers were able to capture already existing but small and inexperienced unions, as well as to found new ones. In several cases, union leaders that had been censured by their base founded new parallel unions with strong financial support from CTRP organizers, which clearly hampered the legitimacy of the CTRP. A low level of knowledge at the base and scarcity of qualified leadership facilitated co-optation of unions by the CTRP.

However, the mobilization created by SINAMOS and CTRP organizers with considerable material resources also increased the CGTP's potential for

[9]The details of these internal disputes only became public much later, in such books as Thorndike (1976) and Béjar (1976). Yet, it was quite obvious all along that there were contradictory tendencies in the role played by SINAMOS. The official emphasis on governmental unity, however, prevented these differences of opinion from being publicly recognized.

organization, due to the propagandization of the need for workers to organize and act collectively in the defense of their interests. How intense the process of mobilization and union organization has been can be seen from the number of new unions recognized per year (Table 6.2). The most striking fact is that the total number of recognized unions almost doubled between 1968 and 1975, and that the number of unions in manufacturing industry more than doubled in this period. Comparing the total number of unions recognized as affiliated to the different confederations between January 1973 and August 1975, one can see that the CGTP and CTRP account for 23% and 25% respectively (Table 6.3). However, the large number of unions for which no in-

Table 6.2
Number of New Unions Recognized per Year

Year	All sectors	Industry only	Cumulative total
1931–1940	52	11	52
1941–1945	124	43	176
1946–1948	213	61	389
1949–1950	11	4	400
1951–1955	51	15	451
1956	35	13	486
1957	71	28	557
1958	50	20	607
1959	39	17	646
1960	47	22	693
1961	143	45	836
1962	240	99	1076
1963	268	98	1344
1964	307	87	1651
1965	184	69	1835
1966	171	79	2006
1967	146	65	2152
1968	145	49	2297
1969	117	31	2414
1970	198	94	2612
1971	384	212	2996
1972	409	203	3405
1973	357	165	3762
1974	303	133	4065
1975 (up to August)	107	44	4172
Before 1968	2152	776	
1968–1975	2020	931	
Total	4172	1707	
Percentage before 1968	51.6	45.5	
Percentage 1968–1975	48.4	54.5	

Source: Register of Unions in the Ministry of Labor

Table 6.3
Number of Unions Recognized by Affiliation, 1973–1975

	Percentage of recognized unions				
Affiliation	1973	1974	1975	1973–1975	N
CTP	1	3	1	2	15
CGTP	22	24	24	23	177
CNT	1	3	3	2	16
CTRP	23	22	36	25	188
Independent	3	16	9	9	69
No information	49	32	27	39	301
Total	100	100	100	100	766

Source: Register of Unions in the Ministry of Labor.

formation about affiliation was recorded in the official register indicates that this table probably overestimates the real strength of the CTRP in relation to the CGTP. It was well known that CTRP-affiliated unions would obtain their official recognition very fast and easily, whereas for CGTP-affiliated unions the procedures could be quite difficult and slow. Accordingly, one would expect all CTRP-affiliated unions to provide information about their affiliation, in contrast to CGTP-affiliated unions, for which withholding this information might be advantageous. In addition, many unions were founded as CTRP unions and switched their affiliation to the CGTP soon after being officially recognized.[10] Since Table 6.3 is based on the register of unions in the Ministry of Labor, which gives the affiliation of a union at the time of recognition, unions that switched their affiliation still appear as CTRP unions here.

An examination of organization patterns by economic activity (Table 6.4) shows that the CTRP's relatively greater success in organization was in the commerce and service sectors, particularly in sales personnel, and transport and communications workers. Transport and communication was the potentially most important area of CTRP organization, since a successful organizational penetration could have rendered paralyzation of activity by militant unions unlikely in these important sectors.[11] However, the CTRP did not manage to develop into the dominant organizational force with control over these sectors either, which became clearly visible, for instance, when the CTP union of microbus drivers paralyzed virtually all public transportation in the Lima

[10]This was pointed out to me repeatedly in interviews with the person in charge of the Union Register in the Ministry of Labor, as well as with union leaders.

[11]An impressive example of the potentially highly disruptive consequences of a paralyzation of activity in these sectors is the Chilean truckers' strike of October 1972. What was done in Chile by private owners of the means of transportation could be done by militant unions elsewhere. Successful CTRP penetration into these sectors, organizing both owners and employees, would have reduced the probability of such militant action in the Peruvian transport system.

Table 6.4
Number of Unions Recognized in Different Sectors by Affiliation, 1973–1975[a]

Sector	Percentage of affiliation in sector							
	CTP	CGTP	CNT	CTRP	Independent	No information	N	Percentage
Agriculture, forestry, fishing	2	4	0	21	8	66	52	100.0
Mining and oil	0	0	2	13	13	72	40	100.0
Manufacturing industry	2	38	2	23	8	28	341	100.0
Construction	0	6	0	6	25	63	16	100.0
Electric and sanitary services	0	0	0	0	34	66	3	100.0
Commerce, banking, insurance, real estate	1	11	2	35	8	43	147	100.0
Transport, warehouses, communication	2	6	2	50	4	35	48	100.0
Services: hotels, movies, hospitals	3	22	3	16	12	45	119	100.0
							766	

Source: Register of Unions in the Ministry of Labor.
[a] N = 766.

area through a strike on July 1, 1976. Commerce and service sectors are generally everywhere less well unionized than production workers,[12] and unions that exist in these sectors have often a decentralized organizational structure with fairly loose coordination and low participation rates of the base in union affairs. Consequently, it was relatively easy for CTRP organizers to set up unions and formally affiliate workers in these sectors without really integrating the workers into the organization. Expansion in these areas added numbers to the CTRP, but not a real power base as counterweight to the CGTP's influence in the labor movement. In the manufacturing industry, where labor was traditionally better organized and more experienced in using its organization as a power base, the CGTP was substantially more successful than the CTRP, accounting for 38% of all unions recognized. Consequently, the CGTP not only retained but even increased its overall influence on organized labor.

In mining, another traditionally well-organized and militant sector crucial for the Peruvian economy, the CTRP was able to affiliate a total of only five unions, which indicates its complete lack of influence in this important sector. For most new mining unions, no information about their affiliation was recorded. Most likely, they were affiliated to one of the strong regional federations of mining unions, particularly in the Center and the South, which were formally independent, but close to the CGTP or attacking the CGTP from the left; or to the National Federation of Mining and Metal Workers, which disaffiliated itself from the CGTP in November 1973.

Geographically speaking, the CGTP was able to organize more successfully than the CTRP in the Lima–Callao area, whereas the CTRP organized somewhat more in the provinces (Table 6.5). However, the large number of unions in the provinces for which no affiliation was reported indicates that the success of the CTRP was quite small in relation to the overall organization rate there, too. (See p. 178 for the assumption underlying this argument.)

Due to the organizational weakness and inexperience of affiliated unions, the national CTRP leadership did not encounter internal opposition to their class-conciliatory and labor peace policies for a considerable time. Under the impact of deteriorating economic conditions, however, the already mentioned criticisms started to be raised. CTRP leadership countered these criticisms by accusations of Communist infiltration, and a successful effort was made to

[12]For instance, figures for Britain show that in 1960 union members constituted 43.2% of the total labor force; in an analysis of membership within separate industries, all commerce and service sectors fell clearly below this average, as they ranged from distribution with only 15% of the workforce organized, to theatres, cinemas, and sports with 39% organized, which was the highest unionization rate among commerce and service sectors. Bain (1970:23). Similar differences hold for the United States: whereas there were no manufacturing industries in 1962 with less than 25% of the wage earners covered by union agreements, less than 25% of workers were covered in such commerce and service sectors as beauty shops, clerical workers, laundries, restaurants, and retail trade. Peterson (1963:151).

Table 6.5

Percentage of Unions Recognized in Lima-Callao and the Provinces by Affiliation, 1973–1975[a]

Area	All	CTP	CGTP	CNT	CTRP	Independent	No information	Percentage
Lima-Callao	75	3	30	3	27	7	30	100
Provinces	25	0	2	0	15	12	71	100

Source: Register of Unions in the Ministry of Labor.

[a] N = 772.

marginalize the Lima bases during the First Ordinary Congress in May 1976. This congress was again subject to strong SINAMOS influence, and a docile new leadership was elected. I interviewed both the former and the new Secretary General, and the Secretaries of Organization of the CTRP, whose responses revealed the same traits:

1. Mechanical recitation of phrases from the *Ideological Bases of the Peruvian Revolution*[13] in response to concrete questions, without any interpretative ability or personal understanding of their meaning;
2. Lack of experience in union affairs, glorified as "real leadership participation from the base;"
3. Lack of knowledge about fundamental provisions of the law of CI, despite strong verbal support for the concept of the CI;
4. Conciliatory attitude toward private entrepreneurs "who deserve their just rewards for their efforts," with the exception of some "bad counterrevolutionary entrepreneurs;"
5. Fundamental hatred toward the CGTP.

Obviously, this type of union leadership was incapable of organizing and holding a union movement together. The little success they did have at all was to be attributed to the material and organizational support provided by state agencies for putting the organization on its feet and carrying out routine activities for its maintenance.

Despite its numerical growth, then, the CTRP just developed into an additional and comparatively weak national union organization. It failed in its central task of penetrating crucial sectors of the industrial working class and becoming the dominant organizational force among labor, capable of providing labor peace and unconditional support for the government's social and economic policies. As the main reason for its failure to penetrate previously organized sectors and to win out in the competition with other union organizers for the affiliation of previously unorganized sectors, one can point to the lack of instrumentality of the CTRP as formal structure serving no clear purpose. Except to its leaders, the CTRP did not provide any special benefits or incentives. Promises and persuasion proved reasonably effective among sectors of workers without integration into a workplace collective and contact with working-class organizations. Among other sectors of workers, however, who experienced a conflict of interest between employers and workers as a collectivity, such as in the industrial sector through the CI, CTRP rhetoric about dialogue

---

[13]The *Ideological Bases of the Peruvian Revolution* were published in various forms, such as brochures, tiny 22-page booklets, etc., and widely distributed by the Central Office of Information, Lima, February 1975.

and mutual respect proved less convincing. Furthermore, experience demonstrated that a show of strength through endurance in a strike increased the chances of demands being satisfied. (Evidence for this point will be presented later in this chapter.) Consequently, the need for strong collective defense of their interests generated among workers by the process of mobilization and increasing polarization rendered them more likely to seek affiliation to a central organization that would provide support and advice in conflicts, than to one that would condemn strikes as contrary to the interests of society.

As a result of the lack of success with the strategies of co-optation and organizational encapsulation, attempts at legal restriction of the action possibilities of unions were given increased emphasis. And enforcement of legal restrictions more and more took the form of repression, which came to dominate the government's policies toward the working class in the Second Phase.

Legal Controls

The possibilities in Peruvian union legislation as of 1972 for control over unions were quite restricted, particularly in comparison to those available to other regimes attempting to restrict autonomous union organization and action, such as Brazil or Mexico. Accordingly, either a comprehensive revision was required of the legislation for an expansion of the government's legal control potential, or an addition of new regulations was necessary. Since the former solution was basically preferred because of its presumed greater legitimacy, but since no consensus on bills for a revised labor legislation could be reached within the government, legal restrictions remained rather ineffective until 1976, when special decrees with repressive provisions started being used very frequently, regardless of their fit with traditional labor legislation.

Apart from the requirement of official recognition, and of notification to the Ministry of Labor in the case of changes in leadership or statutes, Peruvian legislation did not subject unions to any further controls over their internal functioning. Of course, its role in the solution of demands and grievances gives the Ministry of Labor some leeway to reward or sanction unions, but it does not enjoy the legal right for direct intervention in unions. Once a union is officially recognized, the law specifically prohibits its dissolution or suspension through administrative resolution, and its recognition can only be withdrawn if it violates the law (Bonilla 1975:30–31). The only influence possibility provided by the recognition mechanism is temporary withholding of recognition to a new leadership with the argument of violation of statutory election procedures or, in the case of competing leaderships, the recognition of the one that has the approval of the labor authorities. The latter was in fact done in several cases where the Revolutionary Labor Movement (MLR, *Movimiento Laboral Revolucionario*) was involved.[14]

In contrast, Brazilian and Mexican legal control mechanisms over unions extend much further. Brazilian law of the *Estado Nŏvo* provided for funding of unions through a trade union tax, which was collected from all wage earners—union members and nonmembers alike—and distributed through the Ministry of Labor to the unions, to be used for purposes specified by the law. This control over union finances obviously gave considerable leverage to the Ministry of Labor to enforce acquiescence of unions. Furthermore, the Ministry of Labor also had the right to direct intervention in unions, appointing a delegate or junta to administer it (Erickson 1972:142–143).

The most significant and characteristic aspect of the Mexican system of control over unions is its operation through a highly centralized union structure. Top-level union leaders have control over the recognition of lower-level union leaders; if the latter are denied recognition by the former, their local union and its members do not enjoy the protection of labor laws. This clearly enforces compliance of lower-level leaders with directives from the top. The major means at the disposal of lower-level leaders to exercise control over the rank and file is the "Exclusion Clause," which stipulates that a worker who is excluded from union membership automatically loses his job.[15] Thus the government's control task is focused on the co-optation of the top-level leadership, as their compliance ensures compliance of the whole organization. And since the rewards of holding top union leadership positions with governmental approval are considerable, co-optation has been by and large successful. Additional important control mechanisms in the Mexican system are provided by strike legislation: Leaders of large strikes can be jailed under the Law of Social Dissolution (Everett 1967:22); strikes involving violence or property damage (obviously flexible concepts) can be declared illegal immediately; and any strike has to be announced six days in advance by the union in order to be legal.

Minister of Labor Sala Orosco attempted to introduce some of these control mechanisms into the Peruvian system through a revision of labor and union legislation, which he repeatedly announced as being imminent (see, e.g., *La Prensa*, November 24, 1973; and November 15, 1974). According to information obtained in an interview with him, the draft for this legislation included the following major provisions:

1. In order to avoid politicization of union leaderships and the formation of union oligarchies, the period for holding any position as a union leader

---

[14]The MLR will be discussed further in the next section.

[15]This clause only applies in enterprises where union and employer have concluded a closed-shop agreement, which, according to Everett, is quite frequent. The information about Mexican trade unions presented here is drawn from Everett (1967) and Miller (1966).

would be limited to 1 year, and re-election would be prohibited for 3 years.

2. The state (i.e., the Ministry of Labor,) would be given the right to check all books and accounts of unions upon the demand of any group of workers.

3. A strike would have to be approved by 75% of workers in a secret vote before giving notice of the intention to initiate it to the enterprise and the Ministry.

4. The period between giving notice and initiating a strike would be extended from 12 hours to 8 days. During these 8 days a team from the Ministry of Labor, composed of a management specialist, an economist, a lawyer, and a Ministry official would go to the enterprise and solve the issue through compulsory arbitration.

5. The concept of "economic crime" and appropriate sanctions would be introduced into strike legislation, which would subject union leaders to legal prosecution for instigation of irresponsible strikes; the qualification of a strike as irresponsible would be determined by the Ministry of Labor.

Corresponding draft legislation was presented to the COAP by the Ministry of Labor, but a majority of members of the government feared a very strong and costly conflict with unions upon the introduction of such legislation, and consequently none of it was ever enacted. In Mexico and Brazil, in contrast, legislation with stringent control mechanisms had preceded a significant growth in unionization and thus not met with nearly as strong an opposition as was to be expected in Peru in case of its introduction.

Legislation concerning regulation of strikes is composed of a series of decree laws from 1913, 1946, and 1963, the enforcement of which by Peruvian government has varied over time. Violation of any of the rules set forth in these laws makes it possible for the Ministry of Labor to declare a strike illegal. This means that striking workers do not enjoy protection from being fired. Under the 1970 law of security of employment, unjustified absence from work for three consecutive days constituted a reason for being fired. Accordingly, if an illegal strike lasted 3 days, participating workers could be fired. As was mentioned before, this law of security of employment was enacted to solve the problem of massive firings started by entrepreneurs in protest against the law of CI. As a consequence of this law, however, the government's relative strength vis-à-vis unions was considerably hampered (e.g., by delaying the effectiveness of the declaration of a strike as illegal for 3 days). Furthermore, unions could appeal this decision, and it was standard practice for unions to do so. Thus it was not a very frequent occurrence for strikes to last more than 3 days, have their illegality be upheld, and result in the firing of workers. The ones that did occur involved harsh confrontations, sometimes provoking solidarity strikes of federations, and in the case of the factory *Plásticos el Pacífico* in December

1975, even a 1-day solidarity strike of the CGTP. Accordingly, although a
memorandum was circulated by the Ministry of Labor in May 1974, remind-
ing all labor authorities to immediately declare any strike illegal that failed to
fulfill one of the numerous formal requirements, unions were not necessarily
intimidated by the use of this control mechanism due to its frequent but ineffective use.[16] This situation clearly changed in 1976, when the declaration of
strikes as illegal was preceded by the immediate suspension of security of employment in the case of a strike, such as in fishing in February 1976, and in
mining in March 1976. This approach became typical for the Second Phase of
the Peruvian Revolution, after the ouster of President Velasco in August 1975.
Some tendencies of violence and repression were already visible during the
First Phase, but they mainly originated from a small group of ministers, known
as La Misión, rather than being general government policy.[17]

Toleration of Violence and Exercise of Selective Repression

One very controversial tendency, knowledge about which was officially denied by most members of the government, manifested itself in the emergence of
the violent Revolutionary Labor Movement. This movement emerged under
the auspices of the Minister of Fishery, Tantaleán Vanini, and its nature and
purpose were not readily apparent. It was not clear whether it was designed as
a nuclear union organization or as a political party. An after-the-fact official
justification explained the central aim of the MLR as "fighting in support of
the social and economic achievements of the Revolution, and defining the ideologically somewhat confused political panorama."[18] In practice, the MLR
worked mainly as a shock troop with the task of disciplining undesirably independent and militant unions.

Again, an attempt was made to compromise and involve SINAMOS in the

---

[16]For instance, all of the strikes of the CGTP-affiliated Federation of Metal Workers, FETIMP,
were declared illegal, but none of them was followed up by a suspension of the security of employment. These strikes were: 1972, 48 hours; June 1973, 48 hours; March 1974, 48 hours; September 1974, 13 days; April 1975, 48 hours; and December 1975, 48 hours. This information was
given to me in an interview by the Secretary General of the FETIMP, José Chávez.

[17]La Misión consisted of the Minister of Fishery, Tantaleán Vanini, the Minister of the Interior,
Richter Prada, and the Minister of Labor, Sala Orosco. A detailed though, of course, partisan,
account of their actions is given by Thorndike (1976), who was one of the government-appointed
newspaper directors from July 1974 to July 1975. It seems that Velasco's deteriorating health made
him increasingly susceptible to the influence of these ministers, which would explain the arrests
and deportations of July 1975, and the coalition between radical and conservative forces within the
government which brought about his ouster.

[18]Communiqué of the National Committee of the Educational Sector of the MLR; La Crónica,
February 16, 1975.

promotion of this movement. The first public announcement of the creation of the MLR was made in one of a series of lectures sponsored jointly by the Ministry of Fishery and SINAMOS in the presence of Leonidas Rodríguez, then head of SINAMOS, and he expressed "the support of SINAMOS for the MLR [*Expreso*, May 23, 1973]." It seems plausible that this statement was just an adaptation to a situation where he was taken by surprise, being presented with the fact.[19] Given that this happened while the ministerial committee was preparing for the set-up of the CTRP, it seems also credible that the MLR was not part of the government's integral mobilization policy, but rather a manifestation of personalistic manipulatory tendencies and projects. In particular, the MLR was promoted by the Minister of Fishery, in an attempt to build up a personal power base as a counterweight to the popularity of more radical members of the government, and it was supported by the Minister of the Interior. A further indication of the marginality of the MLR in relation to official government mobilization policy at a later stage was the CTRP's denial of any relations to the MLR in response to a self-identification of the MLR as the "armed political arm of the CTRP [see *Cronología Política*]."

Initially, the activity of the MLR was concentrated in the fishing sector. According to an MLR organizer (*Marka*, October 10, 1975), their task was to co-opt the leadership of weak or politically divided unions and to organize new unions. In order to be able to accomplish their task, they received substantial material support from the Ministries of Fishery and Interior, as well as from PESCAPERÚ, the state-owned fishing company which was created after the nationalization of the fishing industry in May 1973.[20] The purpose of their activity was to prevent unions from challenging labor policy and its compensation policy to former private owners.[21] In 1974, the MLR violently attacked several other unions in crucial sectors of the economy, such as the unions in Marcona Mining Company, in SIDERPERÚ (state-owned steel company), in the car manufacturing companies Chrysler and MOTORPERÚ, and Pirelli, in Nicovita, and others.[22]

As the MLR came under increasingly strong public attack, particularly in the socialized newspapers, it became more difficult for the police to tolerate or even protect its violent activities and for the Ministry of Labor to readily recognize MLR-imposed leaderships of unions. Consequently, the MLR faded from the public scene and virtually disappeared in the Second Phase.

[19]This version was confirmed in my interview with a member of the "radical faction" in the Labor Area of SINAMOS, who was transferred after Leonidas Rodríguez left SINAMOS.

[20]An indicator of the closeness of the MLR to the Ministry of Fishery, for instance, is the fact that one of its leaders was on the payroll of PESCAPERÚ as legal advisor.

[21]For a documentation of irregularities in this compensation policy, see Malpica (1975).

[22]Reports about these assaults and the controversy around the MLR can be found in *Expreso*, September to December 1974, and in the *Cronología Política* for the same period.

A more coherent and generally agreed upon policy, which was carried over into the Second Phase, was the use of threats and selective repression against militant unions and their leaders. While constantly reaffirming their commitment to a protection of labor's right to strike as a fundamental right, members of the government frequently attacked strikes as politically motivated, and threatened to prosecute political agitators and instigators of costly labor conflicts.[23] Their definition of "political strikes" was very comprehensive. For example, Minister of Labor Sala Orosco declared a miners' strike in protest against the deportation of their union's legal advisor to be politically motivated, because his deportation was not a labor problem and consequently could not be included in labor claims (*Peruvian Times*, December 14, 1973). Deportations and arrests were the most typical kinds of selective repression.[24]

The use of broader repression in Lima would obviously have had strong public repercussions and consequently political costs. In the provinces, however, repression could be applied more narrowly at crucial sectors—mainly mining—and with less nationwide visibility. Examples where repression escalated in the provinces due to solidarity strikes are the suspension of constitutional guarantees in the Center (Department of Huancavelica, Junín, and Cerro de Pasco) in November 1971, in Moquegua in May 1973, in Arequipa in May and again in November 1973. Yet, selective repression and violence were hardly more effective than co-optation, organizational encapsulation, and legal restrictions in bringing organized labor under governmental influence and reducing its militancy. On the contrary, due to the general increase in mobilization and organization, labor's overall action capability kept growing; and as government policy toward labor became more and more hostile, labor resorted to increasingly militant action in the defense of workers' interests, which showed in soaring strike rates.

Increase in Strike Activity

Table 6.6 shows just how high the strike rate in Peru has been since the early 1970s compared to other Latin American countries.[25] Peruvian strike ac-

[23]See, e.g., *La Prensa*, May 2, 1972, for Sala Orosco's statement that "the state will suppress those who cause labor problems."

[24]Cleaves and Scurrah (1975) have compiled the following figures for deportations between 1968 and 1974: 12 political party activists, 8 union leaders, 18 journalists, 2 social scientists, and 2 priests; a total of 42 persons.

[25]The spotty nature of the table is due to the variable availability of data for different countries in different time periods. The available data from various sources have been checked against each other, and they turned out to be consistent. Most probably, they are all based on figures provided by governmental agencies in the respective countries, which would also explain the blank spots in certain time periods, for which no figures were released, presumably for political reasons.

Table 6.6
Strike Activity in Latin American Countries[a]

Year	Chile 1	2	3	El Salvador 1	2	3	Guatemala 1	2	3	Mexico 1	2	3	Panama 1	2	3	Paraguay 1	2	3	Peru 1	2	3	Venezuela 1	2	3
1962	410	4.5														4	1.5	41.1	380			19	.3	27.1
1963	416	6.1														3	.8	94.5	422			9	.1	15.2
1964	560	7.1								62	.01					2	.2	2.4	398			27	.2	6.8
1965	723	9.0								67	.01					3	.3	1.8	397	7.3	434.8	24	.2	8.9
1966	1073	9.4	974				8	.8	96.1	91	.01					2	.2	4.1	394	6.6	761.8	12	.2	3.8
1967	1114	10.6	937				4	1.4	591.9	78	.12					1	.1	.7	414	7.2	526.2	29	.1	2.4
1968	1124	13.5	1679				3	.6	27.9	156	.06		3	.4	2.5	2	.04	.4	364	5.2	204.9	14	.3	4.9
1969	1277	16.2	529							144	.06		9	.7	2.8				372	4.0	213.7	83	.9	
1970	1819	28.8	1234				36	4.5	87.2	206	.19		6	6.8	50.8				345	4.7	307.8	64	1.0	98.2
1971	2696	12.8	594	12	2.3	421	1	.01	.8	204	.11		280	5.8					377	6.5	550.0	106	1.6	210.8
1972	3325	16.5	703	23	.8	87	4	.8	53.5	207	.10								409	5.0	333.9	172	1.0	47.4
1973	2050	29.2	1026	6	.1	1.2	16	3.5	401.7	13									788	15.2	715.2	250	1.7	441.1
1974				73			53	6.7	799.1										570	12.5	577.9			

Sources: Strikes, Workers Involved, Man-Days Lost: America en cifras, OEA, Washington, D.C., 1975; and ILO Yearbook of Labor Statistics, Geneva, 1975. Non-agricultural economically active population: yearly estimates from 1960 and 1970 data; Statistical Abstracts of Latin America UCLA, Vol. 17, 1976.
[a]The numbered column heads are keyed as follows: 1 = Total number of strikes; 2 = Total number of workers involved as a percentage of non-agricultural economically active population; 3 = Working days lost per 1,000 workers in non-agricultural economically active population.

tivity resembles the Chilean one during the situation of "hypermobilization" preceding and during the Allende years[26] more closely than the one in any other Latin American country.

Apparently the most obvious explanation for the rising strike rates is the increase in union organization. In fact, it has been argued that rising strike rates are typical for periods of rapid unionization.[27] Comparing the Chilean rate of unionization to the Peruvian one, one can see an even steeper rate of increase for Peru (Table 6.7), though one has to keep in mind that Peru started from a much lower base. This explanation can be supported by the findings presented in Chapter 4, which show greater strike proneness in new unions than in older ones. The fight of new unions for recognition and serious considerations of their demands on the part of employers as well as the state bureaucracy frequently involved a show of strength through strike action.[28] Yet, this fight for recognition cannot be regarded as a one-time action, restricted to individual new unions, but rather has to be seen in the larger context of a general struggle for the recognition of the whole labor movement as a sociopolitical force to be reckoned with.

Before accepting this argument and trying to substantiate it, though, the question has to be asked whether the whole increase in strike activity in Peru was not indeed caused by the formation of new unions, or, whether older, better established unions also went on strike more frequently in the years 1973 to 1975. Looking at the number of strikes per recognized union in all sectors and in manufacturing industry only in 1973 to 1975 (Table 6.8), there is no absolute increase over 1965–1967. After a decrease in the early years under the military government, the average number of strikes per union in 1973–1975 reached again the level of the last years under Belaúnde. This might in fact lead one to assume that the whole absolute increase in strike activity was caused by the formation of new unions. In order to conclusively answer this

[26]This terminology is used by Landsberger and McDaniel (1976).

[27]Ross and Hartman (1960:16) argue in their 15-nation study that: "Periods of rapid organization are often marked with industrial conflict. . . . Where union membership has become stabilized, on the other hand, strike activity has generally declined." Whereas their observation that rapid unionization tends to be accompanied by high strike rates is empirically founded and correct, their assertion that stabilization of membership has led to a general decline of strike activity in the industrialized world has to be qualified, as shown by Shorter and Tilly (1974).

[28]In Ross and Hartman's terminology, new unions are preoccupied with organizational, as opposed to economic, conflict. Organizational conflict is characterized by high militancy in strikes, as "unions are struggling to win their place in economic society, and employers are striving to retain their traditional authority. As long as unions are permitted to strike for power but are thwarted in their every bid, only conflict can result [1960:67]." A further characteristic present in the Peruvian situation, which Ross and Hartman identify as being conducive to high strike activity, was political competition within the labor movement. "Rival unionism is a potent cause of strikes where rivalry is pursued on the basis of comparative militancy in pressing grievances and comparative gains in collective bargaining [1960:65]."

Table 6.7
Total Number of Unions in Chile and Peru

	N		Index[a]	
Year	Chile	Peru	Chile	Peru
1960	1770	693	100.0	100.0
1964	1863	1651	105.3	283.2
1966	2870	2006	162.1	289.5
1970	4519	2612	255.3	376.9
1972	6001	3405	339.0	491.3
1973		3762		542.9
1974		4065		586.6

Sources: Chile: Landsberger and McDaniel (1976:518). Peru: Register of Unions in the Ministry of Labor.
[a] 1960 = 100.0.

question, one would want to perform a time-series analysis of strike behavior of unions that were formed before 1968 to establish whether their strike activity remained relatively constant or increased as well.

Such data are not available, but two arguments can be mentioned which suggest that new unions were not exclusively responsible for the overall increase in strikes, and that older unions also went on strike more frequently from 1973 to 1975 than before. First, it has been shown that approximately 25% of the new unions formed between 1973 and 1975 were affiliated to the CTRP, which pursued a clear strike-avoidance policy. As will be shown later in this chapter, CTRP unions accounted for roughly 3% of the strikes in 1974

Table 6.8
Number of Strikes per Recognized Union, All Sectors and Manufacturing Industry Only

	All sectors			Manufacturing industry		
Year	Strikes	Unions	Strikes per union	Strikes	Unions	Strikes per union
1965	397	1835	.22	191	632	.30
1966	394	2006	.20	191	711	.27
1967	414	2152	.19	207	776	.27
1968	364	2297	.16	198	825	.24
1969	372	2414	.15	143	856	.17
1970	345	2612	.13	136	950	.14
1971	377	2996	.13	184	1162	.16
1972	409	3405	.12	259	1365	.19
1973	788	3762	.21	423	1530	.28
1974	570	4065	.14	316	1663	.19
1975	779	4172	.19	427	1751	.24

Sources: Ministerio de trabajo, *Las Huelgas en el Perú, 1957–72*, Lima, 1973; and calculations by the author on the basis of unpublished statistics from the Ministry of Labor.

and 1975 only, which implies that many of these new unions did not go on strike at all. Second, if the increase in strike rates was exclusively due to the formation of new unions, one might expect strikes to have become smaller through time (i.e., involving fewer workers on the average) as unionization expanded particularly to include smaller enterprises. However, as Table 6.9 shows, strikes, on the average, became markedly larger in size rather than smaller. Their larger average size, on the one hand, reflects the participation of big unions, most of which tended to be older, and on the other hand, greater participation in solidarity strikes organized by federations. As will be discussed later, solidarity strikes accounted for a considerable proportion of strikers and of man-hours lost from 1973 to 1975. Thus one has to look for reasons why the militancy of older unions and the mobilization for solidarity strikes had increased by 1975, transforming labor's gains in organizational capacity into increases in strike activity.

To identify these reasons, the introductory remarks to this chapter have to be related to the discussion of determinants of strike behavior in Chapter 1. There it was argued that strikes are a means for labor to expand its power and its share in the distribution of societal resources, and that they can be used vis-à-vis both employers and the government. Great organizational strength and mobilization capacity are a prerequisite for effective strike action, but they are not necessarily causes of high militancy. On the contrary, the greater the sociopolitical strength of a labor movement, the greater its opportunity to pursue its goals without having to resort to potentially costly strike action. In particular, influence on a pro-labor government to effect direct intervention in labor disputes and/or general policies favorable to labor's interests is a highly desirable substitute for strike pressure on employers. Extensive organizational penetration, high centralization of collective bargaining, and high ideological unity are the essential elements for increasing labor's strength as a sociopolitical force—and thus its influence on government, while lowering in turn its dependence on militancy—and thus having a moderating effect on strike rates.

It was further argued that, in developing capitalist systems, both labor's weakness vis-à-vis employers, due to a highly unfavorable supply–demand ratio on the labor market, and a strong tradition of state intervention in labor relations make government the central target for collective action in the pursuit of workers' interests. However, labor movements in developing capitalist countries are typically characterized by the lack of all three essential elements on which labor's sociopolitical strength and influence on government are based. Thus, in the absence of reliable channels for the exercise of political influence, labor remains dependent on mobilization for militant strike action. The Peruvian labor movement is a case in point: It managed to expand its organizational penetration considerably, but has remained characterized by a very low centralization of collective bargaining and low ideological unity. Thus, whereas up to

Table 6.9
Shape of Strikes in Peru, 1965–1975, All Sectors

Year	Size; mean number of strikers per strike	Duration; mean number of man-days lost per striker	Frequency; number of strikes per 100,000 non-agricultural economically active population
1965	342	5.9	20.5
1966	308	12.0	19.5
1967	344	7.35	19.7
1968	296	3.9	16.6
1969	246	5.3	16.3
1970	322	6.5	14.7
1971	428	8.4	15.2
1972	319	6.1	15.7
1973	528	4.7	28.7
1974	636	4.6	19.6
1975	792	4.1	25.6

Sources: Ministerio de trabajo, *Las huelgas en el Perú: 1957–1972*, Lima, 1973; and calculations by the author on the basis of unpublished statistics from the Ministry of Labor, and from the *ILO Yearbook of Labor Statistics, 1976.* The figures published in the 1976 *ILO Yearbook of Labor Statistics* for total number of workers involved and total number of man-hours lost in 1974 and 1975 were somewhat higher than the figures I had collected from the statistics in the Ministry of Labor in the spring of 1976. Since it seems possible that the data collection for the statistics was not fully completed by the time I saw the data, I am using the ILO figures in all the tables. The discrepancies were the following:

	1974		1975	
	My data	ILO	My data	ILO
Total number of strikes	550	570	779	779
Man-hours lost	13,354	13,413	13,839	20,269
Workers involved	259,239	362,737	504,903	617,120

1972, the military government seemed to be somewhat responsive to labor—at least more so than any previous government—this responsiveness was not a result of labor's sociopolitical strength, but rather of the government's policy of national integration, involving an attempt at co-optation of organized labor through persuasion and incentives. Therefore, labor was unable to prevent initial government responsiveness from being turned rapidly and easily into hostility towards autonomous labor organizations. The only action possibility open to labor to defend its autonomy and regain some of the lost influence, then, was to resort to a show of strength through increased militancy. Consequently, a certain restraint in strike behavior gave way to full activation of the newly strengthened mobilization capacity.

In 1971, the government officially recognized the Communist-controlled CGTP, and the Minister of Labor attempted to establish a close working relationship with CGTP leaders and affiliated unions, so as to obtain their loyalty and at the same time further weaken the APRA-controlled CTP. The CGTP had certainly become the strongest force in the labor movement by the early 1970s in terms of its mobilization capacity. And following the Communist Party's line of support for the government, the CGTP was quite ready for a close working relationship. However, it was by no means capable of controlling and restraining all major strike activity, not even among its member unions, due to the low degree of centralization.[29] Furthermore, there were a large number of independent unions, not affiliated to one of the four confederations, that showed considerable militancy. This manifested itself clearly in the 1971 strikes in the mining sector, where the CGTP was not instrumental in exercising a moderating influence. Thus the government could not consider the CGTP a reliable partner in the implementation of its labor policies, and the decision to sponsor the CTRP was taken. In 1972, while organizing efforts for the CTRP were getting under way, relations between the Ministry of Labor and the CGTP had not yet undergone a radical change. Also, real wages were still increasing, since wage settlements remained favorable. Accordingly, the number of strikes increased only moderately. In 1973, however, after the CTRP had officially been recognized and governmental attacks on "irresponsible politicized unionism" grew in intensity, unions resorted to militant solidaristic defense action, and the strike rate rose dramatically. In particular, 1973 saw a number of escalating regional labor conflicts, with clearly political aspects. In 1974 and 1975, with the onset of the economic crisis and the fall of real wages, strike pressure on employers and the government grew even larger, involving even greater numbers of workers.

The contention that escalating conflicts in a number of regions contributed to the extraordinarily great increase in the number of strikes in 1973 is supported by the data.[30] The proportion of strikes in the manufacturing sector outside the Lima–Callao area was higher in 1973 than in the following 2 years, as

[29]A comparison with the French CGT is interesting here. The French CGT is more closely controlled by the Communist Party than is the Peruvian CGTP, presumably because the French Communist Party is much stronger and more disciplined. For instance, in the 1978 Peruvian elections to the Constituent Assembly, the Communist Party received only 6% of the vote, whereas the Communist Party in France regularly polls around 20%. Also, there are many more Communist activists at middle and lower levels in French unions. Thus ideological discipline can compensate to a certain extent for a lack of organizational centralization to ensure unified action of the unions affiliated to the CGT. This is not the case in Peru, where relations between the CGTP and the Communist Party are mainly sustained at the top leadership level, and where this leadership has limited control over affiliated unions.

[30]As data base for this analysis, I was able to copy the information concerning all strikes in the industrial manufacturing sector in 1973, 1974, and 1975 from the original register in the Ministry of Labor. This register contains information not only about quantitative aspects of the strikes, such as length, number of workers involved, etc., but also about qualitative aspects, such as reasons for

was the proportion of workers involved and man-hours lost (Table 6.10). Though susceptibility of organized and nonorganized labor to manipulative policies was generally higher in the provinces than in the Lima–Callao area due to the greater lack of resources needed to build up an organizational infrastructure, there were some quite well organized and ideologically strong regional union federations. Examples are the Regional Federations of Arequipa, of Cuzco, of Puno, and of Mine and Metal Workers of the South of Peru, which took part in the Union Reorganization Committee, out of which the CGTP emerged (Sulmont 1974). Such class struggle oriented federations and affiliated unions showed strong solidaristic reactions in escalating conflicts in 1973. Several such conflicts emerged out of disputes about firings and layoffs. For instance, a bitter struggle concerning arrests and firings in SIDERPERÚ, which originated in a general strike of the Federation of Workers of Ancash in May, escalated to the point of causing a suspension of constitutional guarantees. Further examples of strong conflicts in 1973 in the provinces, where the government resorted to the use of selective repression, are clashes between police and strikers in Moquegua in April, and the declaration of a state of emergency in Arequipa in May and again in November of the same year.

Strike Patterns

In order to further substantiate the above arguments about the impact of changing economic and political conditions on labor militancy, one can look at the development of strike patterns both in longitudinal and cross-national perspective. From 1965 to 1972, Peruvian strike patterns did not show any clear tendencies of change, but between 1973 and 1975 they were on the average markedly larger, shorter, and more frequent than before. In a cross-national perspective, a pattern of short, large, and frequent strikes has been characterized as typical for situations where "newly organized, politically impotent working classes [are determined] to participate in national politics through protest strikes [Shorter and Tilly 1974:326]." This characterization, applied to the French labor movement in the 1950s and 1960s, fits the Peruvian one in the 1970s, particularly 1973–1975, at least in part. A comparison of the Peruvian 1973–1975 pattern with the various patterns distinguished by Shorter and Tilly shows that in size it falls between the 1900–1929 West European and the post-World War II French and Italian pattern, with 500–800 strikers per strike. In

---

strikes, type of organization staging the strike, affiliation of this organization, form of the strike, result, and form of solution. Information about some of these variables has been included only in the register for 1975 and 1974. Consequently, tables using these variables are based only on the strikes in 1974 and 1975, which changes the total N from 1164 to 741 in some tables.

Table 6.10
Strike Activity in Manufacturing Industry in Lima-Callao and the Provinces, 1973–1975

Area	Percentage of all strikes			Percentage of all workers involved			Percentage of all man-hours lost		
	1973	1974	1975	1973	1974	1975	1973	1974	1975
Lima-Callao	74.8	88.2	86.4	74.8	92.9	81.6	70.9	93.1	90.7
Provinces	$\frac{25.2}{100}$	$\frac{11.8}{100}$	$\frac{13.6}{100}$	$\frac{25.2}{100}$	$\frac{7.1}{100}$	$\frac{18.4}{100}$	$\frac{29.1}{100}$	$\frac{6.9}{100}$	$\frac{9.3}{100}$
N	423	312	427	112,196	86,306	133,882	5,295,000	4,597,000	5,445,000

frequency and length, it comes closest to the latter, though Peruvian strikes were both more frequent (20–29 strikes per 100,000 nonagricultural economically active population) and longer (4–5 days).[31] The size of strikes is shaped both by the stage of industrial advance via the corresponding size of enterprises and by the extent of labor's organizational capacity. The average size of enterprises in Peru is smaller than in contemporary France, and is more similar to France before 1930. Whereas the difference in size of strikes between Peru and post-World War II France can be explained by differences in the industrial structure, the difference in length is due to a difference in purpose of the strikes. As will be shown in the subsequent discussion, the figures for average length of strikes hide an important difference between two distinctive types of strikes with respectively different purposes. Peruvian strikes include both types identified as characteristic for the French pre-1930 and post-World War II period (Shorter and Tilly 1974:326). They include strikes aimed at impressing labor authorities to intervene favorably in labor disputes, typical for pre-1930 French strikes, as well as strikes aimed at the government as a symbolic action in support of labor's demands for greater influence and a greater share of the resources, typical for post-World War II French strikes. The importance of strikes aimed at impressing labor authorities in Peru derives from the predominant role that these authorities play in every aspect of labor relations.

Collective negotiations and grievances follow a multistage pattern, where different types of strikes are used according to the stage. In the first stage of the process of collective negotiation, the union presents the list of demands to the employer, and at the same time a copy of it to the Ministry of Labor. If union and employer come to no agreement, the union can bring the employer before a conciliation body in the Ministry of Labor. If the conciliation does not lead to agreement either, the Ministry of Labor issues a resolution as binding arbitration. This first resolution is a divisional or, for the provinces, a zonal resolution, which can be appealed to two higher levels, the subdirectoral and directoral.[32] The strikes breaking out in the direct negotiation phase serve

[31]The 1900–1929 West European pattern (France, Italy, Germany, Belgium, and Spain) shows an average of 300–400 workers per strike, 15 man-days lost per strike, and 6–12 strikes per 100,000 workers. The post-World War II French and Italian pattern shows an average of 1130–1030 workers per strike, 2.3–3.3 man-days lost per striker, and 12.8–18.1 strikes per 100,000 workers. Shorter and Tilly (1974:318–333).

[32]In November 1971, under Minister of Labor Sala Orosco, this procedure was newly regulated in order to render it more efficient. The major innovations were a 30-day limit for direct negotiations, after which the Ministry of Labor would initiate conciliation procedures, and a requirement for authorization of bargaining delegates to conclude binding agreements. The latter provisions were mainly intended to avoid situations in which officials of the Ministry managed to convince union delegates to accept a certain compromise, sometimes after day-long negotiations, which then would be rejected by the base in a vote. Clearly, an extension of the opportunities for personal influence by Ministry officials was sought through this provision.

somewhat different purposes and show different patterns from those breaking out in later phases with direct involvement of the Ministry of Labor.

According to Peruvian legislation, notification about the intention to go on strike has to be given to the employer and the Ministry of Labor 72 hours in advance of initiating the strike. Nonfulfillment of this requirement makes it possible for the strike to be declared illegal, which, however, in the period under consideration only had an impact for strikes that lasted 3 or more days, as discussed earlier in this chapter. The data show that this was taken into consideration by unions that went on strike: For roughly half the strikes, notification was given; for the other half, not. The strikes for which no notification was given had an average duration of 2.9 days, as compared to 9.7 days for strikes with prior notification. These unannounced, short strikes broke out predominantly in the stage of direct negotiation, 95% as compared to 5% in later stages. They include primarily the type of more purely political protest strike, but also strikes over concrete labor disputes. The latter type mainly serves the purpose of demonstrating the union's capacity and willingness to fight for its demands with strike action, and to carry the dispute through several stages. Most of these unannounced strikes (67%) ended with a total rejection of workers' demands, as compared to 36% of strikes with prior notification. At higher stages, then, prior notification of strikes was typically given; strikes were longer and tended to assume the character of endurance tests aimed at forcing employers and the labor authorities to give in so as to avoid continued loss of production and/or a potential escalation of the conflict into solidarity strikes.

In fact, capacity for endurance did increase chances for success. Successful strikes lasted on the average 12 days, partly successful ones 11 days, and unsuccessful ones 2 days. These figures also reflect the higher proportion of short strikes which were staged as expressions of political protest, without chances for a successful resolution.

The difference in results of strikes according to the stage in which they were solved shows that unions did increase their chances of success by pursuing a concrete dispute beyond the stage of direct negotiation (Table 6.11). Whereas 52% of strikes solved in the first stage ended with rejection of workers' demands, only 15% in the conciliation stage did. Chances for full acceptance of demands as well as for a compromise solution increased considerably. However, only 13% of all strikes were solved through conciliation. If either union or employer were intransigent, the dispute was solved through compulsory arbitration. The 86% rejection rate of demands in this form of solution confirms the validity of the consistent complaints by unions about the notorious pro-employer attitude of labor authorities. The problem of corruption and anti-union attitudes among officials in the Ministry of Labor, in Lima and possibly even more so in its provincial branches, was indeed a serious obstacle to the credibility and success of the government's persuasion and incentive strategy

Table 6.11
Form of Solution by Result of Strikes in Manufacturing Industry, 1974–1975 [a]

	Percentage of strikes solved through:			
Results	Direct negotiation	Conciliation	Zonal–divisional resolution	Subdirectoral–directoral resolution	All
Demands accepted	25	44	5	41	24
Demands partially accepted	23	41	9	49	25
Demands rejected	52	15	86	9	51
All	46	13	28	14	100.0

[a] N = 639.

for moderation in labor militancy.[33] Only if unions appealed the decision in first instance and brought the dispute to the highest levels, chances for more favorable outcomes rose again. Only 9% of the resolutions in second and third instance rejected unions' demands flatly; 49% accepted them partially, and 41% even fully.

Obviously, for experienced union leaders this pattern of outcomes constituted a challenge not to accept a rejection from employers in direct negotiations, but rather to pursue the issue through the conciliation procedure, and not to accept an unfavorable resolution in first instance without appealing to higher levels as long as there seemed to be a reasonable chance for a compromise solution. Nevertheless, only 14% of all strikes were solved through resolution in the second and third instance. Also, despite the fact that longer strikes had a greater chance of ending with acceptance of demands, the average length of strikes started decreasing in 1973. This indicates that the purely political type of strike became more prevalent than the battle of endurance over a concrete dispute between particular employers and unions. Relatively short but large strikes were assuming increased importance as a form of protest expressing solidarity against governmental policies in labor organization and wage and price regulations.

Since my detailed data on reasons for strikes, type of union organization involved, etc. are restricted to the years 1973–1975 and to the industrial manufacturing sector, the only evidence for this contention is the tendency of change in overall strike patterns between 1965 and the 1973–1975 period (Table 6.9). However, a number of observations about consistent strike characteristics in 1973–1975 in the industrial manufacturing sector can provide indirect support for this contention. The large proportion of striking workers involved in solidarity strikes is a good indicator of the importance of mobilization for collective expressions of discontent (Table 6.12). Solidarity strikes were neither very frequent nor very long, but due to the large number of workers involved, they were very costly in terms of man-hours lost and thus of considerable economic and political importance (Table 6.13). About one-third of all workers who participated in strikes did so in solidarity with other workers, and almost one-third of man-hours were lost through these strikes. Clearly, federations of

[33]One of the most frequent complaints of labor during the First Phase was about the traditional pro-entrepreneurial orientation of officials in the Ministry of Labor, who kept on solving conflicts according to prerevolutionary standards in contradiction to the spirit of the new legislation. Personal observation had certainly confirmed the existence of a discrepancy between revolutionary humanist rhetoric stressing the dignity of labor, and the behavior of bureaucrats in the Ministry of Labor showing condescending or even outright contemptuous attitudes towards workers and their representatives. An interesting aspect is that the Ministry of Labor pays lower salaries than the Ministry of Industry, for instance. Traditionally, this had been compensated for by "voluntary contributions" from business to acknowledge prompt resolution of problems, and apparently these traditional patterns of behavior have at least partly been carried over into the revolutionary era.

Table 6.12
Reasons for Strike Activity in Manufacturing Industry

Reasons	Percentage of all strikes			Percentage of all workers involved			Percentage of all man-hours lost		
	1973	1974	1975	1973	1974	1975	1973	1974	1975
Wages/working conditions	53.2	54.5	66.3	37.9	33.2	43.5	50.2	50.0	45.8
Firings/layoffs	16.8	10.6	9.1	13.7	11.6	5.3	11.8	7.7	9.9
Union affairs	2.3	1.6	1.9	9.0	1.8	1.3	2.1	0.5	1.7
Solidarity	14.2	6.1	9.1	29.9	33.4	34.0	28.4	32.7	20.9
Others	13.2	27.2	13.6	9.4	20.0	15.9	7.5	9.1	21.7
	100	100	100	100	100	100	100	100	100
N	(423)	(312)	(427)						

Table 6.13
Intensity of Strikes in Manufacturing Industry by Reason for Strikes, 1973–1975[a]

	Mean number per strike		
Reasons	Workers involved	Man-hours lost	Hours of duration
Wages/working conditions	191	11,001	54
Firings/layoffs	230	10,788	46
Union affairs	559	9,410	22
Solidarity	931	35,686	44
Others	246	9,994	44

[a] $N = 1160$.

unions were the most effective organizers of solidarity strikes, though individual unions or informal groups at times also went on strike in solidarity with others. The mobilization potential of federations becomes apparent when one considers that they organized between 2.3% and 2.9% of strikes only, but mobilized between 34% and 38% of striking workers.[34] (Table 6.14).

Actually neither all solidarity strikes nor all strikes called by federations can be qualified as political protest strikes in the strict sense. At times, they were also called in support of the workforce in a particular enterprise, or to pressure the labor authorities for a favorable solution of a serious conflict, typically about illegal firings of union or CI leaders. However, more typical were cases where solidarity strikes developed around the issue of the Ministry of Labor's policies concerning official recognition of union leaderships, particularly as protests against the recognition of MLR leaderships. Or cases where solidarity strikes were carried out in protest against arrests or deportations of union leaders and advisors, or arrests of union militants. Also, strikes called by federations for reasons of wages and working conditions frequently had a clearly political character in that they included demands for legislation about increases in minimum legal wages, or general increases in remunerations to compensate for the rapidly rising cost of living.

The argument that most solidarity strikes as well as most strikes organized by federations had the character of political protest strikes is supported by a comparison of their results with the average success or failure rate of strikes. Only 8% of solidarity strikes ended with acceptance of workers' demands, 30% in a compromise, and 62% with a rejection of workers' demands. The failure rate

[34] The lower figure for 1975 is probably a result of different coding by the statistical office in the Ministry of Labor. If we add the percentage of workers mobilized by strikes coded as caused by a "group of workers," which is 21.3% in 1975 as compared to only 0.3% in 1973 and 1974, to the figure for federations, we obtain 34%, similar to the figures for federations in 1973 and 1974.

Table 6.14
Strikes in Manufacturing Industry by Type of Union Organization

Type of Union	Percentage of all strikes			Percentage of all workers involved			Percentage of all man-hours lost		
	1973	1974	1975	1973	1974	1975	1973	1974	1975
Group of workers	1.9	0.6	0.2	0.3	0.3	21.3	0.1	0	4.2
White-collar union	8.7	6.7	8.4	3.9	1.8	5.1	4.6	2.5	2.7
Blue-collar union	74.7	79.9	85.3	54.5	53.9	58.7	68.6	55.9	78.9
Mixed union	12.1	9.3	3.7	7.8	5.2	1.9	7.0	5.8	1.8
Federation	2.6	2.9	2.3	33.6	38.2	13.1	19.7	34.1	12.4
Industrial community	0	0.6	0	0	0.5	0	0	1.6	0
	100	100	100	100	100	100	100	100	100
N	423	313	428	112,196	86,507	133,942	5,295,000	4,597,000	5,445,000

is even higher for strikes called by federations; only 6% ended with full success, 17% in a compromise, and 76% in failure. The corresponding average for the outcome of all strikes was 24% success, 25% compromise, and 51% failure. The government and the Ministry of Labor took a very purposefully hard line against solidaristic labor mobilization. Frequently, such strikes were severely criticized by members of the government as political and therefore illegitimate strikes, caused by extreme leftist, and sometimes Aprista, agitators. Whereas the qualification of these strikes as political was certainly correct, the related accusation of Communist subversion and outside manipulation of unions in the pursuit of destabilization policies was largely incorrect. The rising strike rate was due to organized labor's efforts to activate its newly strengthened mobilization potential in defense of its autonomy and its previous gains in real wages, against government-supported, sometimes violent, intervention in unions, and against economic austerity measures restricting popular consumption.

Confederations and Strike Behavior

Clearly, affiliation to a strong central organization increased unions' potential for mobilization, and thus the CGTP as the strongest central union organization appeared as the most militant one, being responsible for around 80% of all man-hours lost through strikes in manufacturing industry in 1974 and 1975 (Table 6.15). Again, however, it has to be reiterated that the CGTP was in no way pursuing a destabilization policy, as at least up to the end of 1975 there was some possibility that the process of structural changes would continue. On the contrary, the CGTP was consciously avoiding an all-out confrontation with the government, in order not to strengthen the conservative wing by providing a convenient target for attacks on "economically and politically irresponsible unionism." However, two factors motivated the CGTP to encourage strong militancy short of an all-out confrontation. First of all, demonstrations of labor's mobilization potential were intended to strengthen the radical wing of the government by providing a visible popular-support base; and they were also intended to reinforce pressures for concrete policies favorable to labor. Second, the CGTP had to maintain its credibility as genuine representative of workers' interests in the eyes of its affiliated unions by proving readiness to engage in militant action. The challenge to the CGTP from the left grew in intensity, through attacks on the "oligarchic collaborationist CGTP bureaucrats, selling out the working class." This made it harder for the CGTP to affiliate new unions; it also caused some defections from the CGTP, swelling the ranks of militant unions that did not have an official affiliation and thus weakening the CGTP's mobilization capacity for purposeful collective action in relative terms.

Table 6.15
Strike Activity in Manufacturing Industry by Affiliation of Unions, 1974–1975

Affiliation	Mean number of workers	Mean number of days duration	Percentage of total strikes		Percentage of total workers involved		Percentage of total man-hours lost	
			1974	1975	1974	1975	1974	1975
CTP	128	5.3	7.7	5.8	3.2	2.7	2.2	5.2
CCTP	228	7.4	57.1	61.2	66.1	79.0	78.5	84.3
CNT	44	9.9	1.0	0.9	0.1	0.2	0	1.1
CTRP	142	4.9	2.6	3.7	0.7	3.3	1.0	2.3
None	158	4.5	31.7	28.3	29.9	14.9	18.3	7.2
			100	100	100	100	100	100
All	196	6.3						
N			(312)	(428)				

The figures for newly formed unions 1973–1975 show that almost half of them did not affiliate themselves to any of the confederations. As I mentioned before, this figure probably underreports CGTP affiliations for political reasons of expediency. Nevertheless, the group of nonaffiliated unions appears as the largest one in the figures from the Pacífico Study, which are supposed to reflect the actual state of affiliation of existing unions in 1975, rather than the state of affiliation upon formation of the unions.[35] The CGTP clearly had the largest number of unions with affiliation, over a quarter of the total number of recognized unions, followed by the CTP and the CTRP with roughly one-fifth each; the tiny CNT lagged far behind with roughly 5% only (Table 6.16).

Actually, the figure for the proportion of unions still formally affiliated to the CTP greatly overestimates its mobilization potential. For instance, in the manufacturing sector, CTP unions accounted for 7.7% and 5.8% of total strikes in 1974 and 1975 only, and for an even smaller percentage of total workers involved, about 3%. Traditionally, CTP unions have followed a conciliatory line, with strong emphasis on mutual accommodation through collective bargaining. Their point of view, as expressed by the Secretary General[36] was that strikes were harmful for both sides, and that "class struggle had been overcome by modern unionism, capable of obtaining benefits without sacrifices." Thus, CTP unions were less used to exerting pressure for their demands through militant strike action, but rather to relying on the central leadership for collective agreements. Clearly, in certain cases this attitude facilitated co-optation and sell-out agreements, which in turn caused a great number of unions to disaffiliate themselves from the CTP. The Pacífico Study showed that 42% of unions in their sample had changed their affiliation between the time of their recognition and 1975. Over half of these changing unions had formerly been affiliated to the CTP, and had either become independent or affiliated themselves to the CGTP or CTRP, whereas none of the changing unions affiliated themselves to the CTP. The CTP's loss of mobilization and influence potential over organized labor became clearly visible when calls for general strikes, such as in April and May 1973, and in February 1976 gained only spotty adherence and passed with hardly noticeable effects. (*La Prensa,* April 30, 1973; May 21, 1973; February 2, 1976).

Thus the small proportion of strike activity accounted for by CTP unions does not reflect a politically motivated strike-avoidance policy on the part of the leadership, but rather the latter's continuous loss of influence and mobilization potential. As stressed before, the CTP reluctantly supported certain reforms while basically being opposed to the military government as such be-

---

[35]"Supposed to" indicates that the responses to this question may not always have been fully true—for the already mentioned reasons of official MIT sponsorship of the survey, and because of the well-known anti-CGTP attitude of the majority of the state bureaucracy.

[36]Interview with Julio Cruzado, Secretary General of the CTP, Lima, October 7, 1975.

Table 6.16
Affiliation of Unions to Confederations

Affiliation	Percentage of new unions formed and affiliated 1973–1975	Percentage of total recognized unions affiliated in 1975
CTP	2	20.8
CGTP	23	26.6
CNT	2	5.2
CTRP	25	19.6
None	48	27.7
	100.0	100.0
N	(766)	(173)

Source: Pacífico Sample.

cause of APRA's loss of a political role and influence. Thus, the CTP did not hesitate to call strikes in protest against certain policies. 43% of the strikes of CTP unions were for solidarity or "other" reasons, compared to 25% of CGTP strikes. The category "other reasons" includes protests against business policy of the enterprise and violation of collective agreements, as well as demands for changes of Ministry of Labor and other bureaucrats, and for changes in governmental policies. However, such strike calls didn't have a large mobilizing effect. For instance, no CTP federation carried out a strike in 1974 and 1975. CTP solidarity strikes were apparently actions of individual unions that followed CTP directives and perceived some common interest. I would hypothesize that this was mostly the case for white-collar unions, an example of which were the CTP-supported white-collar protest strikes against a change in pension legislation in April of 1973.[37] In fact, the relatively most significant adherence to the CTP line in the industrial manufacturing sector remained among white-collar unions, through the affiliated white-collar union central organization. This manifests itself in the relatively high strike participation rate of CTP-affiliated unions among white-collar unions, with 14% of the striking white-collar unions being affiliated to the CTP, as compared to only 7% of the striking blue-collar unions. The CGTP accounted for only a slightly higher percentage of striking white-collar unions—18%; most of them were independent unions. I would hypothesize that many of these independent white-collar unions had defected from the CTP due to its loss of credibility and authenticity as a defender of wage-earners' interests, without wanting to affiliate themselves to the blue-collar dominated CGTP.

[37] This new legislation unified the criteria for retirement with pension benefits for white- and blue-collar workers, basing it on age, whereas under previous legislation white-collar employees' rights for retirement with full pension benefits had been based on length of service. The CTP was the only Union Confederation that opposed this new legislation.

As expected, the CTRP did pursue a purposeful strike-avoidance policy. The few strikes of CTRP unions that did occur were relatively short and insignificant in terms of the proportion of total man-hours lost. The small proportion of strikes and the even smaller proportion of workers involved accounted for by the CNT reflects the small number of unions affiliated to the CNT and their small size. On the average, CNT strikes mobilized 44 workers only; or, looking at it in a different way, 86% of strikes by CNT unions mobilized less than 50 workers. It appears that CNT unions tried to compensate with endurance for their small number of workers, for they had by far the longest average duration of strikes—9.9 days—as compared to 7.4 days for CGTP unions, the next longest. Nevertheless, their contribution to total man-hours lost was negligible.

The CGTP clearly had, and had activated, by far the greatest mobilization potential, accounting for between two-thirds and four-fifths of all striking workers in manufacturing industry in 1974 and 1975. Though independent unions were generally very militant, accounting for roughly 30% of strikes, their relatively weaker position in comparison to the CGTP-affiliated unions shows itself in the figures for workers involved and man-hours lost, where their participation was much smaller. On the average, strikes called by independent unions involved 158 workers, whereas CGTP strikes involved 228 workers.[38] Or, looking at the figures in a different way again, only 7% of strikes by nonaffiliated unions involved more than 250 workers, as compared to 29% of strikes by CGTP unions. It is in the average duration of a strike that the relative weakness of nonaffiliated unions becomes most apparent; with an average of 36 hours, nonaffiliated unions had the shortest average strike duration, which is important in the light of the connection between endurance and the chances for success of a strike.

The explanation for this difference in endurance is most likely to be found in the support provided by the union confederations to affiliated unions in the case of a strike, which nonaffiliated unions, of course, were lacking. This support consisted of advice, both practical and legal, as well as some material contributions. For the most part, unions did not have regular strike funds. Two reasons account for this lack: The generally precarious economic situation of blue-collar workers made regular contributions to a strike fund an unacceptable financial burden, and substantial outside financial support of strike funds would certainly have been exposed as politically motivated and therefore illegal. One way to provide material support, however, was through the organization of collections of solidarity contributions for specific strikes among other unions affiliated to the same confederation. Therefore, a strong confederation

---

[38]If strikes by federations are included in the calculation, the figure for independent unions is 211, and for CGTP unions 371 workers. This latter figure indicates the considerable magnitude of the CGTP's mobilization potential.

could provide highly valuable support to affiliated unions, advising them on the basis of experience whether holding out longer would increase their chances of success, and also facilitating such holding out through solidarity contributions. Characteristically, CGTP-affiliated unions had the highest proportion of strikes that were pursued to highest levels, which increased chances of success according to the data presented earlier in this discussion. Seventeen percent of CGTP strikes were resolved through administrative decision in the second or third instance, as compared to 15% of CTP strikes, 8% of CTRP strikes and strikes by nonaffiliated unions, and not a single CNT strike.

On the one hand, then, one would expect a differential rate of success in strikes among unions with different affiliation; but on the other hand, these factors could have been counteracted by politically motivated decision on the part of labor authorities. The latter was clearly the case in strikes of CTRP unions, 42% of which ended with an acceptance of workers' demands. Among the other unions, the hypothesis about the impact of affiliation to confederations with differential strength on chances for success is supported (Table 6.17): CNT-affiliated and nonaffiliated unions that received none or a minimal amount of support from other unions had the lowest overall rate of success. The strength of CGTP unions, which could rely on support from the best-organized confederation, shows itself in their relatively low overall failure rate, which was only slightly higher than for CTRP unions and lower than for all

Table 6.17
Results of Strikes in Manufacturing Industry by Affiliation of Union and Duration of Strike, 1974–1975

Results of strike demands by duration of strike	Percentage of strikes by affiliation of unions					
	CTP	CGTP	CNT	CTRP	None	All
All strikes						
Accepted	30%	25%	0%	42%	20%	24%
Partially accepted	11	26	20	12	26	24
Rejected	59	49	80	46	54	52
N	(46)	(416)	(5)	(24)	(198)	(689)
Less than three days						
Accepted	18	16	0	15	12	15
Partially accepted	9	12	25	15	15	13
Rejected	74	72	75	69	73	73
N	(34)	(231)	(4)	(13)	(130)	(412)
Three or more days						
Accepted	67	36	0	73	34	38
Partially accepted	17	44	0	9	47	42
Rejected	17	20	100	18	19	20
N	(12)	(185)	(1)	(11)	(68)	(277)

other unions. In more than 50% of their strikes, they obtained full or at least partial satisfaction of their demands.

These contentions are further substantiated by an analysis of strike results, controlling for length of strikes. A comparison of the impact of affiliation on results of strikes lasting less than three days, and on those lasting three or more days reaffirms first of all the favorable treatment of CTRP-affiliated unions. They had the lowest rejection rate in shorter strikes and the highest acceptance rate in longer ones. CGTP affiliated unions did not do better in acceptance rate in shorter strikes than other unions, with the exception of nonaffiliated unions, and they did worse in acceptance rate in longer strikes than both CTP- and CTRP-affiliated unions. Looking at rejection rates, the CGTP unions were similar to other unions in shorter strikes, and they even did somewhat worse than the others in longer strikes. Their overall relatively favorable results, then, were mainly achieved by organizing longer strikes, which had clearly higher chances for success.

Thus, CGTP strength and militancy were instrumental in protecting workers' interests in concrete instances of labor conflicts. And they were certainly also instrumental in delaying a shift in governmental policies towards full control and repression of organized labor. However, the sociopolitical strength of the whole labor movement was not sufficient to prevent an eventual decisive reversal of the process of structural transformation in Peruvian society back to a clear consolidation of the capitalist order.

Implications for Relations among the Government, the Private Sector, and Organized Labor

The evidence showed clear tendencies toward increasing militancy and, though to a lesser extent, increasing sociopolitical strength of the Peruvian labor movement during the reform process carried out by the military government between 1968 and 1975. The increase in militancy was explained as a result of the gains in organizational penetration of the union movement, without a concomitant gain of political influence, but on the contrary with a certain loss of access to governmental agencies accompanied by increasingly antilabor policies. Thus the gains in organizational capacity formed the basis for growing mobilization of workers into strike action. Strike action was carried out with two major purposes: to exert pressure on political authorities for favorable intervention in specific labor disputes, and to demonstrate labor's capacity and decision to resist government attempts at both weakening labor organizations and letting the working class pay the costs of the country's deteriorating economic situation. Strikes in 1973–1975 became on the average shorter, larger, and more frequent than before, indicating the growing importance of the role of strikes as expressions of political protest.

The increase in labor's mobilization capacity was not restricted to raising the number of strikes, based on the formation of numerous new unions, but extended also to expanding the size of strikes, based on some consolidation of organizational cohesion. Increasing numbers of workers could be mobilized into coordinated, purposeful, militant action, which constituted a certain gain, however modest, in sociopolitical strength of organized labor. The relatively large proportion of workers involved in solidarity strikes and in strikes called by union federations can be regarded as an indicator of labor's organizational coherence and consequent potential for coordinated collective action.

Thus the government became increasingly concerned both with growing labor militancy per se because of its undesirable economic consequences, and with growing organizational penetration and cohesion because of its contribution to a greater potential for coordinated collective action of labor in support of political demands. The different policies applied with the aim of weakening militancy as well as organizational autonomy of unions, that is, policies of "divide, co-opt, and rule," of organizational encapsulation, and of legal restrictions had all failed to bring organized labor under firm government control. Though these policies certainly did impede the growth of labor's strength as a sociopolitical force in a relative sense (i.e., compared to the strength labor might have achieved without being constrained by these policies) they by no means succeeded in neutralizing unions as autonomous actors providing an organizational power base for coordinated action of the urban working class. The main reason for this failure is the fact that a large number of unions had achieved a considerable degree of organizational consolidation before these policies were applied. A comparison of the failure of the government's policies toward unions with the successful encapsulation of unions and co-optation of their leaders in Mexico on the one hand, and with the successful division of CONACI on the other hand, underlines the greater susceptibility of newly emerging organizations to control-oriented policies. The Mexican system of co-optation and control had its origins in the period of rapid unionization in the 1930s, that is, it did not have to be superimposed upon an autonomous labor movement that had reached an intermediate degree of organizational penetration, as in the case of Peru.[39] The anticipation of strong opposition from and conflicts with unions kept the Peruvian government from introducing

---

[39]A more comprehensive argument, setting the construction of control mechanisms over organized labor in the context of the installation of a corporatist regime is made by Stepan (1978). He uses previous level of organization as one of five key variables predicting success of inclusionary corporatist attempts.

stricter legal controls over unions, as had been proposed by Minister of Labor Sala Orosco. Direct intervention in CONACI, in contrast, was not impeded by any such concerns. The respective experiences with only weak and partial resistance from CONACI against intervention by MIT and SINAMOS officials, and with decided resistance in the form of solidarity strikes from unions against attempted interventions by the MLR and CTRP organizers show the differential strength of the two types of organizations. Unions could build on a certain shared experience of success through collective action. Furthermore, the learning experience that chances of success tended to increase with increasing strike pressure predisposed unions to resort to militant action in defense against governmental controls and intervention, just as they did in the pursuit of their demands in the area of wages and working conditions.

The consequences of the government's abortive attempts to bring both union militancy and capacity for autonomous collective action under control were growing intransigence on the part of employers and unions alike, stronger pressures on the Ministry of Labor as mediator and arbitrator, and stronger pressures on the government for a revision of labor legislation, particularly from the entrepreneurial side. Under these conditions of increasing polarization, the economic austerity measures taken in the Second Phase were bound to provoke harsh confrontations. They also caused the emergence of tendencies toward political unification among various labor organizations, which implied a new potential for growing strength of labor as a sociopolitical force. In this situation, the government resorted to the application of a policy with decidedly greater effectiveness than earlier policies—that of large-scale repression. The following chapter will focus on the circumstances which forced a clear choice on the government between transformation or consolidation of the capitalist order and on the consequences of this choice for the government's policies toward labor in general and toward the workers' participation scheme in particular.

7

Crisis, Polarization, Stagnation, and Reversal of the "Peruvian Revolution"

The discussion of the development of the workers' participation scheme in interaction with dynamics between sociopolitical forces has shown that the CI had a mobilizing effect rather than an integrative one. Yet mobilization in support of a socialist transformation did not effect decisive progress in that direction. Rather, after the coup against President Velasco, the reform process first stagnated, and then, under external pressures in a situation of severe financial crisis, it was clearly abandoned and even partly reversed. Thus, instead of being expanded, workers' participation was curtailed in accordance with larger political processes.

The reason for the change in direction of the Peruvian Revolution from at least partial transformation toward clear consolidation of the capitalist order is the highly limited nature of the military's ideological consensus and the ensuing lack of a coherent strategy of societal transformation. The ideological consensus was limited to two "anti's," anti-imperialist and anti-oligarchic. Anti-capitalist was not included in this consensus, despite consistent official emphasis on the noncommunist, noncapitalist, and genuinely Peruvian third way of development. Thus the government failed to elaborate and implement a coordinated development policy maximizing independence from domestic as well as foreign private capital. The economic power of capital-owning groups and thus their hegemony in civil society were left unaffected. When some of the structural reforms started affecting interests of these groups, the reforms met with firm resistance, and pressures on the military government started mounting, from inside the military institution as well as from outside. Resistance against the reforms from privileged groups that stood to lose was countered by popular mobilization in defense of the reforms and in support of their expansion, which raised the level of social conflict. Increasing societal polarization further aggravated internal disunity in the military government and institution. As long as President Velasco was in firm command, he apparently was able to override conflicts between the various factions. His deteriorating health, however, impaired his ability to keep these factions in check, and this motivated radical forces in the government as well as the others to support a coup replacing him with Morales Bermúdez.

From this point on, the radical members of the government were continuously losing power, and the reform process its impetus. The final break occurred when external pressures in a situation of financial crisis forced a clear choice between consolidation of the capitalist order or immediate economic chaos in case of continued attempts at its partial transformation, and the pursuit of noncapitalist development. The choice of consolidation of the capitalist order required effective repression of all forces promoting a socialist transformation—within the military government and the military institution, as well as within society.

The choice between capitalism and chaos could be forced on the Peruvian government because it had failed to pursue policies preparing and protecting a gradual transition to a noncapitalist, or socialist, model of development. The major flaws from the point of view of a strategy of socialist transformation, mutually reinforcing each other, were the following, which will be discussed in more detail later in this chapter.

1. Continued dependence on foreign financing, despite a change in the patterns of dependence.
2. Pursuit of a rapid, capital intensive industrialization program.
3. Minimal transfer of control and income rights from private capital owners to the state, and consequent lack of changes in the structure of production and distribution.
4. Orientation of the state sector toward the needs of the private sector.
5. Minimal priority assigned to the problem of inequality and unemployment.

Whether an early and decided pursuit of a strategy addressing these problems would have been politically feasible, given the internal power constellations in the government, can not be answered with certainty. However, the radical core group around President Velasco seemed to enjoy considerable influence on government policy and to be able to steer the process in the direction of a socialist transformation. Clearly, the official ideology stressing the construction of a fully participatory society based on a socially owned economy pointed that way. Still, most reforms remained isolated modifications of the existing order rather than constituting coherent steps toward a socialist order. And one potentially crucial reform, the social property sector, had not really gotten off the ground by the time the radical core group lost power.

The Elusive Socialist Alternative

In the policy-making process for the introduction of the workers' participation scheme, the moderate and conservative forces had prevailed, effecting a compromise solution that was aimed at integration of workers into their enterprise and a consequent elimination of class struggle. The participation scheme had the exact opposite effect, since unions were capable of mobilizing workers into collective action in defense of their rights, which were being violated by entrepreneurs. But whereas unions were capable of mobilizing for full development of participation at the enterprise level, they were not strong enough as a sociopolitical force to effect protective and supportive policies at the societal level. This lack of political strength and consequent support meant that the CI was not even consistently implemented according to the legislation. And it certainly prevented mobilized sectors of the working class from successfully turning the CI into an element of socialist transformation. Quite predictably, the responses to these developments were advocacy of return to pure private-property enterprises on the one hand, and advocacy of development of an alternative form of socialist enterprise organization on the other hand. While legislation for these alternatives was developed, however, and their implementation remained highly uncertain as long as no compromise between the two diametrically opposed tendencies could be reached, awareness of the urgent need for a revision of the CI legislation grew within the government. A first indication of the government's concern with such a revision was the public recognition of continued conflict between labor and capital: "The CI does not definitively suppress social conflicts, but it generates new and qualitatively distinct structural conditions within the enterprise because it makes access of the workers to property, management, and distribution of profits possible [Mercado Jarrín, 1973, p. 10]." Accordingly, new mechanisms for conflict resolution were to be designed, in addition to more effective prevention of conflicts through the elimination of legal loopholes for violation of the CI rights. Yet, disagreements between radical and moderate-conservative forces delayed the publication of a new draft law until May of 1975, and the implementation of a new CI legislation until early 1977.

In August of 1974 the *Peruvian Times* published a draft for a new CI law, which reflected the intention to really let the CI develop into an institution of codetermination in a limited period of time. It contained provisions to guarantee an annual progress in ownership of 5%, regardless of the amount of profits declared by the enterprise. Also, it protected the rights of the CI for participation in the board of directors and granted veto-power on board decisions to the CI representative in matters of central concern for the progress of the CI, such as enlargement of the capital base, merger, etc. It also required periodic meetings between management and the workforce, though it did not give the workers any more influence on decisions within the enterprise. Other important innovations were: the distinction between two kinds of CI, with indirect participation in ownership in enterprises with less than 20 workers, and with direct one in those with more than 20 workers; the establishment of limits for differences between the lowest and highest remuneration paid, which was not to exceed 1:30; and the regulation of the 50:50% situation, where the local equivalent of the Securities and Exchange Commission would appoint the chairman of the board of directors from among "qualified university professionals."

The official draft, which was published in May 1975, with an invitation to interested parties to submit comments, constituted a compromise between this proposal and the diametrically opposite position of those moderates and conservatives who favored substituting cash participation in profits in place of participation in ownership and management. This official draft version of the law was essentially aimed at the letting the CI grow according to its original gradual design, but eliminating some conflicts by way of specifically prohibiting certain maneuvers on part of the enterprise. No time limit within which to reach 50% or minimum progress in ownership by the CI was contained in this draft. Certain aspects of the internal functioning of the CI were modified, and the separation between union and CI roles was made more pronounced through the requirement that union leaders make their renunciation 6 months prior to running for office in the CI. The most important innovation in this draft law was the right of the CI to challenge a decision of the board of directors and bring it before the newly created court for Labor Communities. But not even this moderate reform of the CI legislation was implemented, as the forces favoring a greater protection of private enterprise gained predominance and effected a real curtailment of participation rights through the CI in the Second Phase.

The forces promoting a socialist alternative as substitute for the CI achieved a small but symbolically significant advance when their demand that bankrupt enterprises be brought under administration of their CI was partly satisfied with a law in May 1973 (*D.L.* 20023). Particularly the radical forces within CONACI, which had manifested their commitment to a socialist transformation in the Congress of CIs, were pushing for this law, legitimizing their demand by pointing out examples where entrepreneurs had provoked fradulent bankruptcies because of the introduction of the CI, and emphasizing the effect of the law on protection of employment. This law provided for the transformation of bankrupt enterprises into cooperatives, though with the obligation of the workers to assume debts of the former entrepreneurs as members of the new cooperative. By May of 1976, more than 30 such production cooperatives existed in Lima, providing jobs for more than 2500 workers.[1] Though these enterprises were of little significance for the national economy, they had a very significant demonstration effect. They served as examples in support of the argument that workers' self-management was viable, and that consequently the CIs would be able to substitute private capitalists as entrepreneurs. These cooperatives, of course, experienced great difficulties due to their unfavorable initial economic situation. A committee for mutual assistance was formed among them, which received strong support from CONACI, particularly through efforts to publicize their experience and bring coordinated pressure to bear on state agencies for favorable treatment of requests for delayed payments of debts, etc.

Plans for the creation of a socialist alternative to an economy based either on fully private or on complete state ownership and control over enterprises, which had already been announced by President Velasco in 1971 and confirmed by Prime Minister Mercado Jarrín in his concluding speech to the Congress of CIs in 1973, finally received substance at the end of August 1973 with the publication of the draft law for a social property sector, which was to become the dominant sector (*sector prioritario*) in the Peruvian economy.[2] This draft law was published with an explicit invitation for public debate, and participation in the debate was very comprehensive and intense. The various comments resulted in several changes in the legislation, which was finally promulgated in May of 1974, but on the whole the basic outlines and characteristics of the project, consisting in socially owned worker self-managed enterprises, remained unaltered.

The internal governmental disagreements manifested themselves from the beginning in the various interpretations of the term *prioritario*. For the radicals, *prioritario* meant hegemonic in terms of value of production, provision of employment, and allocation of investment, whereas for moderates and conservatives *prioritario* meant at most predominant in official propaganda and public attention, and in absorption of un(employment) employment through labor-intensive projects with a low need for capital investment. In fact, this controversy manifested itself in that an inherent contradiction was built into the law from the beginning, as the law made conversion of existing enterprises into social-property enterprises virtually impossible, while it was abundantly clear that the only way for the social-property sector to become dominant was through such conversions. Due to highly limited allocation of funds for in-

[1]This information was compiled by Shari Berenbach, unpublished manuscript, Lima, May 1976.

[2]For an analysis of the historical background of the project, and of civilian influence on the policy-making process, as well as of the exact provisions of the legislation, see Knight (1975).

vestment in social-property enterprises, the sector developed very slowly, despite widespread popular enthusiasm that resulted in numerous project proposals submitted to the National Social Property Commission. The 2-year plan for 1975–1976 projected an investment of 3000 million *soles* in the social-property sector, out of 200,000 million *soles* of total investment, public and private combined.[3]

By March 1976, there were three fully functioning social-property enterprises, 47 in the implementation phase—some of them already working, with only formalities to be arranged—and 165 projects that had been approved by the National Social Property Commission.[4] Though the general course of the Second Phase led clearly away from the radical conception, the development of the social-property sector still appeared to be an open possibility at that point. In his televised speech of March 31,[5] President Morales Bermúdez confirmed once more that four economic sectors were to coexist in the final socioeconomic order (i.e., the fully private, the reformed private, the state, and the social-property sectors). At the same time he announced that some state enterprises that were not classified as basic industry were to be transferred into another sector. The most common public interpretation of this announcement was that the state-owned tobacco company was to be converted into a social-property firm. This would obviously have meant a symbolic commitment to the social-property sector on part of the government, and consequently aroused strong opposition from the private sector. However, subsequent developments soon made it clear that instead of being strengthened, the social property sector was practically abandoned by the government, this being the direction that the Peruvian process took when faced with growing sociopolitical polarization and economic difficulties.

How weak the socialist component in the elite's ideological commitment really was is underlined by their lack of emphasis on policies designed to increase social equality. Decreasing inequality was very clearly a subordinate goal, but not even elimination of extreme poverty was assigned high priority. Redistribution was a result of structural reforms in various sectors that were to serve specific purposes other than global equalization of living conditions. Thus redistribution remained vertical within productive sectors, whereas the great inter-sectoral inequalities remained unmodified due to lack of horizontal redistribution. For instance, according to Figueroa's (1973:73–74) calculations, the CI transferred one-fourth of the total income of capitalists in the manufacturing industrial sector, which represented 1% of national income, to 5% of the labor force; workers' participation in income rights in the mining and fish-

---

[3]Speech by Minister of Economy and Finance Vargas Gavilano, February 1975, in Desco, *Informe Político*, No. 29, February, 1975.
[4]Figures from the *Comisión Nacional de Propiedad Social* (May 1976).
[5]Printed in full in *La Crónica*, April 1, 1976.

ing sectors together transferred less than 1% of national income to approximately 3% of the national labor force. Altogether, then, about 8% of the national labor force benefitted from these transfers through the redistribution of less than 2% of national income. The salient characteristic of all these redistributive reforms was their sectoral limitation. The 8% of the labor force benefitting from the workers' participation reform belonged to the highest quartile of national income distribution to begin with, by virtue of working in the modern sector. Redistribution from the modern to the traditional sector ranked particularly low on the government's list of priorities, as the goal of equalization in general was subordinate to the goal of growth.

Similarly, the agrarian reform benefitted between 20% and 25% of the rural families only (McClintock 1977:51). The greatest improvements were experienced by the workers in the modern, commercial agricultural sector on the coast, particularly the sugar cooperatives. However, many landless agricultural laborers were left out of the reforms, as were many very small peasant owners. Furthermore, as Webb shows, the whole traditional rural sector benefitted by virtually nothing from the structural reforms and very little through budget transfers (Webb 1975:108–124). In fact, price policies on agricultural products effected a transfer of resources from the traditional rural to both the traditional and modern urban sectors. An improvement of conditions of the rural poor would have required redistribution through price policies and through public expenditures for housing, health, and education, concentrated in rural areas. Such redistribution was not undertaken; on the contrary, the government emphasized industrial investment at the expense of investment in health, education, and housing.[6] Improvements in living conditions of the poor were not to be brought about through redistribution, but rather relegated to the future when increased industrial production and exports would raise the collective wealth of Peruvian society.

Economic Policies and the Financial Crisis

The need for permanent, self-sustained, independent economic development as a key element in the elite consensus, which centered around the concern with integral security, caused the government to assign priority to a reduction of foreign economic dependence. Yet, the implications of a successful attempt to reduce foreign dependence for domestic economic policies were not considered and acted on. The attempt to achieve this goal was mainly based

[6]According to Moncloa (1977:144), the proportion of total government investment allocated to health, education, and housing decreased from 17% in 1968 to 11% in 1975.

on an expansion of state control over direct foreign investment. The means were nationalization of major foreign firms in oil, mining, and fishing in order to bring key resources under direct state control, and strict regulation of foreign investment under Decision 24 of the Andean Pact.[7] The very first instance in which these measures were applied, the nationalization of the International Petroleum Company (IPC),[8] caused a financial blockade against Peru. The U.S. Export–Import Bank and the Agency for International Development froze all loans to Peru. Under pressure from the United States government, international lending agencies also withheld loans from Peru; for instance, from 1969 to 1973 Peru received only one loan from the World Bank. The financial blockade was finally lifted after a settlement for global compensation was reached between the Peruvian and United States governments in February 1974.[9]

Compensation negotiations with individual companies varied widely according to the international connections of the company. For instance, a generous agreement on the price for Chase Manhattan's share in the *Banco Continental* led to favorable treatment of Peru's request for commercial loans in private New York financial circles.[10] During the time of the United States-imposed financial blockade, Peru raised large sums of money from private banks, particularly on the Eurodollar market.[11] When the blockade was lifted, Peru made further ample use of the renewed flow of funds in the pursuit of an ambitious and capital-intensive industrialization program under guidance of the state as a major investor. The compensation agreements constituted a considerable drain on the government's resource base, and therefore aggravated its dependence on public borrowing abroad in order to finance long-term investment projects, such as for the development of oil and mineral production. Thus a reduction of dependence on direct foreign investment (though by no means an elimination of such dependence, particularly in mining and oil) was achieved at the expense of the development of a new pattern of dependence, consisting in financial dependence on private foreign banks and on international lending agencies.

[7]For a general account of nationalization and expansion of state control policies, see Aguirre (1974); Stepan (1978:346–428) assesses the strength of the government's bargaining position vis-à-vis foreign capital and its relative success in reducing dependence.

[8]A subsidiary of Standard Oil of New Jersey.

[9]Under the agreement, the total sum for compensation was distributed by the U.S. government among U.S. companies. This solved the problem of Peru's stern official resistance against granting any compensation to IPC, and U.S. insistence that no foreign-owned company could be nationalized without compensation. Evidence for U.S. pressure on international financial agencies for withholding loans is provided by Einhorn (1974).

[10]See Hunt for several case studies of negotiations about compensation for expropriation (1975:302–348).

[11]For exact figures, see Stallings (1978:29).

Peru's continued reliance and dependence on new loans, in addition to an already tremendous debt burden that assumed crisis proportions by early 1976, gave these foreign finance agencies leverage to demand internal economic measures conforming to classical monetarist stabilization policies, and including more favorable treatment of domestic and foreign private investment. Clearly, the application of these measures constituted a full commitment to a consolidation of the capitalist order and a continuation of dependent development. Part of the reasons for the Peruvian government's failure to significantly reduce dependence were beyond the government's control, but part of them were the already mentioned flaws in economic policy.

The most important among the reasons beyond the government's control was the discrepancy between the projected and the actual quantity of oil to be found in the Peruvian jungle region. Peru's credit-worthiness had been based to a high degree on the prospects for future oil exports, on the availability of which, though not on their quantity, foreign and domestic experts had agreed. Original projections had indicated that Peru could start exporting oil as early as 1977.[12] A large number of oil companies had negotiated drilling rights through profit-sharing contracts with the state company PETROPERÚ, and in 1974 activity in exploration was very high. By 1975 it had already become questionable whether the small amount of actual oil reserves would make investments for exploitation worthwhile, and by 1976 many oil companies had withdrawn. Consequently, Peru turned rather suddenly from a secure into a high-risk borrower, and had to accept stringent conditions in order to obtain new loans.

A second reason beyond the government's control, which contributed to a severe deterioration of Peru's balance of payments was the world recession in 1974–1975. Slackening demand and falling prices for mineral exports, Peru's most important contributor to export revenues, decreased these revenues, while prices for imports kept rising.

And a third reason was the disappearance of the anchovy. Fishmeal had been Peru's second largest export, but in 1972 the fish disappeared due to changing water temperatures and possibly due to overfishing in 1970. This caused a crisis for the whole fishing industry, which was subsequently nationalized. Fishing picked up somewhat in 1974, but the industry did not really recover and kept operating at a loss until 1976.

These three sets of circumstances had a disastrous impact on Peru's balance of trade and balance of payments on the revenue side. In addition, the government's ambitious development project and its failure to gain sufficient control over resource allocation in the private sector put a heavy burden on the expenditure side. The type of development project pursued by the government

[12]Projections from Ministry of Energy and Mines, January 1975.

was based on highly capital-intensive, high-technology projects with long maturity. Investment for these projects came to a large part from the state, financed by foreign loans. This approach neglected two crucial problems of Peruvian development: investment in agriculture in order to promote domestic food production and lessen dependence on food imports,[13] and investment in labor-intensive production of mass-consumption goods.[14] Instead, nontraditional exports were promoted, supposedly to raise foreign exchange earnings. However, production of such nontraditional export goods was based principally on foreign technology, and frequently even on the use of imported industrial inputs, such that the net balance between payments for foreign technology and imports by these enterprises and their earnings from the export of their products was just about even.[15] Furthermore, promotion of nontraditional exports through tax incentives meant that a large part of these earnings remained at the disposal of the respective companies and thus did not contribute to an improvement of the government's resource base.[16]

The government's failure to transfer a significant share of control and income rights from private owners to the state not only increased its dependence on foreign financing but also impeded the implementation of a coherent development plan. Thus, despite some modifications in the structure of ownership, the structure of production and distribution characteristic for a dependent developing capitalist economy remained basically unchanged. Despite the great expansion of the state sector, which grew to include one-third of output and one-fifth of the workforce in the modern productive sector (Fitzgerald 1976:33), and despite expansion of control over the banking system, which brought 63% of the credit market under state control (Fitzgerald 1976:53), the government was unable to ensure a desirable amount of domestic savings and their investment in high-priority areas. Private companies in Peru have been relying largely on self-financing rather than an organized credit market, which greatly constrained the possibilities for government steering of their invest-

---

[13]In 1975, food and industrial inputs of an agricultural nature accounted for 30% of Peruvian imports. Latin American Economic Report, No. 18, 1976. Lack of assistance with credits, etc., remained a constant complaint from beneficiaries of the agrarian reform.

[14]Whereas the contribution of the industrial manufacturing sector to the GNP grew from 13.6% in 1950 to 27.4% in 1975, its absorption of the total national economic population remained virtually stagnant; 13% in 1950 and 15% in 1975. MIT, Evaluación, 1976.

[15]In 1974, 70% of the total Peruvian imports were industrial. One hundred thirty firms, many of them foreign, were using 80% of total foreign exchange used by the industrial manufacturing sector for imports. How outer-directed industrial production remained is indicated by the fact that 40% of industrial inputs were imported. MIT, Evaluación, 1976. There are no data available to document the argument about the net balance, but a high official in the Association of Exporters confirmed it in a personal interview.

[16]In May of 1976, nontraditional exports were exempted from all customs duties, and tax rebates for nontraditional exports were raised to 40%. La Prensa, May 19, 1976.

ments. As far as state-owned companies were concerned, most of them generated low profits, and some of them even had net resource requirements. And
since the state sector did not extend to final manufacturing, its production pattern was oriented toward the needs of the private sector, rather than the production of the private sector oriented toward its needs.

Due to the deficiency of the tax system, with low tax rates both on corporate
profits[17] and on personal income, and with low enforcement of compliance
with tax laws, control over domestically generated surplus was largely left in
the hands of private capital owners. Thus they were in a position to make purposeful use of this control to obstruct the government's development plans and
aggravate the economic problems faced by the government.

As discussed already in Chapter 5, the incentive strategy through the General Law of Industries failed to overcome entrepreneurial resistance and to attract private investment in the first- and second-priority sectors. Consequently,
the Peruvian government was not able to change the structure of the industrial
manufacturing sector, which remained characterized by high capital intensity,
high dependence on imports, and orientation of production toward the needs
of the urban middle and upper class.

The failure to design and pursue a coherent development plan aimed at effectively reducing foreign dependence was aggravated by one of the basic weaknesses of the whole Peruvian reform process, the translation of internal ideological disunity into bureaucratic competition. Divergencies of opinion
between different ministers and their respective appointed top-level personnel
in general gave origin to variations in the enforcement of centrally decided reform policies.[18] In particular, differences between younger and more radical
technocrats in the National Planning Institute, moderate-to-conservative personnel in the Ministry of Industry, and business-oriented management in in-

---

[17]Taxes on corporate profits amounted to only 22% of profits in 1972. Fitzgerald (1975).

[18]The problem of compliance with central directives and correct enforcement of reform policies
reached below the newly appointed top levels down to the lowest levels in the various ministerial
bureaucracies. Traditionally, bureaucratic positions had been awarded on the basis of political patronage, and consequently the military government inherited a bureaucracy in which the bulk of
the personnel had loyalties to traditional parties. This was a particular problem in the provinces,
aggravated in certain regions where one party had been predominant over several years, as for instance APRA in the north. In extreme cases, lowest-level agencies in the provinces simply did not
enforce the reform laws, and supervisors from Lima had to be sent to watch over the implementation of reforms. In Lima, the problem was similar in terms of patronage base for employment
and promotion, though less serious due to closer supervision from higher levels.

Cleaves and Scurrah argue that the dominant rule governing employment in the nonprofessional
levels of the Peruvian bureaucracy are "recommendations" (i.e., influence on the vice-minister of
the hiring agency, previously mainly from the legislative, and under the present government
through personal contacts). For technical or professional personnel, some elements of open public
competition enter into hiring practices, but recommendations remain important. Furthermore,

dividual state enterprises resulted in a deficiency of coordination in economic planning. There was a lack of coherence between the national development plan, the plan for the industrial sector, and plans for individual state enterprises; a lack which was recognized and criticized in the evaluation report of the Ministry of Industry in 1976 (MIT, *Evaluación*, 1976). Thus the Peruvian government's great efforts to improve its economic analysis and planning apparatus, which according to an observer made it the most efficient one in continental Latin America (Fitzgerald 1976:90), did not show the desired and possible beneficial results because of political obstacles.

By the end of 1975, Peru's economic situation had deteriorated to the extent that the government openly admitted that the country was in a serious financial crisis. Foreign exchange reserves had declined to U.S. $150 million.[19] In May of 1976, the country's financial crisis peaked, when there was an urgent need to raise U.S. $400 million immediately in order to meet debt repayment obligations. In this situation, Peru was forced to devalue the *sol* and cut public expenditures as basis for a very stringent economic austerity program. Public admittance that concrete conditions had been set by foreign lending agencies only came on July 26, 1976, in connection with a U.S. $240 million loan from a consortium of private U.S. banks,[20] but the same economic policy measures had been proposed by the World Bank and the International Monetary Fund in 1975 already, and the 31% devaluation of the *sol* on June 28, 1976, was the culmination of earlier weaker measures of the same general type, such as those taken in June 1975 and in January 1976, aimed at introducing an economic austerity and stabilization program.

Choice of Consolidation of the Capitalist Order

If the chosen model of economic development and industrialization was to be pursued further, Peru's staggering foreign indebtedness left no other choice than to accept the conditions first set by private foreign banks in 1976 and then reinforced in 1977 by the International Monetary Fund. These conditions con-

---

certain ministries, like the Ministry of Interior, Foreign Relations, Education, and Labor, do not hire or promote technical and professional personnel to any significant degree, which means that hiring there is done predominantly on the basis of recommendations. Thus, particularly among newly hired officials, loyalty to "their" minister and his top-level assistants was more important than adherence to abstract standards of implementing the letter of the laws, and many reforms became the object of interministerial struggles and contradictory enforcement. (Cleaves & Scurrah, 1976).

[19]Televised speech of Minister of Economy and Finance Barúa, printed in *La Prensa*, January 13, 1976.

[20]*Latin American Economic Report*, No. 30, July 30, 1976.

stituted a typical monetarist stabilization package, with no regard for long-range development prospects, nor for social and political consequences.[21] They included devaluation; price increases; a general cut in public expenditures and, in particular, a cut in subsidies for food and oil imports; more favorable treatment of foreign investment; and a certain reduction of the state's role in the economy relative to the domestic private sector. The primary effects of these combined measures were a restriction of popular consumption, slowdown of economic growth, rising unemployment, and a decrease in what few social services had been provided to the lower classes; in summary, they implied a total abandonment of any reform efforts designed to decrease social inequality. Furthermore, the need to establish a favorable relationship for collaboration with the private sector implied an abandonment of any efforts to protect or strengthen the position of labor vis-à-vis capital. This meant primarily a revision of the CI legislation, but also changes in policies regarding strikes and restrictions on firings.

The only alternative to an acceptance of these conditions would have been a default on debt payments, an abandonment of the capital-intensive development model, an extension of governmental control over internal resources through nationalization of private enterprises, and a fundamental reorientation of the structure of production. This would certainly have resulted in economic chaos in the short run and would have severely affected the living standards of the middle and upper classes, which was clearly unacceptable to the majority of members of the government. The crucial factor forcing a clear choice, then, was external pressure in the situation of financial crisis; and the crucial factor accounting for the type of choice made—consolidation of the capitalist order and elimination of all remnants of attempts at a socialist transformation—was the internal constellation of forces in the governing military elite. However, the strengthening of moderate and conservative tendencies within the elite was facilitated by the dominance of the upper middle and upper class in the balance of power in civil society. Their dominance was a result of the government's failure to restrict their exercise of control and income rights on the one hand, and of its deliberate policies of impeding the growth of popular organizations on the other hand. Popular organizations had not managed to develop their organizational power base enough to overcome their weak structural position such as to constitute an effective counterweight to the sociopolitical strength of private capital owners and provide decisive support for the forces within the government that had promoted a socialist transformation.

Several legislative measures served as indicators of the government's commitment in making concessions to the private sector in order to elicit its col-

---

[21]Several case studies of the social and political as well as economic impacts of IMF intervention are given by Payer (1974).

laboration. One such measure of great symbolic significance was the Law of Small Enterprise (D.L. 21435) of February 24, 1976 (see La Prensa, February 25, 1976). The law responded to demands from small entrepreneurs for legislation specifically protecting and stimulating small-enterprise activity, which had been accompanied by long and harsh attacks against the CI as paralyzing individual initiative and thus impeding the creation of new employment. Under this new law, which applied to all sectors of the economy, small manufacturing enterprises were exempt from the law of CI and were assigned to the sector of pure private property. In small enterprises, workers were to receive a cash participation in profits ranging from 10% to 33% according to the type of activity, but participation in neither ownership nor management. The latter provision effectively dampened the effect of the profit-sharing requirement because it deprived workers of any possibility of controlling enterprise accounts and preventing evasion of profits. The upper limit defining small enterprises was expressed in gross annual income as a multiple of minimal legal wages (i.e., not to exceed 590 legal minimum wages in Lima), which was about three times higher than the previous limit set for exemption from the CI legislation.[22] According to various estimates and calculations, over three-fourths of existing CIs fell below this limit, employing one-fifth of all CI members.[23] Though the law did stipulate that existing enterprises that had a CI and fell below this limit would be required to keep their CI, neither private sector nor workers' representatives were convinced of the effective enforcement of this regulation. In fact, the possibility of dissolving the CI in these enterprises, upon consent of half plus one of its members, was opened up in February 1977 along with the general curtailment of CI legislation. Just how indicative the Law of Small Enterprise was for a change in the government's relations to the private sector could be seen from the latter's highly favorable reaction to it, though most appraisals were accompanied by demands for its application to all existing enterprises, including those with a CI, and for an even further elevation of the defining upper limit.[24]

Pressures on the government from the private sector were intense and aimed at a variety of policy changes, particularly at a harder line in the government's policies toward labor. Entrepreneurs clearly perceived their opportunity to gain influence on governmental policies after 7 years of having been relegated to a passive spectator role vis-à-vis policy making. Through magazines and paid

[22]The previous limit was 1 million soles, which in March 1976 corresponded to roughly $170,000; the new limit corresponded to roughly $500,000.

[23]Marka, June 3, and June 10, 1976; La Jornada Comunera (supplement to La Prensa) March 9, 1976.

[24]Opinión Libre, March 3, 1976; Equis X, March 4, 1976.

communiqués in daily newspapers, private sector demands and views of the necessary course of the "Revolution" were widely publicized. The basic type of argument used was that the private sector was ready to collaborate with the government in trying to correct the mistakes made under the Velasco government, which had brought the country into crisis. The government's receptiveness toward this argument, reinforced by external pressures, manifested itself in increasingly favorable policies toward private-sector activities, not only through concessions to capital at the expense of labor, but also through a restraint on state intervention in economic activities claimed by private capitalists as their prerogative.

A typical example for the latter type of responsiveness to private-sector demands was the repeal of the law which in March of 1976 had reserved urban land development and sales for a state agency. Land speculation and construction had been a favored area of investment during the entrepreneurial investment strike in industry, and this law meant the loss of an area of highly profitable activity for private capital. Consequently, opposition against this law was very strong, and finally achieved its repeal in October of 1976.[25]

The sale of the state-owned anchovy fleet back to the private sector in July 1976 was a further example of the government's changing policy orientation concerning relations between state and private-sector economic activities. The reasons given for the sale by PESCAPERÚ were inefficiency of the company under state management, mainly due to the high labor costs resulting from subsidizing wages during the closed seasons. Also, it was claimed that labor productivity had decreased because workers would feel no need to work hard, having been given a secure job as state employees. Private enterprise was deemed more capable of carrying out the necessary rationalization (i.e., to resort to massive firings and hire workers temporarily during the fishing season).[26]

Despite clear indications of a shift in policies, particularly from January 1976 on, the official rhetoric of the Second Phase kept at least partly reflecting the orientation of the First Phase up to June of 1976. Officially, the government remained committed to the goals of social justice and to a continuation of the Peruvian Revolution, though the emphasis changed from a deepening to a consolidation of the structural changes introduced in society. The continued presence of some radical generals in high government positions held a slight promise for a potential continuation of the process or at least a rescue of the already implemented reforms. Of course, the contents of the negotiations and agreements with the private banks and their implications were not publicly known until July of 1976. Soon after taking power, President Morales

---

[25]*Latin American Economic Report*, October 8, 1976.
[26]*Ibid.*, July 30, 1976.

Bermúdez had announced that the *Plan Tupac Amaru* was to be elaborated and made public, which as successor to the *Plan Inca* was to outline the reform program for the Second Phase. However, publication of this *Plan* was delayed time and again, as the government considered a prior period of reevaluation of the whole reform process indispensable. In his speech of March 31, 1976,[27] President Morales Bermúdez declared that the *Plan* in its present form, shaped by technocrats, had not found the approval of the government and was going to be subject to revision at the highest governmental levels. Yet, before this revision was completed, polarization within the government and in society had proceeded to the point where conservative forces decisively intervened to end the Revolution by force.

Polarization and Repression

The effects of the economic stabilization measures taken in June 1975 and January and June 1976 on the restriction of popular consumption hit the lower urban groups hardest. Despite preventive measures on the government's part, popular resistance through strike pressure was strong. The government attempted to break this resistance, which was countered with efforts by various popular organizations to unify and coordinate their actions in order to further intensify pressures against the new course that the government took. Growing societal polarization threatened to cause violent confrontations in the course of repression of resistance from unified popular organizations. In this polarized situation, the conservative forces in the government managed to purge the last remaining radical members, who served as symbols around which resistance against a reversal of the reform process could rally. This purge also eliminated the last remnants of internal resistance against large-scale political repression.

In order to prevent strong labor protests against the economic stabilization measures and to preempt demands for wage raises in compensation for rising prices, the government decreed an accompanying raise in the legal minimum wage and a compulsory wage raise as an adjustment to inflation, as well as an upper legal limit for wage raises. In addition, the January measures included limitations of issues admissible for collective bargaining in 1976. The extraordinary wage raise decreed in January 1976 amounted to 840 *soles*, which—if one assumes an average income of a blue-collar worker as roughly 5000 soles—corresponded to about a 17% raise, clearly below the 24% inflation rate of 1975,[28] and even further below the 54% yearly rate of price increases noted in the first 2 months of 1976 (*La Prensa*, March 29, 1976).

[27]Published in *La Crónica*, April 1, 1976.
[28]According to a speech by Minister of Economy and Finance Barúa, January 12, 1976.

As further legal control measure against continuing high strike rates, the government announced that strike regulations contained in a decree law from 1913 would be strictly enforced (*La Prensa*, October 9, 1975). This law stipulated that the following documentation had to be brought to the Ministry of Labor 72 hours prior to the beginning of a strike: the original minutes of the assembly in which the strike was decided on, where 75% of the workers of an enterprise needed to vote in favor of the strike; and a list of all the workers that were to go on strike, including their full names and addresses. Clearly, under this law, practically no strikes were legal, but as I argued earlier, the declaration of a strike as illegal only had a potential impact if the strike lasted for 3 or more days.

In February of 1976 this law was suspended and more effective steps taken in important cases. When the anchovy season opened in March and a fishermen's strike threatened to cause substantial losses in export earnings, the government immediately responded by declaring a state of emergency for the sector of extraction and transformation of anchovy, and authorizing PESCAPERÚ to fire all striking workers (*La Prensa*, March 17, 1976). The strike had been called in support of the demand for a solution to the problem of fishermen who were to be laid off during the beginning fishing season; a solution to this had been promised by officials of PESCAPERÚ in a meeting with union representatives and the Minister of Fishery. However, the strike was obviously seen as a provocation by the government, which successfully asserted its control through emergency measures, and the strike was called off immediately. The same decisive action was taken in April 1976 in the mining sector, another crucial contributor to export earnings. In less crucial sectors, a more passive attitude was adopted by the government; mainly, the Ministry of Labor tolerated illegal firings of union leaders and workers by their employers, rejecting unions' complaints and demands as political agitation.

In response to the deterioration of their economic situation and the anti-labor policies pursued by the government, some unification tendencies emerged among unions with different political affiliation. A United Council of Union Organizations (CUOS, *Consejo Unitario de Organizaciones Sindicales*) was formed, with representatives from the CGTP, CNT, and Lima unions affiliated to the CTRP, as well as from independent unions. CUOS called public meetings and demonstrations in support of a common platform of demands. These demands included immediate rehiring of all fired workers, wage raises to compensate for rising prices, and a change in policy towards unions by the Ministry of Labor (*Expreso*, February 26, 1976). However, the potential influence of the CTRP unions participating in CUOS on the future course of the CTRP was successfully neutralized by SINAMOS in the CTRP Congress in May 1976 (see reports in *La Prensa*, April 29 to May 7, 1976). Furthermore, the CUOS encountered opposition against its continued basic support for the Peruvian Revolution from a more radical group of unions that advocated a national strike and total confrontation with the government. Members of this second group provoked incidents of violence in the meeting of May 1 called by the CUOS (*La Prensa*, May 2, 1976), which made the splits in the labor movement highly obvious. Though these continued political divergencies reinforced organized labor's structural weakness, and made it incapable of offering unified resistance to increasing repression, labor militancy in strike behavior and the very fact that unification attempts had been made at all were indicative of a growing polarization in society.

Entrepreneurs on their part were also stepping up attacks, aiming them both at labor directly through illegal firings of workers, and at the government through a strong publicity campaign against the government's labor policies. In particular, the law of security of employment was blamed for protecting labor indiscipline, low productivity, and instigation of conflicts by political agitators. A harder line on the prevention and repression of strikes was demanded as a precondition for the vital contribution of private-sector activity to an improvement of the national economy.

The same polarization between forces urgently demanding a consolidation of the capitalist order, and popular forces defending previously introduced changes as well as further developments toward a gradual socialist transformation, occurred around the issue concerning the future of the social property sector. The first concrete and strong public attacks against the social property sector from the private sector came from the vice-manager (a retired navy officer) of the Honda motorcycle company, denouncing unfair competition by the social property enterprise Moto Andina, under special protective regulations.[29] The example was used as general argument for the inefficiency of social property enterprises and for damage to the private sector that resulted in withdrawal of private investment. A second very strong attack was launched in a paid advertisement in *La Prensa* (April 6, 1976) by the Society of Industries, aimed at publicly discrediting the head of the agency in charge of developing the social property sector, de las Casas. He was accused of stimulating labor conflicts, inducing workers to ruin private enterprises, approving the takeovers of factories, and attacking private entrepreneurs in demagogic terms. As a civilian, he had been promoted to the rank of minister in 1975 and thus it was a convenient argument from the point of view of the private sector to accuse him of abusing the government's confidence to promote socialist ideas alien to the Peruvian revolutionary ideology. Numerous organizations, such as

[29]Open letter in *El Tiempo*, February 20, 1976.

CONACI, CTRP, FDRP,[30] CNA [31] rallied in support of de las Casas. At the same time, the organization of a first national meeting of workers from the social property sector was in progress, another assertive demonstration of forces supporting the development of the social property sector and defending it against attacks from the private sector. Delegates from all social property enterprises and organizing committees of the projects, representing a total of more than 70,000 workers, met from April 29 to May 2, 1976, in Puno. Due to the widely publicized support from other popular organizations, this meeting developed into a strong public manifestation of support for a socialist transformation. In essence, the issue of the social property sector became a symbol of the struggle for survival of the Peruvian Revolution. President Morales Bermúdez himself phrased it in those terms when he affirmed that the government could not accept the failure of the development of the social-property sector, because that would mean the failure of a system that represented the purest postulates of the Peruvian Revolution (*La Prensa*, April 29, 1976). Yet, as the Revolution itself was terminated, so was any further official support for the social-property sector.

Growing polarization and open confrontations in society and within the government on the one hand, and mounting external pressures for stabilization and appeasement of the private sector on the other, brought about a final change in the internal balance of forces in the government, as well as an escalation of repression of radical sociopolitical forces. In June 1976, several people were killed in a battle between the police and several thousand people who supported striking textile workers in Vitarte, an industrial suburb of Lima. From January to March 1976 the number of strikes had reached 159 already,

---

[30]FDRP stands for Front for the Defense of the Peruvian Revolution (*Frente de Defensa de la Revolución Peruana*). The FDRP was supposed to satisfy the need for a political organization in support of the Revolution. It had been launched by President Morales Bermúdez in a speech in Cuzco in November 1975, and in a rather intensive organization campaign, regional and departmental organizing committees were set up. However, in January 1976, the regional organizing committee of Lima-Callao criticized the government's economic measures, which provoked accusations of Communist infiltration from the government. But even after some members had been excluded from this particular committee, other instances of criticism of governmental policies from the FDRP occurred, and by March the organizing drive had already lost impetus.

[31]CNA stands for National Agrarian Confederation (*Confederación Nacional Agraria*). The CNA had been created in 1972 by SINAMOS as a new structure of popular organizations in the agrarian sector. By the time of its First National Congress in October of 1974, it counted with 2500 base organizations, 1500 agrarian leagues at the provincial level, and 20 departmental federations. The CNA was generally regarded as the area of greatest organizational success of SINAMOS, though occasional criticism and transgression of official parameters occurred in the CNA as well as in other government-sponsored organizations.

with 190,879 workers involved and 3.2 million man-hours lost, which would have corresponded to an annual rate of roughly 650 strikes with a total of 750,000 workers involved[32]—slightly fewer strikes than the 779 that occurred in 1975, but involving many more workers than the 617,120 involved in strikes in 1975. However, on July 1, 1976, the government put an end to most open confrontations by declaring a national state of emergency. Strikes were declared illegal, with the provision that any striking worker could be fired immediately. Furthermore, the suspension of constitutional guarantees facilitated rather large-scale arrests of militant union leaders and advisors, as well as of other radical members of popular organizations and of journalists.[33] By December 1976, the Minister of the Interior publicly admitted that there were roughly 240 people held under emergency powers in the country (New York Times, December 24, 1976).

Polarization within the government had been increasing since the beginning of the Second Phase and became clearly visible in October 1975 with the forced retirement of Generals Leonidas Rodríguez, former head of SINAMOS, and Graham Hurtado, former head of COAP, both members of the radical faction. Tensions between government members from the army and the traditionally conservative navy on the one hand, and between junior and senior officers on the other hand grew stronger and more open. The devaluation of June 28, 1976, and the concomitant economic austerity measures finally raised disagreements and polarization to the breaking point, and in a rapid succession of events the last radical figures were purged from the government: On July 7, General Fernandez Maldonado, another member of the original core group of radical officers, who had become Prime Minister in January 1976 despite strong opposition from conservative forces, led a large number of younger officers in a ceremony in commemoration of the 1932 Trujillo massacre of soldiers by Apristas, defying orders from President Morales Bermúdez not to hold such a ceremony. On July 9, a rebellion of a right-wing general was put down, an incident which initially was regarded as a triumph for Prime Minister Maldonado. However, only a week later, on July 16, the forced retirement of Generals Maldonado as Prime Minister, de la Flor as Foreign Minister, and Gallegos as Minister of Agriculture put an end to any presence of radical officers in the government. Arrests of radical officers accused of plotting to reinstate Fernandez Maldonado followed in August. Their demands for a courtmartial

---

[32]Figures from Sociedad de Industrias, published in Equis X, June 3, 1976.

[33]For instance, in July, the former secretary general of the CGTP was arrested, as well as several leaders of the Fishermen's Union because of their protests against the sale of the anchovy fleet by PESCAPERÚ. In August, the editor of the leftist journal Marka was arrested; and in October mass arrests at the National University of Engineering followed. Latin America, Political Report, Nos. 30, 32, 40; July 30, August 13, October 19, 1976.

were denied, and they were simply discharged in order to avoid any further publicity about internal conflicts in the military. Finally, in January of 1977 several prominent members of the Velasco government were exiled: General Leonidas Rodríguez, Admiral Dellepiane Ocampo, Minister of Industry during the introduction of the CI, and General Valdez Palacio, head of the commission that elaborated the legislation concerning the social property sector.[34]

Curtailment of the CI

With the decisive defeat of all forces, inside and outside the government, that had been promoting a socialist transformation, the door was open for a curtailment of the CI, for so long a target for opposition and attacks from the private sector. A fundamental revision of the CI legislation was announced by President Morales Bermúdez in the Annual Conference of Executives in November 1976 (*La Prensa*, November 23, 1976). The major change introduced in the new legislation of February 1, 1977, was a transformation of collective into individual shareholding. The CI remained in existence and continued to receive 15% of before-tax net profits each year, but the rules for allocating this money were changed: 1.5% of profits were to go to the CI fund for administrative expenses, and 13.5% to a special account, the "labor ownership participation account." This account was to grow to an amount equivalent to 50% of enterprise capital, at which point the CI would cease to receive 13.5% of the profits. The money accruing to this account every year would be invested in four different forms, according to the decisions taken by the general assembly of the CI. At least one-third of it has to be invested in "labor shares" issued by the enterprise. The remainder can be invested either in more "labor shares" or in "labor certificates" issued by the enterprise, or in "labor reinvestment certificates" issued by the Industrial Bank, or in "social interest titles" issued by the enterprise. The two types of certificates carry a fixed rate of interest and are redeemable after a period of 5 years. They are owned by workers individually and issued in their name. The "social interest titles" constitute a fund to finance collective social-service programs of the CI; that is, they are common property. The "labor shares," like the certificates, are owned by workers individually, and can be sold after 6 years. They entitle their owners to receive dividends, the same as private shareholders.

[34]These three men had signed a manifesto of a new Revolutionary Socialist Party in November 1976—an attempt to keep the presence of the radical political tendencies of the First Phase of the Revolution alive. Thus it constituted a threat to the new conservative government and provoked repression. (*Latin America, Political Report*, January 14, 1977). Despite such repression, this party obtained six out of 100 seats in the 1978 elections to the Constituent Assembly.

The CI as a collectivity is entitled to representatives on the board of directors according to the proportion of labor shares in relation to enterprise capital. White-collar and blue-collar workers have to be represented on the board according to their proportion in the labor force. If there are only two CI representatives on the board, one of them has to be a white-collar employee.

This combination of provisions renders the achievement of ownership of 50% of enterprise capital, and consequently of 50% representation on the board of directors by the workers virtually impossible. The achievement of this situation would require that *all* funds accruing to the "labor ownership participation account" be invested in labor shares, and none of the workers would sell their shares to the enterprise or to other private shareholders. Given the precarious economic situation of blue-collar workers in Peru, they will hardly be able to resist financial incentives to the contrary. Thus first of all, the enterprise can make labor shares financially much less attractive than labor certificates by paying very low dividends and high fixed interest on labor certificates. Second, given a high enough price, a sufficient number of workers or white-collar employees can certainly be found who would be willing to sell their shares back to the enterprise or to whatever intermediaries one might imagine. Such a sale would *not* reduce the total value of the "labor ownership participation account," but it would change the proportion of labor shares relative to other shares in the enterprise.

Even if a very strong union were to be able to convince all CI members to consistently invest in labor shares, and not to sell any of their shares except to other CI members, an additional safeguard would prevent effective worker influence and possible deadlock in boards of directors with a 50% CI representation. The fact that white-collar employees, who have traditionally guarded a strict social distance from blue-collar workers, are accorded at least one representative on the board renders collective action of labor representatives and solidaristic confrontation with capital representatives highly unlikely. Thus participation of workers in enterprise decision making remains relegated to ineffective joint consultation. The major activity of labor representatives on the board can be expected to center around surveillance of enterprise accounts, as under the old CI legislation. But entrepreneurs can be expected to show renewed confidence in the investment climate, as the specter of an eventual worker takeover has been eliminated for good.

The Peruvian workers' participation scheme, then, was curtailed in accordance with changing dynamics between sociopolitical forces. The crucial force was the elite in control of the coercive apparatus of the state. As long as this elite was united in the determination to carry out a process of structural transformation, even in the absence of a consensus on the ultimate direction of this process, it had sufficient political power to implement reform policies against opposition from dominant socioeconomic groups. However, the elite failed to significantly reduce dependence on domestic capital owners as well as foreign private and public lending agencies in the pursuit of economic development. At the same time, the elite not only failed to strengthen, but even purposefully weakened, popular organizations as power basis for newly emerging sociopolitical forces that had the potential to constitute a counterweight to the predominance of capital owners. Thus, when the internal unity of the elite was disintegrating and it consequently became susceptible to outside influence, capital-owning groups were able to exert the strongest leverage. Their influence first effected a slow shift in policy emphasis away from further structural transformations. And when a clear choice between consolidation of the capitalist order and a rapid chaotic transition to a socialist order was forced, their influence effected a change in the composition of the governing elite in favor of forces protecting the interests of capital.

The mechanism through which the hegemony of capital-owning groups in civil society contributed to the strengthening of the moderate and conservative forces within the military institution and the military government was the penetration of social networks into the military establishment and consequent links of high military officers with economic interests. This argument can be supported by the following interpretation of the interaction between sociopolitical forces and the internal constellation of forces in the military.[35] In the initial situation of political instability and challenges to the established socioeconomic order, elite consensus on the goal of creating a new stable order which would guarantee integral security was sufficient to initiate military rule under strict adherence to institutional procedures and unity. Gradually, a certain radicalization of the reform process took place, promoted by members of the government who were close to Velasco, but whose point of view was probably shared by a minority within the government as well as within the higher ranks in the military. Despite the increasingly obvious disagreements about the basic principles of a desirable socioeconomic order, the moderate and conservative forces abstained from openly challenging the course of the reform process in the interests of preserving institutional unity. Rather, they covertly obstructed the im-

---

[35]The point of view underlying this interpretation is the one of those analysts of the military who contend that two sets of variables have to be taken into account for an explanation of what motivates the military to take certain political actions under given socioeconomic and political circumstances: corporate interests and class background of military officers. A straight class-interest analysis of military political action is inadequate in that socialization in the military institution and a certain confinement of social interaction to military circles constitute forces that countervail the influence of social class background. And interests in corporate self-preservation may take precedence over interests of the social classes to which military officers are linked through social networks. On the other hand, an analysis focusing exclusively on military professionalism and the military as a bureaucratic institution, overlooks the potentially important influence exerted through such social networks. For a good substantiation of this point of view, see North's (1976) discussion of the Chilean military.

plementation of reform policies that tended toward a gradual socialist transformation, and thus tried to protect the interests to which they were linked through social networks.[36] However, when Velasco's deteriorating health caused a certain internal power vacuum and external pressures aggravated the internal polarization to the point of disrupting institutional unity by forcing a clear choice between consolidation of the capitalist order or acceleration of the socialist transformation, which would have affected certain interests in civil society significantly, the moderate and conservative forces rallied and initiated action to restore internal governmental and military unity and to protect the capitalist order through neutralization of all radical forces. Thus sociopolitical forces precipitated the changes in elite composition by way of increasing the internal polarization caused by societal polarization.

The hegemony of social groups linked to domestic and foreign capital interests in civil society contributed to a shift in the internal governmental and military configuration toward a preponderance of moderate and conservative forces. Despite labor's increasing militancy and, to a lesser extent, gains in its capacity for coordinated mobilization, its strength as a sociopolitical force was not nearly sufficient to offer enough effective support to prevent the neutralization of radical forces within the government elite and the ensuing decisive option for a consolidation of the capitalist order, which involved relying on repression to guarantee stability.

This basic constellation of forces crystallizing in the second half of 1976 has persisted, and the same conflicts have continued to manifest themselves. IMF-imposed austerity measures caused severe economic recession, and the financial crisis was worse in December 1977 than it had been in June 1976. Pressures to impose harsher and harsher monetary stabilization policies caused disagreements even among moderate and conservative government members. Such internal conflicts were visible in the rapid changes of ministers. Social conflicts have ever increased in intensity, as protests against economic hardship resulting from the government's policies repeatedly escalated into violent confrontations between protesters and police.

In 1977 the government announced plans for a gradual withdrawal of the military from politics, and in June 1978 elections were held for a Constituent Assembly. These elections took place in a climate of repression, preceded by arrests, deportations of several leftist leaders, and with bans on many leftist publications, and many leftist leaders in hiding. Despite such adverse condi-

---

[36]Obviously, clear evidence to document this argument is hard to come by. One fact that supports the argument is the evidently widespread corruption in the highest military ranks. One book that mentions this corruption is Baella Tuesta (1977); reports to the effect can also by found in *Latin America, Political Report*, No. 34, August 27, 1976. Family connections between military officers and industrial interests, as well as managerial positions in industry held by retired high military officers, further support the argument.

Table 7.1
Election Results in Peru, 1962 and 1978

Presidential election (1962)[a]		Percentage of votes	Election of Constituent Assembly (1978)		Percentage of votes	Number of seats
APRA	right	33.0	APRA		35.3	37
National Union of Odria Followers (UNO)		28.4	National Union of Odria Followers (UNO)	right	2.1	2
			Popular Christian Party (PPC)		23.8	25
Popular Action (AP)	center	31.1				
Christian Democrats (PDC)		2.9	Christian Democrats (PDC)	center	2.4	2
			Other center-right parties		5.9	6
Progressive Social Movement (MSP)	left	0.5	Workers', Peasants', Students', and Popular Front (FOCEP)	left	12.3	12
Communist Party (PCP)		1.0				
National Liberation Front (FLN)		2.0	Communist Party (PCP)		5.9	6
Blank		1.1	Revolutionary Socialist Party (PSR)		6.6	6
			Popular Democratic Union (UDP)		4.6	4

Sources: Neira (1973) for 1962 figures; *Latin America, Political Report*, July 21, 1978, for 1978 figures.

[a] Deputies and senators were elected on the same day as the president.

tions, the legacy of the First Phase of the Peruvian Revolution manifested itself clearly in the comparatively strong showing of the left. Before 1968, the Communist Party had been the only major leftist party, and it received no more than 3% of the vote in the 1962 elections (the Communist vote was split between two candidates). Together with the vote for the Progressive Social Movement, this amounted to 3.5% for the left. In 1978, four major left-wing parties competed and together won 28 out of 100 seats (Table 7.1). However, another prominent characteristic of the left was carried over from the First Phase: chronic disunity, ideological disputes, and infighting. Such disputes led to splits and factionalization among the representatives of the various leftist parties in the Constituent Assembly. Similarly, the First Phase had left its imprint on organized labor in the form of an increased mobilization potential but continued disunity. Rapidly falling real wages, growing unemployment, and political repression facilitated solidaristic, coordinated activation of this potential in the form of a national general strike in July 1977. However, this instance of unity was of short duration, and several subsequent attempts to call a national general strike failed and thus demonstrated the persistent basic disunity and organizational weakness of the working class.[37] Thus, even if a return to civilian rule would take place, which as of the end of 1979 seems less than certain, with rumors circulating about a possible right-wing coup, no significant changes in the pattern of conflict between sociopolitical forces could be expected as a result. Continued predominance of propertied over lower social classes will effect policies designed to consolidate the capitalist order, and concomitant lower-class demands and protests will be met with continued repression. Yet, the legacy of the First Phase lives on in the form of the capacity of broader sectors of the working class to envision the possibility of a transition to an alternative social order that would provide workers a greater share in control rights and in resources for consumption, as well as in the form of greater organizational penetration that would have the potential to develop a stronger unified power base to pressure for such a transition.

[37]Angell (1978) discusses the major disagreements and disputes among organized labor and the left.

8

Conclusion

In conclusion, I will present a short comparative summary of the development of workers' participation in the different cases discussed here in order to substantiate my claim that workers' participation is a highly political issue and that its development has to be understood in terms of the dynamics of sociopolitical forces. An examination of how at every stage the development of participation is linked to the strength and actions of sociopolitical forces will support the usefulness of my conceptualization of the dynamics in the four developmental stages. It will confirm that the issue of workers' participation is at the center of the struggle about the distribution of power and material resources carried on by sociopolitical forces in their promotion of different models of social order. Fully developed workers' participation, or workers' control, is an essential structural element of a politico-economic system modeled after the democratic-socialist ideal type, and its development in the other systems is shaped by the strength of sociopolitical forces promoting a democratic-socialist transformation relative to forces promoting a consolidation of the existing order. The economic and political power base of various forces, and consequently their capacity to promote or impede a process of societal transformation in the direction of a democratic-socialist order, varies of course according to the level of economic development and the type of politico-economic system of a society. Thus, after the following short summary comparing empirical cases, I will conclude with some speculation about possible future developments of workers' participation in societies with different politico-economic systems at different levels of development.

Origins of Workers' Participation

The discussion of the origins of workers' participation in the empirical cases showed that it was by no means a result of managerial enlightenment or of a functional necessity of advanced industrial societies, but rather a result of a

239

challenge to the existing distribution of power and wealth. Workers' participation was introduced in societies at different levels of economic development and with different politico-economic systems. In each case, its introduction was a subject of political dispute, and it aroused strong opposition among status-quo-oriented groups.

France, Germany, and Sweden. In the developed capitalist democracies, the introduction of workers' participation came as a response to a challenge from organized labor to capital owners' exclusive exercise of control over production and their disproportionate share in societal resources. In France and Germany, this challenge originated in a situation of temporary strength of organized labor vis-à-vis capital in the wake of World War II. In Sweden the challenge grew slowly with the increasing organizational strength of labor.

Yugoslavia. In Yugoslavia, a developing socialist authoritarian system, where economic and political power were concentrated in the hands of a small elite, the introduction of workers' participation was an elite response to an external threat that challenged the legitimacy of the existing order. It was the expulsion from the Cominform which induced the elite to search for an alternative to the bureaucratic-centralist type of system that they had upheld as model of a desirable social order before.

Peru. In Peru, a developing capitalist authoritarian system, the introduction of workers' participation was a response of the elite in control of the coercive apparatus of the state to the threat of growing social disorder and instability. This threat originated in a combination of challenges from newly mobilized popular groups with concomitant disintegration of political consensus among dominant groups.

Chile. In Chile, a developing capitalist democratic system, workers' participation was introduced by a leftist political coalition that was able to challenge the control of economically dominant groups over the state due to the latter's political fragmentation and due to growing organizational strength of various popular groups.

Purposes and Designs of Workers' Participation

Just as the origins of workers' participation schemes were not a product of harmonious social evolution and peaceful adaptation to technological change, so the purpose of workers' participation was never the subject of general societal agreement. Consequently, finding the optimal structural design was not a question of developing a correct sociotechnical construction that guaranteed smooth functioning and increases in productivity and work satisfaction. Rather, different designs were promoted to serve the fundamentally different purposes of either consolidating the existing social order or transforming it toward a democratic-socialist order. Status-quo-oriented forces typically promoted incentive schemes emphasizing joint consultation and sometimes participation in income rights that were intended to integrate workers into their enterprise and thus neutralize the challenge to the existing order. The distinguishing characteristic of structural designs promoted by change-oriented forces was their emphasis on transfer of control rights, intended to mobilize workers into demanding and/or exercising full democratic control over the process of production and distribution. In each case, which type of design was introduced depended on the political strength of the forces promoting consolidation relative to the forces promoting transformation of a given order.

France. The designs introduced in France, Germany, and Sweden reflect the varying political strength of labor relative to capital. In the immediate post-World War II period, when labor and leftist political parties in France still enjoyed the political influence they had achieved during the Resistance, they concentrated their attention on nationalization and workers' participation in nationalized industries, and these policies were implemented to a certain extent. Workers' participation in private industry was neglected, and thus only works' committees with joint consultation functions were introduced. However, after this short period of strength, the internally divided labor movement rapidly lost power, and labor and the left remained far from capable of imposing their design of nationalization of industries and establishment of full workers' control. Nevertheless, labor's militancy continued to constitute a challenge to capital's control over production, despite the latters' political predominance. This induced the government in the 1960s to introduce a profit-sharing scheme with a distinctively integrative purpose.

Germany. In the immediate post-World War II period in Germany, demands of labor for nationalization of iron and coal mining and the steel industry, and for the transfer of their administration to the workers, lacked sufficient support from a coherent organizational power base, since unions were just being rebuilt. However, the direct opponents of these demands, representatives of owners of the respective industries, were temporarily in an equally weak political position, and the resulting compromise was one of codetermination. Economic reconstruction caused a faster growth of economic and political power of capital-owning groups than of the labor movement, such that the compromise solution for the workers' participation design in all other sectors of the economy was strongly shaped by an integrative conception, and the actual transfer of control rights to the workers remained highly limited, the main emphasis being on joint consultation. In the late 1960s, increased labor militancy and a slight growth of political strength of labor and the Social Democratic party gave rise to new efforts to expand workers' participation in the form of codetermination to all sectors of the economy. Still, the political strength of labor relative to capital was not sufficient to effect real parity in control rights in the enterprise; the forced compromise solution consisted of formal codetermination, with numerical equality of capital and labor, but with the decisive vote for capital in case of a deadlock, and with mandatory inclusion of two members of top management as representatives on labor's side.

Sweden. In Sweden, the expansion of workers' participation to include an ever larger share of control rights proceeded slowly, with the growing strength of labor and a shift in policy emphasis from societal-level transfer of control and income rights from private capital owners to the state toward enterprise-level transfer of control rights to the workers. When unions did develop an explicit concern with workers' participation and promoted increasing exercise of control rights by workers in the late 1960s, entrepreneurs on their part initiated experiments with job enlargement, self-steering groups, etc., and promoted joint consultation designs, all with clearly integrative purposes. Yet, labor's sociopolitical strength effected the implementation of a structural design that opened up possibilities for a progressive transfer of effective control rights to the workforce, and thus clearly reflected the intention of gradually but fundamentally transforming the capitalist order.

Yugoslavia. In Yugoslavia, no competing designs were promoted initially, since political initiative as well as power were monopolized by a small elite. Since the elite decided to introduce workers' participation as an element in their strategy to transform the bureaucratic-centralist order, the participation design took the form of full transfer of control rights from state representatives at the enterprise level to the workers. There were some internal disagreements among the elite that surfaced in later developments, but in the initial stages the structural design of workers' participation clearly responded to the purpose of transformation.

Peru. In Peru, different members of the military government promoted different structural designs of participation for competing purposes—integration or transformation. The compromise solution between structural designs ranging from simple limited transfer of income rights in the form of profit sharing, to full transfer of control rights to workers acting in combination with communal representatives had a basically integrative character. Its main emphasis was on transfer of income rights, linked to joint consultation on a limited number of issues, excluding any labor relations questions. However, the transformative conception made its imprint on the structural design through the increasing representation of labor in decision-making bodies linked to an increase in ownership, which was ultimately to result in codetermination. This compromise solution, with its lack of clear definition of the final shape of the structural design at the point of 50% participation in ownership and control, was characteristic of the unstable internal configuration of forces in the government, where President Velasco held the balance between factions promoting a full consolidation of the capitalist order and other factions promoting various degrees of transformation.

Chile. In Chile, workers' participation was introduced in the context of a deliberate attempt at bringing about a democratic-socialist transformation. Due to its temporary political strength relative to center and rightist parties, and despite its precariously small margin and its control over the executive only, the coalition of leftist parties, supported by a variety of popular organizations, was able to initiate a process of societal transformation. The government and organized labor jointly elaborated the participation design for the social-property sector with a distinctively transformative purpose, and accordingly the design emphasized the transfer of control rights to workers at the enterprise level.

Development and Effects of Workers' Participation

The political struggle between status-quo- and change-oriented forces not only shaped the design of workers' participation that was introduced in each case, but it continued to affect profoundly its implementation, full development, and effects on integration or mobilization of workers. Though the struggle between forces promoting different designs indicates the great importance attributed to the structure of the design itself, this structure never predetermined the effects of workers' participation. Integrative schemes and compromise solutions did not necessarily have a pacifying and co-optative effect on workers and thus did not necessarily contribute to the consolidation of a given social order. And mobilizing schemes did not necessarily have the intended activating effects, guaranteeing full implementation and generating further support for societal transformation. The structure of the design shaped the motivational predispositions of the workforce, but their activation and the direction in which they were channelled depended on the involvement of actors at the enterprise level with links to sociopolitical forces at the societal level. Developments and effects of one and the same design varied in different enterprises according to the strength and supportive activity provided by local union organizations. And developments and effects of very similar designs varied in different countries according to the strength and supportive activity provided by organized labor and/or other change-oriented sociopolitical forces.

Germany, France, and Sweden. Intranational differences in developments and effects of the same participation design due to varying roles assumed by union representatives at the enterprise level could be observed in Germany. Cross-national similarities in developments and effects of similar designs at the enterprise level due to similar roles assumed by unions could be observed during a certain period in France and Sweden. These similarities later gave way to fundamental differences due to a change in activity of unions in Sweden and due to their much greater strength at the societal level.

Developments of participation at the enterprise level in Germany ranged from integration to no noticeable impact, to generation of demands for further transfer of control rights from capital to labor. In both structural designs—codetermination as well as joint consultation—the dynamics depended on the orientation and mobilizing activity of union leaders and activists. Restricting participation to representation in works councils and on the boards of directors resulted largely in lack of interest and involvement at the base, except where active local union officials managed to mobilize workers into formulating their demands and requiring their representatives to push these demands effectively vis-à-vis the enterprise. Ideological orientation of top-level union leaders and presence of middle- and lower-level activists determined the extent to which appointment of workers' representatives to codetermined company boards by the union resulted in oligarchical and integrative tendencies.

In France and Sweden, designs and developments of participation at the enterprise level in the 1950s and early 1960s were quite similar. Participation through the French works committees, as through the Swedish works councils, was restricted to representation in joint consultation bodies without real influence over any but lowest-level decisions, which hardly elicited any interest from the workforce. Since unions took a passive role, or in certain cases in France an outright negative one, the highly limited designs of participation resulted predominantly in apathy. However, when Swedish unions in the 1960s started taking an interest and mobilizing for participation, the limitations of this joint consultation design became clearly visible, and demands emerged for a correction of its deficiencies to allow for real exercise of control rights by workers.

The sociopolitical strength of labor then determined the extent to which the effects of participation at the enterprise level were fed back into dynamics of societal transformation. In Sweden, demands for an expansion of workers' effective control rights were promoted and transformed into legislation of far-reaching significance by the labor movement's political wing, the Social Democratic party. In Germany, tendencies toward increasing mobilization at the enterprise level generated pressure in support of organized labor's demands for an extension of codetermination, which were promoted by the Social Democratic party. The finally accepted compromise legislation, however, fell short of satisfying labor's demands in two major respects. It did not provide for effective parity at the enterprise level nor for labor's participation in economic planning at regional and national levels. In France, where participation did not have any integrative nor mobilizing effects, but continued high militancy and radical tendencies among workers manifested demands for societal transformation, no progress in such a direction was made, as organized labor and leftist political parties remained in disagreement over the exact nature of the transformation process and were unable to generate sufficient political support for it.

Yugoslavia. Yugoslavia presented an example of a structural design that formally transferred all control rights to the workers, but in practice functioned deficiently due to the absence of a mobilizing force. Workers formally had control over decisions at all hierarchical levels, but its exercise was insufficiently developed. In particular, lower-level workers were not able to realize their influence potential due to the lack of a union capable of motivating them to become involved and providing assistance for effective participation. The participation scheme did have a feedback effect on societal-level dynamics, which however did not originate from horizontal, class-based organized forces, but rather from regional coalitions of political and managerial–technocratic elites. Whereas discontent of workers found no organized outlet but rather manifested itself in wildcat strikes, pressure from these middle-level elites managed to influence policies insofar as it aggravated the breakdown of political consensus within the national elite concerning the central allocation of investment funds. The result was a decentralization of the exercise of income rights from the state to banks and enterprises, and consequently a strengthening of regional as well as enterprise autonomy. Despite the national elite's professed commitment to a democratic-socialist order, lack of political consensus hampered its ability to prevent ever further deviations from this ideal in the form of growing inequalities in the distribution of wealth and power among individuals, social groups, and regions.

Peru and Chile. The Peruvian structural design of participation elicited considerable interest among the workforce, mainly due to its monetary aspects. Thus apathy occurred only when there was a lack of knowledge about the participation legislation. Integration as a result of the participation scheme was largely impeded by entrepreneurial resistance and attempts to avoid granting the legally prescribed benefits. Where the workforce was informed about the legislation, but not unionized, conflicts often remained latent, as workers lacked the capacity to take action in the defense of their rights. Clearly, the monetary aspect of participation was a major incentive eliciting interest among the base despite restriction of participation to representation at highest levels, but only strong unions were able to channel this interest into coordinated action and pressure in support of the worker representative(s) on the board of directors. Involvement in participation was highest, and generation of demands for an expansion of the workers' share in control rights strongest, where ideologically committed and organizationally experienced union leaders assumed leadership positions in the CI.

The contrast between the effects of high union activity and high involvement in participation on strike behavior and productivity in Peru and Chile highlights the crucial importance of the larger political struggle. In Peru, these goals, which were realized in Chile, could not be achieved, despite the explicit intentions of the designers of the reform, because the mediating variables, real grass-roots participation in decision making with significant influence on enterprise operations, were incompatible with private ownership of enterprises in a capitalist system. Whereas such participation was encouraged in Chile, in Peru it was perceived as a threat and consequently obstructed by the economically dominant groups.

Thus class conflict in society was reflected in the conflicts at the enterprise level. In addition to entrepreneurial opposition, though, the scarcity of ideologically committed union leaders and activists greatly hampered the full realization even of the structurally given potential for participation. Personal power struggles among leaders and lack of committed middle- and lower-level activists facilitated outside intervention and manipulation, which involved occasional co-optation of both union and CI leaders, and attempts to neutralize the change-oriented potential of participation. Overall, however, mobilization and demands for a socialist transformation prevailed over apathy and integration among the crucial sectors of the industrial working class. The competition between entrepreneurial demands for a curtailment of the participation scheme and labor's demands for its expansion as part of a process of societal transformation was finally decided in favor of curtailment and consequent consolidation of the existing socioeconomic order due to a change in elite composition in favor of forces promoting the interests of capital.

In Chile, the opportunities for participation given through the structural design were realized to their fullest extent in the enterprises with the most favorably disposed and active union leaders and activists. The social and technical organization of the enterprise, which shaped to some extent the exact features of the structural design, had virtually no influence on the development of participation, once the mobilizing role of unions was taken into account. Overall, the high degree of involvement of unions had a clearly mobilizing effect, not only on the workforce in the enterprises in the social area, but also on the workforce in private enterprises, which caused numerous factory takeovers with demands for the introduction of workers' control. Despite a channeling of these demands by the unions into the political system, the lack of consolidation of political power of organized labor and the coalition of leftist parties brought the process of democratic-socialist transformation to an abrupt end.

Supportive Policies for Workers' Participation

Since the introduction of workers' participation as an integral element of the design of a whole social order is an issue of political struggle, its promotion in different forms has to be seen in the framework of the global political strategy pursued by various sociopolitical forces. The discussion of the empirical examples showed that if workers' participation is promoted with the purpose of contributing to a process of societal transformation, its institutionalization has to be accompanied by a variety of supportive policies. The Chilean case confirmed most dramatically that spontaneous grass-roots action at the enterprise level, even in the context of a high degree of mobilization, is no basis for long-range success in establishing workers' control if it is not accompanied by a consolidation of political power of change-oriented forces. Consolidation of political power requires strengthening of control over the state, and strengthening of state control over the economy through the central exercise of a significant share of control and income rights. The two dimensions are interactive insofar as control over the state is a precondition for transfer of control and income rights from private owners to the state, which in turn facilitates consolidation of control over the state by providing means for strengthening political support and weakening political opposition.

In capitalist democratic systems, strengthening the electoral support base is crucial for protracted incumbency of change-oriented forces, and thus for a gradual expansion of the state's share in the exercise of control and income rights. Through the exercise of these rights, policies to protect economic stability, full employment, and social equality can be pursued, which in turn have a feedback effect on the electoral support base, in addition to constituting desirable achievements in the process of transformation per se. In authoritarian systems, maintenance of elite ideological unity is crucial for purposeful use of state power in the pursuit of societal transformation. In developing countries, the implementation of a coherent model of economic development, aimed at the achievement of a high degree of independence from foreign economic power centers, is a prerequisite for the successful pursuit of societal transformation. This in turn is feasible only through central exercise of a strong share of control and income rights through the state, in capitalist as well as socialist developing countries. A comparison of developments in the empirical cases underlines that global political vision and strategic skills of political leaders were prerequisites for a progress of societal transformation, including a development of workers' participation, but that their ability to implement concrete measures in accordance with their vision depended on the strength of their political support base relative to opposing sociopolitical forces.

France. In France, political unity and strength of labor and leftist parties after 1946 fell far below the level needed to be able to shape policies in accordance with a global strategy of societal transformation. Accordingly, there has been a minimal encroachment on control and income rights of private capital owners for transfer to the state at the societal level as well as for transfer to the workers at the enterprise level. Also, redistribution through the welfare state and full employment remained low on the list of priorities of the dominant political forces in France.

Germany. In Germany, a strategy for societal transformation was elaborated and put forward by union and Social Democratic party leaders in the late 1960s. However, the proposals for transfer of a certain extent of control and income rights from private owners to the state, which were central elements of the whole strategy, met with very strong opposition from capital and allied sociopolitical forces, even more so than the proposals for expansion of codetermination. Whereas a watered-down compromise solution for the latter could be found, proposals to strengthen the state's role in investment planning, in combination with regional and national advisory boards composed of union and employer representatives, completely failed to materialize in policies due to the insufficient political strength of their proponents to overcome stern resistance. Due to the state's limited share in control and income rights, the government's ability to pursue policies of protection against potential capital flight, maintain full employment, and expand the welfare state remained restricted. Some progress in equalization was made under the Social Democratic government, but its overall record did not contribute to a consolidation of its electoral base. As part of the debate about a coherent strategy of social change, a scheme similar to the Swedish wage-earner funds was proposed. The need for accumulating capital without further increasing the wealth and power of private capitalists was clearly perceived within the DGB and the SPD, and the proposed solution was a plan for collective employee-owned investment funds. However, in clear contrast to Sweden, this proposal was modified in negotiations within the SPD–FDP coalition to the extent of bearing little resemblance to the original conception of collective funds. Consequently, it received no further support from the DGB, and by the mid-1970s the debate had virtually faded from the scene, as the balance of sociopolitical forces was too unfavorable.

Sweden. In Sweden, a strategy of gradual societal transformation has been envisioned and corresponding policies have been introduced by the labor movement leadership for several decades, culminating in the proposal for wage-earner funds as the key to socialization of capital ownership. Encroachment on control and income rights of private capital owners for transfer to the state preceded the transfer of certain control rights to workers at the enterprise level. Through the system of investment funds and the Public Pension Fund, a partial protective mechanism to provide for adequate investment was built up. Centrally coordinated labor market policies maintained full employment, which strengthened labor's position on the market, contributed to an equalization of incomes, strengthened labor solidarity, and thus had a positive feedback effect on the electoral support base of the Social Democrats. Redistribution through a comprehensive welfare state advanced Sweden significantly toward the goal of social equality. The mobilization of sufficient political support for the implementation of the system of wage-earner funds would constitute a further significant step in the transition toward a democratic-socialist order.

Yugoslavia. Yugoslavia exemplifies the problems originating from an abandonment of a centrally guided coherent strategy of democratic-socialist transformation. In particular, it highlights the importance of finding a balance between central exercise of control rights and enterprise autonomy, and of retaining central exercise of income rights in order to ensure the effectiveness of central development planning and equalization. Workers' participation in income rights cannot serve as a vehicle for equalization, as it fails to affect important dimensions of redistribution, such as those among regions, sectors of industry, individual enterprises, and employed and not employed social groups. Clearly, such a redistributive function can only be performed centrally through strong state intervention, setting regional and sectoral investment priorities, creating employment, coordinating wage policy, etc. This holds true for a fully developed workers' control system as well as for all transition stages. If equality is promoted in a process of socialist transformation on the basis of the principle "to each according to his work," separation between the exercise of control and income rights is to be advocated because the profitability of an enterprise depends on a variety of factors, such as capital intensity, market share, branch of the economy, geographical location, etc., among which efforts of the workforce are of minor importance. In Yugoslavia, the divestment of central exercise of control and income rights, in the interest of relieving the center of politically difficult decisions, caused the emergence of new "group–private" economic power centers. The pursuit of their economic self-interest in an uncoordinated free market economy led to a failure in the maintenance of full employment and of socialist principles of production and distribution. These problems further aggravated political fractionalization, and thus put the whole future pursuit of a democratic-socialist order into question.

Peru. In Peru, with a developing capitalist authoritarian system, the problems pertaining to the other two types of systems in the pursuit of a socialist transformation were compounded, and thus the lack of elite unity in the pursuit of a coherent transformation strategy was particularly detrimental. The solution of the crucial problems of protection against capital flight, enforcement of central development planning, and reduction of the extremely high inequalities would have required significant curtailment of control and income rights of domestic as well as foreign capital owners, and their transfer to the state. In Peru, transfer of these rights from domestic private owners to the state hardly proceeded at all, and from foreign owners only at great cost. The partial transfer of control and income rights to workers at the enterprise level, then, caused serious political and economic problems. Though capital flight out of the country could at least be partly controlled through foreign exchange regulations, this did not solve the investment problem, and consequently development plans failed to be implemented. Furthermore, the development plans themselves failed to constitute a model for maximizing independent economic development, adequate for the resource base of the country and the needs of the large majority of the population. Neither did they include significant measures to solve the problems of inequality and unemployment. The failure to connect the structural reforms to a coherent strategy of societal transformation, due to the elite's lack of a clear vision of the implications of this failure and of ideological consensus to avoid these implications, rendered the whole process vulnerable to pressures from representatives of domestic and foreign capital interests. The power base of these opponents of the process had hardly been weakened, nor had the power base of supporters been significantly strengthened, and thus growing disintegration of ideological consensus rendered the elite heavily susceptible to pressures from opponents.

Both the Yugoslav and Peruvian example have pointed out the importance of the interaction between forces in civil society and elite composition in terms of ideological orientation and unity. A more important probable threat to the autonomy of an elite in an authoritarian system and to its capacity to pursue a coherent course of societal transformation than actual loss of power vis-à-vis socioeconomic forces is the potential of pressures from such forces to effect internal splits in the elite. A highly unified elite, with a clear vision of the desired model of social order and of a coherent strategy of societal transformation, is not only less vulnerable to outside pressures to begin with, but also has the opportunity to consolidate its power through policies designed to weaken its opponents and to strengthen its supporters.

Chile. In developing capitalist democratic systems, of course, the pursuit of a coherent strategy of societal transformation and the consolidation of political power are even considerably more difficult to achieve than in authoritarian systems, as the Chilean example shows. Initially, the government had a relatively clear and coherent transformation strategy, but political opposition in Congress impeded its implementation. Major disagreements within the coalition then started growing over the issue of how to overcome this opposition; whether to continue respecting legal procedures, or whether to resort to a large-scale mass mobilization and extraparliamentary action. Through redistributive policies, the government was able to strengthen its electoral support base, but it was unable to weaken the economic power base of its opponents. Also, popular mobilization in support of the transformation process increased, manifesting itself in land and factory occupations to bring them under workers' control. However, the government's crucial weakness was its inability to prevent domestic and foreign forces from pushing the country into economic chaos and thus provoking military intervention. Ultimately, control over the coercive apparatus of the state, or rather the government's lack thereof, was decisive for the abortive attempt at a democratic socialist transition. This points forcefully to the central role of the military for any process of societal transformation in developing countries. Accordingly, the military has to be considered as a crucial actor in the following speculations about possible developments of workers' participation schemes in different politico-economic systems at different levels of economic development.

Predicaments and Possibilities for Future Developments

In presenting the following speculations about possible future developments of workers' participation schemes, I will focus first on the chances for successful introduction and development of participation schemes with an integrative–consolidating purpose, and then on those with a mobilizing–transformative purpose, in both developed and developing countries. The first question, then, is whether challenges to the existing order are likely to be countered successfully through the introduction of integrative schemes for workers' participation in developed capitalist democracies. Will participation schemes introduced by politically dominant pro status quo forces as a response to labor militancy or other manifestations of labor discontent, but either in the absence or in spite of explicit union demands for a share in control rights for workers, have the desired integrative effects? They may, provided there is no strong and ideological labor movement with a clear perception of and commitment to the political path toward an improvement of the position of the working class in society and consequent collaboration between unions and a labor party, but rather a depoliticized union movement that supports the participation schemes. The crucial dimension of union presence for integration or transformation is the political orientation and mobilization efforts of union leaders and activists. Presence of sectorally strong, but nonideological unions is conducive to an instrumental–collectivist[1] attitude among workers, aimed at improving their po-

---

[1]The term *instrumental collectivism*, and the corresponding cluster of attitudes and behavior was first defined by Goldthorpe and Lockwood in (1963) and expanded on in their later publications (1968 and 1969).

sition as a group in the existing socioeconomic order. Efforts to improve their position may be aimed at the distribution of income rights only in the sense of expanding the share of labor income vis-à-vis capital income in their enterprise, or they may include the distribution of control rights as well in the sense of expanding their control over their immediate work environment. The distinguishing characteristic of these efforts is their orientation toward improving one group's position within a given distribution rather than challenging the principles underlying this distribution and changing its basic shape. Consequently, workers' participation schemes, which improve the position of a certain group of workers among whom instrumental collectivist attitudes are predominant, may in fact contribute to an integration of these workers into their enterprise and thus to a consolidation of the capitalist order. An additional essential factor required for a lasting integrative effect is continued economic growth, to guarantee security of employment and a more or less steadily improving standard of living.

In developing capitalist countries, possibilities for neutralizing challenges to the existing order through the introduction of integrative workers' participation schemes appear much smaller. Such schemes, introduced as a response to labor mobilization, can only be successful if mobilization is restricted to narrow sectors, either because the country is still in an early stage of modernization and mobilization, or because a stable system of domination has been built up along with the process of mobilization. At an early stage of modernization and mobilization, provision of incentives through workers' participation may have a temporary integrative effect on the most mobilized sectors. Once mobilization reaches beyond narrow sectors, however, scarcity of available resources impedes provision of sufficient benefits for integration out of newly generated wealth, and thus forces a choice between direct redistribution, which would imply significant changes in the existing order, and the repression of popular demands. Continued economic growth of a magnitude to generate sufficient new wealth to satisfy demands of broadly mobilized lower-class sectors is highly improbable, even in countries with a strong natural resource base, given the rate of population growth and the rising expectations resulting from the demonstration effect of the lifestyle of middle- and upper-class sectors. Where a stable system of domination in the form of controls over popular organizations was created during the shift from low to intermediate stages of economic development and social mobilization, but mobilization nevertheless starts exceeding tolerable limits in some sectors, the resource base for incentives to be provided through an integrative design of workers' participation may be sufficient to satisfy the demands in these sectors. Yet, there is a limited number of countries with such stable systems of domination based on low coercive controls existing in reality. Consequently, the possibilities for the introduction and successful development of integrative workers' participation schemes in countries at intermediate stages of capitalist development are equally limited; rather, the predominant response pattern to mobilization is repression.

An assessment of the chances for mobilizing workers' participation schemes to be introduced and fully developed ultimately poses the question of the potential of successful democratic-socialist transformation processes. Where, in which types of politico-economic systems, and at which levels of development, are sociopolitical forces promoting workers' participation as an element of a democratic-socialist transformation most likely to succeed? Analytically, the structural divergencies from the democratic-socialist ideal type are greatest in the authoritarian-corporatist type. Besides the changes in the distribution of control rights required in any type of system in a process of transition, both polity and economy have to be fundamentally transformed in an authoritarian-corporatist system; the nonpolyarchic into a polyarchic polity, and the capitalist into a socialist economy. A transformation of a liberal-pluralist into a democratic-socialist system requires primarily a fundamental modification of the economy, whereas the same transformation of a bureaucratic-centralist system requires primarily a fundamental modification of the polity. In all three types of systems, though, the crucial question is whether sociopolitical forces committed to developing a workers' control system in a democratic-socialist transition are capable of achieving and consolidating political power and of pursuing a coherent strategy of transformation. Clearly, the obstacles to their successful pursuit of such a strategy vary with the level of development of the society.

In developed capitalist democracies, empirically closest to the liberal-pluralist type, it appears possible that a hegemonic labor movement with a clear socialist ideology and sustained mobilization activity is capable of providing sufficient electoral support for protracted incumbency of a leftist political party sharing the same ideology. Long-term wielding of political power enables labor and the left to gradually transfer an increasing share of control and income rights from private owners to the state, and control rights to workers at the enterprise level. And it provides the means to simultaneously educate and mobilize the base for fully exercising control rights and for supporting further societal transformation.

However, the crucial role assigned to unions in the process of development of workers' participation points to a predicament concerning the appropriate structure of union organization. Their ability to influence political incumbency and consequently policies through the provision of electoral support, and to ensure full implementation of workers' participation policies at the enterprise level requires on the one hand organizational and ideological unity and consequently a high degree of centralization, and on the other hand high involvement of middle- and lower-level leaders and activists in individual work centers, which is frequently insufficiently encouraged in highly centralized union organizations. Also, whereas organizational penetration and a link to a strong center is an essential precondition for sociopolitical strength of the union movement, enabling it to effectively promote a socialist transformation, it increases chances for co-optation as well by facilitating the emergence of oligarchic tendencies. Furthermore, the more centralized an organization, the smaller the circle of leaders whose co-optation may bring with it neutralization of the whole organization. Obviously, ideological unity and a strong commitment to a socialist transformation among top union leaders as well as middle- and lower-level leaders and activists effectively neutralizes this danger, which is why they are such crucial prerequisites for the development of a workers' control system. A possible way out of this predicament of centralization versus decentralization seems to be an explicit inclusion of local unions into the participation design,[2] but continued responsibility of the center for collective bargaining, for training of local union representatives for their functions in the participation scheme, and for general political education and mobilization activities.

Political education is a crucial task for a socialist labor movement in order to generate a broad support base for the conception of a new social order and the policies designed to bring it about. In the absence of ideological and organizational penetration of society by a unified labor movement, attempts of a government of the left to introduce and develop workers' control along with other policies for a socialist transformation are hardly likely to be successful. Such a government, dependent on weakly organized middle as well as working-class support, and with it the process of transformation itself, will be highly vulnerable to middle-class defections and opposition, which in turn is certain to be aroused by economic difficulties. Economic difficulties in the period of transformation are virtually unavoidable, given the dependence even of developed capitalist countries on the international capitalist economy. This points to the much debated predicament of "socialism in one country," which has assumed particular relevance in the age of the multinational corporation.

Continued economic growth, essential for the maintenance of political support in a democratic-socialist transformation, requires adequate investments as well as competitiveness on the world market. Crucial providers of investment funds and of technological know-how, essential to maintain competitiveness, are multinational corporations. The impact of multinationals is certainly greatest in developing countries, but even in Western European countries, penetration by foreign-based companies grew to account for an estimated 15% of in-

[2] A strict and comprehensive separation of functions between unions and participatory bodies, such as responsibility for labor relations versus production questions, is impossible to begin with because concerns with labor relations and production questions necessarily overlap. For instance, working conditions as intrinsic elements of general labor relations are intimately related to production planning and organization as well. How unviable such a separation is, is underlined by the failure of the Peruvian attempt to introduce and enforce it.

vestment in the early 1970s (Barkin 1975:19). The activity of multinational companies is concentrated mainly in modern expansive sectors of industry, such as automobiles, oil, computers, chemicals, and food processing. Their possibilities to shift production from one country to another in order to avoid the impact of workers' participation policies constitute an obvious threat to economic growth and stability of employment in the countries concerned.

The most effective way to extend control over multinational companies is through coordinated action among several countries, if such action is clearly regulated in a supranational agreement and carried out with a firm commitment.[3] However, whereas such supranational agreements help to overcome one obstacle to socialist transformation, they may create other new obstacles, particularly if they include provisions for economic integration in addition to provisions for regulations of control over multinational companies. Supranational economic integration agreements can limit the latitude for action in individual member countries in such areas as wage and price policy, environmental and industrial safety standards, and regional development planning, etc., due to economic competition from other member countries. The application of criteria of social costs and benefits for economic policy making, essential elements in a process of societal transformation, is likely to raise prices for certain products and thus render them noncompetitive vis-à-vis imports of cheaper products from other member countries, which in turn has negative consequences for economic growth, and thus may impede progress of a socialist transformation by way of eroding political support for the process.

Clearly, these problems are most serious for small countries with heavily export-dependent economies. The coincidence that hegemonic (or near-hegemonic) labor movements have been able to develop only in such small countries as Sweden and Norway, and to a lesser extent in Austria and Denmark, prevents any strong optimism about possible future development prospects for workers' control along with a socialist transformation in developed capitalist democracies. Nevertheless, Sweden still holds up the promise of potential pioneering developments in this direction.

In speculating about prospects for the development of workers' control in empirical systems approximating the bureaucratic-centralist type, I will restrict the discussion to developing socialist authoritarian systems. A discussion of conditions in the U.S.S.R. and the more developed Eastern European countries is simply beyond the scope of this study. The ideological commitment of the leadership in the dominant ones among these countries to a democratization of decision making at the enterprise level as well as higher societal levels appears very low. The events of the Prague Spring of 1968 testify to that effect.

[3]The Andean Pact agreement on treatment of foreign investment set an example during the time of its actual enforcement.

And an assessment of chances for a possible emergence of forces challenging the political domination of the leadership can not be attempted in the context of these brief final speculations, given the considerable complexity of economy and polity and thus of the potential constituencies for various political forces in the countries in question.

In developing socialist authoritarian systems, with a relatively simple and small economic base, economic as well as political power are concentrated in the hands of a small, military-based or at least supported elite, provided the regime has reached a certain degree of consolidation. Thus initiatives for the introduction of workers' participation in a larger process of transformation have to come from within the elite, be it in response to external challenges or internal ones, such as high labor absenteeism, or low labor productivity, etc. Successful implementation requires primarily that the elite be unified in the commitment to such a process. The two crucial problems are to find a balance between central control and mobilization for implementation at the base, and to build up organizational structures that provide opportunities for popular participation in local as well as national decision making. Transfer of control rights from administrators to workers at the enterprise level can be combined with various degrees of central exercise of control rights through limitations on enterprise autonomy and restrictions on the operation of the market mechanism. The essential elements of workers' control under conditions of scarcity, where central planning is a prerequisite for socially efficient use of resources, are accountability of the directing organs of an enterprise to the workforce, enforced through provisions for election and recall, and direct democratic participation in decision making on all matters of enterprise organization of concern to the workforce.

Whereas limitations on enterprise autonomy through central exercise of income and control rights can solve the problem of accumulation versus consumption, and ensure the implementation of development plans, they may also be a source of tensions in the process. In order for participation to be fully developed at the enterprise level, strengthening of union organization is prerequisite. This strengthening requires that central guidance and support be combined with mobilization at the local level. Yet, local leaders supported by a mobilized workforce may well pressure for reductions of the limitations on enterprise autonomy, in particular for a reduction of the state's share in income rights. As long as the central union leadership supports the need for central planning and is able to control the organization as a whole, such localized challenges are not likely to pose a serious threat to the pursuit of a coherent development strategy. However, the crucial predicament for a socialist transformation under conditions of scarcity lies in the democratization of central decision making. Democratization of the state first requires the creation of an institutional structure providing multiple opportunities for popular participation in decision making, both directly and indirectly through the election of representatives. Institution building is a time-consuming process, and it also demands considerable political skill. Second, democratization of the state requires granting legitimacy to organized opposition, which obviously only a well-consolidated socialist regime will feel secure enough to do. Even in a well-institutionalized and consolidated regime, an increase in the range of participants in political decision making and economic planning increases the chances for disagreements on the allocation of scarce resources, and thus may impede the pursuit of a coherent planned model of social and economic development. Despite all these problems, a democratic-socialist transformation in a developing country has a much greater chance of success in a socialist authoritarian system than in a capitalist democratic or capitalist authoritarian one.

A gradual democratic transition from a capitalist to a socialist order in a developing country is the least likely of all possible paths to full workers' control in a democratic-socialist system. This should be immediately obvious, given that the only formal democratic regimes that have been established and managed to survive in developing countries are those where organization and mobilization of outgroups have remained low. Where interests of dominant groups have been seriously threatened by participation of outgroups in the political process, democratic competition for scarce resources has by and large been terminated even before the initiation of an explicit attempt at socialist transformation. Such a process of transformation would have only a very tenuous chance of success due to the following constraints: First of all, a democratic process of transformation will only be initiated as a result of lower-class mobilization into electoral participation, replacing a government representing the interests of privileged middle- and upper-class groups with one representing the interests of workers, peasants, and the unemployed. Second, the resource base of the society will be insufficient to allow for a satisfaction of the most urgent needs and demands of the newly mobilized popular sectors while a gradual reorientation of the structure of production and distribution is being carried out. Rather than being able to slowly improve the situation of the lower classes through distribution of resources made available through a new pattern of economic growth, the government will be under strong pressure to resort to immediate and substantial redistribution. If it resists these pressures, it may lose popular support and thus ultimately its ability to pursue the process of transformation. If it yields to these pressures, redistribution will invariably elicit decided resistance from the losing formerly dominant groups—resistance which may take legal and illegal forms, and may involve indirect economic sabotage as well as direct use of violence. Counterviolence from mobilized popular sectors will be perceived as a threat by the military guardians of law and order. Thus escalation of violent social conflict will tend to provoke military intervention, ultimately putting an end to the democratic process and replacing it with authoritarian rule based on a monopoly of force.

The question then becomes: What are the chances that a military elite, or a military-backed civilian elite, will use its political power to initiate and successfully execute a process of societal transformation that involves restricting the control and income rights of private capital owners and transferring them to the state, with a partial transfer to workers. The answer is that these chances are rather small indeed, due to a combination of problems centering around foreign dependence, popular mobilization, and elite ideological consensus. The encroachment on control and income rights of private capital owners required for a socialist transformation necessarily affects the interests of foreign capital, and thus would impede the pursuit of an outer-directed path of economic development involving rapid industrialization based on large financial contributions from foreign sources. The only possible exception might be the case of a country with sufficient export revenues from natural resources, such as oil, to expropriate foreign holdings with satisfactory compensation and to continue heavy investment in high-technology industrialization projects out of domestically generated resources. For countries without such a strong independent resource base, however, an indispensable requirement for a socialist transformation is to gain independence from foreign economic power centers by reorienting the model of economic development toward greater self-sufficiency, particularly in food production, and away from capital-intensive, high-technology industrialization. Instead of the production of durable consumer goods for upper-middle and upper income groups, which depends heavily on foreign capital, technology, and industrial inputs, production of food and essential articles for mass consumption with labor-intensive technology need to be emphasized. Such a reorientation of the development model also facilitates the solution of the great problem of equalization faced by developing countries—redistribution from the modern sector to the traditional (i.e., both from the modern urban to traditional urban sectors, and from urban to rural).

However, such a reorientation is extremely difficult: the farther along a country is on the capital-intensive, outer-directed path of industrialization, the more difficult it becomes. In addition to external pressures, domestic opposition presents serious problems, as the reorientation is bound to affect the interests not only of property owners but also of nonpropertied members of the middle class who benefit from their connection to the modern sector. This involves the danger of a loss of badly needed educated personnel through emigration, further aggravating the transformation problems.

Moreover, even a majority of the educated personnel remaining in the country, in leading positions in the socialized sectors, can be expected to adopt a negative or at best a passive attitude towards workers' participation. Thus strong unions as promoters of the full development of workers' participation will be needed, which however creates an additional source of tensions. Scarcity of qualified and committed leaders and activists is characteristic for labor movements in many developing countries, due to the relatively recent growth of unions and their dependence on political forces. Consequently, furthering the organizational growth of unions and the experience and qualification of their leaders is an essential prerequisite for their effectively performing a supportive role in the development of workers' participation. However, such an organizational build-up and concomitant mobilization involves the possibility that competing organizers may try to manipulate the newly emerging organizations for their respective political purposes. The result of such competition is likely to increase labor's militancy rather than its capacity to promote the development of workers' participation through coordinated, unified, purposeful action. Instead of developing a sociopolitical support base for a socialist transformation, such competitive mobilization may have the opposite effect, causing militant disruptions in the economy and consequent political polarization and pressures on the elite, which ultimately may impede a further pursuit of the process of structural changes.

Obviously, such pressures could be resisted by a unified elite, with a coherent vision of the process in relation to the desired final model of socioeconomic order, and with firm control over the coercive apparatus of the state as a decisive power base in society. In the case of a civilian government, this requires continued consent and strong backing from the military elite. However, chances for sustained ideological consensus on the desirability of socialist transformation within a military elite that backs a civilian government, or assumes state power directly in a society at an intermediate level of capitalist development, are low due to a combination of two factors. First of all, the primary uniting bond of a military elite is institutional rather than ideological, and therefore political consensus tends to be limited to begin with. Second, a reduction of foreign penetration will be a prime goal of the transformation process, whereas some members of the elite are likely to be linked indirectly to foreign interests, through social networks connecting them to domestic capitalists allied to foreign firms. Thus the pursuit of a coherent strategy of gradual transformation will probably be jeopardized from the beginning. And difficulties and pressures mounting in the course of the process will greatly increase the likelihood of internal disintegration of the military elite.[4] In the case of a civilian government, this would mean loss of military backing and possibly a coup

[4]Stepan (1971:253–254) makes a similar assessment of chances for military governments to sustain a stable, coherent political course, though his assessment is based on different reasoning. He argues that the tension between the military as an institution and the military as government is likely to cause internal struggles resulting in the possible overthrow of one military government by another group in the military, if the military as an institution feels that its unity is threatened by the political problems caused by the military government.

replacing it with a less change-oriented government. In the case of a military government, this would mean abandonment of the process of gradual socialist transformation.

So far, empirical developments in such cases have gone in the direction of a return to models of dependent capitalist economic development, and a social order based on repression of lower-class mobilization. Theoretically, the opposite development in the direction of accelerated reorientation of the development model and the socialist transformation, with increased coercion directed toward middle and upper instead of lower classes, is an open possibility. However, the farther a country is on the path to dependent capitalist development, and the closer its economic and concomitant political ties to developed Western nations, the less likely it is that this theoretical possibility will materialize in practice. The more advanced the dependent capitalist development, the stronger the social networks tying members of the military elite to foreign and domestic capitalists. And the closer the political ties, the stronger the Western anti-Communist/anti-socialist influence on ideological indoctrination in military training via military assistance.

The summary assessment of chances for the development of workers' participation schemes toward full workers' control in the context of democratic-socialist systems, then, is not exactly optimistic. Among the developed capitalist democracies, only a few small countries meet the preconditions for a potentially successful gradual democratic socialist transition. In developing capitalist authoritarian as well as formally democratic systems, a gradual process of socialist transformation has only a very slim potential for success.[5] There, the more viable path appears to be a rapid transition; that is, a fast and comprehensive transfer of control and income rights from private capitalists to the state; if necessary by force, which implies suppression of opposition. This path, then, would lead to a phase where the politico-economic system approximates the bureaucratic-centralist type. However, as argued above, the military as a crucial actor in countries at an intermediate stage of capitalist development is unlikely to execute or tolerate such a transition. Furthermore, chances for mass-based socialist revolutionary movements to capture state power and destroy the traditional military apparatus as guardian of the capitalist order are low, given the technological sophistication of weapons at the disposal of professionally trained military establishments in these countries.

This leaves mainly countries that are either at an incipient stage of capitalist development or in the process of socialist development as possible places for

[5]Yet, this is not to discount any such chances for success. For instance, the Manley government in Jamaica is trying hard to persist in its democratic path toward a socialist society despite having been seriously hampered by adverse economic conditions that have been aggravated by IMF-imposed austerity measures. One certainly would not want to pronounce a premature verdict on this attempt.

the development of workers' control systems. Countries at an incipient stage of capitalist development have been the most propitious setting for popular revolutions (Tucker 1969; Wolf 1969). Also, in the presence of only a rudimentary national bourgeoisie, the chances that the military will support or tolerate a rapid socialist transition are relatively high. This is particularly true for ex-colonial countries where nationalism and anti-imperialism are identified with anti-capitalism. In many of these countries, some variety of socialism has been adopted already in the wake of wars of liberation, or in the peaceful attempt to overcome the legacies of colonialism and avoid the inequities of capitalist development.[6] However, only a few of these countries are ruled by a unified elite that has managed to consolidate its political power, institutionalize the regime, and embark on a well-defined development plan. And only if these conditions are met can the introduction and successful development of workers' participation or control schemes become feasible.[7] Only then can a regime maintain central planning and control while building up an organizational structure to support mobilization for active participation at the local level. And even after the institutionalization of workers' control and popular participation at the local level, the solution of the problem of democratizaion of national decision-making will only be arrived at through a slow and difficult process.

Thus, even in developing socialist countries, the point where a functioning workers' control scheme in a politico-economic system approximating the democratic-socialist type is likely to be developed appears to be in the rather far future. In the near or middle-range future, Cuba might constitute an interesting test case for the viability of this model for development of workers' participation, since initial attempts to enlarge workers' participation and institutionalize popular participation in political decision making have been made. As for prospects in developed capitalist democracies in the near and middle-range future, the 1976 electoral setback of the Swedish Social Democrats foreshadows a long and arduous political struggle for the full development of workers' participation and a democratic-socialist transition.

Yet, the future success of the Swedish model remains an objective possibility that might have an important demonstration effect, providing empirical proof for the viability of gradual socialization of control and income rights, and their exercise through democratic decision making at the enterprise as well as national level. Such a demonstration effect might serve as a catalyst for sociopolitical forces in other countries, motivating them to unify and strengthen their

---

[6]For instance in Algeria, Libya, Egypt, Syria, Iraq, Ghana, Tanzania, Angola, as well as in Southeast Asia.

[7]Algeria provides an example for a premature introduction of self-management in the agricultural and industrial sector, which failed for the most part due to the lack of central guidance and support, which in turn could not be provided because of the poor institutionalization and consolidation of the regime.

power base for the pursuit of a democratic-socialist transformation. The insights gained from unsuccessful transition attempts might lead to the development of alternate approaches with more coherent and effective strategies to overcome the structural constraints that obstructed such attempts in the past. Social structures not only shape, maintain, and limit collective behavior but they also generate tensions and conflicts between sociopolitical forces, opening up possibilities for change. These possibilities can be realized through purposeful political action based on political will, vision, and organization.

Appendix I

All industrial enterprises are required to file a yearly declaration for industrial statistics to the MIT. From these declarations, I selected all enterprises classified as foreign-owned and mixed enterprises (i.e. with a percentage of foreign capital greater than 49% and between 20% and 49%, respectively). From national enterprises—more than 80% national capital—I selected a 10% random sample, and in addition I included all enterprises with more than 500 workers. For the analysis, the sampled cases were weighed by a factor of 10 in order to arrive at a distribution that represents the universe of CIs. This distribution compares with the one given in the official MIT publication, *Statistics of Industrial Communities*, as follows:

	Enterprises in sample		MIT statistics	
Number of CIs				
Size of CI	N	Percentage	N	Percentage
Under 9 members	80	4	625	19
10–19 members	497	25	1,043	31
20 and more members	1,416	71	1,684	50
Total	1,993	100	3,352	100
Number of workers				
Size of CI				
Under 9 members	680	0.4	4,203	2
10–19 members	6,861	4	23,042	12
20 and more members	183,221	96	168,287	86
Total	190,762	100	195,532	100

The discrepancies that appear can be explained by a lower response rate among the smaller enterprises in declaring industrial statistics, on which my sample is based. However, though my sample represents only two-thirds of CIs due to the underrepresentation of the smaller ones, it represents almost the total labor force affected by the CI, and consequently is a valid base for investigating the effectiveness of the CI in integrating the workforce in the urban industrial sector, or in generating dynamics of socialist transformation.

Appendix II

Coding Scheme

The information contained in the correspondence between the OCLA and individual CIs and enterprises was coded according to the following categories:

Complaints from the CI

(1) Failure to obtain money from the enterprise; (i.e., 10% of profits, or fees accruing to the CI representative on the board of directors, or dividends from shares owned by the CI).

(2) Failure to obtain shares from the enterprise.

(3) Maneuvers of the enterprise to obstruct the development of the CI, such as subdivision of the enterprise; contracts with service or commercial enterprises; change in statutes; increase of capital base without knowledge of the CI; sale of shares.

(4) Measures to decapitalize the enterprise, such as sabotage of production; withdrawal of equipment or raw materials; temporary shutdowns.

(5) Failure to obtain access to information, such as enterprise accounts; minutes of meetings of boards of directors or of shareholders' assembly; declaration for industrial statistics; contracts concluded by the enterprise; payroll.

(6) Irregularities in meetings of the board of directors, such as failure to notify the CI representatives; no prior information about agenda; nonavailability of necessary documentation.

(7) Irregularities in enterprise accounts, such as high costs for inputs; high

remunerations for special people; declaration of personal expenses of owners or managers as business costs.

(8) Obstruction of practical functioning of CI, such as refusal to give time off to representatives; refusal to make room available for assemblies; personal intimidation of CI leaders.

(9) Enterprise accused of breaking agreements with CI or with union.

(10) Firings.

(11) Other labor-related problems, such as injustices in remunerations; violation of labor laws; bad working conditions.

Complaints from the Enterprise

(12) Irregularities in the internal functioning of the CI, such as in elections; in preparation of and procedures in assemblies; in administration of funds.

(13) CI overstepping rights vis-à-vis the enterprise, i.e., undue intervention in enterprise affairs.

(14) Labor indiscipline; declining productivity; sabotage.

(15) Political activities; instigation of conflicts by political agitators.

(16) Abuse of the CI for union purposes; manipulation of CI by union leaders; intervention of CI in labor relations questions.

Complaints from Individuals

(17) Not received due compensation from CI upon resignation or retirement.

Questions from CI or Enterprise

(18) Mode of calculation and distribution of 10% participation in profits to individuals, of dividends, and of compensation upon withdrawal or retirement.

(19) Internal functioning of CI, such as correct election procedures; date for assemblies; use of funds, fines for absence from assemblies; rights of CI vis-à-vis enterprise.

(20) Mode of calculation of before-tax net profits.

(21) Procedures for acquisition of shares by CI.

Other Problems and Actions

(22) Request from CI for visit of OCLA official to assembly, or ceremony, or for advice.

(23) Request from CI for governmental measures in favor of enterprises (e.g., special protective regulations to improve its economic situation).
(24) Problem of formation of a single CI; integration of service workers employed by enterprise into CI.
(25) CI having accounts of enterprise audited.
(26) Declaration of bankruptcy by enterprise.
(27) Occupation of factory.
(28) Letter from CI to the President of the Republic, or to COAP.
(29) Police intervention in conflict between enterprise and workforce.

Actions Taken by the OCLA

(30) Visits of supervisors to enterprise.
(31) Summons of enterprise and CI representatives for conciliation meeting in MIT.
(32) Consultation of other ministerial agencies about problems or conflicts.
(33) Transfer of case to the special court for Labor Communities.

Constellation of Actors

(34) Participation in federation adhering to CONACI or CR.
(35) Collaboration between CI and union(s).
(36) Conflict between CI and union(s).
(37) Internal conflict in CI.
(38) Role of union not mentioned.

Bibliography

Adler-Karlsson, G. *Functional Socialism*. Stockholm: Prisma, 1967.

Aguirre Gamio, H. *El proceso Peruano: ¿ Cómo, por qué, hacia dónde?* Mexico, D.F.: Ediciones El Caballito, 1974.

Alba, V. *Politics and the Labor Movement in Latin America*. Stanford, Calif.: Stanford University Press, 1968.

Alexander, R. J. *Labor Relations in Argentina, Brazil, and Chile*. New York: Praeger, 1962.

Anaya Franco, E. *Imperialismo, industrialización, y transferencia de tecnología en el Perú*. Lima: Editorial Horizonte, 1975.

Anderson, P. "Problems of Socialist Strategy." In *Towards Socialism*, edited by P. Anderson and R. Blackburn. London: Fontana Library, 1965.

Angell, A. "The Peruvian Labor Movement." Unpublished paper presented to a conference at the University of London, Feb. 1978.

Aparicio Valdez, L.; Vásquez, A.; and Alcántara, E. "Ideología y posición política de las confederaciones de trabajadores." Lima: Universidad del Pacífico, Centro de Investigación. *Serie: Documentos de Trabajo*. No. 2, Nov. 1975.

Apter, D. E., ed. *Ideology and Discontent*. New York: Free Press of Glencoe, 1964.

Asplund, C. *Some Aspects of Workers' Participation*. Brussels: ICFTU, May 1972.

Astiz, C. A. *Pressure Groups and Power Elites in Peruvian Politics*. Ithaca, N.Y.: Cornell University Press, 1969.

Baella Tuesta, A. *El poder invisible*. Lima: Editorial Andina, 1977.

Bain, G. S. *The Growth of White Collar Unionism*. Oxford: Clarendon Press, 1970.

Barkin, S., ed. *Worker Militancy and Its Consequences, 1965–1975*. New York: Praeger, 1975.

Béjar, H. *La revolución en la trampa*. Lima: Ediciones Socialismo y Participación, 1976.

Bergmann, J., and Müller-Jentsch, W. "The Federal Republic of Germany: Cooperative Unionism and Dual Bargaining System Challenged." In *Worker Militancy and Its Consequences, 1965–1975*, edited by S. Barkin. New York: Praeger, 1975.

Blumberg, P. *Industrial Democracy: The Sociology of Participation*. New York: Schocken Books, 1968.

Bonilla, F. *A.B.C. del sindicalismo: Legislación Peruana*. Lima: Editorial Mercurio, 1975.

Bourque, S. C., and Palmer, D. S. "Transforming the Rural Sector: Government Policy and Peasant Response." In *The Peruvian Experiment*, edited by A. F. Lowenthal. Princeton, N.J.: Princeton University Press, 1975.

269

Bourricaud, F. *Power and Society in Contemporary Peru.* New York: Praeger, 1970.

Bustamante, A. "La Derecha frente a la Comunidad Industrial." In *Dinámica de la Comunidad Industrial,* edited by L. Pásara, J. Santistevan, A. Bustmante, and D. Garciá-Sayán. Lima: Desco: Centro de Estudios y Promoción del Desarrollo, 1974.

Cameron, D. R. "Inequality and the State: A Political–Economic Comparison." Paper delivered at the 1976 Annual Meeting of the American Political Science Association, The Palmer House, Chicago, Ill., Sept. 2–5, 1976.

Cameron, D. R. "The Expansion of the Public Economy: A Comparative Analysis. *American Political Science Review,* vol. 72, no. 4 (1978): 1243–1261.

Cleaves, P. S., and Scurrah, M. J. "State–Society Relations and Bureaucratic Behavior in Peru." *SICA Occasional Papers.* American Society for Public Administration, Section on International and Comparative Administration, 1976.

Clegg, H. *Industrial Democracy and Nationalization.* London: Blackwell, 1951.

Cleland, S. *The Influence of Plant Size on Industrial Relations.* In Research Report Series, No. 89. Department of Economics and Sociology, Industrial Relations Section, Princeton University, Princeton, N.J., 1955.

Collier, D. "Squatter Settlements and Policy Innovation in Peru." In *The Peruvian Experiment,* edited by A. F. Lowenthal. Princeton, N.J.: Princeton University Press, 1975.

Comisión Nacional de Propiedad Social. *Estado de proyectos y empresas de propiedad social.* Lima, May 1976.

Confederación Nacional de Comunidades Industriales. *Resoluciones del Primer Congreso Nacional de Comunidades Industriales.* Lima, 1973.

Cotler, J. "Political Crisis and Military Populism in Peru." *Studies in Comparative International Development.* no. 6 (1970–1971).

Cotler, J. "Bases del corporativismo en el Perú." *Sociedad y Política.* no. 2 (1972).

Cotler, J., and Portocarrero, F. "Peru: Peasant Organizations." In *Latin American Peasant Movements,* edited by H. Landsberger. Ithaca, N.Y.: Cornell University Press, 1969.

Dahrendorf, R. *Das Mitbestimmungsproblem in der deutschen Sozialforschung. Eine Kritik.* Zweite Auflage. München: Piper, 1965.

Davis, S. M., and Goodman, L. W. *Workers and Managers in Latin America.* Lexington, Mass.: Heath-Lexington Books, 1973.

de las Casas, A.; de las Casas, P.; and Llosa, A. *Análisis de la participación de la Comunidad Industrial en el capital social de la empresa.* Lima: Universidad del Pacífico, Centro de Investigaciones, 1970.

Denitch, B. D. *The Legitimation of a Revolution: The Yugoslav Case.* New Haven: Yale University Press, 1976.

Deppe, F.; von Freyberg, J.; Kievenheim, Ch.; Meyer, R.; and Werkmeister, F. *Kritik der Mitbestimmung.* Frankfurt: Suhrkamp Verlag, 1969.

Durand, J. F. "Origen y desarrollo de las empresas mixtas extranjero-estatales 1969–1974." *Taller de Estudios Urbano Industriales.* Lima: Pontificia Universidad Católica, Serie: Monografías. Apr. 1975.

Ehrmann, H. W. *Politics in France.* 3d ed. Boston: Little, Brown & Co., 1976.

Einaudi, L. "The Military and Government in Peru." In *Development Administration in Latin America,* edited by C. E. Thurber and L. S. Graham. Durham, N.C.: Duke University Press, 1973.

Einhorn, J. P. *Expropriation Politics.* Lexington, Mass.: Lexington Books, 1974.

Emery, F. E., and Trist, E. L. "The Causal Texture of Organizational Environments." *Human Relations,* vol. 18, no. 1 (1965): 21–32.

Erickson, K. P. "Corporatism and Labor in Development." In *Contemporary Brazil: Issues in Economic and Political Development,* edited by H. J. Rosenbaum and W. G. Tyler. New York: Praeger, 1972.

Espinosa, J. G., and Zimbalist, A. S. *Economic Democracy.* New York: Academic Press, 1978.
Espinoza Uriarte, H., and Torres, J. O. *El poder económico en la industria.* Lima: Universidad Nacional Federico Villarreal, 1972.
Everett, M. D. "The Role of the Mexican Trade Unions, 1950–1963." Ph.D. dissertation, Washington University, Missouri, 1967.
Farkas, R. P. *Yugoslav Economic Development and Political Change.* New York: Praeger, 1975.
Ffrench-Davis, R. "The Andean Pact." In *Latin America and World Economy: A Changing International Order,* edited by J. Grunwald. Beverly Hills, Calif.: Sage Publications, 1978.
Figueroa, A. "El impacto de las reformas actuales sobre la distribución de ingresos en el Perú." *Apuntes,* vol. 1, no. 1 (1973): 67–82.
Fitch, J. S. "Toward a Model of the Coup d'Etat in Latin America." In *Political Development and Change,* edited by G. D. Brewer and R. D. Brunner. New York: The Free Press, 1975.
Fitzgerald, E. V. K. "The Political Economy of an Intermediate Regime: Peru since 1968." Draft, 1974.
Fitzgerald, E. V. K. *The State and Economic Development: Peru Since 1968.* Cambridge: Cambridge University Press, Department of Applied Economics, Occasional Papers 49, 1976.
García de Romaña, A. "Comportamiento gremial y político de los empresarios industriales, 1968–1973." *Taller de Estudios Urbano Industriales.* Lima: Pontificia Universidad Católica, 1975.
Goldthorpe, J. H., and Lockwood, D. "Affluence and the British Class Structure. *Sociological Review,* vol. 2, no. 2 (1963): 133–163.
Goldthorpe, J. H., and Lockwood, D. *The Affluent Worker: Industrial Attitudes and Behavior.* Cambridge: Cambridge University Press, 1968.
Goldthorpe, J. H., and Lockwood, D. *The Affluent Worker in the Class Structure.* Cambridge: Cambridge University Press, 1969.
Gomez Cornejo, M. "Historia del Movimiento Obrero Textil." Lima: Universidad Católica. *Serie: Estudios Sindicales.* no. 5, Mar. 1976.
Gorz, A. *Strategy for Labor.* Boston: Beacon Press, 1967.
Gouldner, A. *Wildcat Strike.* Yellow Springs, Ohio: Antioch Press, 1954.
Graham Hurtado, J. *La filosofía de la Revolución Peruana.* Lima: Oficina Nacional de Información, 1971.
Greene, T. *Comparative Revolutionary Movements.* Englewood Cliffs, N.J.: Prentice-Hall, 1974.
Handelman, H. "Struggle in the Andes: Peasant Political Mobilization in Peru." Ph.D. dissertation, University of Wisconsin, 1971.
Handelman, H. "The Politics of Labor Protest in Mexico: Two Case Studies." *Journal of Interamerican Studies and World Affairs.* vol. 18, no. 3 (1976): 267–294.
Hansson, R. *Advances in Work Organization.* International Management Seminar. Final Report. Paris: OECD, 1974.
Harding, C. "Land Reform and Social Conflict in Peru." In *The Peruvian Experiment,* edited by A. F. Lowenthal. Princeton, N.J.: Princeton University Press, 1975.
Hayter, T. (1971) *Aid as Imperialism.* Harmondsworth, Middlesex, England: Penguin, 1971.
Heidenheimer, A. J.; Heclo, H.; and Teich Adams, C. *Comparative Public Policy: The Politics of Social Choice in Europe and America.* New York: St. Martin's Press, 1975.
Hibbs, D. A. "Industrial Conflict in Advanced Industrial Societies." *American Political Science Review.* vol. 70. no. 4 (1976): 1033–1058.
Hibbs, D. A. "Political Parties and Macroeconomic Policy." *American Political Science Review.* vol. 71, no. 4 (1977): 1467–1487.
Himmelstrand, U. "Depoliticization and Political Involvement." In *Mass Politics,* edited by E. Allardt and S. Rokkan. New York: The Free Press, 1970.
Hobsbawm, E. J. "Peru: The Peculiar Revolution." *New York Review of Books.* Dec. 16, 1971, pp. 33–34.

Hoffman, G. W., and Neal, F. W. *Yugoslavia and the New Communism.* New York: Twentieth Century Fund, 1962.

Hunnius, G.; Garson, G.D.; and Case, J. eds. *Workers' Control.* New York: Vintage Books, 1973.

Hunt, S. "Direct Foreign Investment in Peru: New Rules for an Old Game." In *The Peruvian Experiment,* edited by A. F. Lowenthal, Princeton, N.J.: Princeton University Press, 1975.

International Labor Office. "Participation of Workers in Decisions within Undertakings." *Labor Management Relations Series,* no. 33, Geneva, 1969 (referred to as 1969a in footnote).

International Labor Office. "Workers' Participation in Management in the Federal Republic of Germany." *Bulletin,* no. 6. June 1969.

Información política mensual. Lima: Desco, Centro de Estudios y Promoción del Desarrollo, Area de Estudios Políticos.

Jacobi, O.; Müller-Jentsch, W.; and Schmidt, E. eds. *Gewerkschaften und Klassenkampf; kritisches Jahrbuch 1972.* Frankfurt a.M.: Fischer Taschenbuch Verlag, 1973.

Jacquette, J. S. *The Politics of Development in Peru.* Ithaca, N.Y.: Cornell University, Latin American Studies Program, Dissertation Series, 1971.

Jenkins, D. *Job Power.* New York: Doubleday & Co., 1973.

Jovanov, N. "Le rapport entre la grève comme conflit social et l'autogéstion comme système social." Vol. 1. *First International Conference on Self-Management.* Zagreb, 1972.

Karlsson, L. E. "Experiences in Employee Participation in Sweden: 1969–1972." Ithaca, N.Y.: Cornell University: Program on Participation and Labor-Managed Systems; Program on Comparative Economic Development. 1973.

Knight, P. "New Forms of Economic Organization in Peru." In *The Peruvian Experiment,* edited by A. F. Lowenthal. Princeton, N.J.: Princeton University Press, 1975.

Korpi, W. "Social Democracy in Welfare Capitalism—Structural Erosion and Welfare Backlash?" Discussion paper. University of Wisconsin, Madison; Institute for Research on Poverty, 1977.

Korpi, W. *The Working Class in Welfare Capitalism.* London: Routledge and Kegan Paul, 1978.

Korpi, W., and Shalev, M. "Strikes, Power and Politics in the Western Nations, 1900–1976." *Political Power and Social Theory.* vol. 1. (1979).

Landsberger, H., and McDaniel, T. "Hypermobilization in Chile, 1970–1973." *World Politics.* vol. 28, no. 4 (1976): 502–541.

Latin America, Political Report. London: Latin American Newsletters, Ltd.

Latin American Economic Report. Lima: Andean Times.

Likert, R. *New Patterns of Management.* New York: McGraw-Hill, 1961.

Llarena, D.; Trovarelli, R.; and Rodríguez, M. *La Comunidad Industrial, naturaleza económica de la empresa industrial en el Perú.* Lima: Ediciones Universidad Nacional Federico Villarreal, 1972.

Lorwin, V. R. *The French Labor Movement.* Cambridge, Mass.: Harvard University Press, 1954.

Lowell, P. "Lessons from Abroad." In *The Lessons of Public Enterprise: A Fabian Society Study,* edited by Michael Shanks. London: J. Cape, 1963.

Lowenthal, A. F. "Peru's Ambiguous Revolution." In *The Peruvian Experiment,* edited by A. F. Lowenthal. Princeton, N.J.: Princeton University Press, 1975.

MacLennan, M.; Forsyth, M.; and Denton. G. *Economic Planning and Policies in Britain, France, and Germany.* New York: Praeger, 1968.

Malloy, J. "Dissecting the Peruvian Military: Review Essay." *Journal of Inter-American Studies and World Affairs.* vol. 15, no. 3 (1973): 375–382.

Malpica, C. *Los dueños del Perú.* 3rd ed. Lima: Ediciones Ensayos Sociales, 1974.

Malpica, C. *Anchovetas y tiburones.* Lima: Ediciones Runamarka, 1975.

Martin, A. "Sweden: Industrial Democracy and Social Democratic Strategy." In *Worker Self-Management in Industry: The West European Experience,* edited by G. D. Garson. New York: Praeger, 1977.

Matos Mar, J., *et al. El Perú actual; Sociedad y política*. Mexico, D.F.: Universidad Nacional Autónoma de México, Instituto de Investigaciones Sociales, 1970.

McClintock, C. "Structural Change and Political Culture in Rural Peru: The Impact of Self-Managed Cooperatives on Peasant Clientelism." Ph.D. dissertation, Massachusetts Institute of Technology, Cambridge, Mass., 1976.

McClintock, C. "Self-Management and Political Participation in Peru, 1969–1975: The Corporatist Illusion." *Sage Professional Papers*, Contemporary Political Sociology Series, 1977.

Meidner, R. "Employee Investment Funds and Capital Formation." *Working Life*. no. 6 (1978). New York: Swedish Information Service.

Mercado Jarrín, E. "Separata de Participación," no. 2. Lima: SINAMOS, 1973.

Mercado Jarrín, E. *Ensayos*. Lima: Imprenta del Ministerio de Guerra, 1974.

Milenkovitch, D. D. *Plan and Market in Yugoslav Economic Thought*. New Haven: Yale University Press, 1971.

Millen, B. H. *The Political Role of Labor in Developing Countries*. Washington, D.C.: Brookings Institution, 1963.

Miller, R. U. "The Role of Labor Organizations in a Developing Country: The Case of Mexico." Ph.D. dissertation, Cornell University, Ithaca, N.Y., 1966.

Ministerio de Industria y Turismo. *Evolución industrial manufacturera Peruana, 1971–1972*. Lima, 1974.

Ministerio de Industria y Turismo, Oficina Sectoral de Planificación. *Evaluación del proceso de industrialización: Situación actual y tendencias*. Lima, May 1976.

Moncloa, F. *Peru: ¿Que paso? (1968–1976)*. Lima: Editorial Horizonte, 1977.

Montuclard, M. *La dynamique des comités d'entreprise*. Paris: Centre Nacional de la Recherche Scientifique, 1963.

Neira, H. "Peru." In *Guide to the Political Parties of South America*, edited by J. P. Bernard *et al*. Harmondsworth, Middlesex, England: Penguin Books, 1973.

Nie, N. H.; Powell, G. B.; and Prewitt, K. "Social Structure and Political Participation; Developmental Relationships." *American Political Science Review*. vol. 63, no. 2 (1969): 361–378.

Nordlinger, E. A. *Soldiers in Politics: Military Coups and Governments*. Englewood Cliffs, N.J.: Prentice-Hall, 1977.

North, L. "The Origins and Development of the Peruvian Aprista Party." Ph.D. dissertation, University of California, Berkeley, 1973.

North, L. "The Military in Chilean Politics." *Studies in Comparative International Development*. vol. 2, no. 1 (1976).

Obradovic, J. "Distribution of Participation in the Process of Decision Making on Problems Related to the Economic Activity of the Company." vol. 2. *First International Conference on Self-Management*, Zagreb, 1972.

O'Donnell, G. H. *Modernization and Bureaucratic-Authoritarianism: Studies in South American Politics*. Politics of Modernization Series, no. 9, Institute of International Studies, University of California, Berkeley, 1973.

OECD. *Labour Force Statistics 1964–1975*. Paris, 1977.

OECD. *Observer*. 1977; 1978.

Otto, B. *Gewerkschaftliche Konzeptionen überbetrieblicher Mitbestimmung*. Köln: Bund Verlag, 1971.

Palmer, D. S. *Revolution from Above: Military Government and Popular Participation in Peru, 1968–1972*. Latin American Studies Program, Dissertation Series, Cornell University, Ithaca, N.Y., Jan. 1973.

Pásara, L., and Santistevan, J. "Industrial Communities and Trade Unions in Peru: A Preliminary Analysis." *International Labor Review*. vol. 108, (1973): 127–142.

Pásara, L.; Santistevan, J.; Bustamante, A.; and García-Sayán, D. *Dinámica de la Comunidad Industrial*. Lima: Desco: Centro de Estudios y Promoción del Desarrollo, 1974.

Pateman, C. *Participation and Democratic Theory*. Cambridge: Cambridge University Press, 1970.

Payer, C. *The Debt Trap*. New York: Monthly Review Press, 1974.

Payne, J. L. *Labor and Politics in Peru*. New Haven: Yale University Press, 1965.

Perú 1968–1974, Cronología Política. Vols. 1, 2, 3. Lima: Desco, Centro de Estudios y Promoción del Desarrollo, Area de Estudios Políticos.

Peterson, F. *American Labor Unions*. New York: Harper & Row, 1963.

Pike, F. B., and Stritch, T. eds. *The New Corporatism: Social-Political Structures in the Iberian World*. Notre Dame: University of Notre Dame Press, 1974.

Popitz, H.; Bahrdt, H. P. *et al. Das Gesellschaftsbild des Arbeiters*. Tübingen: J. C. B. Mohr, 1957.

Pryor, F. L. *Property and Industrial Organization in Communist and Capitalist Nations*. Bloomington: Indiana University Press, 1973.

Pryor, F. L. *The Origins of the Economy: A Comparative Study of Distribution in Primitive and Peasant Economies*. New York: Academic Press. 1977.

Quijano, A. "Nationalism and Capitalism in Peru: A Study in Neo-Imperialism." *Monthly Review*. vol. 23, no. 3 (1971).

Quijano, A. "Las nuevas perspectivas de la clase obrera." *Sociedad y Politica*. no. 3. (1973): 36–51.

Revans, R. W. "Industrial Morale and Size of Unit." In *Labor and Trade Unionism: An Interdisciplinary Reader*. edited by W. Galenson and S. M. Lipset. New York: Wiley, 1960.

Reynaud, J. D. "France: Elitist Society Inhibits Articulated Bargaining." In *Worker Militancy and Its Consequences, 1965–1975*, edited by S. Barkin. New York: Praeger, 1975.

Roggemann, H. *Das Modell der Arbeiterselbstverwaltung in Jugoslawien*. Frankfurt a.M.: Europäische Verlagsanstalt, 1970.

Ross, A. M., and Hartman, P. T. *Changing Patterns of Industrial Conflict*. New York: Wiley, 1960.

Rus, V. "Influence Structure in Yugoslav Enterprise." *Industrial Relations*. no. 9 (1970): 148–160.

Rusinow, D. *The Yugoslav Experiment: 1948–1974*. Berkeley, Calif.: University of California Press, 1977.

Santistevan, J. "La aplicación de la ley y los conflictos." In L. Pásara *et al. Dinámica de la Comunidad Industrial*. Lima: Desco: Centro de Estudios y Promoción del Desarrollo, 1974.

Sawyer, M. "Income Distribution in OECD Countries." *OECD Economic Outlook. Occasional Studies*. Paris, July 1976.

Schnitzer, M. *Income Distribution: A Comparative Study of the United States, Sweden, West Germany, East Germany, the United Kingdom, and Japan*. New York: Praeger, 1974.

Schoenbach, C. "The Stabilization Programmes of the Federal Government in 1973." *German Economic Review*. vol. 12, no. 1 (1974): 78–83.

Shorter, E., and Tilly, C. *Strikes in France*. Cambridge: Cambridge University Press, 1974.

Sifo, *Indikator*. Stockholm, 1976.

Sodersten, B. "Prospects for Labor Management in Sweden." Paper presented to the Second International Conference on Self-Management, Cornell University, Ithaca, N.Y., June, 1975.

Stallings, B. "Peru and the U.S. Banks: Who has the Upper Hand?" Paper prepared for a Conference on the U.S., U.S. Foreign Policy, and Latin American and Caribbean Regimes, sponsered by the Joint Committee on Latin American Studies of the Social Science Research Council and the American Council of Learned Societies. Washington, D.C., March 27–31, 1978.

Stepan, A. C. *The Military in Politics: Changing Patterns in Brazil*. Princeton, N.J.: Princeton University Press, 1971.

Stepan, A. C. *The State and Society: Peru in Comparative Perspective.* Princeton, N.J.: Princeton University Press, 1978.
Stephens, E. H., and Stephens, J. D. "The Labor Movement, Political Power, and Workers' Participation in Western Europe." *Political Power and Social Theory.* vol 3, in press.
Stephens, J. D. "The Consequences of Social Structural Change for the Development of Socialism in Sweden." Ph.D. dissertation, Department of Sociology, Yale University, New Haven, Conn., 1976.
Stephens, J. D. *The Transition from Capitalism to Socialism.* London: MacMillan, 1979.
Stevens, E. P. *Protest and Response in Mexico.* Cambridge, Mass.: M.I.T. Press, 1974.
Sturmthal, A. ed. *White Collar Trade Unions.* Urbana, Ill.: University of Illinois Press, 1967.
Sulmont, D. "Dinámica actual del movimiento obrero Peruano." *Taller de Estudios Urbanos Industriales.* Lima: Pontificia Universidad Católica, 1972.
Sulmont, D. "El desarrollo de la clase obrera en el Perú." *Serie: Publicaciones Previas.* no. 1. Lima: Pontificia Universidad Católica, Centro de Investigaciones Sociales, Económicas, Politicas y Antropológicas, 1974.
Sulmont, D. *El movimiento obrero en el Perú, 1900–1956.* Fondo Editorial. Lima: Pontificia Universidad Católica, 1975.
Supek, R. "Problems and Experiences of Yugoslav Workers' Self-Management." Paper presented to the Second International Conference on Self-Management, Cornell University, Ithaca, N.Y., June 6-8, 1975.
Swedish Institute, The. "Tatsachen über Schweden" TS99N. Stockholm, Dec. 1973.
Swedish Trade Union Confederation LO. *Industrial Democracy.* Stockholm, 1972.
Thorndike, G. *No! Mi General.* Lima: Mosca Azul Editores, 1976.
Tucker, R. C. *The Marxian Revolutionary Idea.* New York: The Norton Library, 1969.
Vaitsos, C. *Intercountry Income Distribution and Transnational Enterprise.* London: Oxford University Press, 1974.
van Otter, C. "Sweden: Labor Reformism Reshapes the System." In *Worker Militancy and Its Consequences, 1965–1975,* edited by S. Barkin. New York: Praeger, 1975.
Velasco Alvarado, J. *La voz de la revolución.* Lima: Editorial Ausonia, 1972.
Verba, S., and Shabad, G. "Workers' Councils and Political Stratification: The Yugoslav Experience." *American Political Science Review.* vol. 72, no. 1 (1978): 80–95.
Viklund, B. "Education for Industrial Democracy." *Working Life.* New York: Swedish Information Service, May 1977.
Villanueva, V. *100 años del ejército Peruano: Frustraciones y cambios.* Lima: Editorial Juan Mejía Baca, 1972.
Villanueva, V. *EL CAEM y la revolución de la Fuerza Armada.* Lima: Instituto de Estudios Peruanos, 1973.
Vusković, B. "Social Inequality in Yugoslavia." *New Left Review* no. 95 (1976): 24–45.
Walker, K. F. "Workers' Participation in Management—Problems, Practice, and Prospects." Geneva: International Institute for Labor Studies, *Bulletin.* no. 12 (1974): 3–35.
Webb, R. "Government Policy and the Distribution of Income in Peru, 1963–1973." In *The Peruvian Experiment,* edited by A. F. Lowenthal, Princeton, N.J.: Princeton University Press, 1975.
Wilensky, H. L. *The Welfare State and Equality.* Berkeley: University of California Press, 1975.
Wolf, E. *Peasant Wars of the Twentieth Century.* New York: Harper & Row, 1969.
Zimmermann Zavala, A. *Objetivo: Revolución Peruana. El Plan Inca.* Lima: Empresa Editora del Diario Oficial "El Peruano," 1974.

Subject Index

DATE DUE

DEC 1 8 1986		
OCT 6 1988		
OCT 2 7 1988		
MAR 2 0 1989		
DEC 4 1989		
FEB 2 2 1990		
APR 3 1990		
APR 2 3 1993		

DEMCO 38-297